Freedom's Mirror

During the Haitian Revolution of 1791–1804, arguably the most radical revolution of the modern world, slaves and former slaves succeeded in ending slavery and establishing an independent state. Yet on the Spanish island of Cuba, barely fifty miles away, the events in Haiti helped usher in the antithesis of revolutionary emancipation. When Cuban planters and authorities saw the devastation of the neighboring colony, they rushed to fill the void left in the world market for sugar, to buttress the institutions of slavery and colonial rule, and to prevent "another Haiti" from happening in their territory. *Freedom's Mirror* follows the reverberations of the Haitian Revolution in Cuba, where the violent entrenchment of slavery occurred at the very moment that the Haitian Revolution provided a powerful and proximate example of slaves destroying slavery. By creatively linking two stories – the story of the Haitian Revolution and that of the rise of Cuban slave society – that are usually told separately, Ada Ferrer sheds fresh light on both of these crucial moments in Caribbean and Atlantic history.

Ada Ferrer is Professor of History and Latin American and Caribbean Studies at New York University. She is the author of *Insurgent Cuba: Race, Nation, and Revolution, 1868–1898*, which won the 2000 Berkshire Book Prize for the best first book written by a woman in any field of history.

Freedom's Mirror

Cuba and Haiti in the Age of Revolution

ADA FERRER
New York University

CAMBRIDGE
UNIVERSITY PRESS

32 Avenue of the Americas, New York, NY 10013-2473, USA

Cambridge University Press is part of the University of Cambridge.

It furthers the University's mission by disseminating knowledge in the pursuit of education, learning, and research at the highest international levels of excellence.

www.cambridge.org
Information on this title: www.cambridge.org/9781107697782

© Ada Ferrer 2014

First published 2014

A catalog record for this publication is available from the British Library.

Library of Congress Cataloging in Publication Data
Ferrer, Ada.
Freedom's mirror : Cuba and Haiti in the age of revolution / Ada Ferrer.
pages cm
Includes bibliographical references and index.
ISBN 978-1-107-02942-2 (hardback) – ISBN 978-1-107-69778-2 (paperback)
1. Slavery – Political aspects – Cuba – History – 19th century.   2. Haiti – History – Revolution, 1791–1804 – Influence.   3. Haiti – Politics and government – 1804–1844.
4. Antislavery movements – History – 19th century.   5. Revolutions – History – 19th century.   6. Counterrevolutionaries – Cuba – History – 19th century.   7. Plantation owners – Cuba – History – 19th century.   8. Colonial administrators – Cuba – History – 19th century.   9. Cuba – Race relations – History – 19th century.   10. Cuba – Politics and government – 1810–1899.   I. Title.
HT1076.F47   2014
306.3'6209729109034–dc23   2014019409

ISBN 978-1-107-02942-2 Hardback
ISBN 978-1-107-69778-2 Paperback

In memory of
Rita Blanco, 1888–1975
José Luciano Franco, 1891–1989

The world had seen so many changes that the storyteller's "once upon a time" had been replaced by the phrases "before the Revolution" and "after the Revolution."

Alejo Carpentier, *Explosion in a Cathedral*

Contents

List of Figures

Acknowledgments

This book has been long in the making, and I have incurred many debts along the way. The staff at the archives and libraries listed in the bibliography have always been generous and professional, even – in too many places – in the face of crises and cutbacks. I thank them most heartily. This book, like so many others, would be impossible without them.

I owe a huge debt to a wonderful group of colleagues, scholars, and friends whose work and companionship have been a steady source of energy and inspiration. Close to the beginning of the project, a conversation with Josep Fradera at Caffé Reggio, and another with Robin Blackburn on the steps of the John Carter Brown Library, helped me realize that it was slavery that needed to be at the center of this story. The book has also been profoundly shaped by many, many conversations with individual people over many years: Alejandro de la Fuente, Laurent Dubois, Sibylle Fischer, Marial Iglesias, Sara Johnson, Rebecca Scott, and Sinclair Thomson. Rebecca, Sibylle, and Sinclair graciously read all or most of the manuscript in its final stages. For that and for their invaluable feedback and support throughout, I thank them warmly. Other colleagues read individual chapters and shared wonderful ideas and suggestions. My sincere thanks to all of them: Jeremy Adelman, Herman Bennett, Greg Childs, Ana Dopico, Marcela Echeverri, Anne Eller, Marial Iglesias, Sara Johnson, Romy Sánchez, Chris Schmidt-Nowara, Julie Skurski, and Dale Tomich. I am also grateful to Julia Gaffield, who was generous enough to read the entire manuscript in its almost-final form and who provided very helpful comments and corrections.

I received a supportive welcome and much guidance from several Haitianist colleagues; thanks go especially to Jean Casimir, Laurent

Dubois, Carolyn Fick, and David Geggus. I am very grateful to many other colleagues who have read and discussed earlier drafts of parts of this work and shared references, suggestions, doubts, and encouragement: Carmen Barcia, Manuel Barcia, Tom Bender, Lauren Benton, Robin Blackburn, Vince Brown, Matt Childs, Alejandro de la Fuente, Laurent Dubois, Aisha Finch, Reinaldo Funes, the late Gloria García, Malick Ghachem, Olivia Gomes da Cunha, Michael Gómez, Greg Grandin, Keila Grinberg, Jean Hébrard, Martha Hodes, Walter Johnson, Martha Jones, Robin Kelley, Karen Kupperman, Fernando Martínez Heredia, Jennifer Morgan, Chelo Naranjo, Harvey Neptune, Graham Nessler, Sue Peabody, Louis Pérez, Edgardo Pérez Morales, Nathalie Pierre, José Antonio Piqueras, Millery Polyne, Jeremy Popkin, Dmitri Prieto Samsonov, João Reis, David Sartorius, Julius Scott, Mimi Sheller, Cristina Soriano, Richard Turits, Barbara Weinstein, and Michael Zeuske. The list is an embarrassment of riches. On it are many students and former students. To them and to others in my seminars over the years, I offer my humble thanks. My work is much better for their engagement.

In Havana, I counted on stalwart colleagues undaunted by the headaches of getting my visas, in particular, the generous and warm Pablo Pacheco, recently passed. In addition to others already named, Mercedes García, Enrique López Mesa, Jorge Macle, the late Francisco Pérez Guzmán, Ricardo Quiza, Eduardo Torres Cuevas, and Oscar Zanetti were immensely helpful, as were Olga Portuondo in Santiago, and Jean Casimir and Patrick Tardieu in Port-au-Prince. For welcoming me to the Consejo Superior de Investigaciones Científicas in Madrid, my thanks to Chelo Naranjo, Leida Fernández Prieto, Loles González Ripoll, and Inés Roldan. In Sevilla, it was enlightening and enjoyable to share in the riches of the Archivo General de Indias with José Luis Belmonte, Jane Landers, Antonio Santamaria, Sigfrido Vazquez Cienfuegos, and David Wheat.

For their generosity in entertaining sometimes seemingly random questions on topics such as vodou flags, Havana architecture, and Napoleonic conventions (and for sometimes reminding me that not all questions need answers), I thank Roseanne Adderley, Karl Appuhn, Madison Smartt Bell, Zvi Benite Ben-Dor, Rafe Blaufarb, Brian Blum, José Manuel Campa, Jordana Dym, Scott Eastman, Nicole Eustace, Rebecca Goetz, Andrew Lee, Ayo Odiduro, Antonio José Ponte, Emilio Jorge Rodríguez, Jean-Fréderic Schaub, Elena Schneider, John Shovlin, Katherine Smith, Matthew Smith, Edward Sullivan, Gina Ulysse, and Grette Vidal. I was lucky to have research and editorial assistance at various points in this project from Michele Albright, Greg Childs, Jorge Felipe, Joan Flores Villalobos, Pedro Guibovich, Evelyne Laurent-Perrault, Rachel Nolan, Elisa Nolasco, Nathalie Pierre, Romy Sánchez, and Nailah Summers. Anne Eller deserves special mention for finding the image that appears on the cover. Gigi Dopico and Ana Dopico regularly helped with translations of awkward things; thanks are due to both. And to Ana, thanks, too, for everything else.

Research and writing have been supported by the National Endowment for the Humanities, the American Council of Learned Societies, the Social Science Research Council, the Consejo Superior de Investigaciones Científicas in Spain, and New York University. To the staff in the History Department and the Center for Latin American and Caribbean Studies at NYU, a very warm thank you. At Cambridge, heartfelt thanks to Eric Crahan for taking on this project, and especially to Deborah Gershenowitz for seeing it through. Thanks go also to Jeanie Lee, Dana Bricken, Arindam Bose, Hillary Ford, and, of course, the anonymous reviewers for the Press.

My parents, Ramón and Adelaida Ferrer, wonder why I spend so much time pursuing the lives of long-dead people in archives. Their skepticism notwithstanding, I owe to them many of the passions and habits that animate this book. My daughters Alina and Lucía take particular pleasure in reminding me that I have been working on this book for all, or almost all, their lifetimes. I thank them for their levity and inspiration; I have loved sharing this book (and life) with them. Amena Sengal, Julia Sollenberger, and Claire VanRyzin have helped make it possible to raise children and write at the same time. My husband, Gregg VanRyzin, has also shared this book with me for a very long time. The thought of sharing with him a few more books, as well as many other things new and old, is a great part of my motivation.

I dedicated my first book, *Insurgent Cuba*, to the memory of my grandmother, Rita Blanco, born in 1888, whom I met but cannot remember. In researching that book I accidentally discovered that in the late nineteenth century her hometown in Pinar del Río province was nicknamed "little Haiti." A woman of color, who sang and spoke some French, she may have been – among many other things in her life, including mother of twelve and grandmother and great grandmother of hundreds – a product of the kinds of histories told in these pages. Once more, I dedicate this book to her elusive memory.

On my first visit to the Cuban National Archives in Havana in the summer of 1990, historian Fe Iglesias served as my guide. As I headed for the small table just to the right as one enters the reading room, she stopped me and explained that that had been the table of the late José Luciano Franco. Out of respect for him she would not sit there. I never met Franco, who was born in 1891 and who had died just about six months before my first visit to the island. He was without question one of the most important Cuban historians of the twentieth century, having written dozens of books on every important topic in Cuban history and a few on Latin America, the Caribbean, and Spain. I have never failed to learn from his work – from his choice of topics, from his sometimes too-sparse footnotes, from his insistence on putting questions of slavery and race at the heart of political history. For a long time, I avoided sitting at his old table out of regard for him and for Fe, who is no longer able to do research. More recently, with the archives sometimes crowded and with few outlets for computer plugs, I have once or twice had to sit at Franco's table. I do so always with a little trepidation, but also hoping that his archive spirit might inspire my looking. I dedicate this book to his memory as well.

Introduction

The Haitian Revolution and Cuban Slave Society

Of what happened that night there are many accounts, but of this we can be fairly certain: in the French colony of Saint-Domingue, today Haiti, late one night in August 1791, hundreds of men and women held as slaves gathered together at a clearing in a forest called Bois Caïman, or Bwa Kayiman in Kreyòl. It was probably August 21, a Sunday, so some may have arrived at the meeting on their way back from the Cap Français market. If not exactly a day of rest, it was, at least, a day away from the grueling work of sugar, the principal crop of the region. The labor done on one day, by any one of the individuals gathered that night, had been compounding exponentially for years to make Saint-Domingue Europe's most profitable colony and the world's largest producer of sugar, king long before cotton. By the time of the Bois Caïman assembly, the colony had half a million slaves and nearly 800 sugar plantations, producing almost as much as all the islands of the British West Indies combined. French Saint-Domingue was the envy of all Europe, the jewel of the Antilles, the Eden of the Western world.

It was in part the very foundation of that wealth – the brutality of the work and the violence of the coercion imposed on captive Africans and their descendants – that drew so many to the meeting at Bois Caïman that night. They were there to prepare for a radically different future. A leader named Dutty Boukman, himself enslaved, addressed the assembly. In some accounts his words were inspired: he spoke of God and vengeance, closing with a call to "listen to liberty that speaks to all our hearts." At the center of the gathering, a woman lifted a knife and killed a black pig in ritual sacrifice; then the congregants swore an oath to obey their leader Boukman, who was organizing them in rebellion against their masters, and to maintain utmost secrecy so as to ensure the success of their bold endeavor. For additional protection, some took hair from the pig to put in amulets.[1]

We cannot know with what mixture of buoyancy or trepidation the men and women gathered at Bois Caïman walked back to their plantations that night to sleep briefly before daybreak. But the next evening, they did more or less as planned. On Monday night, August 22, they rose up. The strike was substantial from the start: from one plantation to the next, insurgents burned cane fields and buildings, and sometimes killed masters and overseers. By the end of the year, the rebel slaves numbered in the tens of thousands; the property destroyed amounted to over a thousand sugar and coffee farms; and about 400 white colonists had lost their lives. This was the largest and best coordinated slave rebellion the world had ever seen. It made war on the system of slavery at its seat of most extreme and opulent power, and, intentionally or not, it forced the question of slavery on the French Revolution and the world.[2]

Immediately, French colonial authorities sent emissaries to the United States, Jamaica, Cuba, and elsewhere in search of aid: money, men, munitions, hunting dogs, anything that might help them turn the tide and make their world right again. In pleading for assistance, the French painted a grim portrait. The glorious talk of the Antilles' preeminent jewel gave way to laments of devastation and ruin: a veritable paradise turned a mountain of ashes. France, they wrote, was "in imminent danger of losing the colony due to the insurrection of the blacks."[3] Did they believe that? Or

[1] David Geggus, "The Bois Caïman Ceremony," in *Haitian Revolutionary Studies* (Bloomington: Indiana University Press, 2002), 81–92; Carolyn Fick, *The Making of Haiti: The Saint-Domingue Revolution from Below* (Knoxville: University of Tennessee Press, 1990), 93–94, 264–265; Robin Law, "La Cérémoie du Bois-Caïman et le 'pacte de sang' dahoméen," in Laennec Hurbon, ed., *L'Insurrection des esclaves de Saint-Domingue (22–23 août 1791)* (Paris: Karthala, 2000), 131–147; Léon-François Hoffman, "Un Mythe national: La cérémonie du Bois-Caïman," in Gérard Barthélemy and Christian Girault, eds., *La République haïtienne: Etat des lieux et perspectives*, (Paris: Karthala, 1993), 434–448.

[2] C.L.R. James, *The Black Jacobins: Toussaint L'Ouverture and the San Domingo Revolution* (New York: Vintage Books, 1963 [1938]); Laurent Dubois, *Avengers of the New World: The Story of the Haitian Revolution* (Cambridge: Harvard University Press, 2004).

[3] Las Casas to Conde de Campo de Alange, September 15, 1791, in Archivo General de Simancas, Spain (AGS), Secretaría y Despacho de Guerra (SGU), *legajo* (or bundle, hereafter leg.) 6846, *expediente* (or file, hereafter exp.) 79. My research in this archive predated the digitilization project that has since made many of the materials available online at http://pares.mcu.es/. Therefore, some references to AGS, SGU materials do not list the *expediente* number, as those were not always clear before the digitalization.

was that possibility merely a flicker of doubt that emerged sometimes as they narrated the events for the benefit of people who might provide assistance? Even as they prophesied the end of the world as they knew it, they surely believed that the French would ultimately prevail. Africans, slaves, and blacks, they probably thought, would not defeat them. France faced a massive slave rebellion, certainly; but in the late days of August 1791, few in Saint-Domingue or elsewhere – black, brown, white, free, or enslaved – could have imagined that the unrest would become what we know today as the Haitian Revolution.

Yet the process begun that late August evening produced the most unexpected outcomes. The slave rebels persisted, the colonial army unable to subdue them. By April 1792, in hopes of securing the allegiance of free people of color and with it subduing the rebel slaves, France decreed legal equality among free men of all colors. In August 1793, realizing that the strength of the slave insurrection threatened the loss of the colony to Spain and England, colonial authorities began decreeing the end of slavery in the areas of Saint-Domingue under their control: "all the *nègres* and mixed-blood people currently in slavery are declared free to enjoy all the rights of French citizens." A few months after that, the National Convention in Paris followed suit and went further, declaring that "the slavery of the *nègres* is abolished... all men living in the colonies, without distinction of color, are French citizens." The rebellion of enslaved men and women had forced first colonial officials and later European ones to declare the end of slavery not just in Saint-Domingue but in all French territory. In 1795, the French Constitution declared the colonies "integral parts of France... subject to the same constitutional law."[4]

In all this, one former slave, Toussaint Bréda, soon to be Louverture, emerged as preeminent strategist and politician. Black, only moderately literate, and born and raised as the legal property of a white man, Toussaint became commander-in-chief in May 1797 and governor soon after.[5] When Napoleon decided that the colonies would be ruled by special laws, thus paving the way to quarantine particular rights on European soil, it was Governor Toussaint who took it upon himself to author special laws for Saint-Domingue, in the form of a constitution that reiterated that

[4] Translations of the decrees and constitutional articles are from Laurent Dubois and John Garrigus, eds., *Slave Revolution in the Caribbean: A Brief History with Documents* (New York: Bedford-St. Martin's Publishing, 2006), 115–116, 120–125, 129–132, 167–170.
[5] Jesús Ruiz, a PhD student at Tulane University, has recently discovered documentation suggesting that Toussaint might have taken on the name "Louverture" earlier than is generally supposed. "On Becoming Louverture," article manuscript in preparation.

"there can be no slaves in this territory; servitude is abolished within it forever." When Napoleon attempted to reassert French control – to rip every epaulette from the shoulders of those "gilded Africans" – and to reimpose slavery, hundreds of thousands of people fought against the French, winning independence and founding a new country as a way to avoid reenslavement and preserve the right of liberty. Thus, on January 1, 1804, Haiti was born, the second independent state of the hemisphere and the only one ever founded by former slaves and without slavery.[6]

This new country sat in the middle of the Caribbean Sea surrounded by islands that remained European colonies deeply invested in the regime of slavery. On all of them the black population either comprised the majority or was quickly gaining demographic ground. European governors protected and encouraged the slave trade, plantation production, and the violent imperative that sustained both. If the Haitian Revolution was born precisely from the implosion of that kind of system in Saint-Domingue, the new state of Haiti stood as a profound challenge to that order. Not a colony but an independent state, it took an Amerindian name. Its first president – a former slave – proclaimed to have "avenged America," and he denounced France for assuming that human rights were white rights. Blacks, too, were bearers of rights, he said, and henceforth all Haitians would be called black.[7]

In Cuba, just fifty miles distant, no one could have imagined the power of what began at Bois Caïman. But wealthy men there did harbor some hope that the massive August rebellion might work in their favor. Cuban sugar planters had spent the last two decades attempting to emulate the magnificent wealth and power of the Saint-Domingue planter class. Now their model confronted a catastrophe; their competitor faced a colossal handicap. If there was certainly cause for concern, there was perhaps also reason for optimism. "There is no need for doubt. The hour of our

[6] The 1801 Constitution of Saint-Domingue is available at Constitutions of the World Online (http://www.modern-constitutions.de/nbu.php?page_id=02a1b5a86ff13947c0b1c57f23ac196&show_doc=HT-00-1801-05-19-fr). Napoleon's "gilded Africans" statement is quoted in James, *The Black Jacobins*, 271.

[7] *Gaceta de Madrid* (GM), March 23, 1804, 267–268; *The Balance and Columbian Repository*, Hudson, New York, June 17, 1804, and *Journal des débats*, August 7, 1804. On the Delcaration of Independence and the 1805 Constitution, see also Deborah Jenson, *Beyond the Slave Narrative: Politics, Sex, and Manuscripts in the Haitian Revolution* (Liverpool: Liverpool University Press, 2011); Sibylle Fischer, *Modernity Disavowed: Haiti and the Cultures of Slavery in the Age of Revolution* (Durham: Duke University Press, 2004), chaps. 11 and 13; and Julia Gaffield, ed., *The Haitian Declaration of Independence* (Charlottesville: University of Virginia Press, forthcoming).

happiness has arrived," announced the colony's most prominent sugar planter.[8]

If by *our* he meant white planters such as himself, rather than the inhabitants of the colony more generally or the enslaved labor force in particular, his prediction proved more than correct. Sugar took off. In Havana province, center of the boom, the number of mills almost doubled in the two decades after the start of the Haitian Revolution. The average productive capacity of those mills also more than doubled, with the largest ones producing well above that average. With so much more sugar suddenly being produced, Cuba surpassed Saint-Domingue, overtook Jamaica, and became by the 1820s the world's largest producer of sugar, the new pearl of the Antilles.[9]

But in August 1791, none of that was yet apparent. And as the architects of that imminent boom whetted their appetites in anticipation, they soon realized that they were not the only ones hoping for a transformation. The first sign came early and in a most unexpected manner. In Havana, just about three weeks after the Bois Caïman ceremony that launched the Haitian Revolution, members of the city council (*cabildo*) learned of a shortage of pork in the city's meat markets. The scarcity, in and of itself, was nothing out of the ordinary in a city with perpetual shortages and all manner of illicit and contraband business. Yet this time the origin of the problem appeared to be far from routine. "Inquiring as to the cause," the councilor heading the investigation concluded that "it derived from the abuse committed in the slaughter of pigs for some of the insurgents who inspire [with] their perverse ideas those whom we have in our possessions."[10]

How might we read this surprising reference to a shortage of pigs in Havana somehow linked to insurgents from other colonies? The verb used to describe the slaughter is the Spanish *beneficio*, an archaic term for the killing (with a knife), bloodletting, and quartering of animals. According to the councilor's statement, the killing was done not for the

[8] Francisco Arango, "Discurso sobre la agricultura" in *Obras*. (Havana: Imagen Contemporánea, 2005), 1:159.
[9] Manuel Moreno Fraginals, *El ingenio: Complejo económico social cubano del azúcar* (Havana: Editorial de Ciencias Sociales, 1978), 1:68, 3:43–44; Dale Tomich, *Through the Prism of Slavery: Labor, Capital, and World Economy* (Lanham: Rowman & Littlefield, 2004), 75–94.
[10] Archivo Histórico de la Oficina del Historiador de la Ciudad, Habana (AHOHCH), Actas Capitulares del Ayuntamiento de la Habana (AC), tomo 50, f. 247, September 9, 1791. Original: "Yndagando la causa de esta inovación se le havía indicado procedía del abuso que se hacía en el beneficio de los cerdos para algunos de los insurgentes, y estos inspirasen sus perversas ideas a los que teníamos en nuestras posesiones."

benefit of those committing the crime, but rather for insurgents, defined contextually as foreign. Finally, the councilor attributed the insurgents' desire to contaminate local blacks to innate, racial qualities: "the malevolent inclinations of the descendants of Ethiopia are well-known and troubling, notwithstanding the care with which we try to teach them in these dominions."[11]

The mention of the killing of pigs in Havana for the benefit of foreign black insurgents, however oblique, hints at some surprising possibilities. Perhaps the councilor referred to a network by which blacks in Havana sent aid to black rebels in Saint-Domingue. Alternatively, his emphasis on "perverse ideas" and "malevolent tendencies" might suggest an assistance more metaphorical than literal. In the French colony, the killing of a pig at Bois Caïman served as the ritual beginning of the war against the slave regime. Might this brief and enigmatic allusion to foreign insurgents and pork shortages be a documentary trace of the ritual sacrifice of pigs in Havana in support of black revolution in Saint-Domingue?

The potential existence of such a ceremony in Havana would have indicated that "descendants of Ethiopians" in Cuba managed – just days after the start of the Haitian Revolution – to inform themselves of events in the neighboring colony. If the sacrifice of pigs in both places might have suggested a world of shared cultural repertoires, it also revealed the presence of a potent black solidarity in which people across colonial and imperial boundaries provided moral, spiritual, and perhaps material aid to their black counterparts elsewhere: Cuban blacks to Haitian ones by honoring them ritually or aiding them materially; Haitian blacks to Cuban ones by inspiring them to act. Just weeks after Bois Caïman and the war it launched, then, we see perhaps an early and surprising sign of what Julius Scott famously called the "common wind" of communication among black men and women of the African Diaspora in the era of the Haitian Revolution.[12]

That is one way to read the mysterious mention of pork shortages in Havana somehow caused by foreign insurgents. But it is not the only one.

---

[11] Ibid; the remainder of the original statement is: "es constante y de temerse las malas inclinaciones en los descendientes de la Etiopía aun sin embargo del esmero con que se les quiera enseñar en estos dominios." On the terminology of slaughter, see Esteban Pichardo, *Diccionario provincial casi-razonado de voces cubanas*, 3rd edition (Havana: Imprenta la Antilla, 1862), 26.

[12] On African and creole elements of Bois Caïman, see Law, "La Cérémoie du Bois-Caïman." The classic account of the circulation of Haiti's example in the Black Atlantic is Julius Scott, "The Common Wind: Currents of Afro-American Communication in the Era of the Haitian Revolution," PhD dissertation, Duke University, 1986.

That reading is based on the minutes of the meeting of the Havana city council on September 9, 1791, preserved today in Havana's municipal archive, which is housed, along with the Museum of the City of Havana, in the old Palace of the Governor and Captain-General on the verdant and graceful Plaza de Armas. In September 1791, the building was so new it was not yet quite finished. The governor, himself a sugar mill owner and holder of slaves, lived in temporary quarters on the mezzanine floor, the same one on which the city council had its headquarters and meeting hall.[13] Today, on that floor in those quarters sit the handsome leather-bound volumes with neat transcriptions of those meetings' lengthy discussions – about meat shortages and street lights, slaves and sugar. The handwriting in those volumes is so neat and regular that it is hard to imagine the councilors ever raising their voices in disagreement. The script is so perfect that one can almost imagine the steady, precise rhythm of the scribe's pen on paper making him perhaps unmindful of mistakes, of things that might have made little sense had he paused to reread. Could an error in transcription account for the mysterious written record that seems to conjure possible pig sacrifices in Havana?[14]

As is often the case with colonial documents, multiple transcriptions of the same documents are sometimes scattered in several locations. In the Spanish colonial archives in Seville, another partial record of that September 9 meeting has survived, almost by accident. Well into the Haitian Revolution, in February 1794, months after colonial authorities in Saint-Domingue had abolished slavery in French-held territory, the

---

[13] M.E. Martín Zequeira and E.L. Rodríguez Fernández, *Guía de arquitectura: La Habana colonial (1519–1898)* (Havana and Seville: Junta de Andalucía, 1995), 82–83, 126–27; and "Un palacio entre sombras y luces," in *Opus Habana*, Vol. III, No. 2, 1999, 4–15.

[14] In 2002, I spent some time working in the Santiago Municipal Archives reading the minutes of the Santiago city council. Researchers were not allowed to consult the original volumes and instead were required to use the handwritten transcriptions in ink that were then being compiled by one of the archivists. We worked in the same room the whole time: I was reading her transcriptions of the 1790s and 1800s; she was transcribing meeting minutes from well into the nineteenth century. She did this every day, all day. Her transcriptions were neat; sometimes they sloped because the paper had no lines, and sometimes the ink became faint (there were not always ready replacements once the ink ran out). Very occasionally, I encountered a mistake: a line missed, a word repeated. Throughout this book, we will have occasion to consider the archive, in Michel-Rolph Trouillot's phrase, as an institution of power. But it is worth remembering that not all archives are equal, and that such phrases do not take adequate account of the ways in which the contemporary archives that historians rely on in places such as Port-au-Prince or Santiago de Cuba sometimes project insubstantiality as much as power. See Michel-Rolph Trouillot, *Silencing the Past: Power and the Production of History* (Boston: Beacon, 1995).

governor and captain-general of Cuba wrote to the minister of state in
Madrid. The topic of the letter was not too out of the ordinary for that
place and time, conveying as it did his conviction that Cuba was gravely
threatened by the events unfolding in Saint-Domingue. To his letter, the
governor appended the minutes of a Havana city council meeting held
on February 12, 1794. In that 1794 meeting, one of the councilors read
aloud from the minutes of the September 9, 1791 session in which the
members discussed the pork shortages. In that manner, the words spoken
at that September 1791 meeting resurfaced in a different time and form.[15]

In this second transcription, however, the meeting unfolds quite differently. Here, the members of the city council arrive at the same point,
lamenting – with exactly the same words – the ways in which foreign
insurgents could contaminate their own slaves. What precedes this consideration of evil and contagion, however, is not a discussion about the
fate of pigs, but rather a discussion of the September 8, 1791 arrival in
Havana of a slaving vessel named the *Deux Soeurs*.

The *Deux Soeurs* was a slave ship, not unlike the many that were then
arriving and transforming the face and feel of Havana and its environs.
Captained by a Frenchman named Louis Houet de Kehu, it had arrived in
Cap Français on August 9, 1791 from Porto Novo on the Bight of Benin
loaded with 346 captives. It usually took French traders about two to
three weeks to sell their human cargo in the colonies, which meant that
sometime in the middle of that process, Kehu would have found his buyers
suddenly under siege by the slave rebellion in the surrounding northern
plain. Amidst that turmoil, and perhaps unable to finish his business, Kehu
set sail for quieter shores, arriving in Havana on September 8, with 292
men and women to sell as slaves there.[16] Perhaps the 292 enslaved men

---

[15] A partial transcript (quoted here) of the September 9, 1791 cabildo meeting is appended
      to the minutes of the February 12, 1794 meeting, in turn attached to Las Casas to
      Secretary of State Pedro Acuña, February 19, 1794, in Archivo General de Indias, Seville
      (AGI), Estado, leg. 14, exp. 73.

[16] The itinerary of the ship is reconstructed from sometimes conflicting accounts in mul-
      tiple sources. *Voyages: The Trans-Atlantic Slave Trade Database* (hereafter *Voyages*)
      (http://slavevoyages.org/tast/database/search.faces?yearFrom=1791&yearTo=1791&
      shipname=soeurs) identifies a 1791 voyage (31351) of the *Deux Soeurs* as captained by
      a Louis Huet de Relia. Jean Mettas, *Répertoire des expéditions négrières Françaises aux
      XVIII siècle* (Paris: Société française d'histoire d'outre-mer, 1978–1984), 1:758–59,
      gives the captain's name as Louis Houet de Kehu. See also "Estado de los negros
      introducidos en la Habana, Septiembre 1791, in AGI, Santo Domingo (SD), leg.
      2207. Spanish sources sometimes refer to the ship as the *Dos Hermanos* (rather than
      Hermanas) and *Los Hermanos*, and the captain as Luis Quichud. On the timing of
      slave sales in the French colonies, see Robert Louis Stein, *The French Slave Trade in*

and women he brought to Havana represented the difference between the 346 he arrived with in Cap Français and the number he had been able to sell before the onset of trouble there.

The members of Havana's city council had a different hypothesis. They suspected that Kehu was carrying and attempting to sell black insurgents captured in Saint-Domingue, representing them to Havana authorities and buyers as *bozales*, or new African arrivals. That prospect worried the councilors, who imagined that these insurgents, once sold into slavery in Cuba, would ally with local slaves to destroy the emerging plantation order. "Some of the insurgents," they said – using the exact same wording as in the version of the minutes that hinted at possible pig sacrifices – would "inspire with their perverse ideas those that we have in our possessions, for the malevolent inclinations of the descendants of Ethiopia are well-known and troubling, notwithstanding the care with which we try to teach them in these dominions."[17] Potential contagion was an immediate cause of concern in Havana, where – thanks to changes recently underway – there were suddenly many more people susceptible to being contaminated and significantly more wealth for them to destroy.

Neither account of the September 9, 1791 meeting makes it possible for us to know whether its claim was true. The brief inkling of potential pig sacrifices in the first reveals nothing about the participants, nor the place where they gathered, nor the means by which they learned of the insurgents they allegedly honored. Meanwhile, the discussion of captured insurgents illegally introduced in Havana aboard the *Deux Soeurs* provides absolutely no information on who those captive insurgents might have been or to whom they were sold. And information available elsewhere about the *Deux Soeurs* reveals nothing about the people it transported to Havana.[18]

While both claims remain unverifiable, placed side by side they expose perfectly the contradictory effects of the Haitian Revolution in the Atlantic World. One account of the city council meeting suggests a story of black solidarity and the circulation of emancipatory ideas and rituals. The second confronts us instead with the remarkable possibility that the same people making dramatic bids for freedom in Saint-Domingue

---

the *Eighteenth Century: An Old Regime Business* (Madison: University of Wisconsin, Press, 1979), 110–113.

[17] Quoted in minutes of the February 12, 1794 cabildo meeting, attached to Las Casas to Secretary of State Pedro Acuña, February 19, 1794, in AGI, Estado, leg. 14, exp. 73.

[18] *Voyages*, http://slavevoyages.org/tast/database/search.faces?yearFrom=1791&yearTo=1791&shipname=soeurs; and Mettas, *Répertoire*, 1:758–59.

were being captured and sent to Cuba as slaves, transformed in the quick journey across Caribbean waters from participants in a historic struggle for black liberation to hostages in the violent entrenchment of slavery, from protagonists in the Haitian Revolution to targets of Cuba's sugar revolution. In the tension between those two possibilities lies the heart of this book.

At a basic level, liberation in Saint-Domingue helped entrench its denial in Cuba. As slavery and colonialism collapsed in the French colony, the Spanish island underwent transformations that were almost the mirror image of Haiti's. The sugar no longer produced in Saint-Domingue was now produced in Cuba. Machinery, suddenly without a purpose in revolutionary Saint-Domingue, found its way to Cuba; so too did men who worked as sugar technicians and others considered experts in managing slaves. Many of the African captives who would have once arrived in Cap Français or Port-au-Prince were diverted to Havana. The Haitian Revolution thus hastened and hardened Cuba's sugar revolution and the brutal practices of enslavement that came with it. Two decades after Haitian independence, Cuba had emerged as the world's largest producer of sugar and one of the greatest consumers of enslaved Africans in the nineteenth-century world.

To examine the ways in which the Haitian Revolution contributed to the entrenchment of slavery in Cuba, however, is not to deny the profound antislavery power of that revolution. Indeed, the power of the Haitian Revolution derived from the fact that it was forced to operate precisely in a world still committed to the linked realities of slavery, racism, and colonial rule. The Haitian Revolution formally eliminated each of those phenomena in its own territory, but not elsewhere. In the territoriality of its institutional outcomes, it resembled every revolution of the modern world. But the absence of foreign abolition decrees or slave rebellions directly attributable to Haiti does not diminish the significance of the Haitian Revolution. Nor does it mean that its impact was purely in the realm of "symbolic discourse" or "powerful mythos," as Seymour Drescher has argued.[19]

Controversies over the influence of the Haitian Revolution began almost immediately in August 1791, even if participants at the time did

[19] Seymour Drescher, "The Limits of Example," in David Geggus, ed., *The Impact of the Haitian Revolution in the Atlantic World*, (Columbia: University of South Carolina Press, 2001), 10–14. See also Seymour Drescher, *Abolition: A History of Slavery and Antislavery* (New York: Cambridge University Press, 2009), chaps. 6–7.

not yet use the terms *Haiti* or *Revolution*. Debates arose, for instance, about whether the uprising was the result of influence wielded by groups like the Amis des Noirs, or, from the opposing camp, by royalists bent on illustrating the dangers of revolutionary currents, the better to fend them off. As the revolution took root, questions swirled about whether the rebels' example would influence the enslaved elsewhere in the hemisphere. Answers were mobilized to help argue for outcomes such as the expansion or, alternatively, the curtailment of the slave trade in neighboring locations. In staking out positions on these questions, participants used the language of influence ideologically, to couch critiques of revolution or absolutism, or to mobilize support for one or another economic vision. This study then is not concerned with influence *per se*, understood narrowly as the power of one event to produce a similar result elsewhere – in this case, emancipation or rebellion or independence. Instead, it focuses on the quotidian links – material and symbolic – between the radical antislavery that emerged in revolutionary Saint-Domingue and the expanding power of slavery in colonial Cuba.

The majority of Africans transported to Cuba during and after the collapse of slavery in Saint-Domingue ended up on sugar plantations. There, they encountered creole Spanish slaves and perhaps – as the *Deux Soeurs* episode suggests – some transplanted rebels from the Haitian Revolution. Together, these men and women talked, interpreted, and imagined what Haiti might portend. They spoke of black generals who had defeated white ones and then conquered the land, becoming, they said, masters of themselves. They spoke of French declarations of freedom and, later, of the coronation of a black king. At the same time, they shared the experience of enslavement on Cuban plantations. They complained bitterly about the excess of work, the lack of food or free time, and the brutality and frequency of corporal punishment. As they considered their present, enslaved men and women in Cuba grabbed hold of Haiti as a way to think about their enslavement and to imagine other possible futures. How the enslaved understood the world that offered, on the one hand, Haiti as example and, on the other, the intensification of their own enslavement becomes a central question if we are to take seriously the challenges raised by Eugene Genovese's notion of a "revolution in consciousness" wrought by Haiti in the Black Atlantic, or by Laurent Dubois's call to write the "intellectual history of the enslaved."[20]

[20] Ada Ferrer, "Speaking of Haiti: Slavery, Revolution, and Freedom in Cuban Slave Testimony," in David Geggus and Norman Fiering, eds., *The World of the Haitian Revolution*, (Bloomington: Indiana University Press, 2009), 223–247. Quotes are from Eugene

Even though no slave rebellion in Cuba came close to assuming the proportions of the Haitian example, it is clear that the Haitian Revolution, and Haiti itself after 1804, became part of the cognitive world of the enslaved. Masters thought about Saint-Domingue, too, interpreting the everyday actions of their bondspeople in light of what they knew, or thought they knew, about the Haitian Revolution. And as the revolution changed the demographic and economic profile of the Spanish colony, it shaped the way colonial authorities governed, given what they called the "novel character that distinguished the present epoch from all previous ones."[21] The Cuban slave system that emerged at the turn of the nineteenth century, then, was one that had internalized the Haitian Revolution and the liberation it represented: as model, as warning, and sometimes as concrete possibility. The Haitian Revolution – the circulation of its example and the material consequences of its achievement of emancipation and independence – profoundly shaped the experience of enslavement and conceptions of freedom in Cuba and the Atlantic World in the nineteenth century.

The nineteenth century saw the rise of what historians sometimes refer to as the "second slavery." The "first slavery" was that of the early sugar islands, British colonies such as Barbados starting in the seventeenth century, and Jamaica and French Saint-Domingue in the eighteenth. The second wave of slavery in the nineteenth century consisted of the rise of new or reinvigorated slave regimes producing tropical commodities at unprecedented scales in areas formerly marginal to the global economy, most notably Cuba, the U.S. lower South, and southeastern Brazil.[22] To consider Haiti and Cuba side by side then allows us to understand the material links between the collapse of one of the key sites of the first slavery and the emergence of one of the key sites of the second. Such an approach illuminates the metaphorical "hinge" between the first and second slaveries, addressing the broad conceptual questions about the global history of slavery and capitalism while still focusing centrally on how men and women lived those transitions in their lifetimes.

Genovese, *From Rebellion to Revolution: Afro-American Slave Revolts in the Making of the Modern World* (Baton Rouge: Louisiana State University Press, 1979), 96; and Laurent Dubois, "An Enslaved Enlightenment: Rethinking the Intellectual History of the French Atlantic" *Social History* 31 (2006):1–14.

[21] Bando, February 25, 1796, in "Expediente relativo a las precauciones y seguridad..." in Archivo Nacional de Cuba, Havana (ANC), Real Consulado y Junta de Fomento (RCJF), leg. 209, exp. 8993.

[22] On the "second slavery," see the important work of Dale Tomich, *Through the Prism*.

It is important, however, to understand the history of Cuban slavery presented here as part of the "second slavery" in another way as well. Part of what distinguished the second from the first modern wave of slavery is that it developed in an age of ascendant antislavery. Together, the Haitian Revolution and the growing hegemony of British abolitionism constituted a commanding challenge to the institution of slavery. In the latter case, the most powerful country in the globe committed itself to the gradual erosion and eventual elimination of the institution. In the former, the hemisphere's newest and least powerful government stood as an example of the ability of slaves themselves to achieve liberation. Thus, in the second wave of slavery, freedom was always already present. Perhaps that had always been true, for the enslaved did not require prompting from British abolitionist William Wilberforce or even from Toussaint Louverture to see themselves as something other than slaves. But now freedom was present more systematically, not as a desired state for an individual or family or community, but as a possible legal status for all members of society. Everyone – slaves, masters, free people of color, authorities – now understood that a post-slavery society was possible, perhaps in their lifetimes, perhaps in their children's.

This book takes as its point of departure the simultaneity of the Haitian Revolution and Cuba's sugar revolution in order to tell the multifaceted story of the violent entrenchment of slavery in Cuba occurring precisely in the ambit of black freedom in Haiti. Anchored in Cuba, the study tacks back and forth between the two islands to tell a story of freedom and slavery being made and unmade, simultaneously and each almost within view of the other.

Freedom's Mirror is organized in two parts: the first roughly corresponds to the period of the Haitian Revolution, the second to its immediate aftermath. Chapter 1 examines the place of slavery in Cuban society before 1791 and explores the responses to revolution among the island's planter elite and colonial authorities, who saw the French crisis above all as an opportunity. Together, they sought to remake their own colony in Saint-Domingue's image while avoiding the upheavals that had turned Saint-Domingue into Haiti. Of course, powerful white men were not the only ones who imagined opportunities flowing from the events of August 1791. Chapter 2 focuses on those broader understandings and responses to the early Haitian Revolution in Cuba. It shows how the very success of the planters' project – the massive expansion of slavery on Cuban ground – helped make black revolution more thinkable in that time and place. Indeed, it was the very structures of enslavement that helped circulate the example of black people destroying slavery. Chapter 3 focuses on that same encounter between slavery's making and unmaking on very different ground – in Spanish Santo Domingo, where men from Cuba serving in Spain's army became allies and commanders of men such as Toussaint Louverture. The Cubans collaborated with the black rebels, dined with them, occasionally served as their godfathers, sometimes danced with their women. That intimate encounter shaped the way slavery and revolution would be understood in Cuba. At the same time, the proximity of an ascendant colonial slave regime shaped the possibilities and course of the Haitian Revolution itself. Chapter 4 analyzes the ways in which Cuba was implicated in the later Haitian Revolution, as a place of asylum for planters seeking to preserve their hold over other human beings and as an important ally in Napoleon's violent reassertion of colonial authority and racial slavery. At the same time, however, residents of the Spanish colony also encountered the dramatic defeat of the French project. They witnessed the massive evacuation of French troops at the end of the conflict, and they read eloquent proclamations by Haiti's new leaders – proclamations that announced black victory and projected the victor's voice in Atlantic debates around slavery, freedom, and sovereignty.

The second part of *Freedom's Mirror* considers the political, diplomatic, and intellectual effects of having an independent black state in the midst of a Caribbean sea full of colonial slave regimes. Chapter 5 focuses on the very early Haitian state ruled by Jean-Jacques Dessalines. It considers the question of whether the Haitian state promoted antislavery abroad, and it analyzes examples of antislavery movements in Cuba to explore the place of Haiti among their adherents. Chapter 6 is an examination of the profound instability provoked by Napoleon's usurpation of the Spanish crown in 1808 – a crossroads reminiscent of the French crisis that had helped instigate revolution in the Caribbean two decades earlier. As war and confrontation took root across much of Spanish America, in Cuba the presence of tens of thousands of French residents, the violent power of slavery, and the proximity of Haiti gave the "loyalty" that reigned in Cuba a particularly vulnerable cast.[23] Chapter 7 is an extended examination of the now well-known antislavery and anticolonial movement led by the free black carpenter José Antonio Aponte. While some

[23] On the question of Cuban "loyalty" in the nineteenth century, see David Sartorius, *Ever Faithful: Race, Loyalty, and the Ends of Empire in Spanish Cuba* (Durham, N.C.: Duke University Press, 2014).

have recently called into question the movement's antislavery and anti-colonial character, here I argue that the movement was indeed both those things. In some fashion, this argument represents a return to some of the interpretations of the late José Luciano Franco.[24] But I arrive at that conclusion differently, by way of a mysterious missing book that takes us to Rome and Ethiopia in an effort to imagine another Haiti, a new black kingdom in a Cuba without slavery.

That the revolution of sugar and slavery at the turn of the nineteenth century radically transformed colonial society in Cuba is indisputable. But in one regard, it had the opposite effect. Haiti and José Antonio Aponte notwithstanding, in the Atlantic Age of Revolution, Cuba would remain both a powerful slave society and a loyal colony of Spain. Napoleon's invasion of the Iberian peninsula in 1808 set off a complex chain of events that by 1826 had resulted in the independence of all of Spain's American territories, save Puerto Rico and Cuba. That year, an Irish-born sugar planter in Havana addressed himself to Spain's prime minister to explain that divergence. "[Cuba's] property owners," he wrote, "have a direct interest in not separating from the mother country, for they know without a doubt that any movement would lead them to their ruin, and they fear exposing themselves to the fate suffered by the unfortunate victims of Santo Domingo."[25] In 1826, two decades after Haitian independence, as old Spanish viceroyalties and provinces became independent nations called Venezuela, Bolivia, Mexico, and Argentina, Latin America's first independent state, Haiti, faced a world still often unwilling to say its name. The planter's broader point that a fear of a slave revolution – of a new *Santo Domingo* – had kept Cuba attached to Spain, meanwhile, became a statement so oft repeated that it acquired the character of self-evident truth.

Yet the stories told here paint a different picture. *Haiti* was, in the hands of Cuban planters and their allies, a flexible notion and image, invoked strategically in ways meant to strengthen the hand of slavery in Cuba. Thus in 1791, the revolution was an argument for expanding slavery and the slave trade; in 1811, Haiti was justification for postponing abolition. Throughout, the planters were supremely confident that they could manage the risks. Ultimately, then, their decision to remain Spanish

---

[24] Stephan Palmié, *Wizards and Scientists: Explorations in Afro-Cuban Modernity and Tradition* (Durham: Duke University Press, 2002), chapter 1; José Luciano Franco, *Las conspiraciones de 1810 y 1812* (Havana: Editorial de Ciencias Sociales, 1977) and *Ensayos históricos* (Havana: Editorial de Ciencias Sociales, 1974), 125–190.
[25] Peter Fregent to Duque del Infantado, June 29, 1826, in AGI, Estado, leg. 86B, exp. 78.

was one dictated less by fear (even though in moments that might have been what they felt) than by self-interest. Invoking the very real perils of their age gave them the power to negotiate and to win some of the liberties of independence – such as free trade in 1817 – without triggering the confrontations that might bring those risks home.

The issue, however, was that planters were not the only ones considering options and making history. The new state of Haiti also weighed risks, and those risks notwithstanding, it offered its territory as refuge to those who came in search of freedom, whether from Spain or racial slavery or both. Independent Haiti guaranteed the freedom and citizenship of black men and women who arrived on its shores escaping slavery, just as it provided material support to the project of Latin American independence. For their part, the enslaved in territories across the Atlantic World also actively engaged with the Haitian Revolution and later with Haiti itself as a way to think about freedom and to "ease the burden of their enslavement." Those words were spoken in 1806 by Estanislao, a man born in Port-au-Prince, taken from the scenes of the Haitian Revolution, and held as a slave on a sugar plantation outside Havana, where he and his companions plotted liberation in a colony that in becoming the new Saint-Domingue might yet have become a new Haiti.[26]

---

[26] See Chapter 5.

"A Colony Worth a Kingdom"

Cuba's Sugar Revolution in the Shadow of Saint-Domingue

Slavery had existed in Cuba long before the Haitian Revolution, indeed, long before Saint-Domingue had even embarked on its path as plantation power of the late eighteenth century. Yet the story of slavery in Cuba had differed significantly from that of the major slave societies of the French and British Caribbean, where in the two most productive colonies, Saint-Domingue and Jamaica, the enslaved accounted for over 85 percent of the population. There, plantations, monoculture, and slavery together formed the social and economic foundation of the colonies. In mid-century Cuba, slavery was significant, and local elites insistently called for its expansion. But in general, as Franklin Knight persuasively argued some time ago, the Spanish colony was more a society with slaves than a slave society.[1]

That began to change gradually in the last decades of the eighteenth century. With the start of the Haitian Revolution, it changed inexorably. Cuban planters ramped up production, purchasing more and more land and mills and enslaved laborers to fill the world demand for sugar now left unfilled by Saint-Domingue. But they did significantly more than fill an abstract space created in the world market. They remade their society, profoundly transforming the economic and social life of the colony. Allied with the colonial state, they worked to expand slavery and sugar while minimizing the risks of the kind of destruction engulfing Saint-Domingue.

---

[1] See Franklin Knight, *Slave Society in Cuba during the Nineteenth Century* (Madison: University of Wisconsin Press, 1970) and *The Caribbean: Genesis of a Fragmented Nationalism* (New York: Oxford University Press, 1978). On the distinction between societies with slaves and slave societies, see Elsa Goveia, *Slave Society in the British Leeward Islands at the End of the Eighteenth Century* (New Haven: Yale University Press, 1965).

Situated at that crossroads, Cuban planters, authorities, and the enslaved themselves felt the urgency of the moment and the place they occupied. The revolution, planters were sure, was an opportunity, a gift. But as they worked to make slavery and sugar more powerful all around them, they occasionally let themselves wonder if Saint-Domingue might not also be a harbinger of a more dangerous future that their project might help bring into being. It was with these concerns and tensions palpable, always perceptibly in the shadow of the Haitian Revolution, that the Cuban slave system was transformed at the end of the eighteenth century and functioned for much of the nineteenth.

Revolution's Prelude

From the founding of the Spanish colony of Cuba in 1511 to the middle of the eighteenth century, 60,000 African men and women had been brought to Cuba as slaves. These men and women arrived by way of both licit and illicit trade, in most cases from neighboring Caribbean ports. Once in Cuba, many remained in urban settings or on small farms, or *estancias*, on the outskirts of cities or towns. Those more firmly ensconced in the countryside tended to work in relatively small concentrations (by Caribbean and later Cuban standards), sometimes on tobacco or modest sugar farms, or on large cattle estates with small numbers of enslaved laborers. In the middle of the eighteenth century, only four sugar mills on the island had more than a hundred slaves. In the interior of the island, production was geared to internal consumption, and in nearby ports a modest monopoly trade was overshadowed by a substantial contraband trade with British, French, Dutch, and later American traders. Tellingly, at midcentury, the sugar, tobacco, and hides *legally* shipped from Cuba were carried in just three ships sailing annually to Spain (Figure 1.1).[2]

   Even then, however, developments in Europe, the Americas, and Cuba itself were starting to lay the groundwork for the emergence of a different kind of colony. One important portent of change came with the British seizure of Havana in 1762, during the Seven Years' War.[3] The British occupation opened a brief window for dramatic commercial growth. Almost immediately, merchants from England's North American colonies

---

[2] Hubert Aimes, *A History of Slavery in Cuba, 1511–1868* (New York: Putnam and Sons, 1907), 35–36; Knight, *Slave Society*, 4–6, 22; Moreno Fraginals, *El ingenio*, 1:62.
[3] Elena Schneider, *The Occupation of Havana: Slavery, War, and Empire in the Eighteenth Century* (Chapel Hill: UNC/Omohundro Institute, forthcoming).

FIGURE 1.1. View of Havana Harbor, 1760s. Courtesy of the John Carter Brown Library at Brown University.

began arriving and selling their wares: food, horses, linens, wool, and sugar-making equipment. British officials eliminated trade restrictions and abolished taxes on imports and exports, as well as a host of levies used to help finance Spanish military and political power.

Most importantly, perhaps, the new British government in Havana eliminated monopoly arrangements in slave trading and opened up the port of Havana for the entry and sale of enslaved Africans. In the ten months of British occupation, British traders brought unprecedented numbers of Africans to Havana. Estimates of the number of captives introduced during the ten months of occupation vary significantly, with the likely number probably close to 4,000. If not as exorbitant as once assumed, the figure was significant, considering that only about 8,000 had entered in the entire twenty-year period before the occupation, and that it was significantly higher than the number that would have entered in ten months under Spain's monopoly system. In this manner the British helped make real what were already significant calls emerging from the local elite for the expansion of the slave trade.[4] With more enslaved laborers to cultivate and harvest the land and with obstacles to trade removed, sugar exports reached new highs. Precise production figures for the ten months of occupation are unavailable, but the rapid growth of production visible immediately after the British evacuation suggests the acceleration of change wrought by the occupation. The export of sugar in the half decade following British intervention averaged more than 2,000 tons a year, compared with just 300 tons in the 1750s.[5] While the commercial and slave trade bonanza was short-lived, the sudden gains reaped by local planters made of this group the most vociferous proponents of reform and the most eager choreographers of Cuba's sugar revolution.

Soon after the British occupation, the independence of the North American colonies further laid the groundwork for reform. No longer tied through a metropole to British West Indian sugar, the thirteen former

---

[4] For a review of the statistical disputes, see ibid., and Enrique López Mesa, "Acerca de la introducción de esclavos en la Habana durante la ocupación británica (1762–1763)," manuscript in preparation. For an example of local calls for the expansion of the slave trade in the period before the British occupation of Havana, see Nicolás Joseph de Ribera, *Descripción de la Isla de Cuba* (Havana: Editorial Ciencias Sociales, 1986 [1760]), 165.

[5] Knight, *Slave Society*, 6–7; Moreno Fraginals, *El ingenio*, 1:35–36, 3:43; David Murray, *Odious Commerce: Britain, Spain, and the Abolition of the Cuban Slave Trade* (New York: Cambridge University Press, 1980); Louis A. Pérez, *Cuba Between Reform and Revolution* (New York: Oxford University Press, 1988), 57–58; Aimes, *A History of Slavery*, 35–36; Hugh Thomas, *Cuba: The Pursuit of Freedom* (New York: Harper & Row, 1971), 61.

colonies became a tempting and promising market for Cuban agricultural products. Indeed, much of the increase in Cuban sugar production in this period found its way to American rather than Spanish markets. The enactment of limited free trade between Cuba and the new American republic in 1779 strengthened the planters' conviction that there lay a natural commercial partner. There was no way for the Cuban planters to take full advantage of that market legally; but there it was, calling them to consider new arrangements and a new kind of future for their society.[6]

Equally important, Spain's metropolitan government in this period considered and adopted reforms that had the potential to set in motion a profound transformation of Cuban society. In a climate of what has been called enlightened despotism, the metropolitan government rethought many long-standing assumptions of its rule. In these efforts, the colonial question loomed. Up for debate were issues such as the value of agricultural production over mining and the relative perils of enacting free trade versus the seemingly inevitable threat of contraband that came with keeping it closed. An important early figure in this regard was the former finance minister of Spain, José del Campillo, who, in a 1743 treatise first published in 1762, argued for the liberalization of American trade. Others took up the call with enthusiasm. Strongly influenced by Campillo's work, the powerful Pedro Rodríguez, Conde de Campomanes, jurist, economist, and later president of the Council of Castile, took to heart the distinctions between empires of conquest and empires of commerce popularized by contemporary thinkers such as Montesquieu and the Abbé Raynal. Campomanes argued that the present and future success of Spain rested on developing an empire of commerce. It was this reformist energy that resulted in the king's 1765 decision to enact limited free trade for the Caribbean colonies, a concession extended to most of the mainland colonies in 1778 and to New Spain (Mexico) in 1789.[7]

---

[6] Ramón de la Sagra, *Historia económico-política y estadística de la Isla de Cuba* (Havana: Arazoza y Soler, 1831), 134; Ramiro Guerra y Sánchez, *Manual de historia de Cuba* (Havana: Editorial Ciencas Sociales, 1973), 200–201; and Thomas, *Cuba*, 68.

[7] On Spanish political debates on colonial commerce in this period, see Stanley and Barbara Stein, *Apogee of Empire: Spain and New Spain in the Age of Charles III, 1759–1789* (Baltimore: John Hopkins University Press, 2003), 145–345; and Pedro Rodríguez Campomanes, *Reflexiones sobre el comercio español a indias* (Madrid, Instituto de Estudios Fiscales, 1988), including the excellent introduction by Vicente Llombart Rosa. On these debates as they relate to Cuba, Francisco Ponte Domínguez, *Arango y Parreño, estadista colonial cubano* (Havana: Imp. Molina y Cía. 1937); José Antonio Piqueras, "Los amigos de Arango en la Corte de Carlos IV" in María Dolores González-Ripoll and Izaskun

Connected to a growing belief in the utility of freer trade was sometimes a critical questioning of Spain's reliance on mineral wealth. First
Campillo, and later and more emphatically Campomanes, stressed the
urgency of developing tropical commodities as a mainstay of colonial
commerce. In those calls, Campomanes gave the island of Cuba pride
of place. The Abbé Raynal had speculated that the island of Cuba was
"of itself equal in value to a Kingdom." Campomanes agreed, arguing
that by cultivating large-scale tobacco and sugar industries, Cuba would
be capable of competing with the most prosperous French islands, a
claim the Cuban planters were more than ready to believe and help make
real.[8]

As one might expect, every reflection on how precisely Spain might
develop and expand colonial commerce and agriculture led to one place:
the slave trade. Prosperity required agriculture, and agriculture required
laborers. From across the Spanish world, from high ministers in Madrid
to military officers sent to survey the state of the colonies, came insistent
calls for the "liberation" of the slave trade. Writing from Havana, Santiago, Caracas, Cartagena, Santo Domingo, and elsewhere, most colonial
officials concurred: if the state wanted to develop commercial agriculture,
it needed to "facilitate by all means possible the entry of blacks."[9] Against
arguments about the potential dangers inherent in that path, advocates of
an expanded slave trade pointed to other sugar islands of the Caribbean
and asked, "Will we be the only ones more swayed by the imagined risks
of prosperity than by the sure and fatal ones of poverty?"[10]

Álvarez Cuartero, eds., *Francisco Arango y la invención de la Cuba azucarera* (Sala-
    manca: Aquilafuente, 2009), 151–166; Pablo Tornero Tinajero, *Crecimiento económico
    y transformaciones sociales: esclavos, hacendados y comerciantes en la Cuba colo-
    nial, 1760–1840,* (Madrid: Ministerio de Trabajo y Seguridad Social, 1996), 23–34;
    Allan Keuthe, *Cuba, 1753–1815: Crown, Military, and Society* (Nashville: University of
    Tennessee Press, 1986).
8   Rodríguez Campomanes, *Reflexiones*, 70–82, 349–366; Abbé Raynal, *A Philosophical
    and Political History of the Settlements and Trade of the Europeans in the East and West
    Indies* (Glasgow: Mundell and Son, 1804) 4: 163. See also Jeremy Adelman, *Sovereignty
    and Revolution in the Iberian Atlantic* (Princeton: Princeton University Press, 2006),
    25–26; Stanley Stein and Barbara Stein, *Silver, Trade, and War: Spain and America in
    the Making of Early Modern Europe* (Baltimore: Johns Hopkins University Press, 2000),
    231–234.
9   Antonio Narváez y la Torre, Governor of Cartagena, 1778, quoted in Jeremy Adelman,
    Sovereignty and Revolution, 66.
10 Agustín Crame, "Discurso sobre el fomento de la isla de Cuba" (1768), partially
    reprinted in Levi Marrero, *Cuba: Economía y sociedad* (Madrid: Playor, 1983–1984),
    9: 14–15; Leida Fernández Prieto, "Crónica anunciada de una Cuba azucarera," in
    González-Ripoll and Álvarez Cuartero, eds., *Francisco Arango*, 55–65.

The voices raised in support of expanding and opening the slave trade were also, importantly, those of powerful, local-born men. Creole by birth, Spanish in name, members of the emerging Cuban planter class became perhaps the principal and most effective advocates for this particular transformation. They aimed to become masters of their own world by embracing and stretching the limits of the colonial bond, offering their metropolitan rulers guidance on how best to develop their island and place of birth. In the decades that followed Britain's occupation of Havana, petitions to the king from Havana's city council (many of whose members were prominent planters) and even from planters *qua* planters, became almost routine. They asked for an open slave trade, for permission to trade freely with British slave traders, for trade with neutrals in wartime, and so on. In 1780, for example, Havana planters presented a petition to the king arguing that opening up the slave trade would unleash the productive potential of their colony and thus place Spain in a position to better compete with England and France. They concluded – unaware then of how many times and how ardently they would have to repeat the claim in the decades to come – that the prospect of slave rebellion was minimal and that the project of sugar and slavery should proceed quickly and deliberately.[11] Everywhere, everyone with the power to speak and write seemed to agree: the emerging vision of profitable plantation colonies in the mode of Saint-Domingue required a vast and renewable supply of African labor.

Of those creole voices agitating for the consolidation of sugar and slavery in the colony, undoubtedly the most prominent was that of Francisco Arango y Parreño. A wealthy creole planter and lawyer, he became the unsurpassed spokesman for the Cuban sugar elite (Figure 1.2). In 1787, he traveled to Madrid and shortly after became the *apoderado* – or empowered representative – of the Havana city council. In that capacity he addressed himself to the king and his ministers to request one privilege after another. His first formal petition to the court in Madrid was, not surprisingly, a call for "an absolutely unrestricted slave trade" dated February 6, 1789.[12] Three weeks later, on February 28, the king issued a

[11] Murray, *Odious Commerce*, 5. Portions of the 1780 planter petition are reproduced in José Antonio Saco, *Colección de papeles científicos, históricos, políticos y de otros ramos sobre la Isla de Cuba* (Paris: Imprenta de D'Aubusson y Kugelmann, 1858), 1: 404–408. Saco dates the document as 1760, but Hugh Thomas and others as 1780.

[12] Francisco Arango y Parreño, "Primer papel sobre el comercio de negros," in *Obras*, 1:117–121. See also Ponte Domínguez, *Arango y Parreño*; Piqueras, "Los amigos de Arango;" Dale Tomich, "The Wealth of Empire: Francisco Arango y Parreño, Political

FIGURE 1.2. Francisco Arango y Parreño. From Willis Fletcher Johnson, *The History of Cuba*, volume 2 (New York: B.F. Buck & Company, 1920).

decree opening the slave trade and eliminating earlier monopoly arrangements in the transfer and sale of masses of black men and women. If the timing suggests credit due to Arango, in fact, the decree represented the culmination of Madrid's colonial reform projects, changing commercial

Economy and Slavery in Cuba," *Comparative Studies in Society and History*, 45 (2003): 4–28; and Anne Perotin, "Le projet cubain des grands planteurs de la Havane, jalons pour une lecture de Francisco Arango y Parreño, 1769–1839," *Mélanges de la Casa de Velázquez*, Vol. II (1974), 273–314.

prospects in the wake of American independence, as well as the fruit of colonial elites' unyielding pressure and voice.[13]

Much as Arango and others had requested, the king's decree granted permission for any Spaniard to purchase slaves in foreign ports and to introduce and sell them free of duty in designated ports in Cuba, Puerto Rico, Spanish Santo Domingo, and Caracas. Foreigners were also granted the privilege of introducing slaves free of duty, but only in a few official ports and with permission to remain for only twenty-four hours after their arrival. Rather than set fixed prices for the sale of slaves, as the old monopoly contracts had done, the new decree allowed buyers and sellers to negotiate prices directly. The king cast the effort as part of a project to develop colonial agriculture and commerce. Indeed, the development of agriculture was so clearly the objective that the decree imposed an extra tax on those who purchased slaves for domestic rather than agricultural labor. While the planters were thrilled with the measure, they also saw it as limited and imperfect; the restriction of twenty-four hours for foreigners to sell their human cargo, for instance, seemed from the start unworkable. Also, the freedoms it granted were provisional, valid for only two years, at which time the whole enterprise would be reviewed and reconsidered.[14]

Yet despite what some perceived as limitations, the new law also signaled a momentous change. The king and his ministers had ruled with the planters. Spain was now openly and legally committed to the project of transforming Cuba into the kind of colony that might be worth a kingdom. Sugar and slavery were officially ascendant.

Immediately, the number of Spanish and foreign slave ships arriving legally in Havana soared. From an annual average of 1,188 persons a year imported as slaves, the figure jumped almost 600 percent, to 6,683 annually in the first two years of the legally open trade.[15] In Santiago de Cuba, the principal city in the eastern part of the island where foreign traders were not permitted entry even under the new decree, what had

[13] The formulation of pressure and voice comes from Jeremy Adelman, who applies Albert Hirshman's concept. See Adelman, *Sovereignty and Revolution*, 85.

[14] On the opening of the slave trade, see Murray, *Odious Commerce*, 10–12; José Luciano Franco, *Comercio clandestino de esclavos* (Havana: Editorial Ciencias Sociales, 1980), 61–64.

[15] The figures are calculated from tables provided by Herbert Klein in "North American Competition and the Characteristics of the African Slave Trade to Cuba, 1790 to 1794," *William and Mary Quarterly* 28 (1971): 86–102, especially 89–90. See also Aimes, *A History of Slavery*, 36–37. The figures, which do not include illicit and contraband trade in slaves, are necessarily incomplete.

been a petty and illegal regional trade with neighboring Caribbean ports flourished now with the legitimacy of legal commerce. There, the governor spent much time approving requests from Spanish traders to travel to Jamaica and Saint-Domingue in search of slaves. In this manner, 2,665 men and women arrived in the first two years of the open trade, about half of whom were reexported, most to Puerto Príncipe, a growing slave economy in the island's interior with no direct access to the trade, and to Havana, where the vast expansion of the legal slave trade was still not equal to the burgeoning demand for slave labor.[16] If planters and statesmen had long envisioned a prosperity based on tropical commercial agriculture, the opening of the slave trade in 1789 gave them legal access to the black men and women who would make that transformation material.

But, in a sense, that was only the beginning. With Spain now formally committed to the slave trade as a foundation for tropical commercial agriculture in its empire, and with the island on its way to becoming a slave society, slavery itself – and not just the slave trade – appeared to require some thought. Just three months after the free slave trade decree of February 1789, the king approved a second decree designed to regulate the treatment of slaves in his dominions. Predicting that the slave trade decree would result in a "considerable increase in the number of slaves," the state found it imperative to lay down regulations to be "promptly observed by all the owners of slaves." Existing regulations governing the treatment and education of slaves, said the new decree's preamble, were scattered across many pieces of legislation, often dating from centuries earlier. Most contemporary masters and overseers therefore had little knowledge of the Spanish law of slavery and inadvertently committed abuses that violated existing legal principles. The imminent arrival of an unprecedented number of slaves urgently required the formulation of a coherent black code to clarify the obligations and rights of slaves, masters, and the state.[17]

The decree approved by the king reiterated provisions already in effect, at least on paper: the prohibition of work on Sundays, the master's

---

[16] José Luis Belmonte Postigo, "El impacto de la liberalización de la trata negrera en Santiago de Cuba, 1789–1794," *Tiempos de América* (Castellón), no. 14, and "'Brazos para el azúcar,' Esclavos para vender, estrategias de comercialización en la trata negrera en Santiago de Cuba, 1789–1794," *Revista de Indias* v. 70, 249 (2010). 445–467.

[17] "Instrucción para la educación, trato y ocupaciones de los esclavos," Aranjuez, May 31, 1789, reprinted in Manuel Lucena Salmoral, *Los códigos negros de la América Española* (Alcalá: Ediciones UNESCO, Universidad Alcalá, 1996), 279–284.

obligation to feed and clothe his bondspeople; the fostering of marriage among the enslaved; and cumulative fines on masters who neglected the provisions of the laws. The law stated, of course, the slave's obligation to obey and respect the master as a father, and it authorized punishment – by "imprisonment, shackles, chains, clubs, or stocks" – when he or she failed in that obligation. But the 1789 law also specified new and stringent limits on what that punishment could entail, expressly forbidding that the slave be placed upside down when receiving the punishment and specifying that whippings could not cause bleeding nor exceed twenty-five lashes with a soft instrument. Finally, the new law gave the town councils, its syndics, and members of the clergy the right to inspect and report on potential abuses of masters and overseers, and it protected the right of anonymity for denouncers of abuse. The regulation represented, opined its framers, a balance among the imperative to protect the minimum rights of slaves, to allow the expansion of agriculture, and to preserve public order and the security of the state.[18]

Once the new law was issued, the engines of state circulated several hundred copies in Spain's American colonies. Even before its arrival on the other side of the Atlantic, however, rumors of its drafting produced panic and resistance among slaveholders. In Santo Domingo and Louisiana, planters joined forces to resist its implementation. In Caracas, planters persuaded local authorities to suspend its application even before they had received or read it. Despite that, after it arrived, enslaved people apparently attempted to take advantage of its provisions, taking masters to court for infractions of the rules it prescribed.[19] In Havana, the arrival of the decree prompted emergency meetings of the city council. In January, the city's planters – identifying themselves as the "body of sugar planters of Havana" – wrote to the king to persuade him of the "sad consequences and irreparable harm" that would result from the application of the new slave regulations. The brunt of their outrage was directed at the provisions that limited punishment. They objected, they said, not because they wished to exceed the limits established, but because knowledge of the provisions would lessen the fear and subordination of the enslaved, who would abandon their plantations and complain

---

[18] Ibid. See also Manuel Barcia, *Con el látigo de la ira* (Havana: Editorial Ciencias Sociales, 2000).

[19] For a discussion of reaction across America, see Lucena Salmoral, *Los códigos negros*, 108–119. The evidence of enslaved in Venezuela using the new slave code in spite of local officials' refusal to comply with it comes from the dissertation in progress of Evelyne Laurent-Perrault, New York University, History Department.

incessantly to the government. They continued, apocalyptically: "We see already our farms ruined, our families miserable, his Majesty's treasury in incalculable arrears, the income from tithes destroyed, the commerce of our port annihilated, our countryside abandoned, the island overrun with calamities, and our slaves in rebellion." The danger produced by its implementation, they argued, overshadowed any individual instances of abuse, for the majority of masters, they insisted, treated their slaves humanely.[20]

In this manner, Cuban planters touted what they saw as their intimate experience and knowledge of slavery and offered the king an alternative (and clearly self-interested) interpretation of the ideal methods of slave management. It is in this petition to the king that we find the original telling of the story of the "last supper" made famous by Cuban filmmaker Tomás Gutiérrez Alea in 1976. First the 1790 petition and then the 1976 film told the story of a planter, the Conde de Casa Bayona, who celebrated Holy Thursday by washing the feet of his slaves and inviting twelve of them to his table for supper. The master's humility (or arrogance) was repaid with a violent uprising of his slaves. With stories such as this, the planters made the case that mild treatment promoted only rebellion and savagery.[21] They sought to shape perceptions of slaves and slavery and to reserve for themselves a special kind of privilege, the privilege of an ascendant planter class to defy royal orders and to define the very character and quality of slavery in their territory.

The resistance of the planters was so concerted and determined that there was no way to quell it. They invoked Law 24, Title 1, Book 2 of the Law of the Indies, originally dated 1528 and reissued in 1622, which allowed local authorities to suspend application of royal orders in cases where "irreparable harm and known scandal" would ensue. In this manner, with recourse to longstanding colonial legislation, the planters voiced their profound disagreement with the king's mandates. The king yielded, and in 1794 the government in Madrid suspended the execution of the law, weakly asking colonial masters and overseers to respect its spirit. Cuban planters are often portrayed as colonists who remained

[20] La Condesa de Jaruco, el Marqués Justiz de Santa Ana, el Marqués del Real Socorro, et al. to [King], January 19, 1790. The petition was signed by 71 planters, including 12 women. It was sent as an attachment to a letter from Marqués de Cárdenas de Monte Hermoso and Miguel José Peñalver y Calvo to Conde de Floridablanca, Secretary of State, February 5, 1790. The letter identifies the authors of the petition as "el Cuerpo de Hacendados de fabricar azúcar de esta Ciudad." AGI, Estado, leg. 7, exp 4 and 5.
[21] Ibid.

loyal to Spain in a bid to protect slavery; here, the Spanish monarchy was instead committing itself to slavery and the planter elite in a bid to strengthen an empire.[22]

The planters' sense of confidence in themselves and their project comes through even more forcefully in another – much less public – decision made at roughly the same time. As they prepared their petition to the king in objection to the royal decrees on slave treatment, the members of the Havana city council learned that Cuba would soon receive a new governor, Don Luis de Las Casas. With the boon of an open slave trade won and with the current controversy over the slave code unfolding, the planters decided to forge ahead. And so they prepared for the incoming captain-general a welcome sure to make an impression. On his arrival in Havana in July 1790, they presented him with a generous gift: his very own plantation, located in the booming sugar region of Güines, complete with machinery and enslaved labor force. They called it *Amistad*, or friendship (Figure 1.3).[23]

The new governor appears to have taken to the enterprise, for in little time he purchased and developed a second sugar mill, *Alejandría*, one of the largest and most successful in the region. Thus, Luis de Las Casas, governor of Havana and captain-general of the island of Cuba, became also "one more sugar planter." Indeed, he used his role as governor to advance in his role as planter. Spanish law barred him from owning property and interests in the colony, but he, the planters, and other local officials collaborated in the deception, and Las Casas's sugar plantations were registered under the names of relatives and colleagues. Likewise, the intendant José Pablo Valiente, who was in charge of all financial matters on the island, had an illicit but powerful interest in the sugar business. He was co-owner with Francisco Arango of *La Ninfa*, then the largest sugar mill in the world.[24] The planters – confident, aware, emboldened – used their alliance and shared economic interest with the governor and the intendant to continue consolidating their position, asking for and

---

[22] Ibid. See also Lucena Salmoral, *Los códigos negros*, 95, 119–123; Fernando Ortiz, *Los negros esclavos* (Havana: Editorial de Ciencias Sociales, 1975), 334–335.

[23] Moreno Fraginals, *El ingenio*, 1:58.

[24] Guerra, *Manual de historia de Cuba*, 201; Marrero, *Cuba*, 10: 159. On Las Casas and Valiente as sugar planters, see Moreno Fraginals, *El ingenio*, I: 46, 57–62, 140, 290. On the concessions won by the planters in the years immediately following Las Casas's arrival, see José Luciano Franco, *Apuntes para una historia de la legislación y administración colonial en Cuba, 1511–1800* (Havana: Editorial de Ciencias Sociales, 1985), 396–412.

FIGURE 1.3. Ingenio Amistad, engraving by Eduardo Laplante in Justo Cantero, *Los Ingenios. Colección de vistas de los principales ingenios de azúcar de la Isla de Cuba*, 1857. Courtesy of the British Library Board.

receiving more and more concessions. Everything seemed to be working in the planters' favor, even the collusion of metropolitan authorities.

Seizing Opportunity

By the time Las Casas laid eyes on his new sugar plantation, the forces of sugar and slavery's ascent were already clearly in place. To this increasingly visible transformation, many factors had contributed: Madrid's willingness to act on reform impulses, changing commercial relations with the new United States, an activist and vocal planter class, and legal access to a burgeoning slave trade, the linchpin. Then, precisely at the moment when the colony's turn to sugar and slavery seemed secure, the unthinkable began to happen.

In the northern plain of Saint-Domingue so long envied by Cuban planters, several hundred slaves rose up and attacked some of the richest sugar plantations in all the world. The French garrisoned themselves in the capital city of Cap Français, a city that the French called simply Le Cap and that the Spanish persisted in calling *Guarico*, the indigenous name they had retained for it under their own rule more than a century earlier (Figure 1.4). In the months, years, and decades that followed, *Guarico* would become a key word in Cuba and across the Spanish world, used almost interchangeably for the city and region of Le Cap, sometimes for the whole French colony of Saint-Domingue, and, more frequently and capaciously, for the destruction from below that would soon engulf it. In little time, enslaved witnesses in Cuba would be testifying about their desire to make "another Guarico" and authorities ruminating about avoiding one. But the fates of the word and the place were not yet clear on those late August days of 1791, as Le Cap's powerful residents nervously waited, hoping that the conflagration would somehow subside, that the rebels would desist or fall, and that the whites might emerge victorious and once again in command. In the meantime, French colonial authorities dispatched plaintive and urgent missives to Paris, to the United States, and to their counterparts across the region: to the Dutch in Surinam and Curaçao, to the British in Jamaica, and to the Spanish in Santo Domingo, Havana, and Santiago. In this manner began a war perhaps long imagined by the enslaved of Saint-Domingue, one that was poised to shatter all the assumptions on which the emerging Cuban order was based.

In Cuba, few if any imagined what would come in the wake of that initial uprising. The Cuban sugar elite had long sought to match the substantial power and wealth of the Saint-Domingue planter class.

VUE DU CAP FRANÇOIS,

Isle St Domingue, prise de la chemin de l'Embarcadère et de petite Anse. ?

A.P.D.R.

FIGURE 1.4. View of Cap Français, circa 1790. Courtesy of the John Carter Brown Library at Brown University.

Suddenly, their paragon faced a critical challenge to its supremacy. Though nervous about the news of slave rebellion, Cuban planters readily grasped its immediate consequence: a market with higher prices for sugar, temporarily absent its main supplier. And with that boon in mind, they prepared to act.

When the Haitian Revolution began, Francisco Arango, the powerful planter and official representative of the Havana city council, was still in Madrid, linked to the world of Spanish ministers and advocating strategically for policies that would benefit the world of Cuban planters from which he came. Arango's earlier activism had contributed to the opening of the slave trade in 1789 for a provisional period of two years. In May 1791, preparing for the review of that policy by the king, Arango wrote an appeal for the renewal and expansion of the open slave trade for a period of six to eight years. He was not alone; similar petitions were presented by authorities in Caracas, Puerto Rico, and Santo Domingo. In part because of these appeals, but also because the ministers in Madrid were already convinced of the wisdom of expanding the trade and the commercial agriculture it supported, the extension of the open slave trade was looked on very favorably. In fact, it was slated for final discussion and near-certain approval in the Council of State on November 21, 1791.[25]

It was on the eve of that discussion – November 19, to be exact – that the unexpected news of the outbreak of revolution in Saint-Domingue arrived in Madrid. In the press and drawing rooms, dramatic and lurid accounts circulated: of 200 sugar mills laid to waste, 300 white French murdered, and a major city anxiously preparing for a possible attack by the black rebels.[26] Hearing the news, Arango worried that ministers in Madrid might postpone the discussion on the slave trade, or, worse yet, consider closing the trade altogether out of fear and uncertainty. That prospect likely worried him more than the news of insurrection itself.

Arango went to work immediately, and within a day he had drafted a treatise on the causes of the Saint-Domingue rebellion and its implications for Havana and Madrid. Foregoing the customary channels of the Council of the Indies, he allegedly managed to place a copy of his essay in the hands of every individual member of the Council of State.[27] Arango's actions betrayed his conviction that before the metropolitan government decided

[25] Piqueras, "Los amigos de Arango."
[26] *GM*, November 25, 1791.
[27] Francisco Arango, "Representación hecha a Su Majestad con motivo de la sublevación de esclavos en los dominios franceses de la Isla de Santo Domingo," in *Obras*, 1:140–43; Ponte Domínguez, *Arango y Parreño*, 24–27.

on a response to the events of Saint-Domingue, it must first consider the interpretation and interests of Havana's ascendant planter class. He succeeded, and at that first meeting on the revolution on November 21, 1791, the ministers read the reports of the revolution from Havana's governor together with Arango's treatise on the Haitian Revolution.[28] Importantly, then, the very first discussion of the Haitian Revolution at the highest levels of the Spanish government was mediated by the intervention of this spokesman for the Cuban planter class.

Arango's essay on the Haitian Revolution was supremely self-confident. An ocean away from evolving events, he had little information on which to base it, and even the scanty news he had at his disposal would have been about two months out of date. But that was irrelevant. Arango knew already what the Cuban planters wanted; and to make sense of the slave rebellion itself, he relied on the common sense of the age. Terse and to the point, he dispensed with lengthy discussions of the causes of the trouble in Saint-Domingue. The explanation, he said, was simple: one disorder had produced the other. From the subversive actions of masters, slaves had arrived at the idea of rebellion. With that, he moved quickly to consider the implications of those events for Cuba, which, as he reminded the ministers, was practically joined with Saint-Domingue at its eastern-most point at Maisí, near Baracoa. Here, again, he asserted his conclusion as definitive and final. While a fear of contagion under the circumstances might be unsurprising, it was, he insisted, clearly misguided. There was no reason for fear in Cuba. The two colonies were both inherently and conjuncturally different. First, Spanish subjects were content with their king and their system of government. Second, Cuban planters were not engaged in political folly before the eyes and ears of their slaves. Finally, the enslaved in Cuba were better treated by wiser planters and a magnanimous king. For these three reasons, Arango averred, the risks of a major slave rebellion in Cuba were minimal.

Because there was no danger of repetition or contagion, the revolution in Saint-Domingue was above all else an opportunity to be seized. Arango wrote:

No one more than this supplicant sympathizes with the French. I would want at the cost of my own blood to spare them from this disaster. But that being impossible and seeing them immersed in a disaster that – if it does not destroy all happiness in that colony – will surely set it back considerably, it is necessary to view [the French colony] not only with compassion but also from a political

---

[28] Archivo Histórico Nacional (AHN), Estado, Libro 4, Actas, November 21, 1791, f. 131v; AHOHCH, AC, Tomo 51, February 17, 1792, ff. 50v–52.

perspective and, with the faith of a good patriot and vassal, announce to the best of kings the opportunity and the means by which to give to our agriculture on the islands the advantage and preponderance over the French.[29]

It was this pragmatic argument, perhaps more than any historical or sociological comparison between the French and Spanish colonies, that most interested Arango. His immediate purpose was to prevent the ministers from responding to revolutionary news too cautiously by postponing or rejecting the renewal and expansion of the open slave trade. Three days later, Arango had his response in the form of a new royal decree extending the open slave trade for six more years and granting many of the concessions that he and others had long requested.[30]

Beyond the immediate question of the 1791 slave trade extension, Arango sought to persuade the king to carry out more permanent reforms that would allow Cuban planters to take long-term and permanent advantage of Saint-Domingue's crisis. At the time, observers could not yet imagine that Saint-Domingue would never recover, much less that it would become an independent black state in little over a decade. Arango's purpose then was to take intense advantage of what he saw as a significant but temporary opening, so that when France recovered, Cuba would be able to retain its newfound advantage. To this end, Arango concluded his November 1791 essay on the revolution with a proposal to write a second, more detailed piece outlining measures that would give Cuban agriculture a definitive advantage over the French. Arango's offer was discussed and approved at that same meeting of November 21, 1791. Thus, the initial discussion of the Haitian Revolution by the Spanish state explicitly linked that revolution with the expansion of slavery and plantation agriculture in Cuba. Several months later, Arango submitted his famous paper on Cuban agriculture, *Discurso sobre la agricultura de la Habana y los medios de fomentarla.*[31] Generally seen as a foundational document of Cuban history, its direct origin lay in the very first metropolitan-colonial conversation about the Haitian Revolution.

Together, these two documents – Arango's November 1791 paper on the revolution and his 1792 essay on Cuban agriculture – lay out

---

[29] Arango, "Representación hecha a Su Majestad con motivo de la sublevación de esclavos," in *Obras,* 1:142.

[30] On the chronology of Arango's essay and the Royal Cédula, see Ponte Domínguez, *Arango y Parreño.* On the provisions of the *cédula* for the slave trade, see Murray, *Odious Commerce.*

[31] Francisco Arango, "Discurso sobre la agricultura de la Habana y medios de fomentarla," in *Obras,* 1:144–226.

what would become the dominant intellectual approach to Cuban society and economy in the nineteenth century. Arango's *Discurso* systematically made the case for the transformation of Cuba, seeking above all to clear the way for the ascendancy of sugar and the planters who made it. He affirmed that the state should encourage innovation and growth in the industry by exempting entrepreneurial planters from excessive duties and tithes and by expanding the free-trade provisions that guaranteed a market for Cuban sugar. Perhaps most importantly, the state would have to commit itself wholeheartedly to the entry and sale of enslaved Africans, the foundation on which the entire edifice rested. The *Discurso* thus provided a detailed and thorough treatise on the current economic situation of the colony, as well as a blueprint for the state's response to the upheaval of the world's largest producer of sugar. His was no longer a call for Cuba to emulate or compete with Saint-Domingue, but rather a calculated exhortation simply to replace it.[32]

To a very significant extent, Arango's plea was heeded, and authorities in Madrid and Havana confronted the Haitian Revolution with a renewed commitment to making Cuba's sugar revolution. The effectiveness of the response was quickly visible, indeed dizzying. Approximately 325,000 Africans were legally brought to Cuba as slaves between 1790 and 1820, more than four times the number brought in the previous thirty years. Most of these men and women were fated for work in sugar. The nucleus of the boom was Havana, a city that doubled in size between 1791 and 1810. Overtaken by what one witness called a furor to establish *ingenios*, or sugar mills, the city saw the number of mills in its outskirts jump from 237 in 1792 to 416 in 1806. Their average productive capacity more than doubled, from 58 metric tons per mill in 1792 to 136 in 1804. The largest mills, owned precisely by men such as Arango, had production capacities of two and almost three times that average. The island's export figures were equally dramatic: from about 15,000 metric tons of sugar exported in 1790 to almost 40,000 by 1804. The island's share of the world's sugar market grew and grew. Over the course of the 1820s, producing almost 105,000 metric tons a year, it was indisputably the world's largest producer of sugar.[33]

Another clear, if highly imperfect, indicator of the transformations underway was the changing profile of the island's population by race

[32] Ibid.; Tomich, "Wealth of Empire"; Ponte Domínguez, *Arango y Parreño*, 30–45; Marrero, *Cuba*, 10:15–16.

[33] Moreno Fraginals, *El ingenio*, 1:68, 3:43–44; Tomich, *Through the Prism*, 75–94; J. Scott, "The Common Wind," 28.

and status. The census of 1774, the one taken closest to the start of the definitive takeoff of sugar and slavery in the 1790s, estimated the island's population as 56.2 percent white. The 1792 census, taken shortly after the start of the open slave trade, put the white population at 48.7 percent, below the 50 percent mark for the first time in the island's history. The trend would continue well into the nineteenth century: in 1817, on the eve of Spain's largely hollow promise to end the slave trade, the white population accounted for just 43.4 percent of the island's total population. The change was significantly more dramatic in the nucleus of the boom itself. In Güines, home to the most advanced sugar mills of the turn of the century, people classified as white had accounted for about three-quarters of the population in 1775; by the 1820s, they constituted less than 38 percent. If these counts seem undramatic compared to figures for, say, prerevolutionary Saint-Domingue, where those classified as white accounted for less than 10 percent of the population, in Cuba they were experienced as a portent of perhaps greater transformations to come.[34]

From the number of captured Africans imported, to the number of sugar mills established, to the amount of sugar exported, to the perceptible demographic shift unfolding, foundational changes were underway in Cuba in the 1790s. With some important qualifications, the model of settler colony that had predominated for the almost three hundred years of Spanish rule was rapidly ceding room to the increasingly irresistible model of plantation colony.[35] That had been the planters' project already for some time. The elimination of their rival producer of Saint-Domingue only confirmed their choice and made the path to profit and power that much shorter to travel. Slavery, sugar, plantation production, and a somewhat flexible colonial bond would be the organizing principles in Cuba – even (perhaps especially) in the era of the Haitian Revolution.

[34] The figures are taken from the discussions of the 1774, 1792, and 1817 censuses in Kenneth Kiple, *Blacks in Colonial Cuba, 1774–1899* (Gainesville: University of Florida Press, 1976); and Marrero, *Cuba*, 9: 192–194, 217–221.

[35] It is important to note that while sugar did without doubt become king, there continued to be interstitial spaces for other crops, other kinds of landholdings, and other kinds of arrangements between slaves, masters, and free workers. See Consuelo Naranjo Oviedo, "La otra Cuba: colonización blanca y diversificación agrícola" *Contrastes*, 12 (2003), and Antonio Santamaría García and Consuelo Naranjo Orovio, eds., *Mas allá del azúcar* (Madrid: Doce Calles, 2009). Alejandro de la Fuente has suggested that the transformation of slavery in this period was unable to undo some of the legal foundations of an earlier kind of slave system. See his "Slaves and the Creation of Legal Rights in Cuba: Coartación and Papel," *Hispanic American Historical Review* 87:4 (November), 659–92, and "Slave Law and Claims-Making in Cuba: The Tannenbaum Debate Revisited," *Law and History Review* 22:2 (Summer 2004), 339–369.

Seeing Cuba in Haiti's Shadow

The choreographers of Cuba's sugar revolution were nonetheless, on occasion, honest men. They admitted, often explicitly, that their project was not uncomplicated. The fact that the entrenchment of slavery in Cuba occurred contemporaneously with the Haitian Revolution meant that the expansion occurred with the possibility of its unraveling always in mind. Thus, for instance, while Arango's essays sought to convince the king that the Haitian Revolution was the perfect opportunity to consolidate the emerging regime of sugar and slavery, he confessed that the revolution also made that project significantly more delicate. He wrote:

The insurrection of the blacks of Guarico has expanded the horizon of my ideas. Against the noise of that unfortunate event, I have awakened and seen that all my work was built in mid-air . . . that the peace and tranquility of all my compatriots, the enjoyment of all the happiness they were going to attain was hanging by a thread: the subordination and patience of a crowd of barbarous men.

Confident and powerful, Arango confronted, however briefly, the inherent instability of the project he had so long advocated. Its success, even its survival, rested on containing the will of enslaved people. Yet that striking realization appears to have produced barely a moment of doubt. Hesitation in the face of this realization was not reason to abandon the project, said Arango; but it did require foresight and prudence. His warnings, he clarified, were less for the present than for times to come, for when the island would have five or six hundred thousand Africans. "From now, I speak for then, and I want our precautions to begin this minute."[36]

Thus, while planters and the colonial state raced forward to fill the gap opened by the revolution, they also had to confront – sometimes tangentially, sometimes directly – the specter of slave revolution. In a sense, Arango and his clique proposed a delicate balancing act: to follow in the footsteps of Saint-Domingue and to build a prosperity based on sugar, slavery, and colonialism, but to stop emphatically short of the upheavals caused in part by those same institutions in Saint-Domingue. They sought, in other words, to emulate Saint-Domingue, but to contain Haiti.

This perceived imperative to reconcile opportunity with survival, profit with potential destruction, would mark the thinking and the policies of Cuban power holders for decades to come. In the very administration of

---

[36] Arango, "Discurso sobre la agricultura," in *Obras*, 1: 170–171.

the colony, local governors acted both as the institutional handmaidens of slavery's entrenchment and as the guardians of a public order potentially threatened by the very transformations they were helping to bring into being. Governor Las Casas and Intendant José Pablo Valiente, as hidden members of Havana's planter class and owners of large, modern, and prosperous plantations in the fertile sugar valley of Güines, supported and helped advance the planters' requests for new and expanding privileges. But charged with the security of the colony, they also devoted significant attention to questions about how to ensure the subservience and the tranquility of all the king's subjects, especially the enslaved.

To this end, the governor worked closely with the principal institutions of the day: the Havana *cabildo* (city council), the Sociedad Patriótica, and the Real Consulado. All three institutions boasted significant participation by the Havana creole elite, and, in particular, by what one historian has famously called the "sugarocracy," the emerging aristocracy of sugar.[37] As members of these three important organizations, they had frequent occasion to rejoice at the opportunities and happiness that (for them, at least) abounded. But they also frequently challenged one another to think about how to ensure that the slave trade and the economy it sustained would continue to flourish.

The *cabildo* was the oldest of the three institutions, historically composed of representatives of the city's wealthiest and most powerful families. By September 1791, when the body sat down to discuss the outbreak of slave rebellion in Saint-Domingue, the dominant group was completely invested in the project of sugar and slavery. Its members in this critical period included Nicolás Calvo, owner of the *Nueva Holanda*, one of the largest mills of the era, located like so many others in Güines; the Marqués Cárdenas de Monte Hermoso, a prominent planter also involved in the slave trade and in technical projects to modernize sugar production; and at least two members of the extended Peñalver clan, aptly described as "a great family sugar consortium."[38] The group constituted a long-standing arm of the colonial state, but one now intrinsically tied to significantly creole and modernizing interests in sugar and slavery. It was this group that had formally empowered Francisco Arango to lobby the king for more

---

[37] Moreno Fraginals, *El ingenio.*

[38] Ibid., I: 77n, 50, 85, 120. On the disproportionate power wielded in the *cabildo* by particular families, many of whom later became leaders in the transition to the sugar economy, see Marrero, *Cuba*, 8: 106–108, 149–150; María Teresa Cornide, *De la Havana, de siglos y de familias* (Havana: Editorial de Ciencias Sociales, 2003), 294–298.

slaves, for access to other trading partners, and for exemptions from taxes to develop commercial agriculture. As partial guardians of colonial society and of their own personal fortunes, they advocated unrestrained growth of the plantation colony while keeping a wary eye on potential danger emanating from revolutionary Saint-Domingue. Thus, as they addressed the king to advocate a freer slave trade, they also pleaded with the governor to work harder to manage and contain threats, from the possible surreptitious entry of so-called French blacks to the imminent preponderance of people of color.

The same dual concern with security and state building, on the one hand, and with avid economic ambition, on the other, marked the work of the Sociedad Patriótica, founded in 1793 to promote agriculture, commerce, and education. The society published a journal, sponsored contests, and in general worked to encourage scientific and economic thinking in the service of sugar's expansion. It was, for example, centrally involved in projects such as the translation of foreign texts on the modern cultivation of sugar and coffee. As in the case of the city council, its members were overwhelmingly drawn from the ranks of the emerging sugar elite and included members of all the principal sugar families of the day: the Arangos, Calvos, Peñalveres, and others. As the Haitian Revolution wore on, its members even included French technicians fleeing from their losses in their colony and former home.[39]

Perhaps most illustrative of the overlap between colonial administration and private sugar interests was the work of the Real Consulado, created in 1794 under the guiding hand of the planter elite. Traditionally, the Spanish American *consulados* were merchant guilds. In the late eighteenth century, Bourbon monarchs added to these traditional bodies subsidiary committees charged with studying and encouraging economic growth, not only in commerce but also in agriculture and small industry. When Arango drafted his 1792 essay on the development of Cuban agriculture, he proposed the creation not of a *consulado* but rather of a distinct Real Junta Protectora de Agricultura, charged specifically with expanding the colony's agricultural wealth. Madrid seemed unwilling to authorize a powerful and autonomous institution controlled by a local creole elite, but the Real Consulado founded in Havana in 1794 was in effect an amalgam of the late colonial *consulados* and Arango's proposed

---

[39] See Moreno Fraginals, *El ingenio*, 1:112; María Dolores González-Ripoll, *Cuba, la isla de los ensayos: cultura y sociedad, 1790–1815* (Madrid: CSIC, 1999), 164–169, 223–229.

committee. In this joint body, the planter elite was more powerful than in its counterparts elsewhere in the Spanish world. The founding members in 1794 owned among them no fewer than twenty-six sugar mills. The head member, or *prior*, was Ignacio Montalvo Ambulodi, Conde de Casa Montalvo, the owner of two of them. Arango himself became the junta's syndic for life, and in that capacity he set the agenda for what the body would consider. As Manuel Moreno Fraginals made clear in his analysis of the junta's work in its first two years of operation, its main agenda was the consolidation of sugar production based on enslaved labor. It advocated for government loans to mill owners; a reduction in the number of holidays for slaves; the elimination of taxes on the sale of land and mills; ambitious projects for the construction of roads, canals, and docks meant to facilitate the shipment of sugar; the reduction of export tariffs on sugar; and many measures to facilitate the entry of enslaved Africans. Even the group's meeting schedule was designed to accommodate planters' need to absent themselves during the sugar harvest.[40]

If the group's general mission was to encourage tropical agriculture, its most pressing concern on its creation was to reconcile the economic bonanza that came with sugar and slavery with continued peace and prosperity. In one of the junta's first discussions, a consensus quickly emerged that the risk of insurrection was minimal in Cuba, where slaves, they said, enjoyed more privileges than elsewhere and where their numbers were smaller than those of the free population. "We therefore agreed," explained one member, "that since the urgent need for laborers for our fertile lands was so clear, we would quickly seek out all means available to encourage [the slave trade]."[41]

As they worked to expand that trade, however, they added their powerful voices to others urging utmost vigilance. Together with the Sociedad Patriótica, they commissioned and wrote reports to assess the dangers. It was in part the caution provoked by the example and proximity of the

[40] Moreno Fraginals, *El ingenio*, 1: 106–10; Peter J. Lampros, "Merchant-Planter Cooperation and Conflict: The Havana Consulado, 1794–1832" (Ph.D. diss., Tulane University, 1980), 25–87; González-Ripoll, *Cuba, la isla de los ensayos*, 182–194; Archivo Nacional de Cuba, *Catálogo de los fondos del Real Consulado de Agricultra, Industria y Comercio y de la Junta de Fomento* (Havana: Siglo XX, 1943).

[41] "Copia del Expediente no. 134 sobre proponer al Rey un plan para asegurar la tranquilidad y obediencia de sus siervos en esta Colonia en Representación de 10 de Julio de 1799" in ANC, RCJF, leg. 184, exp. 8330. Alexander von Humboldt must have had a copy of this document when he wrote his famous *Ensayo político sobre la Isla de Cuba*, for parts of the chapter on slavery are taken verbatim from it. See Humboldt, *Ensayo político* (Paris: Jules Renouard, 1827), 276n.

Haitian Revolution that led the creole elite in Havana to embark on what
are usually seen as projects of state- and nation-building: surveying distant
territory, counting and classifying the population, and devising programs
for settlement and defense in sparsely populated regions. Starting in 1796,
the group devoted significant energy to rethinking the Cuban countryside.
They devised elaborate rules to minimize the risk of marronage, partially
out of a fear that maroons, or runaway slaves, might readily join an
invading force of rebels from Saint-Domingue or assist slaves rising up
in Cuban territory itself. A set of rules drafted by Francisco Arango and
approved by the king required slaveholders to provide monthly reports
on their enslaved labor force and described the best means by which runaway settlements should be attacked, captured maroons punished, and
captors paid.[42]

Arango, together with fellow sugar planter Nicolás Calvo, also devised
a proposal for rural Cuba that focused on development alongside repression. They proposed the establishment of free public schools in the countryside. But even this project envisioned a link to security in a post-Haiti
world. The schools would soften the habits of rural whites, from whose
ranks would be hired plantation overseers who, as a result of that education, would be more cognizant of long-term interests and less likely to
abuse slaves, thereby helping to minimize the threat of insurrection and
resistance. The first of such schools was to be located in Güines, ground
zero of Cuba's turn to sugar and slavery.[43]

The promise and frenzy of the boom was everywhere in the thinking
of the Havana elite who filled these reform-minded institutions. At the
same time, their work leaves little doubt that almost equally present was
the imperative to plan with Haiti in mind.

The Haitian Revolution did not cause the sugar revolution in Cuba.
Planters had long envisioned and pursued such a transformation. In
their effort to make that transformation real, they were aided by

[42] *Nuevo Reglamento y arancel que debe gobernar en la captura de esclavos cimarrones
aprobado por S. M. en Real Orden expedida en San Lorenxo con fecha 20 de Diciembre
de 1796* (Havana: Impr. de la Capitanía General). For an example of the discussions
about the dangers represented by maroons in the 1790s, see "El Prior y Cónsules de la
Havana elevan un plan que propone la Junta Económica para asegurar la tranquilidad
y obediencia de los siervos de esta colonia" in ANC, RCJF, leg. 184, exp. 8330.
[43] On the public schools proposal, see documents 13 and 14 in the file AGS, SGU, 6865,
exp. 24. For a general discussion of colonial state building in the context of the Haitian
Revolution, see Ada Ferrer, "Cuba en la sombra de Haití: Noticias, sociedad y esclavitud," in María Dolores González-Ripoll et al., eds., *El rumor de Haití en Cuba: Temor,
raza y rebeldía, 1789–1844* (Madrid: CSIC, 2004), especially 203–214.

developments both local and global, from the increasing influence of Spanish reformism, which helped assure allies in the metropole, to the independence of Britain's North American colonies, which guaranteed a market for the sugar they so wanted to produce. The rise of slavery and sugar in Cuba had already been sketched for the colony as its most probable path.

The dramatic outbreak of revolution in Saint-Domingue made the path that much more certain, direct, and profitable. Indeed, it all but guaranteed the success of the endeavor. But if the disruption in Saint-Domingue seemed to hold exceptional promise, planters – and the colonial state with which they were allied – allowed themselves to consider briefly that it might also represent unique peril. Thus, the project of entrenching slavery and sugar in Cuba, precisely because it happened contemporaneously with the Haitian Revolution, was perceived as a delicate balancing act. This balancing act – the drive to emulate prerevolutionary Saint-Domingue and to contain would-be Haiti – was not, however, an abstract proposition. Discussions to that effect may have filled the meeting halls of the city council and the Real Consulado and private parlors of men such as Arango or the captain-general, but the planters' project of reconciling profit and survival had to be made real on the ground.

That ground was challenging terrain indeed. On the one hand, slavery's entrenchment seemed everywhere present, palpable in the changing human landscape of city and countryside, in the rhythms of work and motion at city docks, and in rural cane fields and boiling houses. But on this ground where people confronted slavery's increasing power, they also encountered its antithesis. They encountered the regular traces, echoes, and rumors of slavery's undoing in nearby Saint-Domingue. The same ships that brought the African men and women who were literally making Cuba's sugar revolution also brought news of blacks defeating whites, and of a whole world built upon slavery coming violently undone. From menacing words about making another Guarico murmured on street corners by black men and women, to copies of rebel proclamations circulated from hand to hand, traces of Saint-Domingue's slave revolution circulated easily in Cuba, even as the violence of slavery itself became more and more conspicuous all around them. It was here that men of Arango's stripe strove to balance the expansion of slavery with the maintenance of public order in revolutionary times, here that the divergent projects of the Haitian Revolution and the Cuban sugar revolution met.

2

"An Excess of Communication"

The Capture of News in a Slave Society

Cuban planters rushed in to fill the void left by Saint-Domingue's revolution as if it had been created just for them. But as they worked to expand slavery, the context in which they did so required them always to ponder the possibility of its destruction at the hands of the enslaved. The planters understood that the chaos that now promised to grant them so much economic power had been brought into being by the actions of enslaved men and women just like the ones who were now arriving on Cuban shores in unprecedented numbers. For them and for the people they enslaved, the example of black revolution was not an abstract proposition, but a palpable presence. In Cuba, news, people, and papers from revolutionary Saint-Domingue arrived quickly and vividly. And so as the brutal regime of plantation slavery took root at the turn of Cuba's nineteenth century, stories of black liberation sprouted on that same ground. The proximity of the Haitian Revolution and the ease of contact and communication between revolutionary Saint-Domingue and colonial Cuba made the planters' project of emulating Saint-Domingue and containing would-be Haiti significantly more complicated in practice than in conception.

The Circulation of Revolutionary News

First word of the unforeseen upheaval in Le Cap arrived in Cuba at its easternmost city of Baracoa. Poor, sparsely populated, and surrounded by mountain ranges and water, Baracoa was worlds removed from the plantation society emerging in Havana's hinterland. Founded by Diego Velázquez in 1511 as the first Spanish settlement in Cuba, Baracoa was not of the new Cuba being transformed by sugar and slavery, but of an older Cuba of petty contraband, small settled peasantries, and undeveloped interiors. On a clear day, however, its mountains were visible across fifty miles of sea from Môle Saint-Nicolas in the enviably modern colony of French Saint-Domingue. Easily reachable even from the capital city of Le Cap, Baracoa functioned as Cuba's maritime frontier with the Haitian Revolution.

There, on the evening of August 27, 1791, Lieutenant-Governor Ignacio Leyte Vidal received a M. de Llegart, aide-de-camp to Saint-Domingue's governor, Philibert-François Blanchelande. The Frenchman began his visit by explaining that the black slaves of the northern part of the colony had risen up in what he speculated would soon become a general insurrection across the colony. The rebels, he said, had attacked and burned the plantations, beheaded every white person they encountered, and destroyed even the last standing palm tree – details he surely embellished for effect. To help him convince the Spanish of the horrors he narrated and the imperative of the assistance he sought, Llegart brought with him several wealthy planters and women who had survived the cataclysm. It was seeing these people – "ruined and overwhelmed" – that drove home for Baracoa's governor the urgency of the French plea. Their very carriage and appearance, he suggested, conveyed more than mere words could about their sudden misfortune and vulnerability. Leyte Vidal observed and listened sympathetically, wondering to himself what the news might portend for the territory he governed. He worried, for instance, about the very short distance between Baracoa and the scenes of upheaval, about the possibility that the rebels might seek to escape and regroup in his territory, and about the total insufficiency of his resources should he be forced to repel an invasion from the black rebels of Saint-Domingue.[1]

But however urgent Llegart's plea and however anxious Leyte Vidal's impression, Cuban officials did not apprehend the news they were hearing as in and of itself extraordinary. Certainly, this was not the first time that they had received news of nearby uprisings. Listening to Llegart and reading Blanchelande's missive, Leyte Vidal had no reason to believe that he would not soon receive another report, this time announcing the customarily violent end to the slaves' bid for freedom – leaders caught,

---

[1] Ignacio Leyte Vidal to Francisco Bautista Vaillant, August 28, 1791, in ANC, Asuntos Políticos (AP), leg. 4, exp. 33; and Vidal to Las Casas, August 28, 1791, in AGI, Papeles de Cuba (Cuba), leg. 1435.

hanged, their heads displayed as a warning to potential followers. If officials in Baracoa, or later in Santiago or Havana, were worried by the news, they did not attach to it the significance of history.

Yet in that early and relatively inconsequential conversation in Baracoa can be discerned important patterns of contact and communication that would outlast the insurrection itself. Though it occurred just days into the transformative events, the exchange revealed the major lines of interpretation that would characterize much of the writing and talking about the Haitian Revolution in Cuba and elsewhere for decades to come. First, the description of the events cast the violence of the enslaved as the initial moment of conflict, as the point of origin of all the destruction that was engulfing prosperous Le Cap. The implication of starting the story there was clear: the violence of slavery itself was written out of the sequence of events. Thus, the actions of the enslaved, described simply as "the blacks," became not an action against slavery – and certainly not a conscious intervention in the unfolding of revolution in greater France – but rather simply the natural eruption of the inherent character of these black men – "general enemies of all mankind, barbaric, cruel, sanguinary, lacking the moderation of civilized peoples," as the governor of Baracoa described them after hearing Llegart's tales.[2]

Second, the account given by Llegart to Leyte Vidal, and then repeated by the latter to his own superiors, flatly denied that the slave rebels were acting of their own volition and design. Both men assumed and asserted that the leaders and masterminds of the revolutionary turmoil were emphatically not enslaved people, but rather "some mulattos and white rabble."[3] By default, the revolution's leaders could not be – and therefore were not – enslaved. Slaves were unthinking followers, not protagonists. These two assumptions – that the story of the revolution began with black violence and that its leaders were not themselves enslaved – implied that the causes of this massive slave insurrection were located in the machinations of a few irresponsible free men, not in the political will of the enslaved nor in the injustice of slavery itself. Across the Atlantic world, reports along these lines took flight, appearing and reappearing in newspapers, government correspondence, private letters, and street corner and parlor conversations.

Finally, the conversation between Baracoa's governor and the French officer revealed a third assumption that would immediately mark Cuban

---

[2] Leyte Vidal to Vaillant, August 28, 1791, in ANC, AP, leg. 4, exp. 33.
[3] Ibid.

and other interpretations of the Haitian Revolution across the Atlantic world: that the threat of the revolution was not limited to French soil. Contagion was possible, indeed likely. The emphasis on contagion likened the spread of political turmoil by the enslaved to the natural progression of a physical disease – hardly an act that required forethought or strategy. At the same time, however, that characterization implicitly contained a potential recognition of slaves as political agents. In this view, French slaves sought allies and military conquests; Spanish ones weighed the merit and appeal of potential partners and nearby movements. It may have been that possibility – of example more than contagion – that so worried Cuban authorities. In Baracoa, Leyte Vidal imagined Saint-Domingue's rebels setting their sights on his own coast and territory. Governor Juan Bautista Vaillant in Santiago, receiving the news a day later, confessed that "the force of bad example, especially so near, has me on alert, and I will not sleep as long as my duty calls."[4] Across the island – as indeed in all the neighboring ones across the region – authorities steeled themselves against similar movements, the possibility of which they chose to attribute to the effects of contagion rather than of politics and slavery.

This fear of contagion or example was as flexible and convenient as it was deeply felt. For the French, asserting that the unrest of the slaves was communicable helped bolster their appeal for immediate and generous aid. If the slaves who threatened French life and property could by extension also threaten Spanish or British territory, then the Europeans' interests were truly one and their enemy a common and formidable one. In the same way that such claims bolstered the French government's case for aid, they also potentially bolstered the repressive capacity of the Spanish colonial state. A contagious threat justified surveillance. In the months and years that followed, local governors commissioned spies, and they attempted to limit what people could read and talk about and with whom. In fact, it was precisely in response to the perceived threat of contagion posed by the circulation of news about the French and especially Haitian revolutions that Havana became a principal node of Spanish espionage during this period.[5]

For Cuban leaders, first word of revolution in Saint-Domingue presented an unforeseen dilemma. To governors on the ground – if perhaps

---

[4] [Vaillant] to Conde de Floridablanca, September 7, 1791, in ANC, Correspondencia de Capitanes Generales (CCG), leg. 42, exp. 5.

[5] Eleazar Córdova Bello, *La independencia de Haití y su influencia en Hispanoamérica* (Caracas: Instituto de Geografía e Historia, 1967), 121.

less so to Arango in Madrid – rebellion and violence among local slaves seemed a distinctly possible outcome of the insurrection. Yet a substantial crisis for their principal competitor was just as plausible a forecast, and certainly more welcome. Thus, French entreaties for aid required that Cuban officials – unable in the first instance to wait for guidance from Madrid – weigh competing options: to aid a neighbor and thereby avert potential unrest on their own soil, or instead to deny that aid, risk the expansion of the rebellion, but in the process help create perhaps greater opportunity for Cuban sugar and Cuban planters.

Luis de Las Casas, governor of Havana and captain-general of the island, faced that question just days after the start of the revolution. When Llegart and the French survivors finished their meetings in Baracoa, they went on to Havana to retell the same stories, this time to officials more powerful than those in the eastern coastal town. They arrived in Havana on September 1; there, Las Casas was so much on alert that he refused to allow the French delegation to disembark from its vessel. He read the letter from the French governor, which stated bluntly that he "was in imminent danger of losing the colony due to the insurrection of the blacks." Immediately, Las Casas convened a *junta de generales* and, with its members' support, decided that Havana could not provide any assistance. He based that decision on the king's order of October 10, 1790, which instructed colonial authorities to refrain from intervening in internal conflicts among the French. When a second French ship arrived from Le Cap a week later on the same mission, Las Casas gave the same answer: the Spanish had no help to give, and they were enjoined by their king from intervening in domestic French struggles.[6] Thus, Las Casas – owner of the *Amistad* and *Alejandría* sugar plantations and their enslaved labor forces – denied assistance to the world's most important slave system and Cuba's most formidable competitor.

Llegart's delegation was only the first of many, and the question posed to Las Casas that day would be forced on Cuban authorities over and over again. Thus, if those early conversations in Havana and Baracoa established the principal lines of interpretation, they also presaged important patterns of contact. Just days after the initial outbreak, people in Cuba had detailed news of the event, an invitation to assist in defending slavery and the military rule of European colonizers, and live witnesses and victims to interrogate and anxiously pity. In the weeks, months, and years that followed, this general pattern continued: news of ongoing upheaval

---

[6] Las Casas to Conde de Campo de Alange, September 15, 1791, in AGS, SGU, leg. 6846, exp. 79.

arrived quickly, and Cubans were asked to play different roles: as audiences for dramatic tales of black rebellion, as potential providers of succor and assistance, and as likely targets of contagious and expansive black designs.

Revolutionary news came from multiple quarters. French refugees, perhaps more than any others, became critical conduits of stories and sentiments associated with the revolution of Saint-Domingue. At the beginning of the revolution, and at every critical point thereafter, thousands and thousands of people left – or were taken – to points far and wide, to nearby Cuba or Jamaica, or further afield to New York, Charleston, Philadelphia, Baltimore. They came with stories of what they had witnessed, and, at least in Spanish territory, they were asked to recount their experience in revolutionary Saint-Domingue before receiving permission to remain. Once settled, the refugees strove to remain in contact with what was unfolding in their home colony, some with an eye to returning if circumstances permitted, others to keep track of property they ostensibly owned and people they knew, still others simply to remain informed of political vagaries in times of turmoil. Cuba would receive perhaps 35,000 such refugees. Not all of them remained, as some moved by either choice or force to France or the United States, back to Saint-Domingue, or after 1804, to Haiti itself. Almost everywhere they went, they were viewed with a mixture of awe and suspicion, their very presence a bodily testament to the upheaval in Saint-Domingue.

As the revolution wore on, these human arrivals included not only civilian refugees, but also French officers and soldiers evacuating Saint-Domingue. These men stopped regularly in Santiago and Havana, sometimes in great numbers, sometimes for months at a time, and sometimes in obvious defeat. In 1793, for example, the commander of Jérémie, Vizieu Desombrage, fearing imminent arrest at the orders of new Jacobin authorities, fled and stopped in Santiago, sharing with the governor there all manner of dense revolutionary news: of mulatto ascendancy, of the imminent emancipation of the slaves, of how Spain (then already at war with France after the revolutionaries' execution of Louis XVI) might woo white French colonists to its cause by guaranteeing slavery, racial hierarchy, and tranquility – a tall order in that time and place.[7]

---

[7] Vaillant to Las Casas, April 30, 1793, in AGI, Cuba, 1434; "Interrogatorio evacuado entre el Gobernador de Cuba Juan Bautista Vaillant y el Comandante que fue del partido de Jeremías en la parte francesa de la isla de Santo Domingo," April 29, 1793, and "Noticias que el Gobernador de Cuba ha adquirido y con fundamento estima fidedignas," May 3, 1793, both in AGI, Estado, leg. 14, expedientes 16 and 30, respectively.

The stories that arrived with French officers and soldiers such as these, however, were easily outnumbered by the oral accounts transmitted by the hundreds of ship captains and crew members who plied Caribbean waters, sharing news at ports across the region. The expansion of the Cuban economy, and the growth of the slave trade and commerce with neutral nations authorized in ever more frequent times of war, created ample opportunity for movement, contact, and the dissemination of news. As Julius Scott has shown, whatever product or people these vessels carried, they also brought news and rumor of the revolution in Saint-Domingue.[8] In Cuba, authorities used their power to compel ship captains to provide accounts of what they had seen and heard in Saint-Domingue and to make available any papers they might have acquired while there.[9] The arrival of ship captains coming from Saint-Domingue was so regular, and the news some provided so detailed, that through them authorities in Havana had regular, independent access to the unfolding stories of the Haitian Revolution.

Thus it was that in early November 1791, John Davison, captain of the American schooner *Charming Sally*, sat before authorities in Havana to relay news of his nine weeks in Saint-Domingue, dating from about two or three days before the start of the insurrection. He informed his Havana audience that the slave rebels of the north, whose number he put at about 40,000, had burned forty-two plantations and assassinated some of Le Cap's most distinguished residents. As of mid-October, when he abandoned Le Cap for Port-au-Prince, their dominance continued. In Port-au-Prince, he explained, it was the free people of color who held the upper hand. Indeed, they had forced besieged white residents to agree to their demands and had even provided local authorities with the text of an agreement between the two parties, a copy of which he now turned over to Las Casas. The night before his departure for Havana, the slaves who had joined the free coloreds of Port-au-Prince had been betrayed, and in his presence 350 of them were seized, placed aboard a French ship, to be later drowned.[10]

---

[8] The pioneering and still definitive source on this is J. Scott, "The Common Wind."

[9] Las Casas to Conde Campo de Alange, November 9 and November 13, 1791, in AGS, SGU, leg. 6846, exps. 70 and 65, respectively.

[10] Casas to Conde del Campo de Alange, Nov. 9, 1791, in AGS, SGU, leg. 6846, exp. 65. It is not clear that Davison had the details correct. For example, the number of 350 is higher than the ones noted in many accounts. Davison reported that the men would be killed at sea. In reality, they were supposed to have been sent to the Mosquito Coast. The ship captain, after having failed to sell them in Belize, dumped them on the Jamaican coast, where British authorities detained them and then shipped them back to Port-au-Prince.

Juan Luis de la Cuesta, of a French brig the Spanish called *Descubierta*, arrived in Havana in early 1792, after about a month in Saint-Domingue. It was from him that Havana authorities heard, perhaps for the first time, about Jean-François and Biassou, former slaves who were emerging as the uncontested leaders of a rebel force of about 20,000. Cuesta reported that the two black leaders were offering to negotiate with the French, even proposing to return the insurgents to slavery in exchange for their own freedom and that of their officer corps. Cuesta explained the basic turns in these negotiations: the Le Cap Assembly refused, while the civil commissioners were more receptive. It was with the latter group that negotiations and a meeting occurred. Seventeen white prisoners were returned by the rebels, and some slaves returned to the plantation. But then, as white residents in Le Cap began to breathe more easily, reported Cuesta, the attacks resumed, and on January 1, 1792, black rebel forces took Fort Dauphin, announcing confidently that French troops would soon come in their support.[11] Implicitly, at least, Cuesta's account attributed a political and intellectual position to the insurgent slaves, especially when he told Cuban authorities that the insurgent leaders "wrote in elegant terms, justifying their conduct on the basis of the decrees promulgated by the Assembly in Europe concerning people of color, mentioning them by date and arguing that they should not be excluded from the patrimony and prerogatives signified by the term Rights of Man."[12] In the harbor, selling, trading, and provisioning the vessel, Cuesta and the crew had ample opportunities to retell such stories and share their impressions.

Pedro Ducet (perhaps Peter Duckett), captain of the English schooner *Margarita* (*Margaret*), arrived in Havana in March 1792 and informed authorities that in Les Cayes, capital of the colony's southern province, the impressive black and mulatto forces had been successfully attacked

---

At that point (well after Davison's departure for Cuba), they were imprisoned on a boat; many were executed, and others died of starvation and sickness. A thorough account of the alliance and its betrayal appears in Geggus, *Haitian Revolutionary Studies*, 99–118.

[11] See the monthly customs house register for January 1792, in AGI, SD, 2207; and "Noticias generales de la parte francesa de la Ysla de Santo Domingo... dadas por D. Juan de la Cuesta, encargado del Armazen [sic] de Negros que condujo el Bergantín *Descubierta*," February 8, 1792, in AGS, SGU, leg. 7150. For a description of the historical events described by Cuesta, see Dubois, *Avengers of the New World*, 125–29. *Découverte* appears in the Transatlantic Slave Trade Database (voyage 31773), arriving in Saint-Domingue from northern Congo with 351 slaves. http://slavevoyages.org/tast/database/search.faces?yearFrom=1514&yearTo=1866&shipname=decouverte.

[12] "Noticias generales dadas por D. Juan de la Cuesta," in AGS, SGU, leg. 7150.

by a French detachment from Le Cap. Many white French soldiers had
returned to town carrying the heads of the black insurgents as trophies.
The finality of the display, however, was undermined by the news he
provided next: that the bulk of the rebel force had escaped and gone
deeper into the interior, suggesting more of the same to follow.[13]

Captain José Medina, of the sloop *Santa Rosa de Lima*, which entered
Havana harbor on October 11, 1792, brought news of ambitious French
attempts to restore order. He reported the September arrival in Le Cap of a
new civil commission, accompanied by sixty vessels carrying 8,000 French
troops. The new commissioners posted decrees in the king's name calling
for peace in the colony. Days later, Jean-Jacques d'Esparbès arrived as the
new governor. The rebel leaders again engaged in negotiations involving
a return to slavery for most of their forces, and the new governor posted
more notices, this time threatening death to any French soldiers who used
arms against the rebels without provocation. The Spanish captain shared
with his audience the prevailing consensus that d'Esparbès was hoping to
end the turmoil and subdue the rebels without firing a single shot. But just
one day later, Cuban authorities received an update from another Spanish
seaman, Francisco Fernández, of the American brig *Perseverance*, who
reported that Governor d'Esparbès had been deported.[14]

And the news continued. In January 1793, Captain Luis Beltrán Gonet,
of the Spanish schooner *Nuestra Señora del Carmen*, reported the latest
racial intrigues. The civil commissioners were promoting free men of
color into high ranks in the French army, despite opposition from white
officers. The governor, said Beltrán, had a personal bodyguard of twenty-
four mulatto officers who accompanied him wherever he went.[15]

The proximity of the scenes of unrest and the frequency of Caribbean
maritime arrivals meant that narratives of the revolution were available
in Cuba with only minimal delay. It would be incorrect, however, to

---

[13] See the monthly customs house register for March 1792, in AGI, SD, 2207; Las Casas
  to Conde del Campo de Alange, March 30, 1792, in AGS, SGU, leg. 6847, exp. 55. Las
  Casas identified the witness as Pedro Ducet, captain of the English schooner *Margarita*.
  Presumably, the ship would have been named *Margaret* or *Maggie*; Ducet, likewise,
  might be actually Doucet or Duckett. The names of ships, captains, and crew were often
  Hispanized in the documents, a disadvantage when trying to locate the ships or crew in
  British or French sources.
[14] Both reports are attached to Las Casas to Conde del Campo de Alange, November 13,
  1792, in AGS, SGU, leg. 6849, exp. 38.
[15] Las Casas to Conde del Campo de Alange, January 4, 1793, in AGS, SGU, leg. 6850,
  exp. 1.

view these regular and often detailed updates as a coherent narrative of the revolution. Based on necessarily incomplete eyewitness accounts, rumor, and speculation, they contained precise details that were invariably uneven, disjointed, and contradictory. Alongside the elaborate stories that arrived with incoming vessels, Cuban audiences also received the kind of telescopic updates that conveyed only the most general story lines: "the revolution of the blacks continues" and "the mulattos and blacks continue their hostilities with much rigor." Such were the brief reports of Captain Pedro LaClau of the schooner *Santa Rosalía* and of Captain Francisco Durel of the schooner *Hermana*, both of whom arrived in mid-1792 from Le Cap and Port-au-Prince, respectively.[16] This was, nonetheless, the way the idea and the experience of the Haitian Revolution often circulated throughout the region – in fitful and incomplete accounts that arrived sometimes right away, sometimes after some delay, sometimes as disordered installments in a story that these captains portrayed, by turns, as intricate narratives of internecine battles among the French and as simple stories of black and mulatto vengeance. The danger sensed by authorities in Saint-Domingue was refracted and diffused as authorities in neighboring slave societies kept receiving every manner of dispatch – except, of course, the critical one that would have signaled the end of cause for worry.

An overflow of information emanated from the scenes of revolution as sailors, soldiers, and refugees all plied Caribbean waters and swelled the transient and sometimes permanent populations of Atlantic port cities. In Cuba, authorities sought to capture as much of that moving news as possible. To this end, Spanish authorities in Cuba elaborated on metropolitan strictures already in place since the start of the French Revolution in 1789. In September 1789, the Spanish king had forbidden the introduction and circulation of so-called "French papers."[17] Similar orders were issued and reissued in subsequent years, providing local authorities with the imperative and justification for confiscating papers brought aboard ships or found in the hands of local subjects. It was in this way that governors and their lieutenants acquired copies of French and British colonial newspapers, or pamphlets on the Rights of Man published not only in French territory but also in British and Spanish ones. Personal letters from French

---

[16] Las Casas to Conde del Campo de Alange, June 3 and July 2, 1792, in AGS, SGU, leg. 6848, exps. 16, and 64, respectively.

[17] José Luciano Franco, *Revoluciones y conflictos internacionales en el Caribe, 1789–1854* (Havana: Academia de Ciencias, 1965), 7.

Saint-Domingue were likewise confiscated.[18] "Papers" could be broadly construed, and in one case a local governor went as far as to confiscate fans that depicted scenes alluding to the French Revolution, even though he was sure neither the women nor the retailer who sold them had any idea what they signified. In these times, all things French posed a potential threat.[19]

But the volume and indeed the very manner of the stories' arrival meant that the news was impossible to contain. For every French officer or ship captain who relayed to Cuban authorities stories of black revolution, there were other crew members who would have heard and seen many of the exact same things. Waiting to load and unload cargo, there was more than ample opportunity to share such tales and accounts with local people. Many of these conversations were ephemeral and fleeting encounters between people who perhaps never even exchanged names. Though we cannot recreate such conversations in any systematic manner, their traces are diffused everywhere. In many an official letter between authorities, even in newspaper items, what was reported was not always a verifiable event or certainty, but rather a general public conversation about possible events. "People say," began letters from governors in Havana and Santiago; "people were saying" opened newspaper articles in Havana, Madrid, and elsewhere.[20] This general conversation – in which people of all stations participated – was a kind of echo of the news reported by official messengers and ship captains. The official reports, together with the imprecise allusions to generalized public talk, point to a world replete with possibilities for sharing information, interpretations, and vague but powerful sentiments of fear – or hope, depending on who was doing the circulating. Clearly, the boundaries of such talk and speculation went well beyond the small official circle of those who had the capacity to compel people to talk.

Thus, while authorities endeavored to capture the news, it soon became very clear that they were not the only ones doing so. Nor were they the only ones interpreting the news and considering implications for their own world. While French messengers, Cuban governors, and authors on both sides of the Atlantic constructed powerful and influential narratives about black violence and barbarism, precisely because there was so much talk

---

[18] Vaillant to Las Casas, October 3, 1793, in AGI, Cuba, leg. 1434; Vaillant to Duque de Alcudia, April 16, 1793, in AGI, Estado, leg. 14, exp. 23; Kindelán to Someruelos, October 30, 1799, in AGI, Cuba, leg. 1534.

[19] Antonio de Viana to Las Casas, December 20, 1794, in AGI, Cuba, leg. 1462.

[20] The phrase in Spanish is *corren voces* or *corrían voces*.

and so much news circulating in the region and because so many actors were involved in spreading and receiving it, other, often countervailing fragments of the Haitian Revolution also circulated.

The hint of a supposed ritual sacrifice of pigs in Havana in honor of the Saint-Domingue insurgents, premised surely on other kinds of conversations and other kinds of interpretations, provides a vivid example. The evidence of Bois Caïman's possible echoes in Cuba suggests the circulation not only of dominant narratives of the events – such as the ones that Llegart shared in Baracoa or that Arango assembled in Madrid – but also of the ideological and ritual artifacts of the world's first black revolution.[21] Like the French appeals for aid, they too overflowed the boundaries of Saint-Domingue.

On the night of June 25, 1793, an unusual object arrived in Baracoa, brought by twenty disheveled British men who used the rebels' dramatic burning of Le Cap to escape from prison. Once out of jail, the men quickly stole a "small, damaged boat missing a tiller" and, without provisions or much confidence, rowed to Baracoa. They brought with them not just the news of Le Cap's long-feared (or awaited) destruction, but also an interesting material artifact of the revolution: a rosette or cockade (*escarapela*) carried by the black insurgents, which they presented to Leyte Vidal, lieutenant governor of Baracoa, on their arrival. It consisted of three discrete images: a small heart made of seeds and bordered in gold, a *fleur de lis*, and the word *Constitution*.[22]

The artifact that arrived with the British prisoners combined multiple symbols. Of the three features described, each corresponded to a potential current of political inspiration: the *fleur de lis* associated with the French monarchy; the word *Constitution*, reflecting a newer force on the horizon; and a heart made of small seeds, perhaps similar to the one that would later become a traditional representation of the vodou deity Erzulie. This iconography, in its formality, heightens the impression of ideological syncretism already visible in the well-known example from 1791, when a slave rebel who was captured and executed was reported to have carried in his pocket three things of interest, each drawing on a distinct source of

---

[21] See Introduction to this volume.

[22] Vaillant to Las Casas, June 30, 1793, in AGI, Cuba, leg. 1434. The original reads: "un pequeño corazón de grana bordado de oro, por un lado una flor de liz en el centro, y al contorno una escripción tambien bordado que dice *Constitución*." *Escarapela* might translate as ribbon, rosette, or cockade, the last two usually worn on a military hat to signal one's party. It is hard to imagine all three of these features fitting onto a rosette.

power: gunpowder, an African talisman, and pamphlets on the Rights of Man.[23]

As news of the revolution overflowed the boundaries of French Saint-Domingue, so too did the material and documentary manifestations of its complexity. Governors pondered the meaning of artifacts that drew equally on monarchical and republican symbols, and on European, African, and creole sources of power. Local people of color apparently engaged in ceremonies that seemed to echo those held by the slave rebels of Saint-Domingue. Ship captains such as Juan Luis Cuesta brought news not just of military encounters but also of black slave leaders who cast themselves as beneficiaries – and indeed forgers – of the Rights of Man. Later, in 1795 and 1811, black dock workers in Havana would buy, borrow, and trade printed images (*estampas*) of black leaders such as Jean-François, Toussaint Louverture, and Henri Christophe. In this and countless other ways, news, words, papers, and material artifacts of the revolution circulated in Cuba and across the region. Just as the interpretations of French authorities and white planters made it to Cuba, so too did those of the rebels themselves. Though it was rarely, if ever, commented on as such by witnesses or recipients, traces of the intellectual history of once-enslaved insurgents arrived in Cuba and elsewhere, buried in the profusion of economic and military detail, and in the lurid and dramatic narratives of "race war."

The Capture of News in a Slave Society

To examine the revolutionary news that arrived in Cuba about Haiti is to see how necessarily incomplete and contradictory were the accounts, rumors, and images that people encountered. Nonetheless, the very patterns of its arrival in Cuba may reveal something of an underlying order and logic. Even the brief examination here reveals the existence of a kind of infrastructure for the circulation of Haitian news. Some of this had to do with structures of imperial rule, which dictated that dispatches would be transcribed over and over again, from subordinate to superior officials, to their counterparts across the empire, and to metropolitan authorities in Europe. But an equally dynamic pattern of circulation reflected the infrastructures of Atlantic slavery itself. In Cuba, the transformation of

---

[23] The example is cited by Dubois, *Avengers of the New World*, 102–109; Fick, *The Making of Haiti*, 110–111.

slavery shaped the very manner in which revolutionary news arrived, determining the routes, the carriers, and the reception of Haitian news.

The same ship captains who arrived and shared with local authorities the latest news and emerging narratives of the Haitian Revolution were often, in fact, the captains of slaving vessels. There was ample opportunity to gather information from such vessels. In 1791, the Spanish king had renewed and extended the open slave trade, or the freedom to trade in unfree labor. Under these new concessions, the time allowed for foreign traders to remain in Havana was lengthened from one day to eight. And in 1792, it was extended yet again to forty days.[24] The opening of the trade greatly increased the number of ships and captives entering Havana and Santiago. Importantly, most of the slave ships that arrived in Cuba came from other Caribbean ports, including those of Saint-Domingue. For example, of the 1,261 slave ships that arrived in Havana between 1791 and 1804, an overwhelming number (997) came from the Caribbean, and another 144 were mixed voyages that had stopped in both African and Caribbean ports.[25] In Santiago, the proportion was even higher: between 1789 and 1794, more than 99.7 percent of all slave ships entering that port came from other Caribbean islands.[26]

The captains who provided Havana authorities with the running narrative of the revolution described earlier were in fact all associated with slave-trading vessels. Thus, for example, the *Charming Sally*, whose captain John Davison had informed Las Casas about the outbreak of slave rebellion in Le Cap and of the alliance between whites and free people of color in Port-au-Prince, arrived with thirteen enslaved men to

---

[24] Murray, *Odious Commerce*; and Franco, *Comercio clandestino*.

[25] The 1791–1804 figures are taken from Herbert Klein, "The Cuban Slave Trade in a Period of Transition, 1790–1843," in Herbert Klein, *The Middle Passage: Comparative Studies in the Atlantic Slave Trade* (Princeton: Princeton University Press, 1978), 209–227; relevant table appears on 221. Klein's data comes from monthly customs registers from Havana, located in "Estado de los negros introducidos en la Habana, Septiembre 1791, in AGI, SD, leg. 2207. It should be noted that after 1791, most of the registers record the names and types of vessels, their captains, nationality, and the number of slaves, but not what ports the ships had visited. Klein calculates whether the voyages were Caribbean, mixed, or African on the basis of the holding capacity of the ships and the number of captives carried.

[26] The Santiago figures are based on Belmonte, "El impacto de la liberalización," which are drawn mostly from the Santiago port summaries contained in AGI, Indiferente General (IG), 2822, 2823, and 2824. See also José Luis Belmonte Postigo, *Ser esclavo en Santiago de Cuba: Espacios de poder y negociación en un contexto de expansión y crisis* (Aranjuez: Doce Calles, 2011), 161–162.

sell.[27] Juan Luis de la Cuesta, who had told authorities that black slave leaders were invoking the Rights of Man, was in charge of the *Descubierta*'s cargo of 123 Africans transported for sale in Havana. Pedro Ducet of the *Margarita*, who in March 1792 had informed authorities of the continuation of the war even after French soldiers marched with the heads of rebel slaves on their bayonets, was in Havana to sell nine slaves. Francisco Fernández of the *Perseverance* and Luis Beltrán Gonet of the *Nuestra Señora del Carmen*, both of whom shared the latest news on the governor and the civil commissioners, were in Havana trying to sell 129 and 15 slaves, respectively. The evidence available about the arrival of the *Charming Sally* or any of these other vessels does not broach the question of whether Havana buyers asked about the origin of the slaves they examined – about the possibility that they, like the ship, came from Saint-Domingue in the early throes of the revolution.

The same event – the arrival of a slave ship carrying both captives to be sold and news of black and mulatto revolution – highlighted the simultaneity of the destruction and the rise of Caribbean slave systems. The material infrastructure that disseminated the example of revolutionary antislavery was the very same infrastructure that underwrote slavery's expansion. Thus, news of the slave revolution arrived in the same vessels that were facilitating its antithesis – the entrenchment of slavery – in nearby Cuba.

That some of the ships carrying news from Saint-Domingue also carried enslaved men and women suggests the transfer of the human infrastructure of slavery, as enslaved individuals from one colony in collapse were transported to another in ascent, and as French slave-trading vessels that months before would have sold their human cargo in Saint-Domingue now headed to Havana. Indeed, the monthly figures for arrivals of enslaved Africans in Havana increased dramatically immediately after the start of the Haitian Revolution. In 1791 and 1792, much of that increase derived from the arrival of French ships, which generally carried larger numbers of people than American, Spanish, and British ones. Before August 1791, those vessels would have unloaded and sold most of their cargo in Saint-Domingue. But with the revolution in full force, this had become significantly less feasible. Some stopped there briefly, others not at all. The captains instead diverted their vessels and their cargo to a

---

[27] Davison's translated statement is attached to Las Casas to Conde de Campo Alange, November 9, 1791, in AGS, SGU, leg. 6846, exp. 65. On the slave cargo on arrival in Havana, see the monthly customs house register for November 1791, in AGI, SD, 2207.

nearby place, just recently opened to the frenzy of the trade and, above all, tranquil. Among these vessels were the imposingly named *Assemblée Nationale*, which arrived in Havana in October 1791 with 501 slaves, and the *Nouvelle Constitution* in November, with 464.[28]

The magnitude of French participation in the trade to Havana in this period is striking. Since the Spanish declaration of the free slave trade in 1789, Cuba had been the principal non-French port of arrival and sale for French slaving ships.[29] Turmoil in Saint-Domingue now made those traders readier to trade and sell in Cuba. But because of concerns over the ramifications of the French Revolution, the king's November 1791 order extending the open slave trade had explicitly excluded France. The order took the customary months to arrive. When it did, the captain-general and the intendant, both owners of sugar mills and slaves, decided to suspend enforcement of the exclusion in order to allow additional time for the French in Saint-Domingue to learn of it. When Cuban officials finally began enforcing the order in March 1792 and turned away three French slavers arriving from Le Cap with a total of 786 captives, they did so with great regret, reporting that slave prices were already on the rise. Havana residents – presumably those in the market for slaves – watched disconsolately as the French slave ships headed out to sea, still loaded with African captives. On June 9, the king rescinded the exclusion. But by the time the news arrived in Havana, the French slave trade had already collapsed under the weight of Caribbean revolution.[30]

In making a case against French exclusion, Havana authorities were quick to point out to the king that though these ships often came from Le Cap, their human cargo had been loaded in Africa and was entirely African, thus posing neither a threat against public order nor a potential infraction against the restrictions on purchasing slaves other than those directly extracted from the African coast. But if that insistence served immediate purposes, authorities may have overstated their confidence in the distinction they were seeking to draw. In a different context,

[28] September, October, and November customs registers in AGI, SD, 2207. The *Constitution* (*Nouvelle Constitution*) and the *Assemblée Nationale* appear in Mettas, *Répertoire*, 2:121 and 2:538–39, respectively, as well as in *Voyages*, http://slavevoyages.org/tast/database/search.faces?yearFrom=1791&yearTo=1791&natinimp=10&mjslptimp=31300.

[29] David Geggus, "The French Slave Trade: An Overview," in *William and Mary Quarterly*, Third Series, 58, 1, (Jan. 2001): 125.

[30] José Pablo Valiente to Conde de Lerma, March 28, 1792, in the file "Comercio de negros para el Consejo de Estado," in AGI, IG, leg. 2822. On Spain's exclusion of the French from the open slave trade in 1791, see Murray, *Odious Commerce*, 12.

local authorities had already discussed the difficulty of knowing whether among the multitude of captives carried by French slavers coming from Saint-Domingue there might not hide some captured insurgents. In September 1791, this had been the source of anxiety among Havana authorities with the arrival of the frigate *Deux Soeurs*, carrying 292 people, among whom they feared were insurgent French slaves.[31]

Thus, while the arrival of French slave ships in Havana was generally welcomed, that welcome was not unambivalent. Local planters eagerly purchased the men and women the ships carried. But with mixed emotions of dread and ambition, they listened to their crews' tales of revolutionary upheaval in Saint-Domingue. Authorities and planters were aware of the challenges they faced. They knew that an expanding slave trade in the context of the Haitian Revolution made an increase of danger attendant on the expansion of opportunity. Even as they debated how best to open up the island to the slave trade and the economic growth they imagined would flow from it, they also wrung their hands at the realization that the ships that brought the human merchandise they purchased also brought news that might inspire and instigate those same men and women and others. They also feared that those same ships might sometimes bring captive men and women who had witnessed and perhaps participated in the revolution then unfolding.

Negros Franceses

As news and risks seemed to multiply apace with the growth in prosperity, authorities and their local allies identified no greater threat than the people they called *negros franceses*, or *French blacks*, the term by which Spanish and Spanish American contemporaries referred to African and creole slaves from the French colonies.[32] In Madrid, Havana, and across the Spanish empire, authorities became convinced of the wisdom of keeping out people of color, free and enslaved, associated with the French colonies. This new conviction represented a clear change from earlier policy. For centuries the king had allowed fugitive slaves who arrived in Spanish territory and embraced Catholicism to win their freedom and the privilege of becoming Spanish subjects. That dispensation

---

[31] "Estado de los negros introducidos en la Habana, Septiembre 1791," in AGI, SD, leg. 2207. The *Deux Soeurs* is discussed in the introduction.

[32] For a recent and incisive study of the "fear of French Negroes" that disturbs the usual meaning of the phrase in part to consider black French as subjects, rather than objects, of that fear, see Sara Johnson, *Fear of French Negroes: Transcolonial Collaboration in the Revolutionary Americas* (Berkeley: University of California Press, 2012).

had circulated widely in the Caribbean and contributed, as Julius Scott has shown, to the important phenomenon of maritime marronage, as slaves in British, Dutch, Danish, North American, and even French (and thus already Catholic) territory used it to escape to freedom in Spanish territory.[33] As late as 1789, the policy had been reaffirmed in Cuba. That year, two Jamaican planters traveled to Cuba to recover eleven enslaved people who had absconded there "in search of the privilege of the water of baptism." Instead, the planters were confronted with an uncooperative captain-general, who argued that "the absolute freedom granted to [them] by the laws of Spain . . . [put] it beyond the power of [his] Government to deliver them up . . . or even to permit that [the request] should occasion them the smallest inconvenience."[34]

But that was in 1789. A year later, with the French Revolution in full force, and with the start of rebellion and conspiracy in the French Caribbean, the king rescinded the standing order of transimperial emancipation. In May 1790, he informed his colonial governors that fugitive slaves would no longer be welcome in Spanish dominions. Less than a week later, he went significantly further, expanding the order in two ways. First, he prohibited the entry of all French slaves – not only fugitive ones, but now even those legally purchased from French colonies. He further forbade the entry of any French person of color, including freed or free-born ones, in order to avoid the spread of seditious ideas. That such people were colored and French served as sufficient evidence of their propensity to circulate dangerous notions. The prohibition against the entry of French slaves and French people of color would be repeated and expanded many times over the course of the French and Haitian revolutions. In December 1791, for instance, Spain's Supreme Council of State reiterated the order, now forbidding the introduction not only of French slaves but of "Creole blacks educated and purchased in foreign colonies" more generally.[35]

[33] For a discussion of maritime marronage from French and British territories to Spanish, see J. Scott, "The Common Wind," 93–193; Neville A. T. Hall, *Slave Society in the Danish West Indies: St. Thomas, St. John, and St. Croix*, ed. B. W. Higman (Baltimore: Johns Hopkins University Press, 1992), 124–130; Jane G. Landers, *Atlantic Creoles in the Age of Revolutions* (Cambridge: Harvard University Press, 2010), chap. 1.

[34] Testimony of Martínez, June 9, 1789, and Ezpeleta to Williamson, March 25, 1789, in The National Archives of the UK (TNA), Colonial Office (CO), 137/88.

[35] Circular Reservada, May 21, 1790, in AGI, IG, leg. 2787. For later measures, see Conde de Floridablanca to Vaillant, September 25, 1790, in ANC, CCG, leg. 41, no. 1; and Actas de la Suprema Junta de Estado, December 16, 1791, in AHN, Estado, Libro 4, f. 139. See also Córdova-Bello, *La independencia de Haití*, 117.

The new prohibitions – no matter how many times they were repeated – nonetheless had to confront long-standing trade practices and routes. First in the contraband trade and more recently in the legal one, Cuban planters and the state had long relied on Caribbean (as opposed to direct African) supplies of labor. Whether out of force of habit, the urgency of greed over caution, the lack of sufficient numbers of African voyages landing in Cuba, or a combination of all the above, buyers and sellers seemed to pay little heed to the new restrictions. The state's periodic renewals and expansions of the prohibitions hint as much at authorities' will to curb the influence of so-called French slaves as they do at the very inefficacy of their efforts.

In fact, the multiple legal proscriptions against the entry and sale of French slaves in Cuba were only erratically followed. In Madrid, even as the king and his ministers repeated and expanded the exclusions against French blacks, they also allowed glaring exceptions, in one instance granting a license to a French doctor, then living and working in Cuba as a surgeon attached to the Havana Infantry Regiment, to return to Le Cap, even as revolution already raged all around, and to bring back his own and other slaves to sell in Cuba.[36]

Even in the colonies, officials sometimes ignored or adapted the law. One of the major sources of official access to Haitian news came from slave ships arriving from other Caribbean islands, including Saint-Domingue itself. Yet when these ships arrived, local authorities and planters were much more interested in obtaining news and slaves than in enforcing bans on the inter-island trade they were openly practicing. Before the illegalization of the Caribbean trade, port registers in Havana usually noted the origin of entering slave ships. After the issuance of the ban, the origin of arriving ships was simply not recorded – a convenient oversight in a place where the majority of slaves had come from other Caribbean territories and where those territories were now suddenly off-limits.[37] Still, the only locally published newspaper in Havana, established

---

[36] "Al Visitador Intendente de la Havana, concediendo licencia a Dn Anne Pérez para pasar al Guarico y pueda conducir Negros con arreglo a la Rl. Cédula," Madrid, December 30, 1791, in AGI, IG, leg. 2822.

[37] This is based on my reading of the Havana port registers in AGI, SD, 2207. Through mid-1790, *procedencia* (origin) is often provided; after that date it is rarely if ever noted. Comparing the lists of ship names that appear in these port registers against Mettas, *Répertoire*, or *Voyages* confirms that most of the ships were coming from Caribbean islands that were technically off-limits. Most of the ships do not appear in the database, an indication they were unlikely to represent African voyages; and many of the French ones appear in Mettas as having stopped in Saint-Domingue.

by the captain-general in 1790 and subject to censorship laws, routinely published announcements of slave ships arriving from Saint-Domingue and other Caribbean islands with slaves to be sold in Cuba. Less than an inch above the newspaper's footer "with permission of the Supreme Government," notices appeared announcing the arrival of loaded slave ships from Saint-Domingue: the American sloop *Good Intention* with 10 slaves; the schooner *San Joseph y Las Animas* with 44, the French frigate *Théodore* with 16, and the American brig *Leonor* with 110 enslaved men, women, and children, all of which arrived in Havana from Saint-Domingue in 1792 and 1793, well into the Haitian Revolution.[38]

In Santiago, most of the ships selling slaves were Spanish ones, for even the 1791 extension of the open slave trade did not allow foreign traders access to Cuban ports other than Havana. So Spanish slavers entered the harbor with slaves acquired from neighboring islands, and they continued to do so even after the king had declared the practice of selling French and other creole slaves illegal. When Governor Juan Bautista Vaillant in Santiago first received the 1790 order outlawing the sale of French slaves, he requested clarification: was he really to turn away all foreign slaves even if they came, say, as fugitives seeking to embrace the Catholic faith? The response arrived more than a year later: under no circumstances was he to allow the entry of French – or for that matter, any foreign creole – slaves, fugitive or legally purchased.[39]

In the meantime, however – indeed, even after – small vessels continued to make the short journey between Saint-Domingue and Santiago carrying men and women to be sold as slaves. In Jamaica, where a substantial trade in slaves with Cuba had long existed, merchants complained heartily of a sudden shortage of cash in 1792, which they attributed to the fact that Cuban traders who had before gone there to purchase slaves now went instead to Saint-Domingue, where the revolution had suddenly made the cost of enslaved laborers much cheaper than in Jamaica.[40]

[38] The example of the *Leonor* appears in *Papel Periódico de la Habana*, June 2, 1793. Examples of ships arriving from other Caribbean territories with captives appear on the following dates in 1793: March 10, March 17, March 24, May 30, June 2, September 26, December 22; and in 1794: January 23, August 7. The paper for January 12, 1792, shows the arrival of the following ships arriving from Saint-Domingue to sell slaves: the American sloop *Good Intention*, with 10 captives; the schooner *San Joseph y Las Animas*, with 44; and the French frigate *Théodore*, with 16.

[39] Circular Reservada, dated May 21, 1790; Vaillant, August 11, 1790; and [?] to Vaillant, May 12, 1791, all in AGI, IG, 2787.

[40] "Copy of a letter for a Merchant in Kingston respecting the Scarcity of Specie," September 4, 1792; and Williamson to Dundas, September 4, 1793, both in TNA, CO, 137/90.

The claim suggests indirectly that, well after prohibitions against doing so, local Cuban traders were not deterred from going to revolutionary Saint-Domingue in search of slaves. The port registers and the licenses granted by the local government, at least in Santiago, suggest that the traders went with the implicit consent of authorities. For example, on September 15, 1791, the schooner *Timbala* arrived from Port-au-Prince – where the turmoil had not yet taken root – with 151 slaves to sell. From Le Cap itself, ships arrived sporadically: on November 14, the sloop *Nuestra Señora de la Caridad* with thirty-four, and about a week later another sloop, *La Esperanza*, with fourteen.[41] Sometimes, ships came and went multiple times with exceedingly small (recorded) shipments of people. For example, the schooner *Nuestra Señora del Carmen* arrived from Jérémie on August 3 and again on September 3, 1792, first with six slaves and then with four. The sloop *San Josef* made the trip from Santiago to Port-au-Prince and back again each time with a small cargo of three enslaved.[42]

The modest size of these shipments from Saint-Domingue, their frequency, and the fact that the ships arrived as part of a regular and busy Caribbean trade in slaves with places such as Jamaica and Curaçao made control difficult. Indeed, it is unclear to what extent or how consistently local governors even tried. Thus, on March 14, 1792, Governor Vaillant in Santiago reported to the captain-general in Havana on his efforts to comply with the multiple royal orders prohibiting the entry and sale of creole slaves. For example, among the thirty-four enslaved people transported aboard the *Nuestra Señora de la Caridad*, which had arrived in the port from Le Cap, six were determined to be dangerous: they spoke French and could be classified as *ladino*, the term used to describe assimilated Africans. So those six were apprehended and presumably sent back. The other twenty-eight, though also identified as coming from Le Cap, were classified as *bozales*, or newly arrived Africans, and therefore eligible

See also David Geggus, *Slavery, War and Revolution: The British Occupation of Saint-Domingue, 1793–1798* (Oxford: Clarendon Press, 1982), 97.

[41] See the two lists titled "Estado formado para mi Don Juan Francisco de Salazar . . . para demostrar el número de negros bozales introducidos en este puerto de las colonias extranjeras," June 30, 1792 and January 1, 1794, in AGI, IG, leg. 2823.

[42] The information on incoming slaves ships in Santiago appears in regular port registers. See, in this case, Juan Francisco de Salazar, "Estado formado para mi Don Juan Francisco de Salazar," January 1, 1794, in AGI, IG, 2823. Of course, ship captains may have unloaded larger groups on a beach along the coast in order to avoid detection. This was fairly common practice during later waves of refugee arrivals.

to be sold.[43] How precisely the distinction was drawn in practice is unclear. At times, for the traders to say that the captives they brought from neighboring Caribbean islands were Africans, or *bozales*, seemed sufficient to warrant permission to enter.[44] The policy echoed the vague sentiment expressed by Arango a few months earlier and left implicit in the king's orders: that the danger came from creole slaves educated by the French and not at all from Africans, perceived as somehow passive or apolitical. The distinction may have worked for Arango in the abstract in Madrid, but since at the time of the start of the Haitian Revolution, approximately two-thirds of the enslaved labor force in Saint-Domingue was African-born (many recently arrived), it served as little guarantee that the "safe" Saint-Domingue arrivals had no experience of the revolution then unfolding.[45] It also clearly failed to live up to the letter of the king's order, which had specified that Spanish subjects were forbidden from purchasing any slave who had lived in a foreign colony, no matter for how brief a period.

Perhaps it was this singular interpretation of the law, or the governor's conviction that the proscription was flexible, that prompted Vaillant to advise others on where in revolutionary Saint-Domingue it was safe for traders to travel in search of slaves. Conferring with traders familiar with the business of trading in slaves amidst the turmoil of the place and time, Vaillant felt confident in his assessment of the situation. Thus, in March 1792, he prepared information for his superiors in Havana on the ports in Saint-Domingue that were either safe or off- limits for Spanish slave traders going there to acquire men, women, and children to sell in Cuba. He reported specifically that Le Cap, Môle Saint Nicolas, Port-au-Prince, and Jérémie, among others, were relatively safe locales for slave traders to do business.[46] Another local official saw the list and worried enough to order that public notices be placed around the city reminding residents that it was illegal to purchase slaves from the French colonies. Yet the trade appears to have continued for much of the year with the arrival of ships from the very ports of Saint-Domingue that Vaillant had

---

[43] On Saint-Domingue slaves transported to Santiago by slave traders, see, for example, Vaillant to Las Casas, March 14, 1792, in AGI, Cuba, leg. 1434. A copy also exists in ANC, CCG, leg. 43, exp. 1.

[44] Franco, *Comercio clandestino de esclavos*, 72.

[45] Dubois and Garrigus, *Slave Revolution in the Caribbean*, 8, 13.

[46] Vaillant to Las Casas, March 13, 1792, in AGI, Cuba, leg. 1434. Les Cayes, he said, was also safe. Fort-Dauphin and Tiburón were at the moment relatively safe but more vulnerable, so trips there should be undertaken with extreme caution.

classified as safe, until the practice appears to have either disappeared or become imperceptible in the always imperfect records of ship arrivals.[47]

In addition to the ships carrying enslaved people clearly identified as such, other ships were authorized to travel to Saint-Domingue on official business, yet used that occasion to engage in the profitable business of buying and selling people. For example, the ships *San José de las Animas*, captained by José González, and the *Nuestra Señora del Carmen* were both licensed to sail to Guantánamo and buy cattle in large amounts and then transport the animals to Le Cap and Jérémie as aid to French authorities in their extended moment of crisis. Yet both ships made regular landings in Santiago with small shipments of enslaved men and women, suggesting that they were perhaps doing more in Saint-Domingue than delivering cows.[48] A mobile world of petty trade barely hid the small-scale but regular transfer of enslaved people from revolutionary Saint-Domingue to colonial Cuba.

The number of local ships arriving in Santiago from Saint-Domingue paled in comparison to those arriving from Jamaica. Almost every day, Spanish ships arrived in Santiago from the Jamaican ports of Kingston, Lucea, Port Antonio, and elsewhere, with anywhere from two to 116 men and women carried as slaves. Many times a month, Santiago's governor authorized Spanish traders to travel to Jamaica to purchase slaves to bring back and resell, even though the practice of selling Jamaican slaves was also technically outlawed by the king's orders. But if many of the black men and women carried in this manner were clearly purchased in Jamaica, by admission of colonial authorities in eastern Cuba, many of these Jamaican voyages carried not only Jamaican or African slaves, but also men, women, and children extracted from Saint-Domingue. The ship named the *Bella Angélica*, for instance, had authorization to travel to Jamaica and Curaçao to purchase people. It was for that purpose and with that destination that its captain, Gabriel Gonzáles, left Santiago on

---

[47] On the posting of the notices, see Domingo Morejón to Vaillant, March 30, 1792, in ANC, CCG, leg. 43, exp. 5. On the continuing arrival of small shipments of people from Saint-Domingue through the year 1792, see the two lists titled "Estado formado para mi Don Juan Francisco de Salazar," June 30, 1792, and January 1, 1794, in AGI, IG, leg. 2823.

[48] Both ships appear in the Santiago port registers cited earlier. Their arrivals with slaves are also recorded in the regular reports of port captain Francisco de Varas, scattered in ANC, CCG, leg, 43. On the transport of cattle and, in the case of the *San José de Animas*, the monthly voyages for that purpose, see Vaillant to Maldonado, and the annotations by Ramón Cantero on the backs of the letters regarding the number of cows taken and dates of departure from Guantánamo, in ANC, CCG, leg. 43, exp. 6 and 7.

February 10, 1792. When he returned on March 5, he claimed to have come from Curaçao, as his license allowed, with thirty-three men and one woman to sell. Yet somehow it was discovered that among those thirty-four captives were in fact at least five *ladinos* from Saint-Domingue. On March 10, Governor Vaillant in Santiago reported that the captain was made to take them back to Saint-Domingue. Yet the Santiago port register records merely the ship's departure on March 19 for Havana transporting an unknown number of slaves. In early April, the ship did in fact arrive in Havana, now with nine human beings up for sale. Whether among those nine were the five identified in Santiago as Saint-Domingue creoles is impossible to know.[49]

The willingness to profit from this irregular trade or to purchase slaves cheaply appeared greater than the will to follow or enforce the law. Furthermore, any attempt to enforce the ban on the sale of creole slaves would also have had to confront the fact that the trade was profoundly international and that enforcing the ban would require power not only over Spanish buyers and sellers, but also over a whole cast of Americans, French, British, and others potentially involved in the now outlawed trade.

The case of an American ship named *Juno* provides a glimpse into the temptation to sell men, women, and children from revolutionary Saint-Domingue as slaves in Cuba. The *Juno*, a Baltimore brig, had set sail for Norfolk, Virginia, in October 1793, loaded with 1,156 barrels of flour. In Norfolk, the ship's owner and supercargo, Robert Ellis, planned to purchase slaves and then take both the captives and the grain to sell in Havana. While American ships carrying flour and slaves appeared regularly in Havana harbor, this voyage turned out to be anything but routine. At Norfolk, Ellis was unexpectedly unable to purchase any slaves. Then, en route to Havana with only the flour, the vessel apparently encountered bad weather, and the captain decided to make a stop at Le Cap, "in great confusion by the reason of the success of the Insurgents," according to Ellis. In the midst of crisis and facing severe shortages, Le Cap's municipal council called a meeting of the considerable number of American merchants and ship captains then in the city, in order to urge them to sell their flour and other merchandise before leaving port. Ellis

---

[49] Vaillant to Las Casas, March 14, 1792, in ANC, CCG leg 43, exp. 1. Francisco de Varas, March 24, 1792, in ANC, CCG, leg. 43, exp. 1. On the April 1792 arrival with slaves in Havana, see "Estado de los negros introducidos en la Habana, Septiembre 1791," in AGI, SD, leg. 2207.

refused, but to no avail: either he sold the flour there, or his vessel would not be given clearance to sail.[50] Ellis assented without choice. He sold part of the flour to private residents of the city, among them a man named Newport Bowers, a free man of color from Massachusetts and Baltimore who during a six-month sojourn in Le Cap had managed to set up some kind of shop.

Another portion of the flour Ellis sold to the city itself. In a sign of how much had changed in Le Cap, the municipal council forced him to take as payment for 147 barrels of flour not money but rather forty-four boiler pans used in the manufacture of sugar. Sugar-making equipment seemed useless now in Le Cap; flour, meanwhile, had become a commodity of utmost value. Finally, with significantly less flour than at the outset, the *Juno* sailed for Havana, where selling the sugar pans would surely be an easy task.[51]

A few days later, the *Juno* was captured as prize by the British warship the *Alligator*. Newport Bowers was a passenger on board, headed like the crew for Havana and then Baltimore. Also on board, however, were anywhere from six to eleven – the record is unclear – "Negroes or other slaves." The documentary record is even less clear on who these individuals might have been. Newport Bowers, the only person of color on board the *Juno* who testified before Britain's vice-admiralty court, insisted that "they were people who had been given free by the Commisary and who had agreed to go with [him] to America." "They were," he said, "free negroes and not the property of any person on board." On at least one count, Bowers was unquestionably correct. The *Juno* had left Le Cap on December 4, 1793, months after the civil commissioners had abolished slavery in the territory they controlled. Those black men and women on board were not slaves in any legal sense at that point; they were, according to Saint-Domingue law, French citizens.

---

[50] For a vivid description of Le Cap at this moment, see Jeremy Popkin, *You Are All Free: The Haitian Revolution and the Abolition of Slavery* (New York: Cambridge University Press, 2010).

[51] This paragraph and those that follow are drawn from Case Juno, Master Parker, in TNA, High Court of Admiralty (HCA), 42/261/698 and Julius Scott, "Afro-American Sailors and the International Communication Network: The Case of Newport Bowers," in *Jack Tar in History: Essays in the History of Maritime Life and Labour*, ed. Colin Howell and Richard Twomey (Fredericton, N.B.: Acadiensis Press, 1991), 37–52. On the question of reenslavement, see Rebecca Scott, "Paper Thin: Freedom and Re-enslavement in the Diaspora of the Haitian Revolution," in *Law and History Review* 29 (Nov. 2011): 1061–1087.

But the testimony of every other witness differed significantly from Bowers's. The others – captain, supercargo, co-owner, first mate, and foremast man – all testified that the blacks on board had been sold to Ellis by Bowers himself as payment for the flour, for his own passage on the vessel to Baltimore, and as repayment on an earlier loan from Ellis. Ellis, they testified, meant to sell the men and women in Havana – like the boiler pans, they would sell easily, he surely surmised – and then settle accounts with Bowers. *Juno*'s captain elaborated in a way that made the business seem even more sinister. Bowers, he said, had agreed "to bring off from the shores of the Cape negroes from time to time and that [Ellis] was to pay him money for as many as he should bring." The white officers and crew of the vessel – and perhaps Bowers himself – regarded, treated, and bartered the black men and women as slaves, and they hoped to continue doing so for profit in Havana. They had intended to go there with black men and women acquired in Norfolk, but weather, politics, and war made them willing to improvise and go there with men and women from Saint-Domingue. They were just selling slaves; that they might have been reenslaving French citizens may have never entered their minds.[52]

The officials of the vice-admiralty court never recorded the names of the alleged slaves in question, nor, it seems, did they bother to ask them about their status, their relationship with Bowers, or about how they ended up aboard the *Juno* in the first place. A little over two months after the ship's interception, the court ruled that the prize was good and lawful, and that the time for any potential owners to claim the black men and women had elapsed. So they were ordered sold, the money from their sale to be distributed among the officers and the crew of the war vessel that had seized the *Juno*. Was Bowers, as he himself testified, helping free people travel to Baltimore? Or, as every other witness insisted, was he conspiring with the crew to sell free people as slaves in Havana? We will never know the answer. But that the crew seemed willing and ready to take black men and women from Saint-Domingue to Havana to sell them seems indisputable. French law made those people free, and Spanish law made them unsellable in Havana. Yet both those formalities were insufficient in the face of the habits and profits of the Caribbean slave trade. Had they not been captured by the British, they would have landed in Havana, and the men and women would have there been sold as slaves.

52 TNA, HCA, 42/261/698; J. Scott, "Afro-American Sailors."

When we turn later to the actions of the enslaved on Cuban soil and hear the words of so-called *negros franceses* announcing their liberty or inviting others to rebel, we can wonder if they might have arrived aboard ships like the *Juno*. While the case may have been unique, analyzed alongside Cuban port registers and the licenses issued to traders by local governors, the evidence suggests that the phenomenon of transporting slaves and former slaves from Saint-Domingue for the purpose of selling them in Cuba was not as uncommon as the law, in theory, would have made it. Captains and traders of all nationalities seemed willing to consider the practice. Privateers got in on the action as well. In 1793, armed corsairs operating out of the town of Baracoa, for instance, took twenty people from the coasts of Saint-Domingue and brought them to Cuba to attempt their sale. At least some of the captives were identified by Spanish authorities as brigands, a term usually applied to the nonwhite rebels of Saint-Domingue.[53]

In the end, the precise extent to which enslaved men and women were taken from scenes of unrest in Saint-Domingue and transported to Cuba is impossible to know. First, the practice was illegal, as the king's orders had prohibited the purchase of all slaves not directly brought from Africa. Second, the reality of the Haitian Revolution and the regular talk of danger and contagion would have made the traders involved eager to cover up the origins of the people they were trying to sell. In Saint-Domingue itself, the imperatives of making a revolutionary project and emancipating the enslaved, or, on the other hand, the imperative of subduing black revolution, likely left little energy for or interest in documenting the transfer – and after emancipation, the reenslavement – of people by means of sales to Cuba, or elsewhere. Finally, and significantly, is the character of the slave trade itself. Even in the case of legal voyages, even in the case of large, organized, well-established enterprises – as opposed to this more local, short, improvised trade – slavers and the men who recorded their business rarely paused to gather more information than was absolutely necessary. If they ever thought to record the names of the men and women who passed before them, they never acted on that urge.[54] Against the illegality and the arrogance of the trade, on

53 Vaillant to Las Casas, October 30, 1793, in AGS, SGU, leg. 6851.
54 See http://www.slavevoyages.org/tast/database/methodology-01.faces. "The data set contains thousands of names of ship owners and ship captains, but it contains no names of the millions of slaves carried to the Americas. On the other hand, this web site does provide the African names of and personal information about 67,004 captives who were found on board slave vessels detained by naval cruisers attempting to suppress

the one hand, and the master narratives of revolution on the other, the archive may prove an insufficient tool to trace the movements of the many unnamed men and women taken in this fashion from a slave system under revolutionary attack to another gaining more and more strength precisely as a result of that revolution.

Deeply aware of this confluence – of the special promise and peril of the time and place they occupied – authorities in Cuba responded much in the manner first advocated by Francisco Arango in Madrid: continuing to encourage slavery and the slave trade while exercising vigilant caution in potentially dangerous times. Yet their efforts at the latter were perpetually compromised by slave traders' willingness to purchase and resell slaves, no matter their ties to Saint-Domingue. Local residents, as well, appear to have demurred on such issues, not inquiring too closely about the origins of the slaves they purchased and opting perhaps to live a bit dangerously in the hopes of breaking into the promise of sugar (or coffee) ascendant. The state, for its part, responded in kind, also often choosing opportunity over caution. Thus, as they received and themselves reissued proscriptions on the inter-Caribbean slave trade, local governors seemed willing to overlook infractions in the interest of building on a particular model of economic expansion. The state, as it would for decades to come on almost every legal prohibition against the slave trade, often looked the other way and only erratically followed the new laws designed to impede the entry of so-called dangerous French slaves.[55]

By the mid-1790s, however, local officials were openly worried. Everywhere they confronted signs that the restrictions against importing *negros franceses* were easily eluded and that a significant number of French slaves was living in the territory under their rule. Indeed, the place seemed at times "a swarm [*enjambre*] of foreigners." If French slaves had been considered potentially dangerous since at least the summer of 1791, by mid-decade British slaves now also merited suspicion. With British abolitionism on the march and recent examples of black unrest in British

---

the slave trade in the nineteenth century." For important discussions of some of these difficulties, see Stephanie Smallwood, *Saltwater Slavery: A Middle Passage from Africa to American Diaspora* (Cambridge: Harvard University Press, 2007), 2, 82, 141, 201; and Jennifer Morgan, "Accounting for the Women in Slavery: Numeracy and Race in the Early Modern Atlantic," manuscript in progress.

55 There are some cases from Santiago in which the governor does detain traders bringing in slaves from Saint-Domingue. See, for example, Vaillant to Las Casas, March 14, 1792, in AGI, Cuba, leg. 1434. On the violation of slave trade bans, especially after 1820, see Franco, *Comercio clandestino de esclavos*.

colonies, authorities feared that British slaves, like French ones, could potentially corrupt and incite the Spanish slaves already there. It was this emerging conviction that led the governor to take new and more vigorous action against the illegal importation of slaves from neighboring Caribbean territories.[56] For this, Las Casas did not bother to consult before the fact with metropolitan authorities in Spain. But he did consult extensively with Havana's planters and other local notables.

In November 1795, Las Casas had extensive discussions with both the Real Consulado and the Havana city council. He conveyed his sense of impending danger, reminding both bodies of the proximity and example of the Saint-Domingue revolution and of growing unrest in Jamaica. The problem, said Las Casas, was not just the example, but the fact that there existed an "excess of communication" with these troubled islands. He argued that the principal source of this communication was a badly policed slave trade. After having worked so hard to encourage and expand that trade, Las Casas came face to face with the possibility that the slave trade itself increased the risk of subversion. He suspected that in order to make money and to rid themselves of problems, foreigners were using the trade to send to his island those slaves whom they could not control. The king had already prohibited the entry of French slaves. But this restriction and its imperfect implementation were now severely insufficient to the task at hand. Though he could not (and surely did not want to) alter the king's orders on the "free trade" in captive Africans, he saw the urgent necessity of adopting new measures locally to restrict more severely and punitively the entry of Caribbean slaves. Importantly, he also sought for the first time to evict the ones already there. Since the two groups he addressed – the city council and the Real Consulado – were among the principal advocates for and architects of the expansion of slavery and the slave trade, Las Casas gave them warning and asked for advice on how to proceed.[57]

These notable residents of the city – most of them slaveholders – agreed with the general thrust of the governor's arguments, but they were reluctant to condone the expulsion of slaves without a clearer sense of the gravity and numbers involved.[58] Nonetheless, the governor acted, and on

---

[56] See, for example, Las Casas to Príncipe de la Paz, August 24, 1795, in AGI, Cuba, leg. 1489.

[57] "Expediente relativo a las precauciones y seguridad," in ANC, RCJF, leg. 209, exp. 8993.

[58] For the Junta's reply to the governor, see "Acuerdo de Junta de Gobierno del Real Consulado, Sesión de 2 de diciembre 1795," in AGI, Cuba, leg. 1459. The discussions

February 25, 1796, he issued a new decree, ordering (yet again) that the slave trade to Cuba be strictly limited to Africans directly purchased in Africa, again prohibiting the introduction of any slaves who had lived in any foreign country (outside of Africa) in whatever capacity for whatever duration. Every trader entering Cuban ports with slaves to sell would now be required to sign a sworn statement that none of the captives on board were "illegal." None of this was exactly new by 1796, and the decree was in many ways just a more clearly worded version of royal directives already in place for some time. But this time the governor went further, implicitly conceding that prior laws had not prevented the illegal importation of Caribbean slaves. On his own initiative, and without prior approval of the king and his ministers, he explicitly addressed the issue of creole slaves furtively introduced and presently living and serving in Cuba. Of these, he said, French ones introduced after August 1790 and British ones introduced after 1794 had to be expelled from the island within three months.[59]

The governor's order of expulsion was significantly more forceful than any of the related decrees that had preceded it. First, by legally allowing slaves introduced before those two dates (August 1790 for France, 1794 for Britain) to remain in Cuba, Las Casas in a sense overwrote earlier orders issued by the king himself, who had outlawed the introduction of all creole slaves as of May 1790. With the new order, Las Casas made punishable only the holding of those French and British slaves introduced after the dates he himself had determined, effectively issuing a retroactive pardon for holders of those who had arrived after the king's prohibition but before the new dates he himself determined. The governor thus implicitly conceded that the exigencies of Havana's sugar revolution might take priority over the king's orders. Second, by requiring masters to remove foreign slaves, the governor placed the interests of the state above the private interests of slaveholders. No indemnification was promised, and owners of any of the slaves in question simply lost their property and investment. Las Casas justified the expansiveness of his decree with reference to the "novel character that distinguished the present epoch from all previous ones."[60]

in the city council are recorded in AHOHCH, AC, November 20 and November 21, 1795, Tomo 54, ff. 198–199, 201v–202v.
[59] Bando, February 25, 1796, in "Expediente relativo a las precauciones y seguridad" in ANC, RCJF, leg. 209, exp. 8993. Las Casas identified these dates (August 1790 and 1794) as the ones in which the unrest began in the French and British islands respectively.
[60] Ibid.

For all its boldness, however, the decree provided no guidelines as to how the expulsion was to occur, at whose expense, to what destination, or by what means. The decree required that holders of illegal slaves notify authorities and then make their own arrangements for the expulsion within three months, adding that there was no guarantee that the banished slaves would be accepted at any Spanish port. Everything – the recording of information and the expulsion itself – was to be done with great tact and cunning so as to avoid any unfortunate consequences. Perhaps it is not surprising, then, that enforcement of the new decree was spotty at best. In Santiago, on March 7, 1796, the new decree was "publicly announced" (*pregonado*) with "all due solemnity." Yet local officials there and in Havana – likely the two cities with the highest number of illegally introduced Caribbean slaves – do not appear to have discussed plans for enforcement. And whatever enforcement did occur appears to have left no documentary evidence, suggesting that the effort – if it happened at all – could not have been systematic or concerted. Indeed, through 1796 at least, Santiago's governor continued to grant licenses to local traders engaged in the purchase of slaves in Jamaica and elsewhere, and he permitted the entry of American and other traders in the inter-Caribbean trade who carried men and women to sell to local buyers.[61]

While the decree appears not to have been systematically observed, it did have indirect effects in some parts of the island. Puerto Príncipe, an important provincial city without a major port of its own, had depended on Santiago for access to the slave trade. Indeed, a significant percentage of Caribbean slaves arriving in Santiago were resold in Puerto Príncipe.[62] With a presence of creole slaves from neighboring islands, the town and its surrounding countryside felt the effects of the ban, but not exactly in the way authorities intended.

There, in June 1795, a few months before the ban, two enslaved men had led a rebellion against their masters. The first was named Romualdo, from the eastern village of El Cobre, where enslaved creoles belonging to the Spanish king were already petitioning for their freedom. The second was known as Josef el Francés. The French Joseph, originally from Les Cayes in Saint-Domingue, appears to have arrived in Cuba in late 1794, purchased by a local Catalan trader in Jamaica and then sold to his

---

[61] Franco, *Comercio clandestino de esclavos*, 72–73.

[62] Juan Torres Lasqueti, *Colección de datos históricos-geográficos y estadísticos de Puerto del Príncipe y su jurisdicción* (Havana: Imprenta El Retiro, 1888) 103. On the reexports from Santiago to Puerto Príncipe, see Belmonte, "El impacto de la liberalización."

current master, Serapio Recio, son of a prominent local official. Among the other enslaved men whom Josef and Romualdo recruited for their rebellion were African men, creoles, and at least one other *negro francés*, Juan el Francés, also from Les Cayes.[63]

It was the French Joseph who had managed to confiscate his master's weapons and then bind and restrain him, while announcing that "there were no more masters, that [they] were all free." One version of the story also had him declaring that all men were equal. Having arrived in Cuba sometime in late 1794 – that is, after the abolition of slavery in Saint-Domingue – Joseph carried his own ideas about enslavement, equality, and freedom. Undoubtedly, those ideas were shaped by the dramatic revolutionary events that had unfolded in the region of Les Cayes in 1792, when major conflicts between whites and free people of color forced plantation owners to take refuge in the city and to leave their plantations with their enslaved labor forces unsupervised. Many of these black workers had subsequently joined the rebel forces ensconced in the Platons, the hills surrounding Les Cayes, and from there threatened and burned many of the city's surrounding plantations.[64]

While there are discrepancies in the witnesses' testimony, a basic outline emerges of the 1795 Puerto Príncipe conspiracy in which these transplants from Les Cayes participated. The rebels believed that the captain-general had come to the area to declare their freedom, and they were seeking to appear before him to receive it. Some were willing to destroy the town and kill the whites to reach that end. As details of the event emerged and as authorities endeavored to capture all those involved, the city's residents were in a panic, fearing that they were living on the eve of something akin to the Saint-Domingue revolution.[65]

With all the talk of rebellion and emancipation decrees, white residents and authorities of Puerto Príncipe should theoretically have welcomed the arrival of Las Casas's February 1796 decree calling for the expulsion of all French slaves. Upon receiving it, local authorities posted copies on

[63] Las Casas to Eugenio Llaguno, with attachments, August 18, 1795, in AGI, Estado, leg. 5A, exp. 15.

[64] Fick, *The Making of Haiti*, 142–151; and Geggus, *Haitian Revolutionary Studies*, chap. 9.

[65] "Auto en la Villa de Santa María del Puerto del Príncipe," July 9, 1795, in AGI, Cuba, leg. 1463B; Alfonso de Viana, Teniente Gobernador de Puerto Príncipe to Las Casas, June 14, 1795, in ANC, RCJF, leg. 209, exp. 8993; Las Casas to Eugenio Llaguno, August 18, 1795, in AGI, Estado, leg. 5A, exp. 15.

buildings and roads across the city. But the town council also met and prepared a lengthy response. The lawyer for the town argued that the slaves to be expelled under the new decree numbered fewer than a hundred. Most of them, he said, had been brought to the area from Saint-Domingue before the start of the war between France and Spain in 1793 (still well into the Haitian Revolution and significantly later than allowed either by the king's earlier decrees or the governor's new one). Other creole slaves had been brought from Jamaica, though he conceded that many of these were originally from Saint-Domingue. They had been taken to Jamaica by their French masters and had been sold into the inter-Caribbean trade there. Perhaps this had been the route taken by Joseph el Francés, who had been sold in Cuba by way of Jamaica. Still, insisted the syndic, the vast majority of these French and British slaves had been brought with the explicit permission of local authorities, a plausible claim given the willingness of local governors to grant licenses for small-scale Caribbean slave traders, notwithstanding the king's prohibitions. Many of these slaves were now married to Spanish ones, or they were in the service of small landholders who could not afford to lose them. Finally, he argued that the owners, lacking both access to vessels and money to arrange it, had no way to expel the banished slaves – a complaint that local authorities would repeat for years to come.[66] Without guidelines or resources to enable the expulsion, it does not appear to have occurred.

As soon as the governor's decree about the expulsion of French slaves was published and posted publicly, all kinds of rumors and predictions nonetheless took flight. Across Puerto Príncipe, the enslaved took the new decree to mean that all French slaves in Cuba would now be free. So, thanks in part to the publication of the new restrictions, local planters and authorities now faced vocal French slaves announcing their freedom to each other and to their masters. One enslaved man, left unnamed in the historical record, confronted his master, identified by name as Fernando Rodríguez, to announce that he was free. Unable to persuade the man that no emancipation decree had been issued, Rodríguez sent him to meet with the local governor. The governor questioned the captive about his sources, demanding to know on what basis he considered himself free.

[66] Representación del Síndico Procurador General to Muy Ylustre Ayuntamiento, March 20, 1796, in Archivo Histórico Provincial de Camaguey (AHPC), Fondo Ayuntamiento, leg. 23 (fuera de caja), Actas Capitulares, libro 6. See also Melchor Baptista y Boza to Las Casas, April 4, 1796, in AGI, Cuba, leg. 1464; and Alfonso Viana to Las Casas, March 4, 1797, in ANC, RCJF, leg. 209, exp. 8993.

To this, the unnamed slave replied in a "grand tone of voice" that the blacks of Saint-Domingue were all free, because they had acquired their own liberty, a reference either to the Haitian Revolution generally, or specifically to the emancipation decrees passed in Le Cap and Paris in 1793 and 1794, respectively. The enslaved man then added what the governor referred to as "an assortment of expressions appropriate to an ignorant man awash in weak but seditious ideas and principles." The governor did not bother to record those expressions or ideas, instead ordering the slave's arrest and punishment. He then required that all the owners of French slaves appear with their charges at the central plaza of Puerto Príncipe. That the very category "masters of French slaves" existed and that its members could so easily be identified suggests how ineffective the restrictions against the importation of French slaves had been all along. Before this assembled audience, the governor had the accused don a sign that clearly denied what had already come to pass in Saint-Domingue: "This is the fruit of the imagined liberty of French slaves. In virtue is found true liberty." And then before all the French slaves gathered there, the bound man was whipped and left on display for hours afterwards. The act, the governor believed, guaranteed that the slaves now understood his truth. But just in case, he promised to remain vigilant, to forbid the congregation of slaves at nighttime, and to banish the punished slave from the island.[67]

That the episode happened at all, however, is proof of how necessarily incomplete were the state's measures to contain communication about the Haitian Revolution and to limit the introduction of French slaves. Enslaved men and women from Saint-Domingue entered the island through multiple means, from those who accompanied masters fleeing the revolution to those who entered through what Las Casas identified as a badly policed slave trade. Even once in Cuba, they continued to learn of the conquests of ascendant black armies and of the French and colonial emancipation decrees. The loss of direct access to the revolutionary emancipation taking place in the French colony did not make them less willing to talk about those events with each other.

Local authorities interpreted such talk as the work of mischief makers, or alternatively as the product of delusional thinking. But rumors such as the one spread and believed by the French slaves of Puerto Príncipe might be more appropriately read as evidence of slaves' political engagement.

---

[67] Alfonso Viana to Las Casas, April 9, 1796, in ANC, RCJF, leg. 209, exp. 8993.

For the state to order the expulsion of French slaves – without bother-
ing to address or clarify to what destination – invited several plausible
interpretations by those the order sought to deport. Some might imagine
that the banished slaves would be sent back to the French territory from
which they had come. There, the enslaved knew, legal freedom awaited.
Thus, if a new law banished all French slaves from Cuba, raising the
possibility of a return to French territory where slavery no longer existed,
it was not too big a leap for them to speculate that all French slaves in
Cuba might now or soon become free. Already during the first rebellion
in June 1795, Josef el Francés had insisted that he and his companions
were free. A few months later, he and others likely saw the governor's
decree about the expulsion of French slaves as the latest episode in the
inevitable extension of French revolutionary emancipation: the Cuban
state was deporting them, and in nearby French territory revolutionary
law had already ended slavery. Rumor in this case was not a symptom
of ignorance, confusion, or manipulation, but rather the trace of a sustained and vested engagement with Atlantic legal and political currents
of slavery, emancipation, rights, and revolution.[68]

Scarcely a month later, the same governor, in the same place, reported
another potential conspiracy among a group of three "French slaves"
identified as Luis Santiago, Dionisio Enríquez, and Josef María. Shortly
thereafter came rumors of a new plot involving five French slave leaders.
The local governor was not able in this case to elaborate at all, because of
a "lack of proof or sufficient merit and because the blacks [had] escaped
from the prison."[69] At every turn, the drive to repress and contain the
news and example of the Haitian Revolution seemed insufficient to the
task.

Two years later, in June 1798, a major rebellion erupted in Puerto
Príncipe. On the sugar mills built along the banks of the Tinimá River,
perhaps two dozen slaves put city and countryside on alert. They set fire
to at least one plantation, killed three whites, including two overseers,
and left a fourth for dead. Most of the rebels escaped into the woods,
but were captured a few days later after an unsuccessful attempt to repel
their persecutors, carried out, said one account, to the cry of "Whites,
whites, kill, kill." Here, as in the case of the 1795 conspiracy and the

---

[68] On reading rumor as political engagement, see Steven Hahn, *A Nation Under our Feet:
Black Political Struggles in the South from Slavery to the Great Migration* (Cambridge:
Harvard University Press, 2003), chap. 3; and Ferrer, "Speaking of Haiti."

[69] Viana to Las Casas, May 19, 1796, in ANC, RCJF, leg. 209, exp. 8993.

1796 disputes about the expulsion (or liberation) of foreign slaves, many of the principal leaders and recruits were precisely French blacks.[70]

Indeed, the list of leaders and recruits in the 1798 Puerto Príncipe rebellion makes clear yet again just how untenable had been the state's project of prohibiting the entry and sale of so-called French blacks. For years traders had been able to sidestep those prohibitions by insisting that the slaves they brought from Saint-Domingue and Jamaica were *bozales*, or new Africans, and therefore safe. No set guidelines governed the making of the crucial distinction between *bozal* and *ladino*. Indeed, most of the arriving captives were allowed entry, while only a handful were deemed French or *ladino* and therefore dangerous and inadmissible. Yet planters, slaveholders, and authorities surely understood the insufficiency of that distinction. They knew that what had made prerevolutionary Saint-Domingue so much their model was precisely the seemingly endless supply and arrival of fresh African captives. How surprised could they have been to discover that some of the bondspeople brought from Saint-Domingue were both African *and* "French"? Among those implicated in the violence of the 1798 uprising were Juan de Dios Mandinga and Luis Congo, both belonging to Agustin de Miranda. Another was a man named Manuel, said to hail from Azúa in Spanish Santo Domingo, his master Pedro Vélez. Yet another was Nicolás Carabalí, held by José Arrieta. Every single one of these alleged leaders was "known to be French."[71]

The state had tried to limit the entry of French slaves while continuing to rely on the inter-Caribbean slave trade. It had attempted to resolve the potential contradictions by allowing the trade to continue but drawing abstract and always insufficient distinctions between African or *bozal* and creole or *ladino* slaves in that busy trade. That the rebels could be publicly known as both African and French highlights how obviously imperfect had been the state's solution all along.

Receiving news of the rebellion, the Real Consulado in Havana lamented that over the course of the previous three years, examples of black rebellion had been significantly on the rise. In typical fashion, they attributed the rise not to any inherent features of slavery, and much less

[70] "Noticias acaecidas en la Villa de Puerto Príncipe el día 12 de Junio de 1798," in ANC, RCJF, leg. 209, exp. 8993. Matas to Conde de Santa Clara, August 3, 1798, in AGI, Cuba, leg. 1509; Francisco de Arredondo, "Relación de los acontecimientos políticos ocurridos en el Camagüey," Biblioteca Nacional José Martí (BNJM), Colección Manuscrita (CM) Arredondo, 1903, no. 8.

[71] Matas to Conde de Santa Clara, August 3, 1798, in AGI, Cuba, leg. 1509B.

to those particular to Cuban slavery, but rather to the presence of French and (to a lesser extent) British slaves who, contaminated by events and ideas on their home islands, infected the enslaved in Cuba. Authorities decried specifically the colonial state's inability to put into practice earlier measures for the prohibition and expulsion of foreign creole slaves. The wise decision to expel them remained, they said, largely unenforced.[72] Complaints to that effect would continue for years to come. Foreign slaves, once arrested, often languished in prisons of one kind or another, sometimes to escape or simply to be returned to their masters in the end. Thus, as authorities ruminated on the punishments due to the Puerto Príncipe rebels of 1798, the French ones arrested in the 1795 conspiracy were still in jail without having received public punishment.[73] More than a decade after the illegalization of the Caribbean slave trade, authorities still lamented the "multitude" of Saint-Domingue slaves all around them.[74]

The presence of these foreign slaves signaled the fragility of the economic project that Cuba's planters had undertaken. Planters and authorities would probably not dispute Arango's characterization of this period of Cuban history as that of the arrival of happiness or abundance. But local governors experienced that happiness as a heavy weight on their shoulders. The cornerstone of the planters' project was the expansion of chattel slavery in Cuba, but the context in which that expansion unfolded was one full of perceived danger and uncertainty. For that reason, slavery's implantation depended on containing the example of Haiti's slave revolution. But if authorities succeeded in capturing Haitian news, they continually failed at containing it. They heard accounts of varying degrees of specificity about black revolution. With or without the benefit of rumors to that effect, they envisioned imminent, or at least possible, invasions in Cuba of black rebels from Saint-Domingue. They heard that local blacks might be engaged in rituals to celebrate slave rebellion in Saint-Domingue. They listened with visible consternation to more and

[72] Junta de Gobierno del Real Consulado to Conde de Santa Clara, August 18, 1798, in ANC, RCJF, leg. 209, exp. 8993.

[73] See, for example, Junta de Gobierno, Real Consulado to Conde de Santa Clara, August 18, 1798, in AGS, SGU, leg. 6865, exp. 24; Joaquín de Matas y Alos to Someruelos, October 16, 1800, in AGI, Cuba, leg. 1635; Someruelos to Mariano Luis de Urquijo, January 27, 1800, in AHN, Estado, leg. 6366, exp.2; and Cabildo Ordinario, Ayuntamiento de la Habana, August 17, 1804, in AHOHCH, AC, tomo 60, ff. 128–128v.

[74] Cabildo Ordinario, Ayuntamiento de la Habana, August 17, 1804, in AHOHCH, AC, tomo 60, ff. 128–128v.

more reports of slave unrest on Cuban soil, where so-called French and other slaves confronted their masters and authorities, citing emancipation decrees issued in Saint-Domingue. Everywhere, what authorities learned and heard made its way across city and countryside, seeming to echo and reverberate in the landscape around them. Cryptic statements exchanged on street corners and rural roads, words overheard on the plaza or at the boiling house, all seemed to reflect a surplus of information and danger.

Authorities worked to minimize the threat that came with the confluence of events in Saint-Domingue and Cuba. They tracked population counts and kept close tabs on the proliferation of maroons; they outlawed the entry of French papers and, especially, of French blacks. But with slaves in high demand, and contraband and noncompliance standard practice, their convictions about the threat at hand and their measures to minimize it were inherently inadequate. In the face of Haiti's example, authorities took some precautions, but as a rule they joined with planters to pursue slavery's expansion, pushing for greater access to markets and to enslaved laborers. When asked point-blank if the risks posed by the Haitian Revolution should lead them to consider ending the slave trade, Arango and the planters answered no, quickly, clearly, and loudly.

What authorities only occasionally conceded was that the structures of slavery and enslavement, which they were doing their best to expand, were the very same ones that helped circulate the example and appeal of black and slave revolution. Ships that before would have taken captives to Saint-Domingue now came to Cuban coasts, and planters and authorities welcomed the hundreds of African captives they brought. But the ships that transported their laborers also brought detailed news of the destruction wrought by the enslaved of Saint-Domingue, and in some cases the enslaved men and women who had witnessed and participated in that destruction.

In the decades that followed those first uncertain years of revolution, Cuba deliberately replaced Saint-Domingue as the world's largest producer of sugar. In Saint-Domingue's collapse and Cuba's ascent, we see one of the key episodes in the passage from one chapter to the next in the history of Atlantic slavery. But in Cuba itself – on docks frequented by ships coming from Saint-Domingue, on plantations where French slaves spoke of Haitian freedom, in meeting halls filled with ambitious if somewhat anxious planters, on slave ships plying waters between Saint-Domingue, Jamaica, Cuba, and elsewhere – what we see is not an abstract and neat transition, but rather an extended, violent, and fraught passage between the first and second slavery. People in Cuba – some more than others – bore witness to the intensification of enslavement even as they observed the growing power of revolutionary antislavery, occupying as it were plural time and space in the history of global capitalism and slavery.

3

An Unlikely Alliance

Cuba, Santo Domingo, and the Black Auxiliaries

As slave rebellion became steady warfare in parts of the French colony, substantial flows of news and rumor, liberation and enslavement continued to travel from Saint-Domingue to Cuba. Artifacts of the unfolding conflicts arrived with ship captains and refugees. Men and families who had made their living from slaves and the products they cultivated traveled to Cuba, to wait out events and rebuild fortunes on the basis of the same practices of slavery and commercial agriculture. Men, women, and children who had witnessed and become free in what was undoubtedly the event of their lifetimes were sometimes forcibly extracted and transported to Cuba, where French declarations of freedom were excesses not to be talked about, and where they would be held again as legal chattel.

If much of this movement occurred directly from island to island, a second and crucial avenue of contact between these two societies – one a collapsing, the other a burgeoning slave society – went through Saint-Domingue's closest neighbor, the Spanish colony of Santo Domingo. The New World's first plantation society, it had developed very differently than French Saint-Domingue. An important source of slave-grown sugar in the sixteenth century, by the turn of the nineteenth century it was largely peopled by a mixed-race peasantry, and the economy was oriented inward rather than outward toward international markets. In the 1790s, Santo Domingo, more than any other place, was often the first point of contact between revolutionary Saint-Domingue and the Spanish empire.

Because their territory shared a land frontier with French Saint-Domingue, authorities in Spanish Santo Domingo found themselves enmeshed in the revolutionary unraveling of the French colony from the start. In 1790, Vincent Ogé and Jean-Baptiste Chavannes, leaders of a rebellion of free people of color in northern Saint-Domingue, fled to Spanish territory when their movement failed; Spanish authorities after having promised them safety returned them to the French side of the island, where they met a brutal public execution in February 1791.[1] After the slave insurrection began in August 1791, authorities and residents of Spanish Santo Domingo became, by default, eyewitnesses and interlocutors. By turn allies and enemies, they were soon deeply implicated in what we know today as the Haitian Revolution.

That involvement intensified significantly in 1793, following the French revolutionaries' execution of King Louis XVI, when Spain declared war on its former ally. At that point the frontier between French Saint-Domingue and Spanish Santo Domingo became more than the outer fringe of a slave revolution; it became a contested border, a battlefield between the French Republic and the Spanish monarchy. Faced with this new challenge, and perhaps with new opportunity, the Spanish government opted to pursue "a daring experiment" – to recruit the slave rebels to the king's cause in order to defeat and drive away the French.[2] If the alliance was formally one between the Spanish monarchy and French insurgent slaves, on the Spanish side it was made real on the ground by soldiers and officers of the Spanish army, some from Spain, but many more from Spain's American colonies. They came from Santo Domingo, to be sure, but also from New Spain (Mexico), Puerto Rico, Caracas, and many from the nearby colony of Cuba. By some counts, the expeditionary forces numbered about 6,000, of whom nearly half died. In the first nine months of 1794 alone, the Cuban forces lost 30 officers and 800 soldiers.[3]

The Cuban men came from a world where slavery was expanding as never before. Once in Saint-Domingue, they found themselves in a land where the most profitable of New World slave systems was in the process of being dramatically destroyed. And, implausibly, they were allied with those doing the destroying. The alliance between these Cuban soldiers

[1] On the Ogé and Chavannes rebellion and the Spanish handling of their flight and extradition, see AGI, SD, 1029.

[2] Dubois, *Avengers of the New World*, chap. 7; Geggus, *Haitian Revolutionary Studies*, chaps. 8 and 12; and Jorge Victoria Ojeda, *Tendencias monárquicas en la revolución haitiana: El negro Juan Francisco Petecou bajo las banderas francesa y española* (México, D.F.: Siglo XXI, 2005).

[3] See Antonio José Valdés, *Historia de la Isla de Cuba y en especial de la Habana* (Havana: Comisión Nacional Cubana de la UNESCO, 1964 [1813]), 195–99; AGS, SGU, leg. 6876, exp. 54; Casa Calvo to Las Casas, September 30, 1794, in AGI, Cuba, leg. 1474.

and rebel slaves was not just an encounter between two worlds, but also between the very making and unmaking of slavery. The experience and memory of that encounter, in turn, profoundly shaped the way slavery and revolution would be understood in Cuba, just as it shaped the unfolding of the Haitian Revolution itself.

An Alliance Emerges

In late summer 1791, the pleas for help from French colonial authorities arrived in the hands of Santo Domingo's Spanish governor, Joaquín García, almost daily. So frequent and urgent were the appeals that it was impossible for the Spanish governor to await orders from Madrid, about two months distant by sea. Faced with a magnitude of unrest so novel and threatening, the Spanish governor tried to bide his time, analyzing the complicated scenario before him and hoping that somehow a clear path would emerge. But none did. So to the French he was noncommittal: he lamented the troubled state of their colony, but provided little by way of aid. He justified his reserve with reference to standing treaties, which required him to provide aid only if the colony was invaded by a third power and not, he argued, in this case, in which all contending parties were French subjects.

Still, the French entreaties continued. To his own superiors García expressed apprehension that the conflict would overflow into Spanish territory and utter confusion about what course to follow should that happen. In September 1791, he wrote to Madrid: "Everything is such chaos, disorder, and mystery, that I do not know if my precautions and suspicions should be with the whites, the colored, or with all of them."[4] Two months later his complaint was the same, inflected perhaps by the added frustration – and eloquence – of having already been voiced many times but not yet resolved:

I need the declaration of His Majesty to know among these people who are the bad ones and who are the worse ones and how I should handle them in events of such immediacy. These are matters that require a higher discernment than mine. I will execute whatever is ordered; I do not want to err, surrounded by opportunities to do so and deprived of the wise enlightenment of His Majesty in these current circumstances, which of necessity change the rules prescribed in other very different times.[5]

[4] Joaquín García to Conde de Campo de Alange, Sepember, 1791, in AGS, SGU, leg. 7149. The racial terms García used were *los blancos* and *los de color*.
[5] García to Conde de Campo de Alange, November 25, 1791, in AGS, SGU, leg. 7150.

If García sometimes expressed frustration with the French in general and with what seemed to him their propensity to change course and allies, he was most unnerved by his conflicting impressions of the black insurgents. The Spanish governor (and the officers who reported to him) wrote of the black rebels as barbarians, criminals, and thieves. These impressions became more powerful as the rebellion inched its way closer to their border, and as white French subjects fled east into Spanish territory just ahead of insurgents they called brigands. For example, describing the rebel attack on the French border town of Ounaminthe (Juana Méndez) in January 1792, Spanish officials lingered over the arrival on the Spanish side of a woman covered in the blood of her son, who had been killed in her arms as the two fled on horseback toward the river boundary with Spain. The Spanish description of the aftermath of the attack a day later carefully listed the resting places of the French victims whose bodies had yet to be moved: five in the nave of the church, three in the dais of the main altar, one below the tabernacle, five in the priest's patio, two in his private quarters, four in the cemetery, and so on, for a total of fifty-eight dead.[6] Spanish descriptions such as these stressed the intensity and brutality of the conflict in the neighboring colony and their own presence as reluctant eyewitnesses.

But in spite of, or perhaps because of, Spanish proximity to rebel territory, things were not always so clear to Joaquín García. If he feared the power and actions of the slave rebels, he also seemed at times to regard them as loyal and worthy subjects of a king, potential objects of humanitarian assistance, and eventually perhaps legitimate allies. He wrote in November 1791 that the black armies professed their love of the French king and detested the new revolutionary system, as of course did he.[7] He predicted that the efforts of the civil commissioners to negotiate and return to the *status quo ante* would fail. Speaking specifically of Jean-François – a former slave and longtime maroon before the outbreak of revolution and now perhaps the most important black rebel leader in the north – García wrote that the leader's disposition was to die rather than return to slavery. "There is no doubt about this concept, in my opinion. Slavery is horrifying in the Colony."[8] If he shared with the black rebels a principle of loyalty to one's king, and a measure of disdain

---

[6] See Andrés de Heredia to García, Dajabón, January 15 and January 16, 1792, both in AGS, SGU, leg. 7157, exp. 18; and García to Conde de Campo de Alange, January 25, 1792 in AGS, SGU, leg. 7150.

[7] García to Conde Campo de Alange, November 25, 1791, AGS, SGU, leg. 7150.

[8] García to Marqués de Bajamar, January 25, 1792, in AGS, SGU, leg. 7157, exp. 18.

for the inhumanity of some French forms of slavery, he also seemed somewhat reassured by the respect with which the rebels appeared to be treating Spanish territory. He informed his superiors in Madrid that the slave forces had not, at least for the moment, acted with hostility or aggression toward the Spanish, and in fact they seemed to want to inspire confidence and friendship. He questioned how long this might last or what its motivation might be, but he was nonetheless at a complete loss as to how to treat them.[9] The scenes before him had no precedent, and he confessed openly to being confounded.

After six months of regular appeals for orders and answers from his superiors, García received in February 1792 the Royal Order of November 25, 1791, in which the king, after discussion with his ministers, had laid out a plan of action for his governors on the ground. The king commanded that they observe always perfect neutrality, not favoring or helping to sustain one party over another in what were perceived to be internal conflicts between whites and their government. But, the ruler added, if as a result of all the turmoil there formed "groups of malefactors or pirates or of blacks against whites to destroy them or to commit atrocities or robberies, [Spanish authorities should] offer aid to the persecuted according to the rules of humanity, giving them provisions, arms, and munitions to the extent possible."[10]

If the order seemed prudent and wise during the discussion of the Council of State in Madrid, received half a year after the fact and in the heat and proximity of Spain's frontier with the Haitian Revolution, the instructions seemed imprecise and out of touch. By the time García received them, the insurrection had spread to nearly the entire French colony, and regular reports circulated of the imminent arrival of a substantial French force to put down the rebellion. Once that expedition arrived, García predicted with certainty, thousands of rebels would cross into Spanish territory. It was this scenario that occupied all his thought. And as he pondered the Royal Order, he did not see a clear directive to guide his action. "The black brigands," he wrote, "have respected the lands of the king and give proof that they regard him as a sacred being whom they venerate." If, under attack by a superior French force, the rebels sought refuge in Spanish territory, did not the basic precepts of humanity – and, wondered García, the very Royal Order of November

[9] García to Conde de Campo de Alange, November 25, 1791, AGS, SGU, leg. 7150.
[10] García to Conde de Lerena, February 22, 1792, in AGI, SD, leg. 1029. A copy of the Royal Order was sent to García, as well as to governors in Cuba, Puerto Rico, Trinidad, Cartagena, Mexico, and Santa Fe. See ANC, CCG, leg. 42, exp. 7.

25, 1791 – require that the Spanish offer them asylum? Or was he to repel them at the border with the force of arms?[11]

He never received a clear answer from Spain, and so he improvised as circumstances required. In this improvisation he was guided by his own assessment of the scenes before him. The black rebels declared loyalty to the French king, just as they professed respect for the Spanish one. They had not attacked Spanish territory. And, perhaps most importantly, they vastly outnumbered the forces that he himself could marshal to repel or contain them. Thus, in the absence of direct Spanish action, a *modus vivendi* gradually emerged. On the border, a risky trade developed between the black insurgent armies and the residents – civilian and military – from the Spanish side of the border. Through their secretaries, black leaders wrote deferential letters to García, and they developed a close relationship with the parish priest of the border town of Dajabón, José Vázquez, described as a "Spanish mulatto," through whom they directed themselves to the Spanish governor and others. Slave leaders and Spanish officials seemed to court each other gingerly, in order to have a ready ally should circumstances come to require one.

When France's long-announced expedition of 6,000 troops arrived in the colony in September 1792, the time seemed to have come for the most important slave leaders to pursue that alliance somewhat more boldly. Jean-François – Juan Francisco on the Spanish side of the border – took the initiative and asked the Spanish priest Vázquez to convey a proposal from the rebels to the local Spanish commander, Andrés de Heredia, and through him to the Spanish governor, then the king of Spain, and eventually to the king of France himself.[12] In the proposal Jean-François, Toussaint Louverture (as his second), and all those able to sign their names addressed themselves at once to the Spanish governor and the French king. They offered an interpretation of the origins of their rebellion, the present possibilities for negotiation, and one possible scenario for a postwar society. The signatories made a point of representing their movement not as a rebellion but as an armed and loyal defense of their king, from whom, moreover, they professed to have papers.[13] The bulk of the proposal,

---

[11] García to Conde de Campo de Alange, March 23, 1792, in AGS, SGU, leg. 7150.

[12] The proposal, undated, is attached to Heredia to García, September 12, 1792, which is attached to García to Marqués de Bajamar, September 25, 1792, in AGS, SGU, leg. 7157, exp. 18. Earlier proposals from the rebels have been analyzed most recently by Malick Ghachem, *The Old Regime and the Haitian Revolution* (Cambridge: Cambridge University Press, 2012), chap. 6.

[13] The significance of "having papers" in conspiracies and rebellions of enslaved and free people of color across the Americas merits further analysis. From Saint-Domingue to

however, dealt with immediate circumstances. First, the rebels proposed a negotiation with authorities, on the condition that they come in good will and also in secret, "because the slaves would not understand." Second, the leaders agreed to return the slaves to their plantations, but as free people with a weekly or daily wage until "gradually by rigor and force they were made again to know the yoke of slavery." Third, they insisted, slaves returning to the plantations would not be disarmed until they were settled back into the routine of the plantation. Ostensibly, these demands were directed to the French government, but the drafters of the proposal seemed to have been well aware that their first (and maybe only) readers would be the Spanish, who surely would have been interested to know of the rebels' apparent concession to gradual reenslavement and pacification. In fact, some of the later points in the proposal seem to be specifically addressed to the Spanish. They spoke of their weariness with war and the appeal of peace, but they worried that García might turn them in as he had done with "the mulatto Ogé." Finally, the rebels requested the "opinion and sponsorship" of the Spanish. Thus, as they voiced their loyalty to their own king, they simultaneously represented themselves as people with and through whom the Spanish government might work.

Facing a potentially formidable French expedition, however, the insurgents were also eager to display their force and power. Thus while they proposed to talk about pacification, they also kept fighting vigorously. Just days after presenting their offer of capitulation, the rebels overpowered a French post near Ounaminthe, killing the commander and most of the French force, burning the surrounding area, and making off with all the French rifles, four cannons, and four barrels of gunpowder. Juan Francisco reported the victory to the Spanish commander, Andrés de Heredia:

The honor of the present [letter] is to greet you very humbly and inform you that last night we took a camp of Whites in which we killed many and burned their fields. As good proof I send you the *gola* of the commander of the camp, whose head I have here. I ask you to return it to me once you have seen it. I close wishing good health to you as well as to the Reverend Father [Vázquez], to whom I ask you to convey my most humble debts.[14]

Cuba to the United States, conspirators and rebels often spoke (both to authorities and to each other) about "papers" as a source of legitimacy for the acts of war they were considering. See Chapter 7.

[14] Juan Francisco to Andrés de Heredia, September 30. 1792, in AGS, SGU, leg. 7157, and García to Pedro Acuña, October 1, 1792, in AGS, SGU, leg. 7157.

The word *gola* has several possible meanings. It might have referred to a kind of military collar, often shaped like a half-moon, which was used to protect the neck in battle. *Gola*, however, also meant gullet or esophagus, so Juan Francisco may have here referred to some part of the beheaded victim's remains. How might Heredia have read Jean-François's wish for his good health as he held the physical trace – organic or not – of the violent death of a white military commander much like himself? Easy Spanish advice about neutrality must have seemed glaringly inadequate in this context in which one side – the one whose very existence seemed to challenge existing norms for the conduct of diplomacy, war, and colonial rule – kept making overtures and declarations of fealty in the least abstract of ways.

With time, the dilemma posed to local Spanish officers only grew, as the overtures of the rebels became more explicit and insistent. Finally, in early 1793, the three major leaders of the slave revolution – Jean-François, Biassou, and Hyacinthe – all addressed themselves to the Spanish, asking for a formal alliance against French Republican forces. Jean-François, at the time, commanded a force estimated at 6,650 men, of whom more than 6,500 were said to be fugitives from slavery.[15] On February 13, he addressed himself to the Spanish governor and asserted that he and his men had been forced to wage war on the French, who refused to acknowledge either God or king; for two years they had fought, persevering thanks to God. Even after troops had arrived from France, he and his men had persisted and succeeded in fighting for the king. Now he proposed to the Spanish an "interesting business," one, he suspected, that the governor was "too good" to refuse. He did not ask for men, but he did ask for arms, clothes, and food. In exchange, promised Jean-François, the black forces would "all be under [the Spanish king's] dominion, and He would govern the country . . . and extract its quintessence [*quinta esencia*] and he will make us work as we should, being then his subjects." With Spanish support, he announced, they could control the entire country in two months' time.[16]

---

[15] García to Acuña, June 11, 1793, in AGS, SGU, leg. 7157.

[16] Juan Francisco to García, February 13, 1793, in AGS, SGU, leg. 7157. *Quinta esencia* refers to the extraction of the finest elements of a product, traditionally by way of fire or heat. Here then Jean-François presented the island as a product and the king's rule as the process of extraction itself. The term may have referred to the notion of "the fifth," by which the owner of lands extracted a fifth of the product from tenants, or the king extracted his "royal fifth" (generally *quinto real*) from that produced in his colonies.

BIASOU

Primer Gefe delos Negros de Santo Domingo.

FIGURE 3.1. Georges Biassou, General in the Black Auxiliary Forces allied to Spain. Courtesy of the John Carter Brown Library at Brown University.

The other principal slave leaders took the same path. Hyacinthe wrote to the governor professing his willingness to die for the king, his unwavering refusal to submit to the French Republicans (whom he called brigands, as the white French called him), and his respectful request for Spanish support and asylum. Shortly after, Biassou, having just learned of the execution of the king in France, wrote to the Spanish commander Joaquín Cabrera and offered his own judgment on monarchical succession and European rule in the colonies: in the absence of the French king, the colony now reverted to the Spanish one. We are, he said, resolved to put ourselves under the Spanish flag (Figure 3.1).[17]

---

[17] Jacinto to García, undated, attached to García to Acuña, March 12, 1793, and Biassou to Joaquín Cabrera, March 19, 1793, both in AGS, SGU, leg. 7157.

The Spanish, it seems, had allies who would not be deterred, and García was more than interested in listening. From the start, the Spanish governor had stressed the rebels' desire for friendship and accommodation with the Spanish. Now he received their offers cautiously, not daring to assent formally without orders from his own king, but subtly giving signals of likely interest. He informed the rebel leaders that the king looked favorably on all who defended his party. And, in fact, the king did. Even before Jean-François's offer of alliance reached Europe, Spanish authorities were already weighing the potential benefits of a formal union with the slave army. On February 19, 1793, the Council of State convened an emergency meeting. There the king decided that with war against France very soon to be declared, the governor of Santo Domingo should find the most efficient and discreet manner "to win and attract to our side the Brigands, blacks, mulattos, as well as [white] Royalists dissatisfied with the new government introduced by the French." The order charged García with seeking a specific alliance with Jean-François, Hyacinthe (both identified by name), and other black leaders, who were to make war on the French army and on French partisans of the new system, until such time as they were thoroughly defeated and the island's two colonies were reunited under the Spanish crown. To this end, García was to offer the blacks whatever aid was necessary, the privileges of all Spanish vassals, and, of course, their personal freedom from slavery.[18]

The order arrived in Santo Domingo in mid-April 1793, and García immediately hastened to seal the pact. He gave the task of concluding the alliance with Jean-François to the priest Vázquez and commander Gaspar Casasola, lieutenant colonel in the Cantabria Regiment. The assignment of negotiating with Biassou fell to Joaquín Cabrera, an officer in the Santo Domingo Regiment with considerable experience on the frontier. And the job of dealing with Hyacinthe fell to two officers: Ignacio Caro, a Dominican lieutenant who would later resettle in Cuba and collaborate with sugar planter Francisco Arango, and Justo de la Rocha, a second lieutenant who addressed Hyacinthe in Kreyòl. The new alliance offered for the rebels arms and supplies, and for the leaders immediate asylum for members of their families and juridical freedom from slavery. The Spanish emissaries sought out the black generals and arrived with flattering words and humble gestures. The objects of their flattery responded in kind, offering cries of "Long live the Kings of Spain and France" and promising

[18] Actas del Supremo Consejo de Estado, Consejo Extraordinario, Feb 19, 1793, in AHN, Estado, libro 6, ff. 17–20.

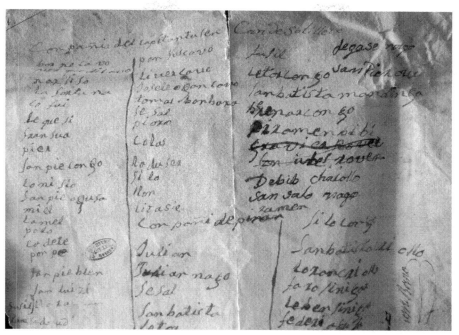

FIGURE 3.2. Fragment from a document that lists the forces of Toussaint Louverture, 1793. Archives Nationales de France, D-XXV 39, 392. Courtesy of the Archives Nationales, Paris.

to spill their last drop of blood before submitting to the French Republic. When it was all over at about four in the morning on May 1, Jean-François asked the Spanish priest for arms; Biassou requested two cows, some soap, and other supplies; Hyacinthe wished to have a horse.[19]

The black generals and their forces had become official "auxiliaries" of the Spanish army. As a result, Spain suddenly found itself with perhaps ten thousand men ready to do battle against republican France, an overwhelming majority of whom had been enslaved until the uprisings of 1791.[20] Thus, the slave revolution of August 1791 was now, in mid-1793, almost entirely at the service of Spain (Figure 3.2).

Governor García and his commanders on the border ordered the black generals to continue their attacks, and with those former slaves as a formidable foundation, the Spanish began achieving things that

---

[19] García to Acuña, May 11, and June 11, 1793, both in AGS, SGU, leg. 7157.
[20] A fixed number for the auxiliary troops is impossible to ascertain. See Geggus, *Haitian Revolutionary Studies*, 179–80.

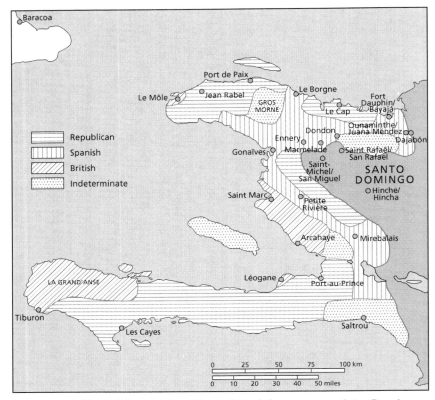

FIGURE 3.3. Map of French, Spanish, and English territory in Saint-Domingue, 1794. Adapted from David Geggus, *Haitian Revolutionary Studies* (Indiana University Press, 2002).

would have been impossible just two months earlier. Immediately, territory on the French side of the border started falling to Spain: Dondon, Ounaminthe, Marmelade, Gonaïves, Limbé, Port Margot, Borgne, Verettes, Petit Rivière, Ennery, Plaisance, and eventually Fort-Dauphin, just about thirty miles east of Le Cap (Figure 3.3).

 If the alliance with armed slaves made it possible for the Spanish to imagine achieving victory over France and regaining territory lost a century before, the alliance also posed challenges that should have been easier for Spanish authorities to foresee. First, the very condition that encouraged the alliance between the Spanish monarchy and rebellious slaves – namely, the declaration of the French Republic and the execution of the king – also made other royalists seek their own alliances with the

Spanish. In exchange for declarations of fealty, García was at the same moment promising white French royalists Spanish protection and respect for their persons, land, establishments, and by extension slavery, still legal on both the Spanish and French side of the border. It is unclear how exactly the Spanish governor expected to maintain the loyalty and support of armed former slaves and beleaguered slaveholders, the latter invested in the restitution of an order that the former challenged by their very existence. García himself recognized the challenge early and explicitly: "I understand the arduous task of reconciling the spirits of the white French with the Blacks our allies whom yesterday they regarded with a superiority and contempt that are notorious. It would be convenient that to the extent possible the actions of both be coordinated and absolutely dependent on us . . . to avoid the flourishing of hatreds."[21] On a half sheet of paper, one Spanish commander wrote with shaky hand: "It is the order of the King of Spain . . . that no black should kill the white French who wish to come under the Dominion of our sovereign."[22] As we will see, intent and practice were often two different things.

Second, even as García forged a formal alliance with black leaders such as Jean-François and Biassou, he confessed his deep skepticism about the dependability of black loyalty. From the start, he suspected that the overtures of Jean-François and others were perhaps less motivated by devotion to the king than by a pressing need for arms, supplies, and asylum if necessary. Thus, at the same time that he ordered his subaltern officers to seal the alliance, he ordered them also to exercise "vigilant zeal" and "constant attention" so that they not be surprised by men "who easily admit into their hearts all parties, or better yet, the most recent and convenient one." Such doubts markedly increased as French colonial authorities began sending their own promises and proclamations to win over Spain's new allies. Sure, on the one hand, of what he identified as an inherent and natural inconstancy of black men and aware, on the other, of French maneuvers to recruit the black leaders, García – only a month into the alliance – admitted that he would not be the least surprised to see the auxiliaries follow one flag today and another tomorrow.[23] This suspicion of imminent disloyalty shaped the experience of the pact for

---

[21] García to [not specified], Santo Domingo, July 13, 1793, in Antonio del Monte y Tejada (Santo Domingo: Imprenta de García y Hermanos, 1890–1892), 4: 62–63.

[22] Elías de Castro, Gimani, August 30, 1793, in Archives Nationales, Paris (CARAN), D-XXV 39, 392.

[23] García to Conde de Campo de Alange, June 25, 1793, in AGS, SGU, leg. 7158. For early discussion of French attempts to win over the new Spanish auxiliaries, see also García

men on both sides. Rumors circulated constantly about the changing of sides of one or another black officer. In the midst of such rumors in July 1793, Jean-François felt compelled to kneel before the Spanish priest Vázquez and swear before God and in the sacred name of the king of Spain his loyalty to their common cause and his willingness to die for Spain.[24]

But displays such as this one seemed to offer only momentary respite from doubt. Convinced as they were that the black men who fought for them were of a race by nature inconstant, the Spanish saw any profession of loyalty, no matter how seemingly genuine, as either suspect or fragile. Moreover, it was only the leaders, such as Jean-François, who made such dramatic and ritualized declarations. The actual power of Jean-François, however, came mostly from his command of six thousand men, whose allegiance could only be assumed. Thus, when Jean-François made almost constant requests for food and clothes to Spanish officers and Father Vázquez, García ordered his men to supply them promptly, so as "not to cause an upset capable of disturbing their loyalty, and [to ensure] that they remain as now adherents to our cause."[25] Similarly, in July 1793, when Biassou refused to accept the authority of the Spanish commander Cabrera and kept requesting more and more money, "the need to live in good order with this leader" led Cabrera to temporize with Biassou and to give him everything he requested.[26] And when the increasingly powerful Toussaint Louverture took the French town of Dondon in July 1793, Cabrera reported that he had turned a blind eye to the forces' confiscation of the goods they found, not only as a concession to their victory, but "also because it was impossible to contain them."[27]

Doubting constantly the loyalty of the forces they nominally commanded, the Spanish lived out the alliance in the most ambivalent and insecure of ways. They demanded proof of loyalty from black officers. But cognizant always of their own weakness – that the force of Spain in Saint-Domingue came principally, even only, from the military feats of the black auxiliaries – they also felt bound to offer proof of their own goodwill and usefulness to the black generals. They gave those generals

    to Conde de Campo de Alange, July 3, 1793, in AGS, SGU, leg. 7158; and García to
    Acuña, July 14, 1793, in AGS, SGU, leg. 7157.
[24] See García to Acuña and García to Conde del Campo de Alange, both dated July 3, in
    AGS, SGU, legs. 7157 and 7158 respectively.
[25] García to Acuña, July 7, 1793, in AGS, SGU, leg. 7157.
[26] García to Acuña, July 14, 1793, in AGS, SGU, leg. 7157.
[27] García to Acuña, July 22, 1793, in AGS, SGU, leg. 7157.

supplies not only so that they could be used in waging war against the French, but also, they increasingly admitted, to keep the former slave insurgents from contemplating waging war upon them.

Newcomers

It was onto this potentially explosive stage that in July 1793, new protagonists arrived. With war between Spain and France declared and the island of Hispaniola its primary colonial theater, the Spanish state redirected regular troops to the frontier between Saint-Domingue and Santo Domingo. Much of the extra force deployed there came directly from the island of Cuba, largely from the Havana and Santiago de Cuba regiments, both of which were by the 1790s significantly creole in composition and leadership. Between the summer of 1793 and the spring of 1794, thousands of men made the quick crossing and arrived at the Haitian Revolution. As a result, the black auxiliaries who were the backbone of Spain's military effort in Saint-Domingue – insurgents to some, loyal subjects of the king in their own words – came into regular and sometimes close contact with men from Cuba. Thus, at the moment when large-scale plantation slavery took root in Cuba, men from that society, some of them intimately involved in that island's sugar revolution, came face to face with the protagonists of a very different revolution.[28]

At the head of two of the Havana battalions deployed to Santo Domingo was a man named Matías de Armona, who upon arriving assumed the title of Commander General of the Frontier. Basque by birth, Armona had served as *regidor* of the Havana city council in 1786, and by the early 1790s, after a long military career that included stints in Baja California, Mexico, and Providence (Nassau, Bahamas), he was completely integrated into the Havana oligarchy. He owned a sugar mill outside Havana named *San Agustín de Campo Santo*, and his wife, María Dolores de Lisundia, daughter of a marquis, was related to the two principal sugar families of Havana: the Arangos and the Calvos.[29]

---

[28] On the arrival of the forces, see Matías de Armona to García, August 4, 1793, in AGS, SGU, leg. 6855. On the increasingly creole composition of the Spanish military in Cuba in this period, see Allan Kuethe, *Cuba, 1753–1815: Crown, Military and Society* (Knoxville: University of Tennessee Press, 1986); and Sherry Johnson, *The Social Transformation of Eighteenth-Century Cuba* (Gainesville: University Press of Florida, 2001).

[29] See the service record for Matías de Armona y Murga, Archivo General Militar-Segovia (AGMS), Expedientes Personales (EP), leg. A2380, and AGS, SGU, leg. 6869, exp. 20. For his property in Havana, see ANC, Escribanía de Guerra, leg. 889, num. 19327, and leg. 891, num. 13357.

A member of the latter family shared with Armona the experience of war in Santo Domingo. Born in Havana, the second Marqués de Casa Calvo, Sebastián Calvo de la Puerta, was a prominent member of Havana society. His father had served in high positions in the colonial state, and his mother was the daughter of the factor of an English slave-trading firm active in Havana. His brother, Nicolás, a close collaborator of Francisco Arango's, owned the *Nueva Holanda*, then one of the largest sugar plantations in Cuba. For his part, Sebastián Calvo owned at least two sugar plantations outside Havana, *Nuestra Señora de Regla* and *Santísimo Cristo de Tigueroa*, one of which was identified by the Cuban captain-general as a "lavish estate."[30]

Another of the prominent Cubans sent to fight on the border between Saint-Domingue and Santo Domingo was Francisco Montalvo, commander of the third battalion of the Havana Infantry Regiment. He was the son of the first Conde de Macuriges and brother of the first Conde de Casa Montalvo. His father and brothers had pioneered the use of French technology in Cuban sugar production; in fact, one of his brothers accompanied Francisco Arango on his 1794–5 trip to study sugar production, slavery, and the slave trade in neighboring empires and colonies. Commander Francisco Montalvo owned a sugar mill on the outskirts of Havana. He was thus not just a prominent military officer but also the owner of sugar property and slaves.[31]

We cannot know with what ideas these powerful men from Cuba arrived in Santo Domingo. Presumably, they went as military men to a war against an enemy nation. They arrived at the border between the

---

[30] The information on Casa Calvo is taken from: Casa Calvo to Las Casas, September 15, 1792, in AGS, SGU, leg. 6849, exp. 17; Las Casas to Conde del Campo de Alange, February 17, 1794, in AGS, SGU, leg. 6851, exp. 54; and Montaño to Antonio Barba, March 8, 1795, in Servicio Histórico Militar-Madrid (SHMM), Colección General de Documentos (CGD), Reel 65, doc. no. 5-4-11-1. For his military service record, see AGMS, EP, leg. C-431. See also Francisco Xavier de Santa Cruz Mallén, *Historia de familias cubanas* (Havana: Editorial Hércules, 1943) 4:119–21; and Mercedes García, *Entre haciendas y plantaciones: orígenes de la manufactura azucarera en la Habana* (Havana: Editorial de Ciencias Sociales, 2007), Appendix 4. On Nicolás Calvo, see Moreno Fraginals, *El ingenio*, 1: 60, 77, and Francisco Calcagno, *Diccionario biográfico cubano* (New York: Ponce de León), 1878.

[31] "Regimiento de Infantería Habana Num. 66. Historial del Regimiento," in SHMM, Historiales de Regimiento, rollo 47 (leg. 8, carp. 5); María Dolores González-Ripoll, "Dos viajes, una intención: Francisco Arango y Alejandro Oliván en Europa y las Antillas azucareras (1794–1829)," in *Revista de Indias*, 62 (2002)(224): 85–102; *Memorias de la Real Sociedad Patriótica*, 1793, p. 34. Montalvo mentions his *ingenio* in an undated letter to Someruelos (likely January 1804), in AGI, Cuba, leg. 1705.

French and Spanish colonies with orders to destroy the French and with the vague idea of conquering French territory and bringing it once again under Spain's dominion. Whether these men were also motivated by the boon that would result from the permanent destruction of the export economy of Saint-Domingue we cannot know with certainty. Some were members of groups such as the Sociedad Económica or collaborators of Francisco Arango, men and institutions that routinely linked Saint-Domingue's demise with Cuba's ascendancy. Many, moreover, had direct ties to the burgeoning world of Cuban sugar. Indeed, it was precisely through such men as Casa Calvo, Armona, and Montalvo that the worlds of Cuban sugar and the Haitian Revolution collided.[32]

The first Cuban forces arrived under Armona's command on July 4, 1793. Armona's initial shock at what he saw was profound. The general poverty of Santo Domingo's border region, the almost total lack of roads, the sparseness of the population, even the intensity of the climate seemed to him to forebode the difficulties of his mission.[33] But what most astonished and disturbed Armona and other officers arriving from Cuba was the army of rebel slaves with whom they would now have to work – at what measure of proximity they could not yet know. How little those black warriors seemed to him like an army: their manner, their aspect, their discipline, all seemed to defy his notion of what constituted a legitimate military force. One month into his mission, he concluded that the Spanish could accomplish little of lasting military value with such men. The Spanish could use them to "fell, burn, and loot the countryside of their Enemy, thus adding to [the latter's] need, anarchy, and confusion. This is the damage we can do with them," he explained derisively.[34] But it was this army, led by Jean-François, Biassou, and increasingly Toussaint Louverture, that was now nominally under his command. Under

---

[32] It would be erroneous to treat the interests of the island's sugar and military elites as one; indeed in key moments (1808, for example) they are better understood as in opposition to one another. Yet, as these brief profiles demonstrate, important military men were by no means strangers to the world of sugar and slavery. On the relationship between the two groups, see Sherry Johnson, "'From Authority to Impotence': Arango's Adversaries and their Fall from Power during the Constitutional Period (1808–1823)" in González-Ripoll and Álvarez Cuartero, *Francisco Arango*, 193–211.

[33] Armona to García, August 4, 1793, in AGS, SGU, leg. 6855. Here Armona's disdain for Santo Domingo seems similar to what was expressed among Cuban and Spanish officials during the reconquest of the colony in 1861. See Anne Eller "Let's show the world we are brothers: The Dominican Guerra de Restauración and the Nineteenth-Century Caribbean," PhD dissertation, New York University, 2011.

[34] Armona to García, August 4 and August 12, 1793, both in AGS, SGU, leg. 6855.

those three black officers, and now by extension and in theory under him and the Spanish, marveled Armona, served the majority of the slaves the French had held in 1789, a number Armona put quite specifically at 434,429.[35]

Even after the arrival of the Cuban forces, the black auxiliary forces retained their structures and command. They reported to the Spanish and received orders from them. But the orders seemed to have been followed, or not, based on decisions taken by the auxiliaries' leaders. As the black auxiliaries conquered French towns for Spain, the forces of the Spanish army entered and worked out the details of capitulation and daily rule, from the swearing of oaths of allegiance by French citizens now under Spanish dominion, to the celebration of solemn masses to mark the transfer to Spain, to the structures of military and judicial rule that would operate.

About the general operations of the auxiliary army, Armona communicated extensively with the black leaders, exchanging regular letters and reports. On any given day, he received updates from all three leaders, Jean-François, Biassou, and Toussaint. The very form of the letters made an impression. Biassou, for example, signed his letters, "Generalísimo de la Armas de Su Majestad," and wrote on paper stamped with an image of a tree of liberty topped with a crown sustained by two naked black men. To Armona, all this was disconcerting. When he commented on these trappings, as he did especially in the first months after his arrival, he could not resist characterizing them as arrogant or pretentious, or else simply as mimicry, which under other circumstances might have been laughable but that current conditions forced him to abide.[36]

If the Cuban commanders bristled at this new contact, it is likely that the black commanders did as well. They now reported to Havana slaveholders who seemed to consume many of the resources that before had gone to them. When Toussaint pressed for weapons from the Spanish in August 1793, Ignacio Caro explained that the guns he had promised Toussaint had already gone to the new Spanish arrivals. "Rocks," added Caro, "I have already given him plenty."[37]

---

[35] Armona to García, August 14, 1793, in AGS, SGU, leg. 6855. Armona does not explain how he arrives at such a precise number.

[36] Armona to García, August, 12, 14, and 23, 1793, all in AGS, SGU, leg. 6855. Leonardo del Monte to Marqués de Casa Calvo, February 22, 1794, in del Monte, *Historia de Santo Domingo*, 4: 186.

[37] Ignacio Caro to Juan Esteban Nova, August 7, 1793, in CARAN, D-XXV 39, 392.

In moments of confidence, Armona laid aside his shock and confusion and wrote of his intention to subdue what he called the black leaders' arrogance, to soften their habits, and to make the auxiliary army more obedient, subservient, and grateful for the recognition and privileges offered so magnanimously by the king of Spain. He explained to his commanders that he wanted to temper the auxiliaries' pride, to make them act like humble vassals of the king.[38] But for the most part, Armona's behavior was otherwise. He answered the rebels' letters, no matter how pretentious or arrogant he judged them, with words of flattery and respect, addressing Biassou, for instance, as a most valued friend, whose letters he received "with all respect and esteem."[39] Perhaps he was advised to adopt this style by a M. Virou, who had served as secretary and interpreter to Toussaint Louverture, and now worked as Armona's principal French scribe and translator.[40] Armona treated the black leaders, he confessed, as the circumstances of the day required, accommodating himself to their style and customs. He invited Biassou to dine at his camp with his officers and guards. At banquets and other gatherings hosted by the black generals, the officers of both armies – black former slaves and Cuban-Spanish planters – broke bread.[41] In late February 1794, when gold medals with engravings of the king of Spain were awarded to the three black leaders in honor of their service to Spain, it was precisely the battalions from Havana and Santiago who performed the ceremony. They paraded around the town square with the black officers; they played the military music that served to give the occasion the necessary pomp; and when it was all over, the Cuban men sat down at the table with former slaves turned generals, feasting and toasting their achievement and bravery.[42]

---

[38] Armona to García, August 24, 1793, in AGS, SGU, leg. 6855.

[39] Armona to Biassou, August 11 and 12, 1793, both in AGS, SGU, leg. 6855.

[40] Juan Lleonart to García, April 30, 1794, in AGI, Cuba, leg. 170A.

[41] See Armona to García, August 23, 24, and 27, and December 16, 1793, all in AGS, SGU, leg. 6855.

[42] It was García's idea to award the medals as a means to ensure the loyalty of those leaders honored in such a dignified manner. The three gold medals were awarded to Jean-François, Biassou, and Toussaint Louverture. See García to Acuña, June 11, 1793, in AGS, SGU, leg. 7157; García to Duque de Alcudia, February 18, 1794, in AGS, SGU, leg. 7157; and García to Conde de Campo de Alange, February 18, 1794, in AGS, SGU, leg. 7150. For a detailed description of the awarding of the medals and the participation of the Cuban regiments in the festivities, see Antonio Barba, "Continuación de las noticias de la Ysla de Santo Domingo hasta 25 de Marxo de 94" in "Relación de lo ocurrido en la Ysla de Santo Domingo con motivo de la guerra con los franceses," in SHMM, CGD, Reel 65, doc. no. 5-4-11-1.

Much of this kind of contact served the purpose of military ritual. The awarding of medals, for example, was suggested by Governor García as a means to flatter and thereby help ensure the loyalty of their powerful allies. But there was other contact as well – less formal and less likely to receive approval from the king and his ministers. The archbishop of Santo Domingo complained frequently, for example, of an illicit trade in which the officers and soldiers of the Cuban regiments participated actively. He accused them of forcing local Spanish residents to sell them livestock at very low prices and then turning around and selling them at a premium to the black forces (even after some of these were already enlisted on the French side), as well as to British soldiers, who were also waging war against France. The Cuban men were also said to buy from the black troops jewels, furniture, money, and valuables of all kinds taken during attacks on French towns and plantations. Rumor had it that some of the officers had sent to Cuba thousands of pesos acquired through this kind of illicit trade.[43]

Importantly, the Cubans also purchased sugar-making equipment taken from the French plantations attacked by the auxiliaries. The Marqués de Casa Calvo, owner of two sugar estates in Havana, purchased up-to-date sugar-making equipment from the black insurgents who had acquired it during their attacks on French property. He purchased so much of this kind of material that the hallways and patios of his residence were said to be almost impassable, so crowded were they with drums, cylinders, and other pieces of sugar machinery, all waiting to be shipped to Havana. Casa Calvo, it seems, had come to a literal interpretation of Arango's early argument that Saint-Domingue's revolution represented "an opportunity" for Cuba. It was this kind of behavior that led the archbishop to refer to the Cuban battalions as a group of low and ambitious businessmen. Even the Cuban commanders themselves sometimes confessed that they and their troops participated in at least some illicit trade with their black allies, less for the purpose of profit than of survival, as they also purchased much of their food from people in the camps of the black forces.[44]

---

[43] Archbishop of Santo Domingo to [Consejo de Estado], October 24 and November 24, 1794, both in AGS, SGU, leg. 7161; and "Causa contra el Brigadier D. Matías de Armona...." in AGI, Cuba, leg. 1774B.

[44] For examples of these accusations, see Archbishop of Santo Domingo to [Consejo de Estado], October 24 and November 24, 1794, both in AGS, SGU, leg. 7161. For the admission, see Juan Lleonart to Conde del Campo de Alange, February 22, 1795, in

The contact between Cuban men and black auxiliaries was sometimes more indulgent and festive, though still clearly extraofficial. For example, in the almost nightly dances in Bayajá (Fort-Dauphin) in late summer and fall of 1794, the town's Cuban commander, Casa Calvo, allegedly found time to dance with and pay court to the wife of Jean-François.[45] Whatever ceremonial contact was ordered by king and governor, in the routine practice of war and occupation, white and black men (and sometimes women) did interact, engaging in the mundane business of survival, petty commerce, and even pleasure. As Armona would later note, not entirely metaphorically, these were the men with whom they dined and slept.[46]

Whatever ideas of war and honor the Cuban forces arrived with, contact with the day-to-day conditions on the border between the Spanish colony and a revolution of former slaves left them at the very least confused. Armona met the black auxiliaries and their leaders; he communicated with them regularly, and he worked to manage territory newly acquired as a result of their efforts. Yet he was at a loss as to how to describe and understand the whole endeavor. His letters are full of confessions of incomprehension. Even such simple tasks as naming the black allies confounded him. In fact, for his first months in Santo Domingo, Armona seemed almost incapable of seeing or designating the black force under his nominal command as an army. For him, these forces were simply "*palenques de negros*," or "maroon people who aided" them in war. As if aware that the term "runaway slave" was inadequate to describe the people before him, Armona also scattered his descriptions with allusions to the Christian reconquest of Muslim Spain or to North Africa more generally, using terms such as "Saracens" and "seraglio" to refer to the black auxiliaries and their encampments. He compared Biassou, who he said commanded 16,000 soldiers, and Jean-François, who commanded another 20,000, to the emperors of Morocco and Algiers.[47]

Armona marshalled a succession of awkward terms to fix the character of the men before him. But often he did so with a budding recognition

---

AGS, SGU, leg. 6855. On Casa Calvo's sugar mills, see M. García, *Entre haciendas y plantaciones*, Appendix 4.

[45] Antonio Barba, "Continuación de lo ocurrido en esta Ysla" September 25, 1794, in "Relación de los ocurrido en la Ysla de Santo Domingo con motivo de la guerra con los franceses," in SHMM, CGD, Reel 65, doc no. 5-4-11-1.

[46] Armona to Manuel del Barrio y Armona, et al., February 9, 1795, in AGS, SGU, leg. 6855.

[47] See, for example, Armona's letters to García dated August 4, 12, 14, 20, and 27, 1793, all in AGS, SGU, 6855; The August 4 letter also appears in AGI, Cuba, leg. 170A.

of the futility of his effort. He conceded hesitantly that the categories
and terms he tried to use to describe the moment tended not to correspond to those used by the black officers and soldiers themselves. In
fact, he routinely recorded such discrepancies. "They," he said, referred
to their positions as encampments, but he called them "palenques." He
mentioned that they referred to themselves as generals, brigadiers, and
lieutenants. He seemed about to record a difference in the way the Spanish named these same leaders, but then added, almost sheepishly, that his
forces called them that too. His discomfort seemed to suggest that the
very power of the black armies was making old labels (such as *maroons*)
inappropriate, and new ones (such as *general* for a former slave) credible,
but still not so natural as to go unmarked.[48] What emerges here is a spas-
modic attempt to classify the political situation they now confronted, an
attempt to reconcile unprecedented scenes with already existing language
and categories.

This kind of incongruity between existing categories and the complicated and unprecedented reality that surrounded Armona and his men did
not produce a simple narrative that "silenced" the Haitian Revolution or
its black insurgents. Rather, the gap between preexisting categories and an
outsized, unprecedented set of events became clearly audible in Armona's
efforts to narrate the history in which he himself participated. In the process of day-to-day talk and interpretation, specific acts of naming came
into contact with other competing ones. The sources, then, reveal a kind
of tug of war – the competing efforts of narrators and actors to contain these events in categories that would not allow them to fit. It is in
these routine, day-to-day acts of speaking and writing and thinking that
what Michel-Rolph Trouillot has referred to as "silences" emerged. But
they emerged not fully formed, but rather in the process of being made,
as actors – black, white, and brown; free and enslaved; African, creole,
Spanish, and French – put forth interpretations that vied for ascendancy
in fluid and volatile contexts, at the time and long after.[49]

The discrepancies in the very terminology used to describe the revolution and the alliance between the Spanish army and the black rebels
also affected the routine mechanics of that alliance. Problems arose all
the time between black leaders already used to fighting their own war

[48] Armona to García, August 12 and August 14, 1793, in AGS, SGU, leg. 6855.
[49] Ada Ferrer, "Talk About Haiti: The Archive and the Atlantic's Haitian Revolution," in
Tree of Liberty: Atlantic Legacies of the Haitian Revolution, edited by Doris Lorraine
Garraway (Charlottesville: University of Virginia Press, 2008); and Trouillot, *Silencing
the Past*.

their own way and Spanish officers who saw those leaders as fugitive slaves, or, at best, as auxiliaries who owed them subservience and gratitude. Jean-François, for example, ran into trouble with the local Spanish commander in Ounaminthe when he rebuffed his orders, insisting that *he* was the ranking officer, and that he owed obedience only to the king and governor. Biassou did the same with Cabrera.[50] In general, the Cuban officers noted the rebels' troublesome aspiration to equality and status. Armona wrote of men who gave themselves grandiose titles (which he and his companions were forced to accept) and who went around "trying to act like our equals, and even with a certain air of superiority, or as if *we* were the ones who *needed* and had to please *them*."[51]

Santo Domingo was for these Cuban officers a practical school of revolutionary politics. Once-abstract ideas about allying with masses of insurgent former slaves in the interest of elite and imperial political goals confronted a recalcitrant reality. In practice, the alliance was impossible to oversee and manage. Cuban officers who shouldered the task of making material the alliance between the Spanish king and armed former slaves betrayed an almost constant sense of frustration, a sense of being in an impossible place, stuck between unrealistic orders issued by distant superiors and the actions taken by the black army immediately before them.

So, when Biassou, in the midst of a conflict with Jean-François, decided to head for the capital city of Santo Domingo for a personal meeting with the governor, García wrote to Armona in panic, telling him to forbid Biassou to do any such thing. García did not want the black army at the door of the Spanish capital. Armona replied with incredulity:

You promoted him and there is no longer any remedy; the blacks are far from the point where we can treat them like officers in an army; they are *bozales* or maroons; they do not understand our language; they do not have payment, prest, or ration, nor anything other than what they can steal and loot and whatever necessity (which knows no Law) authorizes them to do.... Allow me to speak to you frankly and amicably: either you have not the slightest idea what is happening in the territory under your rule, or [you are waiting for] someone else to rush in and fail.[52]

---

[50] Juan Antonio de Urizar, Regente de la Real Audiencia de Santo Domingo, to Acuña, August 25, 1793, in AGS, SGU, leg. 7157.

[51] Armona to García, August 12, 1793, in AGS, SGU, leg. 6855. Emphasis added.

[52] Prest refers to an advance of money given to men enlisting in an army. Armona to García, September 10, 1793, in AGS, SGU, leg. 6855. Jean-François and Biassou reconciled sometime that fall, as García reported to Acuña on December 14, 1793, in AGS, SGU, leg. 7157.

No wonder, perhaps, that the governor would be so eager to court-martial Armona once the whole experiment collapsed less than a year later.

In the meantime, even routine matters – such as provisioning the army to which Spain owed all its victories – were constant sources of aggravation and worry. The insurgents assailed Cuban commanders continually with requests for meat, clothes, arms, and all kinds of supplies that the Spanish officers could not readily supply. Yet the Spanish felt they absolutely had to – first, because the auxiliaries needed the supplies to achieve victories in Spain's name. For better or worse, the auxiliaries were the "only resource they had" – "the all of the war," in Armona's words.[53] Second, the Cuban commanders also feared that not giving the auxiliaries what they asked for might cause them to turn on their erstwhile Spanish commanders and allies. Armona wrote to the governor saying that he felt obliged to give in to their incessant requests so that they did not become "turncoats" (*casaca*). Months later, he was still making the same argument, asserting that if they did not satisfy the auxiliaries' requests for meat at Dajabón, Dondon, Grande Rivière, and Gran Boucan, "we can fear a tragedy."[54]

With arms, the problem was even more complicated. The auxiliaries asked for weapons to use in their battles on behalf of the Spanish. Already, the armed victories of these troops had brought a vast expanse of territory, stretching all the way to Gonaïves on the west coast, under Spanish control – at least in name. The Spanish, of course, wanted the military conquests to continue. Indeed, in February 1794, the captain-general himself relocated to the recently conquered town of Bayajá, founded as a Spanish settlement in 1578, ceded to France in 1697, and in January 1794 retaken by Spain, thanks in part to the actions in arms of its black auxiliaries. It was from fortified Bayajá (called Fort-Dauphin by the French) that the Spanish command hoped to launch a daring attack on Le Cap, just under thirty miles distant. Using the forces of the black auxiliaries and the Spanish army, with the support of a Spanish naval squadron, García expected to reclaim for Spain the once-opulent sugar country.

But however much they wanted the victories to continue, Spanish authorities were torn as to whether to comply or not with the auxiliaries' insistent requests for arms and munitions. They feared that those weapons, once in the hands of the black forces, might one day be turned against them; or, at the very least, they worried that well-armed auxiliaries

[53] Armona to García, August 12 and September 10, 1793, in AGS, SGU, leg. 6855.
[54] Armona to García, August 19, 1793, and January 12, 1794, in AGS, SGU, leg. 6855.

would be that much harder to control and contain. Local commanders on the ground were the ones stuck trying to reconcile those fears, on the one hand, with the desire for military power, on the other. Armona put it to García with characteristic bluntness:

I repeat what you must certainly know. That the swarm of wasps, this school of crustaceans, or black French rebels, neither you nor they themselves have any idea how many they are.... They alone have waged this war and they are waging it for us. How do you want them to win victories and make significant progress, and at the same time you charge and order us all the time to not give them Arms or Munitions with which they can defend themselves from the Attacks they face every day? Look for someone else, my friend, who knows how to put things in order [*atar estos cabos*], because I do not know how to execute it. Wake up ... from so long a sleep.[55]

Armona's pessimism was palpable. For him, and indeed for much of the Spanish command, it was inconceivable that the black forces would not choose at some point to change sides or to rebel against their new Spanish commanders. Sometimes they predicted that that betrayal would come because the Spanish were unable to meet all the demands for food and arms; other times that it would come precisely because they had been too generous in providing arms. Whatever the cause, Spaniards and Cubans repeated the prediction with fearful certainty: when the auxiliaries ran out of French targets, they would inevitably turn on the Spanish, if only because of what they saw as the inherent nature of black men.[56]

This deep discomfort was further exacerbated by events unfolding on the French side of the island. In August 1793, Civil Commissioner Léger-Félicité Sonthonax abolished slavery in the northern part of the French colony, extending the emancipation decree to the west and the south in September and October, respectively. The black auxiliaries, whose allegiance and constancy the Cubans and Spanish already doubted, began receiving copies of French proclamations and letters that boasted of the superiority of the French Republic and French liberty. The French now offered to give the men equivalent ranks in the French army and to grant freedom to all the enslaved. According to Armona, "There is not one chief among the Auxiliaries who does not have a copy of the declaration ... and other facts and offers even more flattering than that one." Biassou, for

---

[55] Armona to García, September 10, 1793 in AGS, SGU, leg. 6855.
[56] Predictions of this sort abounded; see García's letters to Conde de Campo de Alange and Acuña, scattered in AGS, SGU, 7150 and 7157; Armona to García, August 4, 12, 19, 1793; and Vázquez to Archbishop of Santo Domingo, December 3, 1793, in AGI, Estado, leg. 11B, exp. 98.

example, received a letter from a French officer in Le Cap, who contrasted Spanish slavery with French freedom; in French Saint-Domingue, only liberty and equality reigned. The letter arrived with many copies of the emancipation decree, in the hope that Biassou would accept the offer to turn French and distribute the decree among others as proof of the worthiness of the French cause.[57]

"All men," read the proclamation, "are born and remain free and equal. . . . All blacks and mulattos currently in slavery are declared free to enjoy all the rights attached to the quality of French citizens." The declaration specifically addressed those blacks currently fighting under Spain: "Do the Spanish free their own slaves? No, surely not. On the contrary, they will likely weigh you down with chains as soon as they no longer need your services."[58] While the French challenged the permanence of the individual freedom granted by Spain, the Spanish governor issued competing proclamations. He did not offer general emancipation, but rather disputed the legitimacy of the French authorities who had done so. García wrote personally to Jean-François, extolling his virtues and reminding him of the privileges he had acquired as a vassal of the Spanish king. Then the governor, and all the other Spanish and Cuban officers, waited and watched. Whose assertions would the black leaders believe? What would be the response of the black armies to the enactment of general emancipation in French territory?[59]

García wanted desperately to believe in the auxiliaries' loyalty. He, after all, had been the main architect (along with Jean-François and Biassou) of this alliance to begin with. The possibility that the leaders whom he had courted, honored, and supplied would now turn their backs on the Spanish army filled him with dread. Just as politics was making the loss of Spain's black allies significantly more likely, García seemed to abandon all his early warnings and to cling urgently to the notion that the black forces would remain steadfast and loyal. Forced to report the betrayal of one after another black officer, García still advanced interpretations that stressed the loyalty of his black allies. He surmised that Jean-François was devastated by the treason of his subaltern officers and

---

[57] "Copia de carta de Maire y Municipalidad de Guarico al General Negro Biassou remitiéndole ejemplares de la Proclamación de los Comisarios Civiles sobre la Libertad General de los Esclavos," Sepember 9, 1793, in AGS, SGU, leg. 7157.

[58] "Proclamation au nom de la République," attached to Armona to García, September 10, 1793, in AGS, SGU, leg. 6855.

[59] García to Conde de Campo Alange, September 12, 1793 and October 22, 1793, both in AGS, SGU, leg. 7151.

would avenge it. He trusted that Toussaint, eager to prove his love of Spain and his loyalty to the king, would continue fighting for Spain with the same astonishing effort and success as before.[60] He insisted that when the black leaders received the French letters and proclamations they were overcome with all the proper emotions: horror, indignation, and offense at the insolence of the French; gratitude, submission, and love for the Spanish. For him, the fact that the black leaders immediately turned over to the Spanish commanders their copies of the French documents offered positive proof of their loyalty.[61] Of course, Jean-François and others may in fact have handed over the French offers as a powerful reminder of their own supreme importance to the Spanish, enhancing their ability to negotiate and solicit more supplies or privileges for their men, and perhaps putting the possibility of a broader emancipation on the table. García nonetheless insisted on the reading that confirmed the wisdom of the path he had chosen for the Spanish.

However interpreted, French emancipation made even more precarious the ties that bound many black insurgents to a Spanish king who defended slavery. It also made the practice of war – and of governing the towns coming under Spanish rule – significantly more complicated. To gain the loyalty of white French royalists, the Spanish had formally promised to protect their persons and their property, sometimes even giving them salaries to act as a local police or military force. At the same time, the Spanish had attempted to keep the loyalty of their black allies, former slaves who had achieved their power precisely by attacking the white French now coming under Spain's protection. Thus, as the war unfolded in the context of general emancipation in French territory, questions and tensions multiplied over how to reconcile the allegiance of white French royalists, most deeply invested in slavery, with the allegiance of black insurgents whose very existence challenged the institutions of enslavement and racial hierarchy. Increasingly, García found himself making contradictory promises to each group – freedom, arms, and protection to rebel slaves; protection and slavery to slaveholders.[62] But one set of promises implicitly challenged the other.

---

[60] See García to Conde de Campo de Alange, September 12, 1793, in AGS, SGU, leg. 7151; García to Duque de Alcudia, January 3, 1794, in AGI, Estado, leg. 14, exp. 89; García to Duque de Alcudia, February 18, 1794, in AGS, SGU, leg. 7157.
[61] García to Conde de Campo de Alange, October 22, 1793, in AGS, SGU, leg. 7151.
[62] On promises made to white French colonists, see, for example, García to Conde de Campo de Alange, June 25, 1793, in AGS, SGU, leg. 7158.

The spectacular and relatively bloodless conquest of Bayajá/Fort Dauphin is a case in point. When the town was taken by combined Spanish and auxiliary land and naval forces in January 1794, its prominent French citizens elected to pledge allegiance to Spain if the Spanish consented to several conditions.[63] The French called for the protection of the political rights of "men of color, [their] brothers." Did those rights include freedom from slavery for those enslaved before the French emancipation? No answer was made explicit. At the same time, the Spanish agreed to "religiously protect" the lives and property of all French citizens. Did that property include slaves? Again, the answer was not spelled out. Slavery in Bayajá had been abolished by the French commissioners several months earlier, suggesting that, in a legal sense, in the first instance, the protection of property would not have included property in human beings. If the Spanish and the French at Bayajá and elsewhere imagined that the protection would extend to property in black men and women, then they were envisioning a collective reenslavement – the conversion of French citizens into Spanish slaves. But the white French and Spanish, surrounded by Jean-Francois and thousands of black insurgents just outside the town, had neither the power nor the inclination to implement such a policy, nor even to express such desire explicitly. So the issue was addressed obliquely. And on the ground – between French and Spanish rule, and between slavery, emancipation, and reenslavement – everyone improvised on the edge of catastrophe.[64]

The Spanish conquest of Bayajá produced an influx of people to the town and surrounding countryside. French subjects from neighboring towns, seeking to escape republican rule and perhaps especially emancipation, crowded into newly Spanish Bayajá offering to exchange their vassalage for the king's protection of their persons and property. In just two days in early February 1794, at least 204 French citizens arrived from the nearby town of Yaquesi. While some arrived destitute and ruined, others managed to arrive with some of their belongings and with black men and women whom they and their new Spanish authorities called slaves. Meanwhile, the black auxiliaries and others attached to them made frequent visits to the town for purposes of military consultation, petty trade, and

---

[63] On the Spanish victory in Bayajá in January 1794, see Beaubrun Ardouin, *Etudes sur l'histoire d'Haïti, suivi de la vie du général J.M. Borgella*, (Port-au-Prince: Éds. Fardin, 1789–1801), 2: 82–87; del Monte, *Historia de Santo Domingo*, 4: 178–181.

[64] The phrase is borrowed from Joseph Ellis, *Founding Brothers: The Revolutionary Generation* (New York: Vintage, 2002), 216.

pleasure. Those forays into town – and the sight again of white masters and black slaves – would have provided firsthand experience of Spain's concessions to reenslavement.[65]

Aware of the potential volatility of that encounter, authorities tried to limit contact between mobilized black men and the white French in Bayajá. When the town authorities swore allegiance to Spain, one of their conditions had been a prohibition on the entry of the black auxiliaries. Partly in response to the French request, the Spanish issued orders to Jean-François's army, camped on the outskirts of town. They were banned from entering the town in any military capacity; entry was permitted only with a written pass and with no weapons. They were expressly forbidden from engaging in arson, extortion of residents, looting, and theft, including the taking of sugar cane or foodstuffs from neighboring plantations, under threat of punishment by whipping. This, even though the Spanish code provisionally drafted for Bayajá had forbidden the use of the whip as punishment for crime.[66]

It was, however, the final point of the order transmitted to Jean-François that was most elaborate: "It is forbidden under penalty of the most severe punishment to perturb those blacks who have remained loyal to their masters.... You will also allow the return of all those who voluntarily seek to return to their plantations to work in that useful and important labor." The order did not speak of reenslavement, but it made the auxiliaries complicit in an order that protected and expanded servile black labor under former masters. Perhaps as additional encouragement to any black auxiliaries who might think of returning to their masters, García added that they would return as "free men" – a condition and a right they had achieved by concession of the Spanish king. The order did not mention that if the town had remained French, slavery would not have existed.[67] There is no indication in the record that any of Jean-François's men voluntarily answered the invitation to become plantation laborers once more. But the order itself highlights the malleability of terms such as

[65] García to Duque de Alcudia, February 21, 1794 in AGI, Estado, leg. 14, exp. 85; March 6, 1794 in AGI, Estado, leg. 14, exp. 79; March 10, 1794 in AGI, Estado, leg. 14, exp. 77; March 19, 1794 in AGI, Estado, leg. 14, exp. 75; and del Monte *Historia de Santo Domingo*, 4: 178–205.
[66] García to Vicente Antonio de Faura, Bayajá, February 28, 1794, and "Orden para el Exército de Gral. Juan Francisco," signed Joaquín García, Bayajá, March 3, 1794, both in del Monte, *Historia de Santo Domingo*, 4: 190–195.
[67] "Orden para el Exército de Gral. Juan Francisco," signed Joaquín García, Bayajá, March 3, 1794, in del Monte, *Historia de Santo Domingo*, 4: 195.

"slave" and "free men" in that very volatile and changing context. And that very malleability increased everyone's sense of distrust.

While the fate of slavery in the formerly French towns now ruled by the Spanish was perhaps uncertain, the Spanish and Cuban military men who occupied those towns day to day acted as if it were not. Indeed, they worked actively to expand their own capacity to exercise powers associated with the ownership of property in persons.[68] Within days of their arrival in Bayajá, members of the Cuban forces began purchasing "slaves" from former French subjects who had just sworn allegiance to Spain. The Marqués de Casa Calvo, owner of two sugar mills in Havana, purchased one black man named Eli, who appears to have remained to serve him in Bayajá. Gabriel de Aristizábal – commander of Spain's naval forces in America, head of the force that helped take Bayajá, longtime resident of Havana, and married into the creole nobility – purchased a man named Ignacio. José María de la Torre, an officer in the Havana Regiment and owner of a Havana sugar mill, purchased five people. Juan Lleonart, son of the man who would soon replace Armona as commander of the frontier, also purchased some.[69]

These and other recently purchased "slaves" were sent to Havana together with French prisoners of war, some identified as white and free, others still as slaves. In Havana, where the captain-general and his allies strove to prohibit the entry of so-called French blacks, the people who arrived as slaves were refused entry, and an angry captain-general sent word to his subalterns on duty in Santo Domingo: stop buying *negros franceses*. Havana's refusal of these particular French slaves caused no small loss and disappointment among Cuban officials stationed in Santo Domingo.[70]

If this particular shipment of people appears to have been sent back, not all were. In Santiago de Cuba, the governor complained repeatedly about *negros franceses* being taken from territory conquered by Spain in Saint-Domingue and sent to his territory for sale. He tried his best to

[68] The notion of "powers attaching to a right of ownership" is developed in Rebecca Scott, "Under Color of Law: *Siladin v. France* and the Dynamics of Enslavement in Historical Perspective," in Jean Allain, ed., *The Legal Understanding of Slavery: From the Historical to the Contemporary* (Oxford: Oxford University Press, 2012), 152–164.

[69] García to Yntendente de la Habana, Bayajá, February 10, 1794, with enclosures, in AHN, Ultramar (Santo Domingo), leg. 6209, 2a parte, exp. 49. Lleonart to Mi estimado amigo, April 17, 1794, in del Monte, *Historia de Santo Domingo*, 4: 205–207.

[70] Lleonart to Mi estimado amigo, April 17, 1794, in del Monte, *Historia de Santo Domingo*, 4: 205–207.

impede the practice and, indeed, he was sometimes aided by the refusal of local people to believe the sellers' claims that the men for sale were African and not implicated in the Revolution. Still, he was at a loss as to what do with them once he discovered them. Surely, he could not send them to other Spanish territory; sending them to colonies held by allies would be improper; returning them to the enemy would be to replenish its ranks.[71] Thus, the thorny and recurring problem of how to restrict and remedy the entry of French blacks in Cuba was now made even more complex by the presence of Cuban soldiers as slave buyers on the borders of Saint-Domingue itself.

In theory, the taking of Bayajá signaled a substantial victory for Spain. Captain-General García moved his headquarters there to prepare for what he hoped would be a definitive Spanish attack on Le Cap. The Spanish, it seemed, had cause for optimism. But the details of actual Spanish rule became increasingly difficult to manage. The arrival of white emigrés from neighboring towns strained resources and public order, forcing the Spanish to recognize and pay a local French police force. The confusion over the current and future status of slavery itself – especially given the increasing pull of French emancipation – was potentially more explosive. Formal documents made no mention of the preservation of slavery, but in daily practice white French royalists and Spanish and Cuban military men assumed the continuation of enslavement, and they bought, sold, and commanded accordingly. Their behavior would have been readily known among the thousands of mobilized former slaves who were camped on the town's outskirts and in regular contact with its residents.

Not just in Bayajá, but across the war zone, Spanish commanders conveyed how difficult it was to govern this war in practice, especially after the decree of general emancipation added new sources of tension and conflict. Even before French emancipation, the frustration of commanders such as Armona over the day-to-day difficulties of managing the alliance had resulted almost in insolence. "Wake up," Armona had said harshly to the governor. Now Armona, like others, forwarded news of more and more defections. The letters read like lists, reporting the desertion of one auxiliary officer after another: Adan, Blancazenave, Petit

---

[71] Vaillant to Las Casas, June 12, 1794, and Las Casas to Vaillant, July 29, 1794, in ANC, CCG, leg. 47, exps. 5 and 7. Though Vaillant complained of a general practice, he also specifically identified Juan Colás as the captain sending the slaves to Cuba for sale. Colás sent the slaves with written permission from Santo Domingo governor Joaquín García, suggesting that they were sent from Bayajá, where García had his headquarters at the time.

Thomas, Bernadin, Macaya, Barthélemy, Chevalier.[72] In the context of escalating defections and uncertain allegiances, rumors and predictions flew about imminent betrayals, massacres, and reenslavement. By late winter and early spring 1794, in Le Borgne, a coastal parish west of Le Cap surrounded by Republican forces on two sides, the Spanish officer in charge reported to Armona that the town was "smoldering" (*ardiendo*). Briefly overseen by Spanish troops, it was now under the watch of the black auxiliary troops, who were apparently spreading rumors that the Spanish planned on killing all the whites. The black commanders there also allegedly stole and burned property and goods, and they maintained not-so-secret contact with black soldiers of the Republic who suddenly seemed to be everywhere. Within the month, the local auxiliary troops switched to the side of the French.[73]

Facing urgent requests for more Spanish troops, for more food, for more munitions, for more everything, Armona lost what little faith and patience he had brought to the project. He was, he said, "disillusioned, tired, chastened, and resolved to no longer stain [himself] in this dark coal pit."[74] In February, this man who had seen campaigns from Portugal to Nassau to California before entering the world of sugar in Havana, overcome with the weight of having to make material the alliance between the king of Spain and the rebel slaves of Saint-Domingue, took sick leave.

Armona remained in Santo Domingo, but on February 12, 1794, his job fell to the younger and fresher Juan Lleonart. The Cuban-born Lleonart was so young and fresh that he even volunteered for such formidable tasks as the governor's projected attack on the French capital city of Le Cap.[75] But difficulties soon accumulated all around. His initial orders sounded simple and measured in writing, but were vague and perhaps unrealizable in practice: to control the leaders of the auxiliaries while not offending their honor in any way.[76] Such a charge would have been difficult to fulfill months before; now the growing power of French emancipation made it impossible. Old difficulties continued. The auxiliary forces kept insisting on more money, arms, meat, and supplies. Lleonart's appeals to the governor met with somber responses about the lack of resources at the capital, just as the governor's requests to

---

[72] Armona to García, February 8, 12, and 14, 1794, in AGS, SGU, leg. 6855.

[73] Armona to García, January 25, 1794, in AGS, SGU, leg. 6855.

[74] Ibid.

[75] Armona to García, March 2, 1794, and Juan Lleonart to Conde de Campo de Alange, December 19, 1794, both in AGS, SGU, leg. 6855.

[76] García to Lleonart, March 21, 1794, in AGI, Cuba, leg. 170A.

neighboring colonies and to the metropole itself met with equivalent replies. In times of war, each set of urgent needs prevented the possibility of assistance to those down the hierarchy.[77]

Lleonart faced new conflicts as well – and of significant proportions. Biassou and Toussaint each appealed to Lleonart to take sides in their own growing rivalry. In late March 1794, Toussaint attacked Biassou's camp, perhaps in retaliation for Biassou's earlier attack on his camp at Marmelade, or to avenge the violent arrest of his nephew Moïse, or, as other historians have suggested, to punish Biassou for his participation in an illegal trade in human beings.[78]

Whatever the immediate cause, the attack seemed to portend a change in Toussaint's allegiance. Spanish commanders noticed that Toussaint's forces were engaged in suspicious behavior in places such as Ennery and Dondon. Rumors circulated that Toussaint was preparing an attack on the Spanish at San Miguel. And shortly before April 30, his troops allegedly staged an uprising in Marmelade, about which no details appear to have survived.[79]

It was, however, at Spanish-controlled Gonaïves that the long-predicted assault materialized. There, in late April 1794, the forces of Toussaint turned on the Spanish command, killing about twenty of them and then attacking the French residents of the town. Toussaint himself was nowhere to be seen, leaving the distraught Spanish agonizing over whether the man who by then had become the most powerful black leader was turning on them or instead losing command of his subalterns. Toussaint himself claimed innocence, forwarding to Lleonart copies of his alleged correspondence with the rebellious black officers. Toussaint's letters chastised his subaltern officers and professed his love of Spain. But he also forwarded to the Spanish a letter written by his officers, a move that allowed him to air scathing condemnations of the Spanish without voicing the accusations himself. [80]

---

[77] Lleonart to García, March 14, 1794, and García to Lleonart, March 17, 1794, both in AGI, Cuba, leg. 170A.

[78] "Continuación de la noticias de lo ocurrido...en el mes de Abril de 1794," and "Novedades ocurridas en esta vanda del Sur desde el Correo anterior de April de 94" both in Antonio Barba, "Relación de lo ocurrido en la Ysla de Santo Domingo con motivo de la Guerra con los franceses," in SHMM, CGD, Reel 65, doc. 5-4-11-1. On the conflict over slavery between the two leaders, see Geggus, *Haitian Revolutionary Studies*, 129–130; Ardouin, *Etudes sur l'Histoire d'Haïti*, 2: 87–91.

[79] Geggus, *Haitian Revolutionary Studies*, 119–124, 133–145.

[80] On the attack on Gonaïves, see Lleonart to García, April 30, 1794 in AGI, Cuba, leg. 170A; "Novedades ocurridas en esta vanda del Sur desde el Correo anterior de April

The officers excoriated the Spanish, who, they said, offered nothing but empty promises, florid words with no substance, and looked upon them as "a zero in number." They – the black auxiliaries – were the ones fighting the war for Spain and receiving precious little in return, while the French émigrés received subsidies from the Spanish and did nothing. Where, they asked, were the protection and privileges promised by the Spanish king, when all their black brothers were mistreated at the hands of the Spanish? What they identified as mistreatment was a very specific practice. The black officers writing to Toussaint – among them Christophe, later king of Haiti – accused the Spanish of illegally and immorally trading in people. Toussaint's officers wrote:

The same people who offer us protection and liberty enslave [our brothers] and bargain over our blood, engaging in a vile commerce, removing them and *sending them to their possessions*. There is not one Spanish officer, nor any from the Troops who does not have slaves purchased for three or four *portugueses* a head. This is their beautiful protection.[81]

They complained – and insisted they had already complained many times before – that Biassou was selling people – including children from Toussaint's camps – to Spanish officers and soldiers, who as a general practice bought them cheaply and then shipped them off to other Spanish possessions. In the port of Gonaïves, for instance, small vessels went back and forth to Santiago and elsewhere in Cuba, carrying goods in both directions, making a modest, surreptitious trade in people logistically plausible.[82] While the governor in Havana worked to keep people – and especially French slaves and people of color – from entering Cuban territory, Cuban and Spanish officers in Saint-Domingue worked to buy

---

de 94," May 11, 1794, in Antonio Barba, "Relación de lo ocurrido en la Ysla de Santo Domingo con motivo de la Guerra con los franceses, 1795," in SHMM, CGD, Reel 65, doc. 5-4-11-1; and the letters of commanders Ramón Salazar and Santacilia to Brisbane, May 1794, in TNA, CO, 137/93.

[81] Emphasis mine. Jean-Baptiste Paparel, et al., to Toussaint Louverture, Marmelade, April 25, 1794, and Toussaint Louverture to Oficiales, Sargentos, Cabos y Soldados del Exército, [April 25, 1794?], forwarded by Lleonart to García, April 30, 1794, in AGI, Cuba, leg. 170A. Lleonart claims that the letter allegedly written by Toussaint's officers was actually written by Toussaint and his secretaries; as evidence of this he cites a conversation with a M. Virou, who had served as one of Toussaint's secretaries and later served as Armona's *amanuense* (scribe).

[82] Raimundo Salazar to Vaillant, May 1 or 10, 1794 and Vaillant to Salazar, June 4, 1794, in ANC, CCG, leg. 47, exps. 2 and 5.

them – even if they came from the mobilized forces of Toussaint Louverture – and ship them home to Havana and Santiago.[83]

The events at Gonaïves, more than any other, have been interpreted as the immediate and critical preamble to Toussaint's *volte-face*, when he switched allegiance from a monarchical Spain still committed to slavery to a republican France opting for emancipation. David Geggus has argued persuasively that this critical *volte-face* may have had less to do with French offers of freedom than with Spanish moves to restore slavery.[84] Part of this seemingly imminent restoration of slavery involved the return of white French refugees to their homes in what was now Spanish-controlled territory, and the efforts of these returning French to humiliate and reassert control over black men and women.

The behavior and interpretations of Toussaint and his officers, however, strongly suggest that the Spanish restoration of slavery was more than a local phenomenon. It involved the well-known purchase of black men, women, and children by Spanish army officers. But in many cases, the soldiers who purchased them sent them off to other Spanish colonies as slaves. Toussaint himself would repeat the accusation months later, after he was openly fighting for the French, when he exhorted the residents of Mirebalais to help expel the Spanish. "You should understand the price we pay for that foreign protection; how many of your brothers under that apparent protection have been sent to foreign countries to labor under the yoke of the cruelest slavery."[85] Thus, the restoration of slavery that figured so centrally in Toussaint's *volte-face* was indirectly linked to the growth of plantation slavery in Cuba, which Cuban soldiers and officers – erstwhile allies of Toussaint – were eager to facilitate.

From the moment of the attack on Gonaïves in late April 1794, Toussaint's words and actions became objects of the closest scrutiny.[86]

---

[83] One such dispute over the fate of slaves purchased by Cuban commanders and shipped to Havana appears in García to Las Casas, April 3, 1794, in AGI, Cuba, leg. 1474. Some of the soldiers and officers sent slaves to Santiago, home to the other regiment that sent soldiers to Santo Domingo. Vaillant to Las Casas, June 12, 1794, and Las Casas to Vaillant, July 29, 1794, in ANC, CCG, leg. 47, exps. 5 and 7.

[84] Geggus, *Haitian Revolutionary Studies*, 129.

[85] Toussaint to "havitantes de la parroquia de Miravalé," undated [September 1794], translated and transcribed in Lleonart to García, September 20, 1794, in AGI, Cuba, leg. 1774B. Another copy appears in AGI, Cuba, 170A.

[86] As David Geggus has noted, it is impossible to fix with certainty the exact date or even location of Toussaint's about-face. In this Spanish military correspondence, there are detailed descriptions of the attack by Toussaint's men on Gonaïves, but there are

Lleonart, struggling to understand what had happened at Gonaïves, read Toussaint's behavior backwards. Had it meant anything when Toussaint arrived at his camp on April 23 with 150 armed and mounted men (as opposed to the usual 25) without announcing his arrival or waiting for permission to enter (as was his custom)? Toussaint's manner on that occasion had not had its usual modesty or submission, noted Lleonart. Should he read something into the fact that after having accepted his invitation to dine together on April 29, Toussaint failed to appear? What about the noticeable limp, which had confined him to his bed while the attack on Gonaïves occurred? Feigned, decided the Spanish, after some inquiry.[87]

If the Spanish and Cuban officers had from the start of the alliance engaged in sweeping predictions of disloyalty based on what they believed to be the inherent nature of black men, they now engaged in something different: minute observation and interpretation of the words, gestures, and absences of one black man in particular. Their fates, they were beginning to conclude, might depend on it. Lleonart almost immediately came to the worst conclusion possible: Toussaint had turned. But whatever evidence he and others marshalled in support of that conclusion – and there was much of it – did not lead the Spanish command to acknowledge that probability in public. So, with Toussaint himself, they kept up appearances, pretending they believed his expressions of loyalty to them and their king. And for the most part, the military rituals of submission and discipline continued. Their letters, less frequent perhaps, displayed the same attention to ceremony and honor. The Cuban forces continued to supply his troops with provisions, and Toussaint's people, now potential rebels and enemies, entered Spanish camps and towns freely to sell vegetables and plantains at, complained one officer, exorbitant prices.[88]

numerous and imprecise references to attacks on Ennery (on Biassou), Dondon (once referred to as an attack on Biassou), and an incident of insubordination among Toussaint's troops at Marmelade. See Lleonart's letters in AGI, Cuba, leg. 170A, and Antonio Barba's in SHMM, CGD, Reel 65, doc. 5-4-11-1; García to Conde de Campo de Alange, July 5, 1794, in AGS, SGU, leg. 7159; and Armona, September 1, 1794, in AGS, SGU, leg. 6855. For a discussion of the difficulties in fixing the exact timing of Toussaint's turn to the French, see Geggus, *Haitian Revolutionary Studies*, chap. 8.

[87] Lleonart to García, April 30, 1794, and Toussaint Louverture to Lleonart, April 29, 1794, both in AGI, Cuba, leg. 170A; and "Novedades ocurridas en esta vanda del Sur desde el Correo anterior de April de 94," May 11, 1794, in Barba, "Relación de lo ocurrido en la Ysla de Santo Domingo con motivo de la Guerra con los franceses, 1795," in SHMM, CGD, Reel 65, doc. 5-4-11-1.

[88] See, for example, the testimony of Santiago Cabanis and Manuel de Molina, in "Causa contra el Brigadier Matías Armona..." in AGI, Cuba, 1774B.

Lleonart faltered in this charade of business as usual only once, when he decided to keep Toussaint's wife and children under something like house arrest in San Rafael at the time of the attack of Toussaint's troops on Dondon in early May, an act he later feared had sealed Toussaint's enmity toward him.[89] Toussaint strayed from the script much more often. Yet even as he attacked the black forces remaining loyal to Spain, he wrote to the Spanish as a loyal subject. As late as September 1794, about four months after what would seem like Toussaint's about-face following the Gonaïves attack – and by which time the power and reach of the British in Saint-Domingue had surpassed the challenge posed by Spain at the beginning of the war – Toussaint wrote respectfully to Lleonart that the British had tried to win him over to take control of Gonaïves and that he had resisted, asserting that he was loyal to the Spanish. Lleonart and García were perplexed: no Spanish force had been in Gonaïves since May.[90] Toussaint had attacked the forces commanded by the still-loyal Jean-François and Biassou at Gros Morne, Ennery, Plaisance, Marmelade, and more. He wrote letters to the French residents of other towns identifying himself as republican. Clearly, he had ceased being loyal to the Spanish. But still, though they knew otherwise, they hoped that maybe there was a chance. So they sent him a Spanish flag to repost at Gonaïves. Unable to settle on another course of action, they pretended to believe his increasingly less-frequent gestures of loyalty.[91]

In a sense, there was nothing else they could do, as they did not have the forces to attack Toussaint. In the meantime, Lleonart did as Armona had done, complained frequently of illness and asked to be replaced.[92] García, for his part, ordered his subalterns to bide their time with Toussaint, to "neither trust him nor reveal [their] distrust," and in the meantime to do everything possible to retain the services of those still-loyal black auxiliaries. To Madrid the governor wrote with circumspection and more than an ounce of deception, never explicitly reporting Toussaint's turn of allegiance to the French, explaining only that it was hard to decipher

---

[89] Lleonart to García, April 30, 1794, in AGI, Cuba, leg. 170A; and "Novedades ocurridas en esta vanda del Sur desde el Correo anterior de April de 94," May 11, 1794, in Barba, "Relación de lo ocurrido en la Ysla de Santo Domingo con motivo de la Guerra con los franceses, 1795," in SHMM, CGD, Reel 65, doc. 5-4-11-1; Armona, dated San Rafael, July 27, 1794 in AGS, SGU, leg. 6855; and García to Lleonart, August 14, 1794, in AGI, Cuba, leg. 170A.

[90] Salazar to the people of Gonaïves, May 12, 1794, in TNA, CO, 137/93, no. 106, 108.

[91] Fascinating letters between Lleonart and Toussaint in this period of feigned loyalty and feigned belief in that loyalty are transcribed in AGI, Cuba, leg. 1774B.

[92] Lleonart to García, April 30 and May 8, 1794, both in AGI, Cuba, leg. 170A.

Toussaint's intentions from afar and that his true loyalties were not really known.[93]

Meanwhile, the edifice of Spanish domination in former French territory collapsed. The Cuban troops were on the front lines, implicated in and eyewitnesses to one of the key turning points of the Haitian Revolution. There, on the frontier, they tried to make tangible the most difficult of orders, and they watched closely as Spain's delicate project of using armed slaves in support of imperial political goals unraveled in dramatic fashion.

Thus it was that on July 7, 1794, a Jean-François ostensibly loyal to Spain entered the Spanish-held town of Bayajá and, before the eyes of the troops of the Havana Regiment, killed between six hundred and seven hundred white French subjects, all of whom had sworn loyalty to Spain in exchange for that government's protection. The massacre was covered in international papers in the United States and Europe, many of which heaped almost equal blame on Jean-François's troops as on the Spanish ones who had not prevented or stopped the massacre, and some of whom were said to have joined with the black soldiers in the subsequent looting of the town. In Madrid, authorities were horrified not only by the massacre, but also by the strange inaction of their soldiers and by the widespread international attention it received, all to the discredit of Spain.[94] When Britain, working with the Spanish, captured the town of Petite-Rivière shortly after the massacre, white French residents begged to be placed under the protection of the British, "absolutely refusing" Spanish rule.[95]

The reports of how the massacre at Bayajá started are contradictory. Rumors had been circulating for days about an impending attack by republican forces, perhaps with the aid of resident white émigrés. The mood was tense. One of the few French survivors saw the purposeful and unexpected approach of Jean-François with seven hundred or eight

---

[93] García to Lleonart, June 2, 1794, in AGI, Cuba, leg. 1774B; and García to Conde Campo de Alange, July 5, 1794, in AGS, SGU, leg. 7159, and August 6, 1794, in AGS, SGU, leg. 7161.

[94] Irujo to Muy Señor mío, London, September 27, 1794, in AGS, SGU, leg. 8150; the letter was discussed in Consejo de Estado on October 24, 1794; see AGS, SGU, leg. 7159.

[95] Lleonart to García, September 10, 1794, in AGI, Cuba, leg. 170A. See also correspondence between Toussaint and Raimundo Salazar, Captain Thomas Brisbane, and Antonio Santacilia, TNA, CO 137/93.

hundred armed men, and he warned Francisco Montalvo, commander of the third Havana battalion, a distinguished Havana nobleman, a career military man, and a sugar planter. Montalvo thought to disguise the Frenchman as a Spanish soldier, and thus was the latter able to escape to tell the tale.

On the morning of the massacre, Jean-François and his troops entered the town – in violation of standing orders issued by the Spanish military command, but with permission of the Spanish priest Vázquez, who informed the others that he had orders from Governor García to let them enter. Governor García himself was absent that morning, for having used the town as his headquarters for several months, just three days before the massacre, he had fallen ill and relocated with his scribes and assistants to a small farm some fifteen to twenty miles away.

On entering the town, Jean-François marched to the government house to meet with the Spanish. Armed, standing, and with a loud, authoritative voice, he demanded that all the French in town be evacuated within the hour. Spanish commander Gaspar Casasola saw no choice but to accede to the evacuation and sought more time to organize it. Jean-François rejected the proposal, announcing that they (the French) would all perish and giving the signal to his men to begin the attack.[96] Then the killing began. Spanish accounts describe the massacre as indiscriminate and general, and indeed, the majority of white French residents in the town were killed. Still, some hints of a pattern emerge. For example, Jean-François's men immediately freed all the people of color held in jail, and they targeted first the officers of the *maréchaussée*, or rural police, and then its members. The body had been reinstated by the Spanish and given the task of maintaining order, in part, against the very men and women attached to Jean-François's troops who came often into town. The killings and looting that followed were accompanied by cries of "Long live Spain!"[97]

Jean-François himself provided a very different account of events. He prefaced his account of the massacre with a sinister story of intrigue and collaboration between the white French residents of Bayajá and the republican forces of Toussaint, who plotted together against the Spanish and

[96] Gaspar Cassasola to García, July 12, 1794, in "Relación de lo ocurrido en la Ysla de Santo Domingo..." in SHMM, CGD, reel 65, doc. no. 5-4-11-1, a copy of which also appears in AGS, SGU, leg. 6855.

[97] Antonio Cumulat to Vaillant, July 11, 1794, in ANC, CCG, leg. 47, exp. 7.

against his own person. He claimed to have arrested spies and messengers who gave credit to this conspiracy. His intention had been to enter the town, arrest all the white French, and then interrogate them to ferret out and punish the guilty. But his men had misunderstood his instructions and launched the massacre without his approval or authorization, and, despite his best efforts, he had been unable to stop them. The looting that happened afterward, he added, was the work of the Spanish troops and not his men. In short, while he lamented the violence, he claimed credit for saving the Spanish from what he regarded as a confirmed conspiracy of French republicans.[98]

The Spanish ambassador in London, who had read about the event when it was excoriated in the British press and who appears to have had contact with some French survivors, laid the blame squarely on García, echoing the irreverent attacks García had received on the ground from Cuban commanders such as Armona. The ambassador accused García of foolishly placing all his trust in Jean-François and believing that even his own existence would not be secure if Jean-François abandoned him. This fear, he argued, prompted García to give in to Jean-François's plan to sack Bayajá only days after García's convenient withdrawal from the town.[99]

Conspiracy theories notwithstanding, the massacre of July 7 must be understood broadly in the context of Spanish policy on the Haitian Revolution. In allying with the black army of Saint-Domingue in 1793, the Spanish had offered individual freedom to its members. As that army conquered more and more territory for Spain, however, the governor offered the white French respect for their property and their economic endeavors, a promise that was interpreted by the white French as a forthcoming restitution of slavery. This set the two groups of new Spanish subjects on a collision course. In Bayajá (as perhaps in Gonaïves with Toussaint's troops), these competing expectations were one trigger to the violence, as white French there repeatedly insulted the black troops, boasted of the vengeance they would enact on the blacks, and spread rumors of the

---

[98] "Relación de Juan Francisco de los echos [sic] que fueron la causa de la función que sucedió el Lunes 7 del presente," July 11, 1794, in SHMM, CGD, Reel 65, doc. no. 5-4-11-1, ff. 150v–154. Other accounts give credit to Jean-François's insistence on rumors of a republican conspiracy. See, for example, Antonio Cumulat to Juan Bautista Vaillant, July 11, 1794, in ANC, CCG, leg. 47, exp. 7. Accounts by Aristizábal and other Spanish officers are in Archivo General de la Marina (AGMAB), Sección de Expediciones a América (EA), leg. 18, carp. 7.

[99] Irujo to Muy Señor mío, London, September 27, 1794, in AGS, SGU, leg. 8150.

imminent restoration of slavery. It was this context that contributed to the volatile day-to-day tensions that produced the calamity of July 7.[100]

Whatever its causes, the massacre was directly witnessed by Cuban troops, some of whom appear to have rooted around the bloody remains to retrieve artifacts of value. They saw with their own eyes the acts that standard accounts would regard as emblematic of the Haitian Revolution – the massacre of white colonists. In the immediate aftermath of the episode, some of the Cuban forces – some out of illness, others perhaps out of terror – fled to Santiago de Cuba, where they were given care, lodging, and the opportunity to tell of the remarkable event they had just witnessed.[101]

But what they witnessed was not only the conduct of war at a particularly violent moment, but also the dramatic unravelling of a complicated arrangement whereby the Spanish state (their state) had tried to use rebel slaves to its own ends. The alliance, from the start, had been delicate: its success relied on the willingness of an army of former slaves to accept some sort of subservience to a Spain that still defended slavery and whose vision for the restoration of a united Hispaniola under Spanish rule included the continuation of enslavement. When after some initial successes the precarious edifice of the alliance began to collapse, Cuban soldiers and officers were there to witness it. They saw firsthand how promises of freedom and talk of reenslavement could become animated agents in the conduct of insurgency and counterinsurgency.

Though the events of July 7 made clear the limits of the alliance between the Spanish and the black auxiliaries, after the massacre things continued much the same. In ravaged Bayajá, the discredited Casasola was replaced by the Cuban sugar planter, Sebastian Calvo de la Puerta, the Marqués de Casa Calvo. Weeks after the massacre, Casa Calvo reported that Jean-François and his troops had professed their loyalty and love of Spain and that they had returned to their camp on the outskirts of town, entering the town only with permission and in general observing some measure of military discipline. While he seemed pleased with this new state of affairs, he also lamented that in order to ensure that this

<hr>

[100] On this in Bayaja, see "Relación de Juan Francisco," in SHMM, CGD, Reel 65, doc. 5-4-11-1, ff. 150v–154; Irujo to Muy Señor mío, London, September 27, 1794, in AGS, SGU, leg. 8150; and Casa Calvo to Las Casas, September 3, 1794, in AGI, Cuba, leg. 1474. On these tensions in Gonaïves and elsewhere, see Lleonart to García, June 7, 1794, in AGI, Cuba, leg. 170A; and Lleonart to Conde de Campo de Alange, December 19, 1794, in AGS, SGU, leg. 6855.
[101] Vaillant to Las Casas, July 17, 1794, in ANC, CCG, leg. 47, exp. 8.

would continue to be the case, they were "forced to bear contact with the Blacks and people of color." He continued, "we have not lost our honor, but our pride suffers much."[102] And as before, the Spanish Cuban commanders felt obliged to provide everything in order to avoid being attacked. Armona wrote with his usual derision that the Spanish army now functioned as the blacks' tributaries – paying tribute in liquor or livestock in order to stave off an attack – and contributing to what he saw as the auxiliaries' inflated sense of superiority. The Spanish continued to do this even with the troops of Toussaint Louverture, even after these were clearly in the camp of the French enemy. As late as October 14, 1794, Lleonart supplied Toussaint with twenty cows and six barrels of *aguardiente* (liquor).[103] Clearly, the alliance envisioned by the Spanish governor and king in the days following the execution of Louis XVI had devolved into something else entirely.

So too had the war itself. The impressive Spanish conquests of late 1793 and early 1794 were reversed, and Spain's complete reliance on the black auxiliaries was made manifest. Their old ally, Toussaint Louverture, having reclaimed for France most of the territory he had earlier helped win for Spain, decided now to advance and attack territory nominally Spanish since the sixteenth century. His eyes were fixed on the town of San Rafael. Close to Dondon and Marmelade, the area around San Rafael was a kind of contact zone where Cuban troops engaged in commerce with Toussaint's troops, trading in food or buying from them objects they had taken in war. After the Bayajá massacre, San Rafael also served as general headquarters of the Spanish command.[104]

On October 15, 1794, just one day after receiving the cows and liquor from the Spanish, Toussaint sent a letter to Lleonart asking him to send a trustworthy person for a personal conference. Lleonart sent his own aide-de-camp, Joseph Boville, escorted by four dragoons and accompanied (without Lleonart's knowledge) by two lower officers of the Havana Regiment. All but one were arrested; Boville would be held captive for

[102] Casa Calvo to Duque de Alcudia, August 31, 1794, in AGI, Estado, leg. 14, exp. 63.
[103] Matías de Armona to Antonio de Armona, et al., July 16, 1794, in AGS, SGU, leg. 6855. Santo Domingo critics of the Cuban regiments argued that this illicit trade with Toussaint's troops occurred on the Cubans' own initiative and that they claimed falsely to trade and supply the "brigands" under orders from García. See Archbishop of Santo Domingo to Consejo de Estado, October 24, 1794, in AGS, SGU, leg. 7161.
[104] Barba, May 15 and July 11, 1794, in SHMM, CGD, reel 65, doc. no 5-4-11-1; and Lleonart to García, August 17, 1794, in AGI, Cuba, leg. 1774B.

over five months. Toussaint sent one of the dragoons back to Lleonart unarmed and with a written ultimatum: evacuate the town within two hours, or else his troops would enter with blood and fire, observing in their acts of war no distinctions of age or sex. Having for over a year ordered black auxiliaries to attack French towns, the Cuban commanders, as they had long predicted, saw the former auxiliaries turn on them. According to Lleonart, his troops resisted valiantly. Overwhelmed by a lack of resources, by the enemy's numerical superiority, and by the mounting rate of civilian and military casualties among the Spanish, Lleonart called a meeting of high-ranking officers and notable civilians of the town and opted to evacuate.[105] In his account, and that of his predecessor Armona, their withdrawal was wise and honorable: they protected innocent residents from sure and savage death at the hands of the invading forces. No act captured the worthiness of their regiments' actions, they reported, as aptly as the valiant efforts of a Havana Regiment cadet, Martín Rubio, who risked his life to save the sacred paraphernalia from the altar of the town church just ahead of the entry of Toussaint's troops.[106]

In powerful accounts, the governor and other witnesses, however, cast the evacuation as something else entirely. Supported by detailed declarations of dozens and dozens of local residents, they insisted that the evacuation had been unnecessary, cowardly, and premeditated.[107] Everyone in town knew, locals testified, that the Cuban officers had already sent their baggage ahead to other towns, and even joked openly about how they only kept with them two changes of clothes, so ready were they

[105] For accounts of the attack and withdrawal, see "Causa contra el Brigadier D. Matías de Armona..." AGI, Cuba, leg. 1774B; Juan Lleonart, "Relación del ataque que hizo el General Toussaint Louverture de San Raphael, San Miguel y Villa de Hincha"; Lleonart to Conde de Campo de Alange, December 19, 1794, and February 22, 1795; "Confesión de Matías de Armona," August 19, 1795; and "Cabeza, pie y conclusión de la Declaración del Brigadier Dn. Matías de Armona," March 1795, all in AGS, SGU, leg. 6855; José María de la Torre to Lleonart, November 8, 1795, in "Oficios y documentos presentados por D. Juan Lleonart," in AGI, Cuba, leg. 170A. See also Barba, "Relación de lo ocurrido en la frontera del Oeste el 16 del pasado," November 25, 1794, and "Copia de la intimación al Gral. D. Juan Leonar [sic] por el Tusén rebelde," both in SHMM, CGD, reel 65, doc no. 5-4-11-1. Boville's service record and details of his captivity appear in AGMS, EP, B-3311. D Jose Maria Boville.

[106] Lleonart to Conde del Campo de Alange, February 22, 1795, in AGS, SGU, leg. 6855.

[107] For this opposing view, see especially García to Consejo de Estado, October 25, 1794, and Archbishop to Consejo de Estado, November 24, 1794, both in AGS, SGU, leg 7161. The colonial state gathered testimony from over fifty witnesses, many if not most of whom criticized the actions of Lleonart and the Cuban leadership and troops. The testimony appears in "Causa contra el Brigadier D. Matías de Armona..." in AGI, Cuba, leg. 1774B.

to leave the vulnerable town of San Rafael. The archbishop and others argued that the enemy had barely shown his face when Lleonart ordered the evacuation; that he had his troops fire at no one in particular before the enemies' arrival, only to run away when they finally appeared. The archbishop further claimed that the Cuban troops (as in Bayajá) participated in looting and took from local Spanish residents the treasures they were trying to save in their flight. In this telling, not only did the cadets from the Havana Regiment not save the sacred artifacts of the church, they actually appropriated them from an indignant priest for their own profit. It was no wonder that local Spanish residents, he argued, had begun to say that their "true enemies [were] the Spanish soldiers and officers."[108]

After the dramatic flight from San Rafael, the Cuban commanders quickly ordered the evacuation of the nearby towns of San Miguel and Hincha, both also Spanish since the sixteenth century. The Spanish were outraged and greeted news of the losses with accusation and blame laying (Figures 3.3 and 3.4).

It was the governor's view that held sway, at least immediately. Lleonart, Armona, and four other officers from the Cuban regiments were arrested, held for months in a fort in the capital city, and then court-martialed.[109] The court-martial of these six officers of the Havana and Santiago regiments captured perfectly the conflicts and contradictions in the relationship of the Spanish empire to the Haitian Revolution. Those immediately responsible for the decision to surrender the towns naturally defended their actions. But in their testimonies and defense, they also crystallized a sharp critique of Spain's policy *vis à vis* the revolution of slaves, echoing the one that they had already expressed on the ground and in close contact with the black auxiliaries. Above all, Lleonart and Armona made the case that the blame needed to be placed squarely at the feet of the man who designed the policy to begin with: Governor García. His whole military campaign against France relied almost

---

[108] Archbishop to Consejo de Estado, November 24, 1794, in AGS, SGU, leg 7161; and Archbishop to Conde de Campo de Alange, August 24, 1795, in SHMM, Ultramar, Santo Domingo, leg. 5646. In fact, much of the testimony taken from local residents, including the parish priest, does corroborate the story of Rubio saving the church valuables. See "Causa contra el Brigadier D. Matías de Armona, el Coronel Lleonart ... " AGI, Cuba, leg. 1774B.

[109] Barba, " Continuación de lo ocurrido en esta Ysla en este mes de Diciembre de 1794," in SHMM, CGD, reel 65, doc. no 5-4-11-1; Archbishop to Conde del Campo de Alange, January 2, 1795, in AGS, SGU, leg. 7151; and Armona to Manuel del Barrio y Armona, et al., February 9, 1795, in AGS, SGU, leg. 6855.

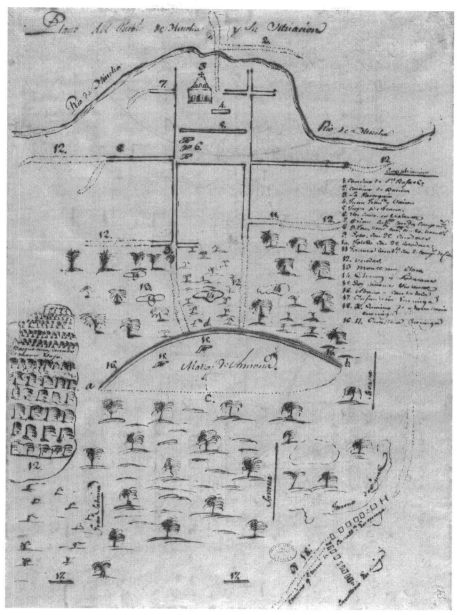

FIGURE 3.4. Map of Hincha by Matías de Armona, 1795. It shows the road to San Rafael (1) and the situation of the Santiago and Havana regiments (11 and 16, respectively). The location of the enemy infantry and cavalry are marked 17 and 18, respectively. The legend identifies 4 simply as Jean-François and Biassou. Archivo General de Indias, Mapas y Planos, Santo Domingo, 580. Courtesy of Archivo General de Indias.

exclusively on the black auxiliary forces. That reliance made the Spanish highly vulnerable not only in the face of their French enemy but also in relation to their own black allies. The more the Spanish provided by way of arms and munitions, the more potentially vulnerable they were. This had reached the point of absurdity. Toussaint, who was clearly in the French camp, continued to receive provisions, safe-conducts, and respect from the Spanish up to the eve of his attack on San Rafael. So too with Jean-François, who while loyal to Spain had still attacked the town of Bayajá. Indeed, he continued to receive honors and even silver medals for some of his officers.[110] Simply put, a total dependence on an ill-conceived alliance doomed the governor's "illusory [and] chimerical" project.[111]

Not only was the project ill-conceived, they suggested, it was ineptly managed from above. The financial and military weakness of the Spanish government in Santo Domingo made it impossible for the Cuban regiments to comply with all the promises made by the governor to the white French in newly captured towns. They were supposed to receive stipends from the governor, funds for which were not available. Facing deafening complaints, the governor acceded to their desire to resettle on their old plantations, a policy that all the commanders on the ground knew would fail because of the consternation and outrage it would create among the black auxiliaries. This had been the pattern in both Gonaïves and Bayajá.

All these problems, argued Lleonart and Armona, were clear on the ground and almost from their arrival. Duty had bound them to inform the governor. But so invested was he in the project of his design that he refused to listen. He failed to reply, or replied in ways that did not address the problems they enumerated. Thus, when Lleonart reported on the attack on Gonaïves by Toussaint's troops and speculated with solid foundation that Toussaint had switched sides, the governor only chastised him, saying that his very doubt might push Toussaint into the arms of the French. When Armona wrote in despair that everything had gone to hell, García quickly accepted his resignation. But rather than replace him with the next logical choice, Colonel Joaquín Cabrera, who knew both the region and the auxiliaries well, the governor chose instead Juan Lleonart, who had arrived from Cuba only days before and who was "without any notion

---

[110] Besides the declarations cited earlier from AGS, SGU, leg. 6855, see García to Conde de Campo de Alange, April 23, 1795, in AGS, SGU, leg. 7151.

[111] Armona to Manuel del Barrio y Armona, et al., February 9, 1795, in AGS, SGU, leg. 6855. The arguments discussed in these paragraphs are condensed from the many letters and documents provided by Armona and Lleonart in their defense, most of them from AGS, SGU, leg. 6855 and AGI, Cuba, leg. 170A.

of this Island, its frontiers, and these enemies."[112] It was, they suggested, as if García, finally beginning to perceive the magnitude of the failure, was already reaching for a scapegoat. Lleonart and Armona rejected the blame, turning it around and impugning the governor's judgment.

Finally, in the court-martial, Lleonart and Armona mounted a spirited defense, drowning the prosecutors in thousands of pages of documents to cast doubt on the accusations against them. Among them was a document given to Lleonart by José María de la Torre of the Havana Regiment, who happened to be his son-in-law and whose father was being tried alongside Lleonart. The younger de la Torre had been taken as prisoner of war by black republican forces during García's aborted assault on Le Cap in spring 1794. During the court-martial following the San Rafael evacuations, de la Torre went out of his way to clear the names of his commanders and his father. Shortly after the peace treaty was signed and the Spanish side of the island had been ceded to France, he traveled to Le Cap, met with Governor Etienne Laveaux, and requested information – from a French perspective – on the disputed events of October 1794. Laveaux provided a kind of synthesis based on the reports of Toussaint, in which the number of soldiers attacking the Spanish was put at 4,800, and in which the Spanish heartily defended their post and caused Toussaint the loss of almost 200 men. Never, said the French report, had their troops encountered such a challenge.[113]

It would be impossible for us now to verify one or another account. The court-martial, in essence, sought to fix the blame for the ultimate loss of the entire Spanish colony. But it was also implicitly a retrospective trial on the larger policy of working though rebel slaves to arrive at Spanish ends: the defeat of the regicide French, the reunification of Hispaniola under Spanish rule, the destruction of the most prosperous rival colony of the hemisphere. The trial crystallized the limits of that policy, which had assumed – incorrectly – that local Spanish commanders could contain and ultimately subdue the forces mobilized by Jean-François, Biassou, and Toussaint.

[112] Armona to Manuel del Barrio y Armona, et al., February 9, 1795, in AGS, SGU, leg. 6855.

[113] Joseph María de la Torre to Lleonart, Bayajá, November 8, 1795, enclosing "Extracto de los diarios recividos por Estevan Laveaux General de la Ysla Francesa de la América a Sotovento de los acaecimientos relativos a la toma de San Miguel y de San Rafael," 12 Brumaire año 4, in "Oficios y Documentos presentados por D. Juan Lleonart," AGI, Cuba, leg. 170A. The enclosure is a copy of a translation of an alleged original. As with the translation of Toussaint's ultimatum of October, we have no way to prove its authenticity.

If the trial offers a window into that policy and its failure, it also reveals competing visions of the future of the Spanish empire. Dominican leaders had sought an alliance with black leaders in the service of Spanish interests, but they also appeared to take very seriously the rebels' oaths to the king and, in turn, the inviolability of the obligations incurred by the king and his representatives. García requested more silver medals for Jean-François's most worthy officers, and with the war and the colony lost to France, he reminded Madrid of their government's obligations to these men and their forces. García's vision was an old-regime one of incorporation, in which black men served the king and received privileges and honor for their service.[114]

A different vision, however, emerged among the Spanish officers arriving from Cuba. From the start, they saw the policy as ill-advised. They arrived from a colony making a full-fledged transition to plantation agriculture organized around slave labor and export production. The war brought them to a frontier region where former slaves set the agenda, commanded as generals, and were addressed as such by high-ranking Spanish officials. They tried to go through the motions, but they did so, they confessed, with significant loss of pride. And everywhere they revealed their commitment to a vision of a different kind of colony, as they amassed money, slaves, and sugar equipment to send back to a rising plantation world in Cuba. Local residents of the Spanish border towns lambasted the Cuban men for their efforts to convert the local spoils of war into sugar profits in Cuba. Their testimonies quote at length all the negative things the Cubans had said about the colony of Santo Domingo. According to one witness, "Among all the men from Havana and Santiago it was common to hear it said that the King would not regret the loss of this Island, which gave him nothing and cost him much." Such attacks, said the Dominicans, constituted an attack on the king himself.[115]

---

[114] García to Conde del Campo de Alange, April 23, 1795, in AGS, SGU, leg. 7151; and García to Príncipe de la Paz, October 21, November 9, and December 17, 1795, in AHN, Estado, leg. 3407.

[115] See the testimony in AGI, Cuba, leg. 1774; quote is from f. 44. See also Domingo de Ugarte to Conde del Campo de Alange, June 25, 1795, in AGS, SGU, leg. 6855. Ugarte was Armona's defender in the trial and a captain in the Havana Regiment. Unsigned to Luis de las Casas, Aranjuez, January 24, 1796, in AGS, SGU, leg 6855. While some of the Dominican residents and leaders took offense at the Cuban officers' disparaging remarks about their colony's lack of value, the Cuban view seemed to echo the thinking that had already emerged in Madrid. For example, Manuel Godoy, the Minister of State who negotiated the 1795 peace treaty, believed that the loss of Spanish Santo Domingo represented little if any sacrifice, as the cost of maintaining the colony outweighed

Joaquín García had put the Cuban commanders on trial as a way to avoid an indictment of his own policy. But in the process, two opposing visions came face to face: one represented by García and his insistence on the sanctity of the ties that bound the monarchy to the slaves it had armed; the other represented by the Cuban commanders, whose vision was much more in line with the emergent model of plantation slavery from which they had come.

Leaving Santo Domingo

With the end of the war, these visions came into open conflict, with the monarchy itself stuck in the middle. News of peace between Spain and France and the cession of the eastern part of the island to France arrived in Santo Domingo in October 1795. García immediately drew attention to the fate of the black auxiliaries. He noted with distress that none of the manuscript copies of the treaty that had arrived contained the slightest mention of what would happen to them. In late October, Jean-François and his men turned in some of their arms at Bayajá and, like the governor, prepared to await orders.[116] But the presence of large numbers of black troops loyal to Spain in the context of a peace governed by France seemed to García potentially explosive. On his own, without waiting for orders, García resolved to send the men to Havana and to let the governor there determine where to locate them. On November 9, he wrote to Governor Luis de Las Casas, reminding him that as Spanish authorities they were "committed to them solemnly and with the King's approval." He explained the dangers these men posed in a Santo Domingo in the process of being evacuated and ceded to France. And he reported their imminent transfer to Havana with the confidence and casualness of common sense.[117]

In Havana, the news was received otherwise. Word of the forthcoming influx arrived piecemeal. First, in a letter from the governor in Santo Domingo, Las Casas read that he would soon face the notorious Jean-François and his staff. Then, from two officers of the Havana Regiment recently returned from Santo Domingo, he heard that the

---

any benefit to Spain. See Manuel Godoy, *Memorias* (Madrid: Atlas 1965 [1836]), 1: 104, 110; and Godoy to Marqués del Socorro, April 12, 1795, in AHN, Estado, leg. 883, 1a parte, exp. 16.

[116] A. Ocarol, Comandante del Apostadero de Bayajá, to Juan Araoz, Comandante Principal de la Marina de la Habana, October 27, 1795, in AHN, Ultramar (Santo Domingo), leg. 2776, exp. 7, doc, no. 1.

[117] García to Las Casas, November 9, 1795, in AHN, Estado, leg. 3407.

transfer was not just of a few officers but of hundreds of members of the black army.[118] News of the impending arrivals from Saint-Domingue was spreading rapidly all over Havana. White residents, the governor reported, imagined the certain rebellion of their slaves. Black residents, meanwhile, began organizing events to honor and receive the black generals.[119]

The Havana city council met and appealed to the governor to refuse entry to the arriving black army. The governor wrote urgently to Madrid, sparing no reference to the likely destruction that would ensue from the resettlement of the black auxiliaries in Cuba. The rising economic power of Havana and the Cuban colony was much too promising to subject it to such a risk. The reaction of Havana authorities exemplified perfectly a recurring and convenient retort of the Cuban colonial state – intimately tied to the interests of sugar – in the face of the Haitian Revolution. Paramount was the categorical prediction of turmoil on Cuban soil if the example of Haiti was not contained. The arrival of Jean-François and the others became the harbinger of "the same sad Catastrophe as in the fields and cities of Guarico." Not only did authorities need to fear direct contact between the black military figures and local slaves, but the very presence of the former was a menace. It would inevitably lead local slaves to dangerous conclusions. Wrote the Cuban governor:

A servant, who is looking at another one already freed from slavery, occupying an honorable position, having arrived at this happy state by virtue of infidelity to his master, will have in that image a powerful incentive to choose the same perfidy. He will reflect on how that same man had he stayed faithful to his master would still remain in slavery, and from that he will conclude that insurrection is a means to shake off so heavy a yoke.[120]

The governor insisted that the very *sight* of the black auxiliaries – "miserable slaves yesterday, today heroes of a revolution, triumphant, opulent, decorated" – constituted a threat to public order. He continued:

Nothing engraves itself in the minds of most men with as much intensity as those perceptions received by the sense of sight. And it is not easy to predict the depths of the impression made, or the potential trouble among the rabble [*populacho*]

[118] Las Casas to García, December 17, 1795, in AGI, Estado, leg. 5A, exp. 24.
[119] Las Casas to Príncipe de la Paz, December 16, 1795, in AGI, Estado, leg. 5B, exp. 176; and José Luciano Franco, *La conspiración de Aponte* (Havana: Consejo Nacional de Cultura, 1963), 10.
[120] Las Casas to Príncipe de la Paz, December 16, 1795, in AGI, Estado, leg. 5B, exp. 176; and Cabildo ordinario, December 4, 1795, in AHOHCH, AC, tomo 54, ff. 204v–205.

of people of color caused by the presence of Jean-François, decorated with the sash that serves as the insignia of the Generals of the Army and Armada of the King, with a great following of his subaltern generals and brigadiers, outfitted in the symbols corresponding to the ranks they have been given, showing off with astonishing pomp a magnificent coach of six horses ... much superior to anything this public has ever seen even among the Captain-General of the island, nor others among the most distinguished persons of these regions. Putting in plain sight of a public in which the number of slaves is so large a subject of this nature, whose name resounds in the ears of the masses like that of an invincible hero, redeemer of slaves; introducing him [here] in an age where everywhere resounds the voice of liberty and everywhere sprout the seeds of insurrection, would be the same as exposing our countryside to a shock of perhaps powerful consequences.[121]

The governor surely exaggerated, giving free rein to his imagination to paint a picture of the black general surrounded by luxury and indulgence in plain sight of Cuban slaves. It is curious, however, that Las Casas volunteered that people in Havana thought of the black general in such heroic terms, as "a redeemer of slaves." Jean-François had, after all, fought on the side that lost the war. He had sold free people as slaves and had sided with a Spanish monarchy that recognized slavery over a French republic that did not. Despite this apparent discrepancy, the figure of Jean-François would continue to resonate as a symbol for future black conspirators in Cuba.[122]

In 1795, however, everyone close to the governor in Havana shared his conviction that the black army had to be turned away: the members of the town council, the Real Consulado, local sugar planters, and members of the Cuban regiments, who had just fought in Saint-Domingue with these same black allies. Each group seconded the Cuban governor's insistence on refusal.

The Marqués de Casa Calvo, the Spanish commander of Bayajá, the man who had allegedly paid court to Jean-François's wife and had accumulated sugar machinery from Saint-Domingue to send back to Havana, wrote directly to the governor with a warning that was hard to ignore. These men, he said, believed themselves equal – indeed superior – to the Spanish. He had felt forced to treat them as such because the war necessitated the alliance and because the governor and king had so ordered. But now, with the war over, those privileges needed to end. The auxiliaries had left Santo Domingo, he wrote, "full of the flattering idea that they would be settled in Havana and enjoy [there] the same distinctions,

---

[121] Las Casas to Príncipe de la Paz, December 16, 1795, in AGI, Estado, leg. 5B, exp. 176.
[122] See Chapter 7.

prerogatives, luxury and indulgence [as in Santo Domingo].... Could I be ... so bad a Vassal of the King, so ungrateful a son to my Country, as to propose such an absurdity?" He then urged the Cuban governor

> not to lodge or settle in the bosom of the flourishing island of Cuba, loyal and faithful to her King, nor within the boundaries of Havana, these venomous vipers.... I am almost an eyewitness to the disgraceful day of the 7th [of July], I am as well of the desolation of this whole Colony, and I have stepped on the vestiges of their fury. They are, even if painted with different colors, the same ones who assassinated their Masters, raped their Mistresses, and destroyed all who had property on this soil at the beginning of the insurrection. Why more reflections, if with these alone the human heart is horrified.[123]

In fact, the Cuban governor had already arrived at the same conclusion: he would not grant the black auxiliaries entry to Havana. He quickly sent a ship to Bayajá to impede the black army's embarkation for his island. But it arrived too late, and the hundreds of black men in question were already en route to Havana. On January 8, 1796, Biassou appeared in Havana aboard the *San Lorenzo* with an entourage of twenty-three. A day later, three boats arrived carrying Jean-François and 780 others, slightly under half of them women and children. Immediately, the governor convened a meeting of his top-ranking military men, and then, reflecting the gravity of the situation, twice again on January 11 and 14. Together they decided that Jean-François and his top officers would be sent across the Atlantic to Cádiz, the most important port in Spain's colonial trade. The rest would be dispersed and sent to Florida, Mexico, Guatemala, and the island of Trinidad, still Spanish in 1796. All this Governor Las Casas decided without authorization from the king, motivated by a fear and conviction that made the decision unassailable in his eyes. He found some solace and foundation in the royal order of May 1790, which had prohibited the entrance on the island of blacks from the French colonies, or of any other person capable of spreading dangerous ideas.[124] The risk of possibly overstepping his authority paled in comparison to the sure peril he associated with the entry and settlement of the black army in Cuba.

This decision, so sound in his own view, brought him into heated dispute with Governor García in Santo Domingo. Here again, the competing visions of colonial development that were already in conflict in the

[123] Casa Calvo to Las Casas, December 31, 1795, in AGI, Cuba, leg. 1474.
[124] Las Casas to García, December 17, 1795, in AGI, Estado, leg. 5A, exp. 24; Las Casas to Príncipe de la Paz, January 25, 1796, in AGI, Cuba, leg. 1489; Barba to Francisco Savatini, January 25, 1796, in SHMM, CGD, reel 65, doc no. 5–4–11–2.

war-torn frontier of Hispaniola reemerged. García challenged all of Las Casas's objections, insisting that the auxiliaries, if given land and religious guidance from priests of "good character," would be valuable vassals, submissive and productive. Indeed, the future that García imagined for the auxiliaries may not have been that different from the one imagined by Jean-François himself in his many dealings with Spanish authorities in Santo Domingo, Cuba, and eventually Cádiz. Jean-François expressed his desire to stay with his men and together form a community of small farmers and artisans, who would be always ready to defend king and nation when called to do so by Spanish authorities.[125] But for Las Casas, one of whose principal endeavors in Havana was to facilitate the hegemony of slave-based sugar production, there was little room for this kind of community on his territory. The risks were, he concluded, too great, and the payoff minimal compared to that offered by the system he was helping to erect in Cuba.

This dispute notwithstanding, there they were – 780 men and women with Jean-François alone, among them almost three dozen decorated black officers in full uniform. Jean-François asked to stay in Havana, if not permanently then at least until the priest José Vázquez arrived. Las Casas denied the request. Jean-François then suggested traveling to Santo Domingo to meet with and receive orders directly from Governor García. Las Casas denied that request as well, reminding the black general that he was bound to follow the orders of the king, no matter who conveyed them. Waiting for a final decision about his destination, Jean-François demanded in frustration that the Cuban governor clarify their situation: were they vassals of the king of Spain or prisoners of the state?[126]

Jean-François and his companions remained in this uncertain state in Havana harbor for two weeks, at which time he sailed with his twelve most important officers and their families and dependents for the Spanish port of Cádiz. Over the next several months the rest of the group were sent to Campeche, Trujillo, Florida, and Portobelo; the last 86 members

[125] García to Las Casas, January 25, 1796, in AGI, Cuba, leg. 1474. Jean-François's vision of this kind of future emerges piecemeal. See, for example, the description of the conversation between Jean-François and Ignacio Maria de la Torre in the latter's letter to Casa Calvo, Dajabón, September 25, 1794, and Casa Calvo to Las Casas, December 31, 1795, both in AGI, Cuba, leg. 1474; and the numerous letters from the governor of Cádiz after Jean-François's arrival there, in AGI, Estado, leg. 3, exp. 10.

[126] Jean-François to Monsiuer le Colonel [Francisco Montalvo], January 12, 1796 in AGI, Cuba, leg. 1489; Las Casas to Príncipe de la Paz, January 25, 1796, in AGI, Estado, leg. 5A, exp. 28. See also AGI, Estado, leg. 5A, exp. 23.

of the group were not deported from Havana until August 23, 1796, after more than an eight-month stay.[127]

Little is known of the black auxiliaries' day-to-day life during their Havana sojourn. While authorities had reported that the city's black *cabildos*, ethnic African brotherhoods, had planned festivities to welcome and celebrate the black heroes, no record of such a celebration, if it in fact occurred, has survived. Historian José Luciano Franco wrote that authorities confined the hundreds of black combatants to their ships, and that no contact was established between the auxiliaries and local people of color. But we cannot know for sure. The ships were anchored at a spot in the bay between the Morro castle and Casa Blanca, a modest but growing maritime settlement across Havana harbor, where ships often anchored for repairs and layovers, and where black sailors, artisans, and petty merchants were a common sight. Interactions would have been hard to police there. If Cuban authorities did not provision the men with food, local people may well have come out on small boats to sell supplies to those on the ships, and perhaps to trade in material artifacts of the revolution from the neighboring colony. More than a decade later, in 1811–12, when some of these same men passed through Havana again (this time on their way back to Santo Domingo), they did indeed have contact with the black and mulatto communities of Havana. That contact occurred as part of the routine of daily life in a busy port, and only came to light later as part of the investigation into a subsequent conspiracy among slaves and free people of color. In the extensive investigation into that conspiracy, many of the free suspects of color testified that some of the most damning evidence against them – printed images of Haitian leaders, for instance – had been acquired at the docks precisely during the evacuation of Bayajá, suggesting that these revolutionary portraits may have been exchanged by black auxiliaries and local residents of Havana in 1796 when Jean-François and his men were there.[128] Whether or not actual contact occurred, the troops were there for some time, sitting in the harbor, visible to many Havana residents, perhaps especially so to the communities of urban slaves and free people of color who frequented the docks.

With the cession of Santo Domingo to France, other former residents of the colony arrived in Havana as well. One Spanish officer had the

[127] Las Casas to Príncipe de la Paz, February 22, 1796; Las Casas to Ministro de Guerra, March 11, 1796; and Las Casas to Ministro de Estado, September 2, 1796, all in AGI, Cuba, leg. 1489.

[128] See Chapter 7.

foresight to send the remains of the body of Admiral Christopher Columbus. Several orders of nuns eager to elude French rule also made their way
to the Cuban capital.[129] These postwar arrivals only continued a pattern
already established during the war, in which some of the movable spoils
of the war had found their way from the Spanish/French frontier of Santo
Domingo to the island of Cuba – from the French prisoners of war, who
would be guarded in Havana by members of the free black and mulatto
(*pardo*) militias of the city, to the French "slaves," so eagerly and illegally
purchased by Cuban officers.[130]

Starting in late 1795, Spanish residents who chose not to continue living in the colony once power was transferred to the French began leaving
in sizeable numbers. More than four thousand would arrive in Cuba in
the decade following the cession of the colony. The first wave of migrants
consisted largely of property owners and slaveholders. With them arrived
sizable entourages of slaves, some legitimately Spanish, others transferred
from Saint-Domingue. Of the 633 Santo Domingo migrants who arrived
in Havana in January 1796, 476 were people of color. The colonial
government in Havana resolved to investigate and to expel those who
might conceivably pose a threat. It also established a junta (presided over
by Francisco Arango himself) charged with helping the new (free) residents by providing pensions, jobs, and other assistance. Rural settlements
(*colonias*) were established, with plots of land given to the refugees, in
the hopes not only of providing aid but also of helping to populate areas
of Cuba perceived to be dangerously low on population. Many of these
migrants arrived penniless, telling stories of lives and fortunes lost to the
revolution in Saint-Domingue.[131]

The Spanish and Cuban military men who had traveled to and participated in the Haitian Revolution were among the first to make their
way back to Havana. In November 1795, the court-martial of Armona,
Lleonart, and the officers of the Cuban regiments was transferred to
Havana; thus arrived the accused, the lawyers, and apparently incomplete

---

[129] On the transfer of the nuns and Columbus's remains, see Archbishop, December 21,
1795, in Archivo del Ministerio de Asuntos Exteriores, Madrid (AMAE), Política Exte-
rior, República Dominicana, leg. 2372.

[130] Las Casas to Príncipe de la Paz, January 3, 1796, in AGI, Estado, leg. 5A, exp. 22.

[131] Las Casas to Príncipe de la Paz, November 14, 1795, and April 5, 1796, both in AGI,
Cuba, leg. 1489. Two important sources for the study of this migration are AMAE,
Política, República Dominicana, leg. 2372, and AGI, Cuba, leg. 1693. For a useful
overview and a brief discussion of the 633 migrants arriving in January 1796, see Carlos
Esteban Deive, *Las emigraciones dominicanas a Cuba (1795–1808)* (Santo Domingo,
Fundación Cultural Dominicana, 1989), pp. 7–8, 21–25.

sets of all the relevant papers, which – even incomplete – numbered in the thousands of pages. The accused remained under house arrest in Havana, and the business of the court-martial continued. With the transfer, the tone of the proceedings shifted. In Havana, defense lawyers criticized the very manner in which the trial had been conducted in Santo Domingo, where testimony taken from slaves, people of color, and women was given weight equal to that taken from Spanish military officers and soldiers.[132]

About half a year later, the bulk of the soldiers and officers of the Cuban regiments returned, in an evacuation organized by the Cuban commander in Bayajá, the Marqués de Casa Calvo, and the Admiral Gabriel Aristizábal, in apparent violation of García's order that they remain in Santo Domingo.[133] While still in Santo Domingo during wartime, they had sent back material and artifacts, and we can assume that they did the same on returning definitively. But, if nothing else, they returned having seen and taken part in one of the most important and dramatic events of their lifetime. They had been allies and commanders of armed black men recently escaped or liberated from slavery. They had participated in waging the same war. They had dined together, they had traded together, and, in the end, many had faced off against (or fled from) some of those former allies.

The military officers returned to a Havana already well aware of the war in which they had participated. Collections to support the Spanish cause in Saint-Domingue had been taken up routinely in churches and among artisan guilds and city neighborhoods, and notices soliciting donations had been posted across the city.[134] French prisoners of war captured by the Cuban and Spanish officers had been sent to Havana, where, though imprisoned in the city's fortresses, they had some limited freedom to move around the city – often guarded by the city's free colored militia. They piqued the interest of local residents as they bought food and other supplies from vendors and artisans in city markets. Some of the prisoners appear to have had contact with well-heeled Havana residents, who sometimes petitioned for French prisoners with knowledge of sugar-making technology in Saint Domingue to be pardoned and allowed to

---

[132] García to Las Casas, November 26, 1795, in AGI, Cuba, 1474, and "Causa contra Matías Armona...," especially Domingo Ugarte's defense, starting f. 958.

[133] See Las Casas to Ministro de Guerra, June 24, 1796, in AGI, Cuba, leg. 1489, and García to Miguel de Azanza, July 18, 1796, in AGS, SGU, leg. 7161.

[134] See, for example, Vaillant to Las Casas, June 8 and July 27, 1793, in AGI, Cuba, leg. 1434.

establish residence and work on local sugar estates.[135] Through word of mouth and the press, news of the war in which their countrymen participated was already well known in Havana. And in a city where the names of Jean-François and Biassou resounded, said the governor, like the names of great conquerors or dreaded villains, residents certainly would have been keen to find out more from the direct witnesses now returning.[136]

Even before his return to Cuba, Matías Armona had written to friends and family members of meals with black generals, insisting that he engaged the black officers as "equals" – not out of conviction, he clarified, but out of necessity. Letters written to his nephews and other relatives offered scathing attacks on the conduct of war in Santo Domingo and on the ill-conceived policies that he said accounted for the end of Spanish rule in Hispaniola.[137] He returned to Havana in November 1795 as a nobleman under the cloud of a court-martial, heavily indebted, but hoping to pay off his creditors with sugar produced in his mill.[138] Perhaps he spent his evenings at his house on Oficios Street, sitting on the large porch, sharing stories with the Barba family next door, one of whose members, while stationed as engineer in Bayajá, had lamented the close contact between their forces and black military and civilians. Armona's son, who followed in his footsteps as a high-ranking officer in the colonial army, earned a name for himself as the commander of a band of sixty men commissioned to chase criminals and maintain the peace in the countryside around Havana in the early 1820s, a task that might have had particular meaning for him given his father's stories of the ultimate disorder in a society that in many ways resembled the rapidly transformed countryside around Havana.[139]

---

[135] On prisoners being guarded by militias of color, see Havana intendant José Pablo Valiente to Diego Gardoqui, April 7, 1794, in AGS, SGU, leg. 6852. On petitions regarding French prisoners involved in sugar, see, for example, "Sr. D. Nicolás Calvo pide que se recomiende al Gobierno los extrangeros D. Julián Lardiere y D. Juan de Lage," November 11, 1795, in ANC, RCJF, leg. 201, exp. 8915. For discussion of other similar petitions, see Actas de Sesiones de la Junta de Gobierno del Real Consulado, in ANC, RCJF, libro 161, passim.

[136] Las Casas to Príncipe de la Paz, December 16, 1795, in AGI, Estado, leg. 5B, exp. 176.

[137] His letters to Armona family members appear in AGS, SGU, leg. 6855.

[138] See ANC, Escribanía de Guerra, leg. 889, exp. 19327, and leg. 891, exp. 13357.

[139] See AGMS, EP, 1a Seccion-1a División, leg. A-2380; for his and his family's position in Havana, see *Historia de familias cubanas*, 5:33–38; Calcagno, *Diccionario biográfico cubano*; AHOHCH, AC, March 23, 1786 and March 1, 1792, tomo 51, f. 69v.; and ANC, Escribania de Guerra, leg 889, exp. 13327, and leg. 891, exp. 13377.

The Marqués de Casa Calvo had participated in the Spanish siege on Bayajá and became the town's commander shortly after the massacre of July 7, 1794. Brother of Nicolás Calvo, often referred to as the island's second most important sugar planter, and owner himself of two sugar plantations, the Marqués had connections to the world of Havana sugar that were readily visible in his comportment in Santo Domingo. He had been accused of engaging in suspicious, even immoral, trade with the black troops, purchasing sugar equipment that they had apparently taken from French victims (even as their corpses still steamed, alleged one critic). The Marqués had then shipped the equipment to Havana. From French subjects brought under Spanish rule at Bayajá, he had purchased men and women to send back to Havana as slaves. When the troops of Jean-François were evacuated, Casa Calvo appeared also to have accepted the commission of selling for the black general a substantial number of horses, cows, and pack animals, in order to remit the money to him later. In 1803, Jean-François was complaining from Cádiz, Spain, where he lived the last years of his life, that Casa Calvo had taken the animals and never remitted any money. Jean-François makes no mention of the sale of people as part of that transaction, but the behavior of both men in and after Santo Domingo leaves room for speculation.[140]

Whatever the dimensions of the profiteering that Casa Calvo engaged in, he was indisputably a wealthy Havana native from the booming world of sugar and slavery who had found himself suddenly the governor of a formerly French and now Spanish town reeling from a violent massacre just days before. It had fallen to him to reestablish order, to try to ensure the loyalty of the remaining auxiliaries, and to stave off actual attacks from external enemies (Toussaint) and potential ones from supposed friends (Jean-François). Just remaining in the town, he said, required living in "a constant state of war." Under his rule, the Spanish forces had regular – and perhaps symbolically freighted – contact with the black auxiliaries. Casa Calvo referred to Jean-François as his godson; Jean-François

---

[140] The accusations regarding the purchase and shipment of sugar equipment appear in Archbishop of Santo Domingo to [Consejo de Estado], October 24 and November 24, 1794, both in AGS, SGU, leg. 7161; and Barba, "Continuación de lo ocurrido en esta Ysla," September 25, 1794, in "Relación de los ocurrido en la Ysla de Santo Domingo con motivo de la guerra con los franceses," in SHMM, CGD, Reel 65, doc no. 5-4-11-1. On the purchase of slaves from French prisoners of war, see the various lists of people sold and sent to Havana, February 1794, in AHN, Ultramar, legajo 6209, box 2, exp. 49. On his responsibility for selling goods on behalf of Jean-François, see Jean-François to Excellent Seigneur, May 10, 1803, in AGI, Estado, leg. 3, exp. 10.

addressed Casa Calvo as his dear godfather. In Bayajá, under Casa Calvo's command, the members of the Cuban expeditionary force – unlike the earlier and much smaller French garrison of the town, who had largely confined themselves to the fortifications – associated with the black and mulatto residents of the area. And there, in the waning days of war, Casa Calvo reported repeated rumors of other July 7ths. In his mind, and among those who spread and reported the rumors, the massacre, the conflagration, was – as Haiti itself would later be – eminently repeatable.[141]

Casa Calvo may or may not have relayed these experiences in the letters he appears to have written home to his mother, the countess of Buenavista. Did he tell her, for instance, about his cousin, José Santiago Justiz, who was one of the men taken as a prisoner of war in the preamble to Toussaint's attack on San Rafael in October 1794? At the very least, given the world in which he moved in Havana and the depth of his experiences in the lands of the Haitian Revolution, he was surely asked to elaborate in person after his return.[142]

Much less is known about Juan Lleonart, Armona's successor and the man most responsible for the decision to abandon the towns of San Rafael, San Miguel, and Hincha as Toussaint attacked in October 1794. He too had significant contact with the black troops, as did some of his close relatives. Lleonart's son, Juan Bautista Lleonart y Echevarría, accompanied him on the campaign to Santo Domingo, where he accumulated thousands of pesos that he sent back to Havana in currency and merchandise. When Lleonart y Echevarría died in Havana in 1827, he left an estate that included twenty-five slaves, at least one of whom he may have acquired during his time on the Spanish frontier of Saint-Domingue, for even his father conceded that the younger Lleonart was involved in the illegal buying of slaves in Saint-Domingue/Santo Domingo.[143]

[141] Casa Calvo to García, September 30, 1794; Jean-François to Casa Calvo, September 24, 1794; and Casa Calvo to Jean-François, September 25, 1794, all in AGI, Cuba, leg. 1474.

[142] Justiz's story is related in García to Consejo de Estado, October 25, 1794, in AGS, SGU, leg. 6855, and Lleonart, "Relación del ataque que hizo el General Tousaint Louverture a los Pueblos de San Raphael..." 1794, in AGS, SGU, leg. 6855. His service record (AGMS, EP, leg. S-1695) shows him surviving the capture and returning to Cuba to serve as Captain in the Havana Regiment. On his connection to the Calvo family, *Historia de familias cubanas*, 2: 230–231. Casa Calvo's letter to his mother is extracted in Las Casas to Príncipe de la Paz, May 31, 1796, in AGI, Cuba, leg. 1489.

[143] On Lleonart's service, see AGMS, EP, LL-142; Lleonart to Duque de Alcudia, February 23, 1795, in AGI, Estado, leg. 18, exp. 9; and Lleonart to Conde del Campo de Alange, February 22, 1795, in AGS, SGU, leg. 6855. On his son's activities in Santo Domingo,

Lleonart shared the experience of Saint-Domingue with Antonio María de la Torre, leader of a prominent Havana family and his son's father-in-law. In the end, the elder Lleonart and de la Torre were court-martialed together for the retreat from San Rafael, San Miguel, and Hincha, and both were exonerated in Havana in 1804, though by that time de la Torre was no longer alive. Two of de la Torre's sons also went to the war of Santo Domingo. One son, Ignacio, was killed by the French during the retreat from San Rafael in October 1794. Another son, José María de la Torre, had been held captive for three days by black republican forces during the start of a projected Spanish attack on Le Cap that was aborted by Governor García in spring 1794. De la Torre survived the experience and, in the fall of 1795, he traveled to Le Cap, where he met with French governor Laveaux and received from him an official account of Toussaint's attack on San Rafael, one that he hoped would prove the worthiness of Lleonart's resistance and help exonerate him (and his father) of all charges.[144]

Like Casa Calvo, José María de la Torre had also purchased men and women from Saint-Domingue as slaves and then shipped them to Havana. Years later, back in Havana where he appears to have owned multiple farms, de la Torre's intimate contact with the Haitian Revolution continued. In early 1804, de la Torre traveled to Cádiz, where he met with his old ally and auxiliary Jean-François. We do not know who initiated the meeting nor for what purpose, nor if the two men greeted each other as friends or as old collaborators bent on settling a debt. But the outcome of their meeting seems certain: De la Torre purchased from Jean-François two people he designated as slaves. One was Tomás, 35, born in Le Cap, a member of Jean-François's troops, and part of the entourage that had traveled with him to Havana in 1796. The second was Tomás's wife, María Josefa, 28, apparently born in the Kingdom of Kongo, enslaved, and raised in French Bayajá. After the town's fall to the Spanish, she had served a mulatta woman named Marie-Françoise, who was the sister of Bernardin, one of Jean-François's officers. It was as a servant of the

Archbishop [to Consejo de Estado], November 24, 1794, in AGS, SGU, leg. 7161; and Lleonart to [?] in del Monte, *Historia de Santo Domingo*, 4: 206–207. His will appears in ANC, Escribanía de Guerra, leg. 657, exp. 10454.

[144] Antonio María de la Torre in AGMS, EP, T-772; and Joseph María de la Torre to Juan Lleonart, Bayajá, November 8, 1795, enclosing "Extracto de los diarios recividos por Estevan Laveaux General de la Ysla Francesa de la América a Sotovento de los acaecimientos relativos a la toma de San Miguel y de San Rafael," 12 Brumaire año 4, in "Oficios y Documentos presentados por D. Juan Lleonart," AGI, Cuba, leg. 170A.

family of this officer that she had traveled to Havana in 1796 and then to Cádiz, where in February 1804 she had married Tomás. She testified that it was on the "verbal order" of Jean-François that de la Torre had taken them to Havana. (Intriguingly, the black general had promised to join them there two months later). In Havana, Tomás and María Josefa served de la Torre in his house in the city. Soon after their arrival, de la Torre began making repeated threats: to cut off Tomás's hands, to sell one or both to a sugar plantation in the countryside. So the couple ran away. When they were captured by local authorities, Tomás and María Josefa protested that they were free; they had after all been followers of Jean-François, all of whom were freed by the king of Spain. Authorities avoided the issue and quickly resolved to ship them back to Cádiz at de la Torre's expense. But in typical bureaucratic fashion, the deportation took at least five years to materialize.[145]

Francisco Montalvo – wealthy Havana officer and planter – may have known or seen Tomás or María Josefa in Bayajá. He had been there on July 7 and witnessed the famous massacre; he had intervened to save the life of at least one French resident, whom he disguised as a fellow soldier. When the war was over and the evacuations began, Montalvo was given the task of accompanying the black auxiliary leaders – men he clearly identified as assassins – as they left Santo Domingo for Havana. There he served as mediator and messenger between Las Casas, who wanted nothing to do with them, and Jean-François, supremely certain of his claim to respect. In 1803, years after returning from Santo Domingo and in the midst of trying to sell one of his own sugar mills, Francisco Montalvo was again called into direct contact with the Haitian Revolution. The Cuban governor, the Marqués de Someruelos, chose him to head the effort to provide temporary refuge to the multitude of French officers and soldiers evacuating Saint-Domingue on the eve of Haitian independence. Montalvo personally arranged lodging for French soldiers and officers in a small town outside Havana. For more than two months, from late

[145] José de la Torre, in AGMS, EP, T-772. On his capture by republican troops, see "Cabeza, Pie i conclusión de la Declaración del Brigadier, D Mathías de Armona y su adicción a ella," in AGS, SGU, leg. 6855; on his meeting with Laveaux, de la Torre to Lleonart, November 6, 1795, in "Oficios y Documentos presentados por Juan Lleonart," in AGI, Cuba, 170A; on rural property in Havana, "José María e Ignacio de la Torre. Traslado de dotes," in AGS, SGU, 7227, exp. 44; on his purchase of slaves in Saint-Domingue, see AHN, Ultramar (Santo Domingo), leg. 6209, box 2, exp. 49; on his purchase of slaves from Jean-François in Cádiz, see "De oficio contra los negros Tomás y María Josefa, naturales del Guarico, sobre su introducción en esta Plaza [Havana] por el Teniente Coronel D. José María de la Torre," in AGI, Cuba, leg. 1778B.

November 1803 to early February 1804, Montalvo lived there alongside French general Jean Lavalette, 35 officers, and 279 soldiers. There, as Lavalette recovered from the physical and emotional exhaustion of his Saint-Domingue service, the two men conversed regularly about the revolution both had witnessed and about the fate of France's once-rich sugar colony.[146]

Francisco Montalvo went on to become a pivotal figure in Cuban colonial politics, ascending to a position as commander of the Spanish army on the island, a post that made him second in command only to the governor. He later played a decisive role in the 1808 defeat of the proposal to create an independent governing junta in Havana following Napoleon's usurpation of the Spanish throne. In 1809, he would be instrumental in crushing a popular rebellion against the French residents in Havana. And in 1813, he defeated a proposal by the black and colored militias to serve under officers of color. This man with direct experience of the Haitian Revolution, witness to one of its most violent massacres and reluctant collaborator of Jean-François, thus returned to Cuba to use his growing power against independence, popular mobilization, and the ascent of black military figures.[147]

In their mission to Santo Domingo, members of the political, economic, and military elite of the colony had traveled to the very scenes of the Haitian Revolution. There, they attempted to exert command over armed former slaves and their black leaders. With those men, the Cubans had contact of many kinds, both hostile and amicable. They purchased sugar-making equipment no longer needed in a world where slavery had been destroyed by these same allies. They purchased black men, women, and children to send home to Cuba. They were direct witnesses to dramatic massacres of French whites at black hands. Some were taken hostage by black forces who had earlier served as their auxiliaries; others faced their erstwhile allies on the battlefield.

Necessity made them would-be readers of black men, forcing them to try to interpret their behavior and their words as signals of things to come. In making such predictions, the commanders of the Cuban expedition found themselves forced not only to treat the allies with some measure of outward respect, but also to concede that these men whom they inwardly

---

[146] See the correspondence between Montalvo and Someruelos, January 1804, in AGI, Cuba, 1705.

[147] See Francisco Montalvo's service record, AGMS, EP, M-3747; Kuethe, *Cuba*; Sherry Johnson, *Social Transformations*.

scorned were political subjects, who read, interpreted, judged, and ultimately participated in the production of imperial politics of freedom and
governance. This contact was significant, intense, and material. Thus, the
shadow of Saint-Domingue that hung over the transformations of Cuban
slavery was very far from abstract. In Cuba, the Haitian Revolution was
not spectral; it was real.

In Saint-Domingue itself, as the revolution embraced general emancipation, the prospect of enslavement and reenslavement continued to be all
too imaginable. Former slaves, now French citizens, confronted threats
to their freedom from multiple quarters, from white royalists who hoped
to use Spain's rule to maintain or reassert their mastery, from black
insurgent leaders who were willing to sell some of them into slavery,
from ambitious Cuban officers and soldiers who were willing to overcome fears of contagion and purchase *negros franceses*. The proximity of
the Cuban sugar revolution, then, meant that the progress of revolution
and emancipation in Saint-Domingue would also have to contend with
Cuba's shadow, with the continued and indeed accelerated entrenchment
of slavery, which itself further threatened the stability of the freedom the
black revolutionaries were making.

4

Revolution's Disavowal

Cuba and a Counterrevolution of Slavery

Rain and wind on the morning of May 9, 1799, prevented Nicolás Calvo from making the journey back to Havana from his sugar estate, the *Nueva Holanda*. What might have been an uneventful morning was interrupted by the arrival of a stranger, dressed in uniform, wet and muddy from a long journey across bad roads in a downpour. The man was Salvador José de Muro y Salazar, the Marqués de Someruelos, on his way to the capital to assume his new post: governor of Havana and captain-general of the island of Cuba.[1]

It is fitting that the new governor's welcome to the island consisted of an extended visit with Nicolás Calvo at *Nueva Holanda*. Calvo was one of Cuba's richest sugar planters and the brother of the Marqués de Casa Calvo, the former commander of Bayajá. The *Nueva Holanda*, meanwhile, was the largest and most mechanized mill on the island, thanks in part to innovations introduced by its Saint-Domingue technician, Julian Lardière. No account of the conversations during Someruelos's five-day visit with Calvo has survived. We can imagine that, once the weather cleared, the new governor was treated to a tour of the impressive estate. Surely, the two men spoke about sugar and slavery and politics. Calvo may have explained his successful campaigns to buy out local tobacco growers and expand his sugar enterprise. Perhaps he skipped telling the new governor about a recent rebellion of slaves on the plantation in 1798. In any case, the governor whom local lore would soon describe as having been "rained from the sky" began his tenure much as Luis de las Casas

---

[1] Álvaro de la Iglesia, *Tradiciones cubanas: Relatos y retratos históricos* (Havana: Ediciones Géminis, 1911), 65–73.

had in 1790, establishing warm, personal links with the island's creole sugar elite.[2]

History, however, would soon put the governor in touch with men of a different sort. In May 1799, with Spain and France allied in war against Britain, Cuba's closest allied territory was the French colony of Saint-Domingue. Someruelos's counterpart in that colony was Commander-in-Chief and Governor Toussaint Louverture. Still new to his office, Someruelos pondered letters from the French governor, and as he put pen to paper to respond, he turned over in his mind a very practical question, one that he had probably not anticipated before arriving in the Caribbean. And no number of conversations with sugar planters like Calvo would have answered it satisfactorily. What was the proper salutation for a man who was the legitimate representative of a foreign ally, yet also black and a former slave? He consulted the letters of his predecessors for guidance that was not forthcoming. Flummoxed, he looked to Madrid for instructions. Toussaint, he said, addressed him as *vos*, a form of *you* usually used to address eminent persons. Other French officers had used the same pronoun to address Cuban governors in the past, and most had replied in kind. But now, facing a *vos* from a black governor and general, Someruelos was not sure what to do: "the use of *vos* is rare among us and General Toussaint is black." Please clarify, he requested, the proper form of address in these unusual circumstances (Figure 4.1).[3]

For all his uncertainty regarding the proper epistolary form for addressing a high black official, Someruelos was less than forgiving if others erred in their choice of tone or address. When Sebastian Kindelán, governor of Santiago de Cuba, besieged by shortages of food and grain in 1800, received aid from Governor Toussaint in Saint-Domingue, Someruelos seemed less perturbed by Kindelán's recourse to a foreign government than by the very words the latter had used to address Toussaint. It was inappropriate, he said, to have given the honorific title of "your excellency" to the *caudillo* (chief) Toussaint, when such treatment had never been given by his own office to any person of Toussaint's color. That he would use the term *caudillo* to refer to the French governor of Saint-Domingue suggests perhaps that the radical transformations underway had not unseated long-standing assumptions. Yet, enough had changed

[2] The 1798 rebellion is mentioned briefly in Vidal Morales y Morales, *Iniciadores y primeros mártires de la revolución cubana* (Havana: Cultural, 1931), 1:250. On the *Nueva Holanda*, see Moreno Fraginals, *El ingenio*, 1: 73n, 75.
[3] Someruelos to Mariano Luis de Urquijo, August 8, 1799, in AGI, Estado, leg. 2, exp. 14.

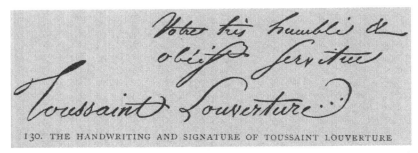

130. THE HANDWRITING AND SIGNATURE OF TOUSSAINT LOUVERTURE

FIGURE 4.1. Signature of Toussaint Louverture from Sir Harry H. Johnson, *The Negro in the New World* (New York, 1910). Courtesy of the New York Public Library, Schomburg Center for Research in Black Culture.

to make the Cuban governor take note of disjunctures between old categories and new realities. Thus, Someruelos (or his secretary) crossed out the rebuke and reworded it. The *caudillo* Toussaint became *General* Toussaint, and the reference to Toussaint's color was deleted. The problem with using "your excellency" was not Toussaint's blackness, but the fact that such a label was incompatible with the new French system of government.[4] The rise of men of color as prominent political leaders dealing with foreign governments had destabilized the very habits of routine interaction and communication.

At the outset of the Haitian Revolution, many of the accounts that had circulated in Cuba and elsewhere were undergirded by images and stories of enslaved people rising up against their masters. But as the revolution took root, it ceased to be a slave rebellion in any technical sense. As more and more of the black armies allied with the French Republic – a development in which Cuban soldiers and officers were deeply implicated – the men and women who had initially made the Haitian Revolution ceased being rebels – or slaves – and became instead French citizens. Their leaders, no longer brigands or *caudillos*, became representatives and agents of the French Republic (Figure 4.2).[5]

---

[4] Toussaint to Kindelán, 9 Pluviôse An 8 (March 7, 1800); Kindelán to Toussaint, April 6, 1800; Kindelán to Someruelos; April 29, 1800; and Someruelos to Kindelán, May 15, 1800, all in AGI, Cuba, leg. 1534.

[5] It is important to note, of course, that there were still black rebels who continued to fight against the French Republic, even one represented by Toussaint. On this "war within the war," see Michel-Rolph Trouillot, "The Three Faces of Sans Souci: Glory and Silences in the Haitian Revolution," in Trouillot, *Silencing the Past*, 31–69.

FIGURE 4.2. Toussaint Louverture negotiating with the British. 1821 Engraving. Courtesy of the New York Public Library, Schomburg Center for Research in Black Culture, Prints and Photographs Division.

This fundamental shift necessarily shaped the news that circulated across the Atlantic World. That already "unthinkable" revolution took on a different character, became more unthinkable perhaps, as the black and mulatto men who led it ascended the rungs of power to become high-ranking leaders of the French Revolution in the New World. In Cuba, as surely elsewhere, men such as Someruelos and Kindelán found themselves forced to conduct the business of state with an ally represented by a black man, a former slave who had defeated their own army in battle. Coming face to face with the echoes of the Haitian Revolution, then, meant not only trying to assimilate the unprecedented phenomenon of slavery's unmaking at the hands of former slaves, but also the emergence of a new category of person: the former slave turned formal political leader.

Yet the transformation of former slaves into political and military leaders, and the power of the antislavery positions more and more of them occupied, did not eliminate the forces that worked to expand the reach and practice of enslavement. Under Napoleon Bonaparte, metropolitan France relegalized the slave trade, exerted brute force over its errant colony, and attempted to reimpose slavery and to subdue Saint-Domingue's powerful black leaders. In these endeavors, France sought an ally in the expanding slave system in Cuba. Thus, the late Haitian Revolution reached Cuban shores in ways that made manifest both tendencies: on the one hand, the rise and consolidation of a powerful black antislavery leadership and, on the other, the continuing power of enslavement even amidst that unprecedented challenge.

The Figure of Toussaint in Cuba

Perhaps the most telling sign of how much things had changed in Saint-Domingue was the growing power of Toussaint Louverture himself. Born enslaved, he had been long free by the start of the revolution in 1791. Two years into the war, he had already showed himself to be an unusually gifted military and political tactician, allying first with the Spanish monarchy and then leading the French Republic in Saint-Domingue in its defeat of Spain in 1795 and Britain in 1798. By that time, he was governor of the French colony. As news of Toussaint's promotions and victories reached Cuba, Spanish authorities found themselves having more direct contact with him.

The rise of a black man to the highest position of military and political power in Saint-Domingue, however, produced vociferous critics in the French colony, and Cuba's contact with Toussaint was also forged indirectly, through his opponents. This was the case, for example, during the War of the South in 1799–1800, the year-long military struggle that pitted the ascendant Toussaint and his army of about 40,000 men, mostly former slaves, against André Rigaud, southern Saint-Domingue's most prominent military leader, who enjoyed strong support from formerly slave-holding and long-free people of color like himself. Citizen G. Pothier, who was Toussaint's official representative in Santiago, secretly favored Rigaud; so too did Anton Chanlatte, official French representative in formerly Spanish Santo Domingo. Both men regaled Cuban authorities with stories condemning Toussaint, whom they characterized as, among other things, "the executioner of the human species."[6]

As Toussaint's victory over the forces of the South became certain, Cuban authorities wrung their hands about two distinct possibilities. First, they feared an exodus of defeated Rigaud officers and sympathizers to Cuba. They anticipated correctly, and by August 1800, more than 700 had arrived in Santiago. Cuban officials sought explicitly to replicate the protocol observed with Jean-François and Biassou in Havana in 1795–6, attempting to keep Rigaud and his people in confinement and away from local residents. In practice, however, authorities entertained and admitted significant exceptions to the stated policy. When Guy Bonnet, aide-de-camp to Rigaud, arrived in Santiago, the governor allowed him to stay to conduct some business. Bonnet "understood that this was an authorization to remain ... and that for fear that protecting them openly would create difficulties with the captain-general in Havana, [Kindelán] pretended to forget about them."[7] In fact and in practice, thousands of French refugees ended up or passed through Cuba, a great many of them people of color, a great many of them hostile to Toussaint.[8]

[6] See, for example, Roume to Kindelán, 28 Messidor An 7 (July 16, 1799) and Someruelos to Kindelán, July 31, 1799, in AGI, Cuba, leg. 1534; Rigaud to Someruelos, June 30, 1800, and Rigaud to Pothier, July 14, 1800, attached to Someruelos to Urquijo, August 12, 1800, in AHN, Estado, leg. 6366, exp. 16.

[7] Guy-Joseph Bonnet, *Souvenirs historiques de Guy-Joseph Bonnet, général de division des armées de la République d'Haïti, ancien aide de camp de Rigaud. Documents relatifs à toutes les phases de la révolution de Saint-Domingue, recueillis et mis en ordre par Edmond Bonnet...* (Paris: Auguste Durande, 1864), 97.

[8] Isidro Josef Limonta to Conde de Santa Clara, November 14 and December 30, 1798, in AGI, Estado, leg. 1, exps. 58 and 57, respectively; Someruelos to Urquijo, March 5 and May 20, 1800, in AHN, Estado, leg. 6366, exps. 4 and 14, respectively; and Rigaud to Someruelos, July 14 and August 12, 1800, both in AHN, Estado, leg. 6366, exp. 16; Kindelán to Someruelos, July 18, 1800, in AGI, Cuba, leg. 1549. On French people

Authorities also feared that an increasingly powerful Toussaint, having defeated his internal enemies, might set his sights outward. Rigaud's agents fanned those fears. Some reports referred to a conspiracy apparently hatched by Isaac Sasportas, a radical French Jewish republican born in Saint-Domingue. Sasportas proposed to travel to Kingston, Jamaica and unleash a rebellion of the enslaved, who would receive the support of troops from Saint-Domingue. Sasportas had already attempted something similar in Curaçao – with no success – just a few months before. From there he traveled to Santiago de Cuba, where he met with fellow conspirator Barthélemy Dubuisson, before heading to Kingston in December 1799. By that time, however, Toussaint – who had already developed close commercial ties with the British – warned Jamaica's governor. The conspiracy was thwarted, and its leaders executed.[9] Even though Toussaint had revealed the plot and undermined the rebellion, the story that circulated in Cuba portrayed Toussaint as eager to bring race war and emancipation to Jamaica by force. Surely, some speculated, if he aspired to take Jamaica, his sights would not be satisfied there alone. From French interlocutors in Saint-Domingue, local authorities heard of Toussaint's imputed ambition to seize Puerto Rico, Mexico, Cuba, "and finally perhaps the whole globe."[10]

Confirmation of Toussaint's alleged designs at least on Spanish territory came in January 1801, when Toussaint occupied eastern Hispaniola, technically French but still full of Spanish residents and authorities. Rumors of the occupation had been arriving in Cuba for months, so neither the public nor the state seemed that surprised to hear of the new

---

of color in Santiago in this period, see Olga Portuondo Zúñiga, "La inmigración negra de Saint-Domingue en la Jurisdicción de Cuba," in her *Entre esclavos y libres de Cuba colonial* (Santiago: Editorial Oriente, 2003), 97. On the work of Rigaud's agents in Cuba and Santo Domingo, see Franco, *Revoluciones y conflictos internacionales en el Caribe*, 52–54.

9 See J. Scott, "Common Wind."

10 Predictions of Toussaint invading Spanish territory and Cuba specifically are numerous. For some examples, see "Traducción de una carta de Santo Domingo entregada en confianza al Gobierno de Cuba por el ciudadano Pothier," attached to Kindelán to Someruelos, June 30, 1800, in AHN, Estado, leg. 6366, exp. 16; Kindelán to Someruelos (enclosing several letters), April 14, 1800, in AGI, Cuba, leg. 1534; Kindelán to Someruelos, July 26, 1800, in AGI, Cuba, leg. 1534; Kindelán to Someruelos, January 26, 1801, in AGI, Cuba, leg. 1535; Santiago Cabildo Extraordinario, February 17, 1801, in Archivo Histórico Municipal de Santiago de Cuba (AHMSC), Actas Capitulares (AC), Tomo 16, ff. 86v-87v; and Someruelos to Pedro Cevallos (enclosing letters of Ministro de España en Philadelphia), November 21, 1801, in AHN, Estado, leg. 6366, exp. 39.

development. Officials received word of Toussaint's deft maneuvering, in which he used the pressure of the formerly enslaved to push Commissioner Philippe-Rose Roume into assenting to the occupation, which was waged against the practice of illegal enslavement on the formerly Spanish side of the island.[11] First from captains and ship crews, Cubans received copies of Toussaint's public proclamations to the people of Santo Domingo. It was, however, the stories of the Spanish refugees fleeing Santo Domingo that were most often repeated on the ground in Cuba. As Spanish subjects, the new refugees appealed to the king and his local representatives for assistance, money, land, and jobs. In hundreds of petitions, the refugees testified about their flight amidst violent danger; they wrote of losing members of their families to the incoming army, of being robbed en route from the frontier region to the capital of Santo Domingo, and of being attacked by pirates once aboard a boat headed to Cuba. They too were victims of the catastrophe of Saint-Domingue, they insisted.[12]

Thus it was – through the visits of the enemies he had defeated and through firsthand accounts of his occupation of Santo Domingo – that people in Cuba became increasingly familiar with the name and spectacular ascent of Toussaint Louverture.[13] To ponder his rule as governor, to speculate about his designs on Cuba, to wonder at his dealings with England, was to have moved beyond early images of mass slave rebellion to something perhaps more challenging: the rise of black political power. And its principal bearer, Toussaint Louverture, had, for the moment, undisputed power in the French colony.

---

[11] "Traducción de una carta de Santo Domingo," attached to Kindelán to Someruelos, June 30, 1800, in AHN, Estado, leg. 6366, exp. 16. For a description of the events, see James, *Black Jacobins*, 237–239.

[12] Kindelán to Someuelos, February 15, 1801, and Francisco Barba to Kindelán, February 3, 1801, both in AGI, Cuba, leg. 1535; Joaquín García (with enclosures), January 15, 1801, in ANC, AP, leg 8, exp. 28; and "Relación dirigida por Doña Francisca Valeria al Presbítero Doctor Don Francisco González y Carrasco," in Emilio Rodríguez Demorizi, *Invasiones haitianas de 1801, 1805 y 1822* (Ciudad Trujillo: Editorial del Caribe, 1955), 71–79. Individual testimonies of people leaving Santo Domingo in this period, as well as discussions in the Junta de Emigrados, of which Cuban planter Francisco Arango was president, can be found in AMAE, Política, República Dominicana, leg. 2372; AGI, Cuba, legs. 1693 and 1733; AGI, Santo Domingo, legs. 1038–1039 and 2372; SHMM, Ultramar, leg. 5646. See also the compelling account of Francisco Arredondo, [November, 1805] in AGI, Santo Domingo, leg. 1038.

[13] Kindelán to Someruelos, August 31, November 11, and November 24, 1801, in AGI, Cuba, leg. 1535.

Napoleon and Counterrevolution in Cuba

In metropolitan France, however, that authority was disputed quite force-fully. There, a general unease with the growing power of Toussaint, a desire to reverse what were viewed as excesses, and ultimately Napoleon's option for reenslavement resulted in the ambitious and ill-fated expedi-tion led by Victor Emmanuel Leclerc. The Leclerc expedition arrived off the coasts of Hispaniola in February 1802 with more than 20,000 troops and hundreds of copies of public statements that promised prosperity, order, and eternal liberty. Napoleon's basic premise was that recent pol-icy in Saint-Domingue was illegitimate and that Toussaint's revolution had to be undone by the force of tens of thousands of French soldiers. In secret, Leclerc carried orders for the destruction of Toussaint Louverture and, it was generally believed, for the return of slavery.[14]

The Leclerc expedition would intensify still further the links between revolutionary (and counterrevolutionary) Saint-Domingue and Cuba. In eastern Cuba, news of the expedition's imminent landing arrived first, as was often the case, in Baracoa, where a French schooner brought word that forty-five ships were poised to disembark at Le Cap, that Toussaint had already ordered his officers to resist the French landing, and that the city's white women were crying disconsolately in the streets in presentiment of what might happen. Baracoa's commander traveled on horseback from farm to farm, conveying the spectacular news to his charges.[15]

With more delay but in regular installments, the *Gaceta de Madrid*, which was readily available in Cuba, provided news on the expedition in almost every edition. The frequency and nature of the reports turned the news into something like a serialized novel. The number of ships leaving Brest grew and grew; fresh French troops arrived in successive waves, with a purpose the readers were left to imagine. And as in a novel, details of the unfolding events were sometimes quite intimate. So, for example, the gazette published moving descriptions of Toussaint's reunion with his two sons, who had been sent to France to study and who now accompanied the expedition on Napoleon's orders.[16] Soon, readers began hearing about

---

[14] Philippe Girard has recently cast doubt on the contention that Napoleon sought to reimpose slavery in Saint-Domingue. See "Napoleon Bonaparte and the Emancipation Issue in Saint-Domingue, 1799–1803," *French Historical Studies*, 32/4 (2009): 587–618.

[15] Joseph Murillo to Kindelán, February 10, 1802, in ANC, CCG, leg. 61, exp. 1; and Franco, *Revoluciones y conflictos internacionales*, 56–57.

[16] Both appear in *GM*, May 21, 1802, 489–491.

the response of the black generals who had exercised so much power of late. Arriving at Ravine-à-Couleuvres near Gonaïves, the expedition encountered resistance, cannon shots, and hand-to-hand combat from Toussaint's men. Arriving at Le Cap, the black leader Christophe refused to grant them entry without the previous authorization of Toussaint. In Port-au-Prince, the rebels set fire to the town before French troops could disembark. Alongside the detailed descriptions of such encounters were reprinted extracts from official reports by Leclerc to French ministers in Paris.[17]

But in Cuba, it was not just news of the expedition that arrived; it was the expedition itself. In Santiago, the French frigates *L'Indienne* and *La Creole* arrived to pick up French men of color to serve with the expeditionary army. The expedition, which included André Rigaud and other prominent leaders of the free people of color earlier defeated by Toussaint, heartened the many men of that class then resident in the eastern city. "Hope was reborn in the heart of the exiles," reported Santiago resident Guy Bonnet, Rigaud's old aide-de-camp. Bonnet and almost 400 men of color left Santiago to accompany Rigaud and Leclerc, prepared, if need be, to fight against Toussaint. Spanish authorities were happy to help. Local mayors and their deputies searched neighborhoods and farms for French free people of color to send on the expedition, grateful for the opportunity to make long-standing bans perhaps finally effective.[18] On March 15, two frigates and a host of smaller private vessels took off with some 600 returning refugees. Not all those who returned were people of color. White French also left, some hoping to recoup losses or to put affairs in order. When French Admiral Latouche-Tréville arrived on May 14, 1802, to pick up more French to return to Saint-Domingue, Kindelán replied that there were few left. As historian Agnès Renault writes, "Government authorities in Cuba had put as much hope on the Saint-Domingue expedition as the French."[19]

[17] GM, April 2, 313–316; April 6; April 9, 338–341; April 20, 376–377; April 23, 385–386; May 18, 477–479; and Someruelos to Sec. de Estado, 25 May 1804, in AHN, Estado, leg. 6366, exp. 78.
[18] Bonnet, *Souvenirs historiques*, 99–100. See also "Minutas de una comunicación dirigida al Gobr. de la Ysla," February 21, 1802, and February 26, 1802, in ANC, AP, leg. 8, exps. 45 and 47; Pedro Pérez, Alcalde del Caney, to Kindelán, March 1, 1802, in ANC, CCG, leg. 60, exp. 5; and Louis Félix Boisrond-Tonnerre, *Memoires pour servir a l'histoire d'Haiti* (Paris: France, Librarie, 1851), 82.
[19] Agnès Renault, *D'une île rebelle à une île fidèle: Les Français de Santiago de Cuba (1791–1825)* (Publications des Universités de Rouen et du Havre, 2012), 66.

In Havana, as well, the Leclerc expedition served to strengthen ties with the turbulent French colony. In early February 1802, just after the arrival of the expedition, a formal French delegation appeared in Havana. Among its members was the Spanish admiral Federico Gravina, who commanded a seven-vessel Spanish fleet that formed part of the expedition from Brest to its arrival and initial deployment in Saint-Domingue.[20] Gravina presented Governor Someruelos with a request from Leclerc for substantial financial assistance and for 1,000 soldiers. Someruelos convened a meeting of top officials to discuss the request and to hear the latest news from Gravina, who had landed at Le Cap with the French forces. They discussed the vigorous resistance of the black forces and the hardships being suffered by the French troops. Local residents were so distraught, explained Gravina, that the French command had given them their own rations. Newly arrived, the expedition was already floundering; greater Spanish aid was imperative. Though imperial law prohibited the dispensation of money from the treasury without prior approval from Madrid, the captain-general, with the concurrence of those in attendance, decided to grant Leclerc's request for supplies and money. Someruelos argued that the goal was worthy and the consequences of failure too high for the good of their ally, and perhaps for their own good. The soldiers, however, could not be spared.[21]

After that initial commission, many more arrived. Even as Someruelos was considering the request brought with one French envoy, another would arrive asking for more. As a result of this insistence, and as a measure of self-interest in preservation, the government in Havana, as in Santiago, sent considerable sums of money, as well as many shipments of flour, dried beef, wood, and livestock. The French sent ships to be repaired in Havana, soldiers to convalesce, and, surreptitiously, wine and other products to sell. As the expedition began to make inroads against the rebels and to "pacify" the colony, this kind of contact between the two islands became completely routine.

France's pacification of Saint-Domingue, however, was illusory and short-lived. By early summer, many things threatened the precarious

20 On the Spanish part of the expedition, see Cesareo Fernández Duro, *Armada Española desde la unión de los Reinos de Castilla y de Aragón* (Madrid: Museo Naval, 1972–1973), 8: 228–229. The papers of the Spanish portion of the expedition are in Museo Naval (MN), Campaña de Brest, mss. 0864 to 0874.
21 Someruelos to Secretario de Estado Pedro Cevallos, February 24, 1802, with attached minutes of the Junta de Generales, Havana, February 22, 1802, in AGI, Estado, leg. 2, exp. 29.

truce: Leclerc's deportation of leaders such as Toussaint and Rigaud, the scourge of yellow fever among the French troops, the campaign to disarm the rural population, the circulation of the news of France's restitution of slavery in other colonies. Indeed, by early fall of that year, much of the colony was in open and generalized rebellion against France. It was no wonder then that French appeals for monthly payments and regular shipments of attack dogs grew so desperate and urgent.[22]

Donatien Rochambeau, who became governor and captain-general after Leclerc's death of yellow fever in November 1802, sent semipermanent agents to Havana. It was largely through them that the incessant requests for aid were conveyed. French agents met regularly with the governor and other officials to discuss matters of trade, intercolonial policing, and disputes over privateers and their prizes. Perhaps not surprisingly, their requests utilized some of the same arguments that were used at the start of the conflict, when French authorities appealed for critical assistance from their neighboring colonies. They argued, as they had in 1791, that in the face of the current enemy, their interests were one; for the sake of both France and Spain, this dangerous enemy must be definitively vanquished. And the attainment of that goal undoubtedly required commitments from Madrid and Havana. If anything, French appeals would have sounded and felt more urgent and desperate in 1802 and 1803 than they had in 1791, when the scope, duration, and trajectories of the rebellion were still unthinkable.

With a sense of entitlement, the French agent Captain Reynaud wrote to Someruelos practically demanding money and men. "Our cause today is a common one and the dangers we face identical; the enemy is at your door with a dagger in hand; he destroys our properties and will quickly threaten yours."[23] Brigadier General Louis Noailles, another of Rochambeau's representatives in Havana, ventured that success was possible, but that the continuation of the French campaign required Cuban assistance. Without that aid, the rebels would

very quickly take fire and knife to their neighbors. The island of Cuba will be infested, and, encouraged by their success, they will find accomplices among the

---

[22] On the history and fate of the Leclerc expedition, see Claude Auguste and Marcel Auguste, *L'expédition Leclerc, 1801–1803* (Port-au-Prince: Henri Deschamps, 1985); and Philippe Girard, *The Slaves Who Defeated Napoleon* (Tuscaloosa: University of Alabama Press, 2011).

[23] Ciudadano Reynaud, Capitán de Navío y Jefe del Estado Mayor de las Fuerzas Navales de Santo Domingo, to Captain General Someruelos, December 27, 1802, in AGI, Estado, leg. 2, exp. 61.

island's laborers. The planter, the merchant, the artisan will be forced to abandon their properties, or they will be assassinated in their homes by a homicidal beast.[24]

French officials thus echoed arguments that had been circulating in Cuba since 1791, as statesmen and planters weighed political choices with the possibility of "another Guarico" in mind.

Rochambeau himself used similar arguments, but he went further in detailing their implications and in advocating an even more repressive stance from the colonial state. At issue, he said, was the whole "chain of colonial possession of Europe in the new world." The survival of the entire system, he argued, required the preservation of the French link in that chain. To this end, he insisted that both colonies – and, indeed, all the European nations with colonies in the Americas – needed to form a "police alliance" to do battle against their common enemies. Revealingly, he identified these enemies not as the black and mulatto rebels against whom his troops now waged war, but rather all "the blacks who work the land and the blacks employed in manufacture, the very existence of which they threaten." The danger derived from the fact that *all* blacks, *all* agricultural workers were now the presumed and targeted enemy. Starkly, ominously, he predicted a regional and permanent state of aggression and warfare.[25]

Whether it was the power of their arguments, or the unrelenting insistence with which they wore down their audience, the French in Saint-Domingue managed to wrest substantial aid from the Cuban governors. As Someruelos confessed to the secretary of state in Madrid, he felt compelled to provide "some quantity with which to quiet the clamors of a request everywhere so agitated."[26] That aid was ultimately insufficient, in the view of the French. But from the perspective of the Havana authorities who gave it repeatedly without metropolitan authorization and in light of their own necessities, it was substantial nonetheless. Rafael Gómez Robaud, the intendent of Havana, put the figure of direct monetary aid by February 1803 at over 722,150 *pesos fuertes*, a contemporary currency that had a fixed and guaranteed conversion rate in precious metal. Whatever the final figure, most of it was not reimbursed by either France or Madrid, and most of it appears to have been issued without direct

[24] Louis Noailles to Someruelos, January 20, 1803, in AGI, Estado, leg. 2, exp. 61.
[25] Rochambeau to Someruelos, March 31, 1803, in AGI, Cuba, leg. 1706.
[26] Luis de Viguri to Préfet Colonial Daure, January 4, 1803, in Service Historique de la Défense, Département de l'Armée de Terre, Vincennes (SHD-DAT), B7/12; and Someruelos to Cevallos, February 22, 1803, in AGI, Estado, leg. 2, exp. 61.

prompting or approval from the latter.[27] The figure also did not include the costs of repairing French ships or maintaining and transporting French troops in Havana, nor the substantial aid sent in other forms, such as food, lumber, and animals. For example, after some delay, Havana had begun sending attack dogs that were bred locally to hunt fugitive slaves: 400 in February 1803, another hundred a month or two later. By the time most of the dogs arrived, however, the French were already reduced by battle and yellow fever and faced an ascendant and general rebellion. The dogs had become immaterial to the outcome of war: they cowered at the sound of gunshots, and many ended up being eaten by starving French soldiers.[28]

The spirited and continual requests for assistance, and the grudging and partial willingness to concede, were premised on a fairly extensive set of contacts between the two governments. The captain-general in Havana met with the many messengers and more permanent delegates sent first by Leclerc and later by Rochambeau. In considering the French requests, the governor routinely convened meetings of the high-ranking military personnel in the city, and he conferred as well with members of the Real Consulado. As the governor consulted with prominent planters and residents, so too did the French agents. Indeed, some took up residence or spent time on nearby plantations. They conversed with planters about the utility of hunting dogs; they requested their help in cajoling the governor into letting them sell French flour in violation of standing imperial restrictions.[29] Thus, in Havana, there was in late 1802 and early 1803 a

[27] Rafael Gómez Robaud, *Manifiesto documentado en respuesta a los hechos que se sientan en el papel del capitán de fragata José Luyando . . .* (Cádiz: Imprenta de Don Diego García Campoy, 1813), 12–13. See also Arango to Rochambeau, April 26, 1803 (with attachment), in Sección Nobleza, Archivo Histórico Nacional, Toledo (SN-AHN), Almodóvar, leg. 36, exp. 1. Someruelos, in his letter to Rochambeau, dated January 4, 1803, in AGI, Estado, leg. 2, exp. 61, refers to at least two separate loans or payments, one of 530,000 and another of 123,000 *pesos*. Some of the money given by Someruelos to Rochambeau appears to have come from the Viceroy of New Spain, or the Mexican *situado*, the longstanding subsidy from Mexico to Cuba that was intended to cover the costs of Caribbean defense and fortification, but that had also been used in the past to help support the development of the sugar industry.

[28] Lequoy Mongiraud to Someruelos, March 6 and April 5, 1802, both in AGI, Cuba, leg. 1709; Someruelos to Rochambeau, February 12, 1803, in AGI, Estado, leg. 2, exp. 61; and *GM*, November 8, 1803. On the use of the dogs more generally, see Sara Johnson, *The "Fear of French Negroes,"* chap. 1; and Girard, *Slaves,* 106, 239–246.

[29] See, for example, Captain Kroehm, Captain of the *San Genaro*, to Someruelos, July 16, 1802, in AHN, leg. 6366, exp. 49–50; Luis de Viguri to Ignacio Acosta, June 30, 1802, in ANC, CCG, leg. 61, exp. 4; Viguri to Someruelos, February 5, 1803, in AGI, Cuba, leg. 1705.

substantial conversation – in Spanish and in French – about the present and possible futures of Saint-Domingue, and about what all that might mean for a growing sugar economy and colonial slave society such as Cuba's. Each decision to award or not award assistance assumed these multiple background conversations.

One very important Cuban participant in such conversations was Francisco Arango y Parreño. Over a decade earlier, Arango had played a critical role in lobbying for the colonial reforms that enabled the Cuban boom in sugar and slavery. In 1791, he became the principal interpreter of the Haitian Revolution for the Spanish state. The Council of State's first recorded discussion of the revolution was accompanied by Arango's recommendations for taking advantage of the disaster for the benefit of Spain and Cuba. To say he was interested in the events of the revolution would be a gross understatement. By the time of the Leclerc expedition and its unraveling, Arango was back in Havana, serving in several capacities that made him a central voice in the day's discussions and debates. When Rochambeau's agents met with local planters and authorities, we can be sure that he was foremost among them.[30]

As the relationship between Rochambeau's government and Someruelos's became more entwined and as Rochambeau's agents became fixtures in Havana circles, Someruelos decided that it was time to send his own agent to Rochambeau. For this task he picked Arango, a choice thoroughly unsurprising. Arango was to travel to the French colony to discuss a host of issues, from disputes over privateers, to trade arrangements between the two colonies, to the repayment of some of the money provided by Havana. He was named for the post on February 19, 1803, and departed shortly after. With him went a sizable retinue. Ignacio Caro was appointed as his secretary. Caro was an officer in the Spanish army, a native of Spanish Santo Domingo, who in 1793 had helped persuade the black rebel leader Hyacinthe to join the Spanish forces against France. Caro made the journey with considerable knowledge of the formerly Spanish part of the island and with personal experience of the Haitian Revolution itself. Arango's entourage also included scribes, cooks, butlers, other servants, and a man named Felix held as property by Arango himself. Whether as gifts to be presented or merchandise to be sold, Arango also took 200 pounds of good chocolate, 130 pounds of cigarettes, 120 pounds of snuff, and dozens of boxes of candy and

---

[30] He refers to his conversations and meetings with Noailles, for example, in Arango to Hector Daure, dated le Cap, April 5, 1803, in SN-AHN, Almodóvar, leg. 36, exp. 1.

nougat. At about the time of Arango's arrival in Saint-Domingue, another shipment of Cuban dogs arrived; whether on the same boat, we do not know.[31]

While Arango submitted an extensive report of his impressions and findings, there appears to be no surviving account of the many meetings and conversations he had while there. We know that he met with Rochambeau, whom he impressed deeply, and with Hector Daure, the official prefect of the colony.[32] The three men discussed giving preferential treatment to Cuban and Spanish products entering Saint-Domingue ports (which both sides seem to advocate enthusiastically). Arango petitioned for the right of Spanish residents of former Spanish Santo Domingo to emigrate with their slaves (a request that suggests that Leclerc had indeed restored slavery there in 1802), and for the right of the Spanish to board French warships in Cuba. Rochambeau denied both requests, arguing that the first was in violation of the treaty that had ceded the colony to France and that the second was against French law and custom. For his part, Rochambeau proposed a new form of Spanish aid to Saint-Domingue: a permanent monthly stipend. Part of it would be paid in sugar and other colonial exports, one more sign of how much things had changed in the French colony.[33]

Arango visited Saint-Domingue during the heat of war, long after the conflict had become a war of independence and a war against the reimposition of slavery. The rebels were by then calling themselves an indigenous army – the army of the Inca – and Jean-Jacques Dessalines and his allies controlled much of the mountains and countryside. Before his death, Leclerc had characterized the conflict as a "war of extermination." Rochambeau took that course even further, embarking on a program of brutal and violent repression premised on finishing off with all "the blacks" in the colony and then importing new ones. "*Peau nouvelle*," Rochambeau had explained to Arango. But "surely," the latter pondered, taking in the scenes before him, "the objective of France cannot be the conquest of a desert."[34]

[31] Ponte Domínguez, *Arango*, 158–69; and Gómez Robaud, *Manifiesto documentado*, 12n–16n.

[32] His correspondence with Rochambeau while in Saint-Domingue appears in SN-AHN, Almodóvar, leg. 36, exp. 1.

[33] Ibid, and Rochambeau to Someruelos, 20 Floreal An 11 (May 1803), in AGI, Cuba, leg. 1706.

[34] Dubois, *Avengers*, 290; Arango, "Comisión de Arango en Santo Domingo," in *Obras*, 1: 343. On the usage of Inca and *indigènes* by Dessalines and others, Manuel Guevara

Among Arango's many interlocutors was a French officer named Pascal Sabès, who had arrived in Saint-Domingue with the Leclerc expedition. When Arango met him a little over a year later, he was the commander of the city of Le Cap. But it was what had happened in the intervening period that made Arango so willing to listen to and remember what Sabès said. Shortly after his arrival, Sabès and a fellow officer, Jean-Baptiste Gemon, were sent on a mission to deliver a message to Dessalines. Instead, they were captured and held hostage for over two months. During his time in captivity, Sabès said he witnessed before his eyes the brutal executions of about ten thousand victims. One day Dessalines ordered that he and Gemon be executed along with fifty other *blancs*, yet the two men managed to survive and to be sent as messengers once more, this time to Toussaint.[35] Arango talked with Sabès regularly, and the conversations made an impression. When drafting his final report on his mission to Saint-Domingue, Arango drew on those conversations to answer the question about the likely number of insurgent and pacified blacks. He concluded forcefully that the distinction itself was meaningless. With only minimal exceptions, "even the women and children are obstinate rebels." And to give the claim authority, he added: "I proceed with the authority of those persons with most experience and judgment," including that of Sabès, "who having been prisoner among them for over two months deserves more trust than others and who assures me that he has seen the very young children amuse themselves using their little sabers to wound the dead or dying."[36]

Vasconcelos to Ministro de Estado, January 4, 1804, in AGI, Estado, leg. 68, exp. 3, and Geggus, *Haitian Revolutionary Studies*, 213–215. On possible connections between its use in Saint-Domingue and revolution in the Andes, see Sinclair Thomson, "Sovereignty Disavowed: The Tupac Amaru Revolution in the Atlantic World," manuscript in preparation.

35 The details of Sabès's service and captivity appear in SHD-DAT, 2YE, classement alphabetique 1791–1847, "André Pascal Sabès." A more extensive and melodramatic account is provided by the captain with whom he was captured, Jean-Baptiste Gemon, in his *Précis des evènements arrivés à la députation envoyée a Port-au-Prince*, http://mornegue .free.fr/evenem.htm. Like so many other eyewitness accounts, it combines exceptional and dramatized detail with the obligatory disclaimers about the insufficiency of narration: "Les évènements que j'ai a décrire sont d'un tel caractère, que je ne puis me concevoir moi-même." Finally, a semifictionalized account of Sabès's imprisonment and eventual release appears in Madison Smartt Bell's novel, *The Stone the Builder Refused* (New York: Vintage, 2006), 382, 526–528. The accounts differ on how the two men managed to escape execution in the end. The service record attributes the escape to the firmness of Sabès; Gemon's account credits the intervention of Dessalines's wife; Bell's novel credits Louis Daure Lamartinière, once an ally of Rigaud and by 1802 a firm subaltern of Toussaint's.

36 Arango, "Comisión de Arango en Santo Domingo," 1: 348.

Arango's presence in Saint-Domingue put the world of ascendant slavery in Cuba once more in physical contact with its antithesis in Saint-Domingue. And this, of course, was not lost on Arango, who realized from the start that it was precisely the once-ordinary enslaved black agricultural workers who were now "the bitterest enemies of agriculture and order." It was their actions – whatever the cause and wherever the blame – that had reduced the globe's richest and most flourishing colony to ruin. And, like many narrators facing the same task, he confessed that "his pen fell from his hands" as he pondered how to begin describing that process.[37]

Unable or unwilling to elaborate on unfolding events, Arango focused much of his report on the possibilities for pacifying the colony and Cuba's role in that effort. Here, he echoed the French officers in Cuba who argued, sometimes testily, that it was Cuba – as much as or more than France and Saint-Domingue – that stood to gain by saving the French colony. Arango, the same man who had been so eager to take advantage of France's misfortune in 1791, was now deeply disturbed by the prospect of a total French defeat in Saint-Domingue. His concern was less that the victorious rebels of newly liberated territory would somehow invade or instigate revolt in Cuba. His concern, rather, was that without French control, the newly independent state would prove an insurmountable obstacle to all Cuban maritime trade. Its ships and its seamen would jeopardize and attack vessels coming in and out of Cuba, making all commerce highly vulnerable. Such a development would endanger the Cuban boom he had so diligently worked to produce. From what Arango saw, he knew Saint-Domingue would never return to its so-called days of glory. Cuba was safe from that economic threat. But he also knew that a French defeat was entirely possible, and that it would usher in an uncontrollable set of risks that could indeed jeopardize what Cuba was fast becoming. That alone justified the privileges for the French that he advocated in the report: for instance, the concession of loans and monthly payments and the exclusive right (to be shared, of course, with the Spanish) to introduce African slaves in Cuba.[38] By then Napoleon had reopened the French slave trade and reestablished (or maintained) slavery in the rest of France's colonies.

The new alliance between Saint-Domingue and Cuba thus had its roots in the counterrevolutionary resurgence of slavery in the French empire and the growing and very profitable dependency on the institution in the

[37] Ibid., 1: 343, 340.
[38] Ibid., 1: 364.

Spanish. But, as will soon become clear, it was the very convergence of those two realities that sometimes made the alliance so difficult.

By the time Arango returned to Havana in May 1803, already tense relations between the captain-general and Rochambeau's agents had become even tenser. More and more petitions and requests for aid were denied, with feigned outrage and righteousness expressed on both sides. Already in April, Someruelos seemed reluctant to deal with the agents at all, arguing that their mission had been completed and that he did not have the authorization to negotiate with a permanent delegation. The letters back and forth exuded sarcasm and impatience, and the bottom line seemed always the same: no, no more aid was possible. The shift in Havana was echoed as well in Santiago, where Kindelán had earlier been fairly receptive about shipping cows, food, wood, and other supplies to his French counterparts in Leclerc's and then Rochambeau's Saint-Domingue. But the reluctantly given aid of the early Leclerc expedition had, by early spring of 1803, almost completely stalled.[39]

This gradual shift in policy, which predated the resumption of war between France and England in May 1803, reflected in part Cuban authorities' growing frustration with a French practice that they interpreted as a dangerous and unacceptable affront: French collusion in the movement of black men and women between the two colonies. The fact that in one society slavery was collapsing and in the other it was expanding gave that movement a potentially subversive cast and alarmed Someruelos and his men almost to the point of distraction. For the black men and women involved, the movement between colonies could signal very different things: for some a chance to reach soil about to become free, for others the grim reality of reenslavement.

Movement, Marronage, and Reenslavement

In the period of the Leclerc expedition and the Haitian War of Independence, many dozens of French ships docked in Cuban waters. Ostensibly, they came for very brief stops, but, in fact, relatively quick stops sometimes developed into extended stays of a month, or two, or six. In that time, the crew disembarked, and as crews had done in Havana since the beginning of the Spanish fleet (*flota*) system, they passed the time

---

[39] See, for example, the letters between Someruelos and Noailles, Reynaud, and Vermonet, especially in April and May, 1803, in AGI, Cuba, leg. 1706.

talking, dancing, trading, drinking, gambling, and cavorting. Crew members entered a world already itself fairly cosmopolitan, one with vibrant, diverse, and polyglot communities of color, and in the process, exchanges occurred that the state did not like – not just exchanges of information, but exchanges of people. Some crew members appear to have liked the life of Havana and sought to escape duty on their ships to spend time there, maybe with someone they had just met or simply to feel firm land under their feet for a time. Meanwhile, some local slaves used the ships to escape, joining crews or stowing away to freedom on the sea or perhaps back to a Saint-Domingue where black men were now succeeding in taking all the land.

To authorities this kind of exchange represented the absence of all control and security; it seemed to them absolutely essential to police, yet at the same time virtually unpoliceable. They warned the French that they would arrest black crew members they found on land. And they did, but in perhaps typical fashion, they seemed unable to control them even then. When French ships ready to set sail demanded the return of this or that crew member, the governor would discover that there was no such person in jail in Havana. Whatever the reason, some people eluded the control of their French captains and their Cuban jailers. Havana authorities also tried demanding lists of all black crew members from French captains, yet the lists rarely materialized.[40]

The French vessel that the Spanish referred to as the *San Genaro* arrived in Havana harbor in April 1802 to make some quick repairs. It remained in the harbor, however, for more than four months. As it prepared to leave, its captain provided Cuban authorities with a list of forty-four people currently being held in prison who sought to leave with his ship. Two of them were clearly original crew members who, for being black and on land, had been picked up by the Havana police. But with many of the others there is significantly less clarity: the man identified as Emeni whom authorities suspected was a fugitive slave from New York, or a host of blacks and mulattos from places such as Calcutta, New Orleans, or Guadeloupe who from jail volunteered for service on the ship, even though it is not clear that they were on it to begin with.[41]

---

[40] For more on agreements to police the entry of black French crew members in Cuban territory, see Noailles to Someruelos, undated; Someruelos to Reynaud, February 12, 1803; Someruelos to Noailles, February 19, 1803; and Rochambeau to Someruelos, March 12 and March 31, 1803, all in AGI, Cuba, leg. 1706.

[41] See the exchanges between *San Genaro*'s captain Kroehn and Someruelos from April through August 1802, in AGI, Cuba, leg. 1706.

Among the would-be passengers on the Saint-Domingue-bound vessel were other men who, enslaved in Havana, sought to reach freedom in Saint-Domingue. Some had been born or had lived in Saint-Domingue and now sought to return. Among them were eighteen-year-old Domingo; Jean-Bar, in his early twenties, who was a baker with maritime experience; and Lorenzo, forty-five, who "played a kind of guitar made from a gourd with a very long neck and who sang in French though always the same melody." Importantly, a few were the property of prominent Cuban military men who had spent time on the Santo Domingo/Saint-Domingue border in 1793–5. Agustín, formerly from Saint-Domingue, was held as property of the estate of Antonio Barba, a military engineer stationed in Bayajá (Fort Dauphin) in the 1790s.[42]

Carlos el Francés belonged to the prominent merchant-planter Gabriel Raimundo de Azcárate. A member of the Real Consulado and the Sociedad Económica, Azcárate was completely immersed in high-level conversations on slavery, sugar, trade, and revolution. In 1789, he was one of the planters who passionately convinced the king that it was foolhardy to implement the new code on the treatment of slaves. In 1799, he was among a group of Real Consulado members who clamored against the application of a canonical law that would require parishioners to attend church. Requiring attendance at church, he said, would result in the congregation of a handful of whites and tens of thousands of black slaves, too grave a danger to bear. Whatever dangers he had signaled then, they were not sufficient to keep him from holding as slaves black men and women from Saint-Domingue. It is impossible to tell when he first acquired the man named Carlos, whom he claimed as his slave. From 1792 to 1796, Azcárate was part of an association that received slaves in consignment from traders arriving in Havana and resold them wherever demand determined. Finally, Azcárate was also a member of the Havana Regiment, some of whose members were stationed in Santo Domingo during the war and where some were involved in the illegal acquisition of human beings they held and sold as slaves.[43]

Also on the *San Genaro* was a Congo man who was handed over by Antonio del Valle Hernández, secretary of the Real Consulado, to the

[42] Somervelos to Cevallos, Sept. 27, 1802, in AHN, Estado, leg. 6366, exp. 51. On Barba, see Chapter 3.

[43] On Azcárate's participation in the 1789 petition to the King, see AGI, Estado, leg. 7, exp. 4 and 5; on his participation in the 1799 declaration against the Ley Canónica, see Real Consulado to Somervelos, July 5, 1799, in AGI, Cuba, leg. 1651. On his participation in the slave trade consignment association, see Sherry Johnson, "The Rise and Fall

captain of the vessel for him to take to an associate in Saint-Domingue. Thus, as the French ship set sail, two members of the Real Consulado that had so ardently condemned the proliferation of dangerous *negros franceses* in their territory revealed suspect ties to those very people, who now sought to return just as the tide turned definitively against the French.[44]

From another black ship passenger in Havana, we get a different kind of pressing for rights – less a prescient invocation of Haiti as free soil than an appeal to an *ancien régime* understanding of the juridical possibilities open to the enslaved. María Sofía, born in Le Cap, had been brought to Havana aboard an unnamed brig by the Vicomte Cormillón, whom she identified as her master. That she arrived in Havana from Saint-Domingue in 1802 identifying someone as her master is in and of itself remarkable. The viscount had allegedly forbidden her to leave the ship and kept her in chains when necessary to prevent it. Despite this considerable handicap, she somehow managed to connect with a local notary and submit a petition to the captain-general asking him essentially to ignore the many royal decrees that prevented her sale and establishment in Cuba and to recognize her right (traditionally granted as a legal prerogative in Spanish Cuba) to seek a different master. In fact, she said, she had already found one in Havana.[45]

When Someruelos appealed to French agents in Havana or to Rochambeau himself in Saint-Domingue asking for help in stemming the tide of black movement between the two colonies, he mentioned that the public in Havana was alarmed and that rumors circulated about black men and women from Saint-Domingue taking advantage of the intensified contact of the period in order to stay in Havana. As from the beginning, nothing seemed to signal danger so clearly as groups of unpoliced *negros franceses* capable of destabilizing the peace and prosperity of their territory.[46]

Often, the complaints were not just about black maritime movement, which in a sense would have been familiar, even if perceived now with

of Creole Participation in the Cuban Slave Trade, 1789–1796," in *Cuban Studies* 30 (1999): 52–75. On his membership in the Regimiento de Caballería de la Habana, see AGS, SGU, leg. 6850, exp. 35.

[44] Some of the fugitives were recovered some months later and returned. See Someruelos to Cevallos, May 26, 1803 in AHN, Estado, leg. 6366, exp. 54.

[45] Draft of Someruelos to Reynaud, June 18, 1803, and María Sofía's declaration, dated Havana, June 30, 1802 [sic?], both in AGI, Cuba, leg. 1706.

[46] For a regional perspective on this, see J. Scott, "The Common Wind," and Sara Johnson, *The "Fear of French Negroes."*

heightened alarm. Some involved the sale *as slaves* of black French men, women, and children from Saint-Domingue. The issue had been a contentious one in the early periods of the revolution. Masters preparing to leave the colony sold slaves to traders to garner cash for their relocation. Insurgent leaders such as Biassou and others had "stolen" black women and children to sell on the Spanish side of the island, many of whom were then taken to other Spanish colonies. French officials charged with banishing rebel slaves or drowning them at sea, tried to elude orders and make money by selling them at foreign ports.[47]

In 1802, with the French decision in July to maintain slavery in the territories returned by the British in the Treaty of Amiens, followed by slavery's reimposition in Guadeloupe, there was perhaps renewed incentive for people to engage in this kind of trafficking. For example, soon after the slave trade in Martinique and Guadeloupe reopened, traders loaded a ship with 250 black men, women, and children to sell in Spanish ports.[48] In another case, rebels from the recent insurrections in Guadeloupe were loaded on five ships, clad in loincloths so as to pass for new Africans, and sent to the coast of Caracas to be sold as slaves. Turned away there, some of the ships headed to Cartagena, where they met the same fate, and then Jamaica, where their number was put at 1,500 and where they were likewise turned away and then followed to ensure that the crews did not unload the rebels on some unguarded coast. Reading of boats full of banished black rebels being sold as slaves and looking for furtive and safe landing, Someruelos charged his subalterns with utmost vigilance. It did not take long for Leclerc to realize that such contraband acts, clearly against Spanish laws that required that all slaves sold in Spanish territory be *bozales*, were undermining his appeals for assistance.[49]

---

[47] For captured insurgents sold by French officers in other colonies during the early revolution, see the extensive file in TNA, CO, 137/90, beginning at f. 87.

[48] Captain-General of Caracas Manuel de Guevara Vasconcelos to Cevallos, September 20, 1802, in AGI, Estado, leg. 60, exp. 29.

[49] Circular by Havana Intendant to his Subdelegates in Matanzas, Remedios, Trinidad, Puerto Príncipe, Bayamo, [Santiago de] Cuba, Baracoa, and Batabanó, September 13, 1802, in ANC, AP, leg. 8, exp. 50. The news of their arrival in Jamaica says the load of 1,500 captured rebels was sent from Guadeloupe to Cartagena from where they were to be taken to New Spain and put to work in mines. See John Duckworth to Evan Nepean, August 7, 1802, in TNA, Admiralty (ADM), 1/252; and Leclerc to Minister of the Marine, 15 Vendémiaire An 11 (October 7, 1802), in University of Florida, Rochambeau Papers, item 1178.

Because Leclerc died of yellow fever very soon after making that observation, the task of trying to cajole the Spanish out of their suspicion fell to Rochambeau. But his protestations were so effusive – and the evidence against the French so damning – that suspicion if anything only grew. In December 1802, shortly after taking command of Saint-Domingue, he wrote to Someruelos that

[France,] faithful to its principles of loyalty, has preferred to accumulate in its own territory the evils of the insurrection rather than take to the colonies of our neighbors the seed of rebellion and discord by ridding itself of the black insurgents who desolate its colony. None of these rebels has been sent to Spanish possessions by order of General Leclerc nor by mine.[50]

Indeed, there is no evidence that Rochambeau ordered or approved of illegal slave trafficking to Cuba or other Spanish colonies. And Someruelos took him – or at least pretended to take him – at his word; he trusted in his honor too much to doubt his innocence in the matter. In a questionable sign of faith and good will, he informed him he was sending 400 maroon-hunting dogs to be used against the rebels.[51]

But even if Someruelos absolved Rochambeau of personal responsibility for authorizing the illegal traffic, he had no doubt that it was indeed underway and that French state officials were involved. This was the case, for example, with at least two French vessels named the *Necker* and the *Courrier*, both of which took captured black rebels to Havana to be sold as slaves. Deeply suspicious, Someruelos had an agent pretend to want to buy captives off the French ships, and the steward aboard the *Necker* offered to sell him four of them. Another confidant of the governor learned from an officer aboard the *Necker* that about sixty blacks brought by one or more of these vessels had been sold in that manner and, now reenslaved, were already working on unnamed plantations in the area. The governor offered local residents cash rewards for denouncing French slaves and the masters who held them. The Spanish were livid, and the French understood; indeed, they confessed among themselves that the case of the *Necker* had attained a kind of notoriety in Havana.[52]

---

[50] Rochambeau to Someruelos, December 9, 1802, in AGI, Estado, leg. 2, exp. 61.
[51] Someruelos to Rochambeau, February 12, 1803, in AGI, Estado, leg. 2, exp. 61.
[52] Someruelos to Cevallos, November 6, 1802, in AGI, Estado, leg. 2, exp. 30; Someruelos to Rochambeau, February 19, 1803 in AGI, Cuba, leg. 1706; Someruelos, "Instrucción que se da al Sr. D. Francisco de Arango para la Comisión con que pasa al Guarico," March 5, 1803, in Arango, *Obras*, 1: 332–333. Commissaire de Marine Vermonnet to Daure, 22 Pluviôse An 11(February 11, 1803), in SHD-DAT, B7/13; and Noailles to Rochambeau, 29 Pluviôse An 11 (18 February 1803), in AN (CARAN), 416AP/1.

Occasionally, authorities were luckier: in one instance, they were able to locate eight people from Saint-Domingue who had just been sold and return them to their ship. The number of the plausibly more frequent cases of people not recovered is impossible to establish.[53]

According to Arango, who had been charged with speaking to Rochambeau about this during his mission to Saint-Domingue, the selling of Saint-Domingue blacks in Cuba was the result of a flourishing and profitable private contraband trade and not a concerted effort by French officials to undermine Cuban stability. While authorities were engaged in diplomatic maneuvering around the infractions in Havana, Arango was convinced that significantly more black French were being sold illegally in eastern Cuba (in Santiago, Baracoa, Bayamo, Holguín, and Puerto Príncipe), as well as Puerto Rico.[54]

Rochambeau, however, continued to insist that there was no problem. First, he was a man used to being obeyed: he had issued strict orders against the practice, and there was not the least cause for worry. Arango could not resist pointing out that, precisely as Rochambeau was giving them earlier assurances to that effect, new cases were being discovered. Second, Rochambeau argued, the Cubans were almost certainly exaggerating: "There has been a lot of noise for nothing...the mountain labored and gave birth to a mouse."[55] For whatever infractions had occurred, he blamed the Cubans. "Permit me to complain," he wrote, "of the secret and inquisitorial methods your subalterns have used to tempt the greed of those who have been weak enough to succumb."[56]

Wherever the blame for any specific case, the practice suggests that if the French were willing to sell people in Cuba, local people were also prepared to ignore the law in order to buy them. Indeed, Cuban traders were even then petitioning for licenses to travel to Saint-Domingue for the purpose of the slave trade. In September 1802, the captain-general in Havana was stunned to receive news of events in Saint-Domingue that had been gathered from the captain of the schooner *San Juan Bautista*, which had just returned to Santiago from a trip to Le Cap precisely to

[53] ANC, RCJF, leg 112, exp. 4703.
[54] Arango, "Comisón de Arango en Santo Domingo," 1: 342, 351–352.
[55] Rochambeau to Arango, Port-au-Prince, 12 Floréal An 11; and Arango to Rochambeau, Port-au-Prince, May 3, 1803, both in SN-AHN, Almodóvar, C. 36, D. 1.
[56] Rochambeau to Someruelos, March 12 and March 31, 1803, both in AGI, Cuba, leg. 1706.

purchase slaves.[57] Apparently, the captain had received authorization to travel there in September 1802, after Toussaint's deportation, after news of the restitution of slavery in Guadeloupe, and after black rebellion against the French had reemerged in response.

With or without official French knowledge of the infractions, a smaller version of the old clandestine slave traffic between revolutionary Saint-Domingue and Cuba was reemerging. The Cuban governor felt caught. On the one hand was the seeming inefficiency – or, he feared, unwillingness – of the French colonial state to police the transfer of local black men and women to Cuban ports. On the other was the clamoring of his public and of the main institutions in the city – the town council and the Consulado – that there were simply too many *negros franceses* in the city. In the year that the French agents had been in Havana, involved in all that contraband and all those conversations, five minor slave conspiracies and rebellions were discovered in the area: three linked ones in 1802 on a coffee farm in San Antonio de los Baños; one in May 1802, on the sugar mill *San Juan Bautista* in Managua owned by the Márques de Cárdenas; and another in February 1803, involving forty slaves on the sugar mill owned by the Conde de Casa Barreto in Rio Hondo.[58] There were other kinds of challenges as well. In Bayamo, where Arango had speculated that traders were selling reenslaved black prisoners, authorities asked for help in dealing with numerous cases in which foreign blacks held as slaves were "demanding their freedom on the basis of various titles."[59] Authorities clearly feared that, perhaps especially with the independence of the Saint-Domingue rebels now a distinct possibility, the presence of so-called *negros franceses* in Cuba had the capacity to make incidents such as these, and the general climate of low-grade intranquility, that much more explosive.

[57] Someruelos to Kindelán, Havana, October 14, 1802, ANC, CCG, leg. 61, exp. 14; Kindelán to Someruelos, no. 836, May 10, 1803, ANC, CCG, leg. 63, exp. 3; Kindelán to Someruelos, November 8, 1802, AGI, Cuba, leg. 1536B; Joseph Murillo to Kindelán, January 8 and January 28, 1803, in ANC, Gobierno General, leg. 529, exp. 27084; "Nota remitida por el Sr. Prior Marqués de Casa Peñalver, RCJF session, February 16 and February 28, 1803, in ANC, RCJF, leg. 112, exp. 4703.

[58] Gloria García, *Conspiraciones y revueltas: la actividad política de los negros (1790– 1845)* (Santiago: Editorial Oriente, 2003), 32–34; "Expediente relativo a los ecsesos cometidos por los negros del ingenio San Juan Bautista," June 2, 1802, in ANC, RCJF, leg. 150, exp. 7407; and Real Consulado to Someruelos, February 24, 1803, in AGI, Cuba, leg. 1651.

[59] Actas de sesiones de la Junta de Gobierno del Real Consulado, November 17, 1802, in ANC, RCJF, Libro 165, ff. 255–256.

The conflict and mistrust over the clandestine entry of black Saint-Dominguans contributed to a decline in the civility of the exchange between Someruelos and the representatives of the French state. And as the months wore on, the already reluctantly given aid dried out. By May 1803, almost every single request for aid was denied. To make matters worse for Rochambeau, Britain and France were again at war, and the prospects of preserving Saint-Domingue all but nullified. The already very shaky edifice of French rule collapsed.

Not surprisingly, tangible evidence of that collapse quickly reached Cuban shores. In Havana and Santiago, hundreds of sick and wounded soldiers arrived. Soon those arrivals were not convalescents but evacuees – hundreds of them. Troops, men who looked, according to one witness, like "living skeletons," were unloaded on the coasts, and without transportation or resources, many died before making it any further.[60] The troops of Lavalette, who on arrival in Santiago had numbered at around 1,300, were later sent to Havana and settled in a small town outside Havana named San Felipe y Santiago. It was Francisco Montalvo, planter, officer, witness years before to the Bayajá massacre of July 1794, who found them the housing, lived with them, and, we might imagine, spent evenings with Lavalette, comparing notes, lamenting Haiti, while being served by men and women held as slaves in Cuba. Some defeated soldiers found work as guards on sugar plantations, some in garrisons protecting city and countryside against threats. According to one historian, they bore on their faces the look of tragedy. Someruelos could not wait to be rid of them, but neither he nor they had the resources to organize their return to France. Nonetheless, the Havana government decided to spend the money – even though no one else would reimburse them – and requisition boats for their return. Many thus left in 1804 and 1805.[61]

It was a shared commitment to slavery, and to containing black power, that served as the foundation for the 1802–3 alliance between France's representatives in Saint-Domingue and the colonial state and planters of Cuba. But the presence of increasingly desperate French officials in Cuba in 1803–4 revealed the fragility of the alliance's project. Cuban support had not saved Napoleon's scheme of reversing the revolution

[60] José María Callejas, *Historia de Santiago de Cuba* (Havana: La Universal, 1911), 64–66.
[61] See the correspondence between Someruelos and Montalvo between November 1803 and January 1804, in AGI, Cuba, leg. 1705; Rolando Álvarez Estévez, *Huellas francesas en el Occidente de Cuba: siglos XVI–XIX* (Havana: Ediciones Boloña, 2001), 35.

in Saint-Domingue. Indeed, the French were in Cuba, having just suffered a cataclysmic defeat, their very presence on the Spanish island a reminder not of the containment but of the victory and power of black revolution.

Revolution's Disavowal: The French Evacuation in Cuba

The defeated soldiers and officers making their way to Cuba were soon joined by an even greater number of civilian refugees (*colons*), also hurriedly evacuating Saint-Domingue. Unlike the soldiers, they immediately set about establishing themselves in Cuba. In the process, they expanded the reach of slavery and plantation agriculture in the Spanish island, working to create an enclave somehow immune to the tumult and influence of black revolution. What they sought to create was in some sense a counterrevolutionary space of slavery, one that represented a material disavowal of the Haiti that was at that moment coming into existence.[62]

Even before the evacuation of late summer and fall of 1803, waves of Saint-Domingue refugees had landed and settled in Cuban territory at key moments of the revolution: the initial rebellion, Sonthonax's emancipation, the defeat of Rigaud in the South, and so on. But these waves paled in comparison to the deluge that would come in the final months of Saint-Domingue's existence. Already in late 1802, the governor of Santiago, Sebastián Kindelán, began to predict the exodus, insisting that preparations be made for the arrival of massive numbers of French soldiers and citizens. He was correct: starting in late June 1803, and over the next few months, thousands of Saint-Domingue residents arrived on the shores of Santiago de Cuba. Men, women, and children of all colors came on French ships that sometimes landed in Santiago but that, to elude the required inspections, often dropped passengers on deserted coasts nearby. The British did the same with many of the French prisoners they captured now that war had recommenced. And so the refugees arrived, on the order of hundreds a day. On June 23, Kindelán reported the arrival of six ships loaded with an unknown number of French families. A week later, he reported the arrival of five other vessels, together carrying more than 500 people. The next day, the governor heard of more

[62] The term "disavowal" is borrowed from Sibylle Fischer, who uses it to describe the cultural and political process by which Haiti's challenge was suppressed even as it emerged. Here I give the term a more economic and material application. See Fischer, *Modernity Disavowed*.

ships arriving in nearby Baracoa. All in all, between June and December, 1803, over 18,000 Saint-Domingue residents arrived in Santiago, a figure roughly equal to the entire population of the city in 1791.[63]

The number is staggering; and almost immediately everyone – new arrivals, long-term residents, and local officials – understood that a crisis was at hand. The housing stock was insufficient, food supplies dwindled, and nerves frayed. In September 1803, the governor of Baracoa reported that all foodstuffs were gone; there had been no flour in the city for fifteen days, and even plantains, which substituted for bread in times of scarcity, were impossible to find.[64] The demands placed on cities such as Baracoa and Santiago as a direct result of the influx of people evacuating Saint-Domingue meant that Cubans, in their own way, also experienced the final, dramatic prelude to Haitian independence, that they too encountered the tangible evidence of the defeat of slavery and colonialism at the hands of former slaves and men of color.

Faced with a flood of arrivals more substantial than all the earlier ones, local authorities had to decide quickly on a policy: how would they deal with the thousands of foreigners requesting asylum? As allies of France, authorities seemed to have felt little choice, and they simply reaffirmed long-standing policy. As the ships arrived, captains submitted formal requests for "hospitality" from the Spanish. In order to receive the benefit of that refuge, the migrants were required to talk, to explain the motive of their hasty and desperate flight.[65] In one such request for hospitality, the ship captain stressed the fact that England and France were again at war and that their town was under threat of British invasion. The governor,

[63] The total population of Santiago in 1791 was 19,703. Kindelán to Someruelos, November 11, 1802, in AGI, Cuba, leg. 1536B; Kindelán to Someruelos, June 25, June 30, July 1, and August 15, 1803, all in AGI, Cuba, leg. 1537A; and Kindelán to Someruelos, September 30, November 15, November 30, and December 15, 1803 in AGI, Cuba, leg. 1537B. The figure for the period 1800–1804 is 19,635; see AHN, Estado, 6366, exp. 66, cited in María Elena Orozco Melgar, "La implantación francesa en Santiago de Cuba, 1800–1810," in Jean Lamore, ed., *Les Français dans l'Orient cubain* (Paris: Karthala, 2006), 48.

[64] Joseph Murillo to Kindelán, Setempber 26, 1803, attached to Kindelán to Someruelos, November 29, 1803, in AGI, Cuba, leg. 1537B.

[65] The declarations of these refugees appear in Kindelán to Someruelos, June 30, 1802, in AGI, Cuba, leg. 1537A. Many others are scattered in that bundle, as well as 1537B. For recent work on families from Jérémie resettling in Cuba, see Rebecca Scott and Jean Hébrard, *Freedom Papers: An Atlantic Odyssey in the Age of Emancipation* (Cambridge: Harvard University Press, 2012), chap. 3; and Marial Iglesias Utset, "Los Despaigne en Saint-Domingue y Cuba: Narrativa microhistórica de una experiencia atlántica," *Revista de Indias* 71 (2011): 77–108.

hearing this request, showed little compassion and was inclined to deny refuge. If the threat was a British attack, then why not flee to another point in the colony? It was not, he added, as if they were threatened by black troops or black rule. Having expressed this doubt and suggested an alternative, he overdetermined the nature of the narrative that would ultimately be produced. Formally requesting hospitality days later, that is, stating the official reason for their flight, the refugees' petition now requested hospitality in a more urgent and conformist language. We left of absolute necessity, they wrote, because we were about to be killed by the blacks.[66] Thus, the power and authority of the governor – and the very process of producing routinized documents of empire in that chaotic moment – shaped the record of the archive and turned several possible narratives – for example, of imperial war between Britain and France, or of anticolonial struggle between black rebels and their metropole – into a much simpler, starker story of blacks violently sacrificing whites.

After interrogations of this kind, white refugees were allowed to remain. But people of color were subjected to a different fate.[67] Those identified as slaves or servants by their putative masters would be allowed to remain only if deemed necessary. Necessity, of course, was not always an objective or transparent quality, and many, in fact, were allowed to remain. Sometimes it was evacuating French officials who came in with so-called slaves. The former military commander of Port-au-Prince, for instance, arrived as part of Lavalette's entourage in October 1803, with "a number of blacks he extracted on his exit" and whom he then appears to have sold in Santiago. Indeed, notarial records in Santiago for 1804 and 1805 are full of references to the sale and, to a lesser extent, the manumission of slaves from Saint-Domingue.[68]

Men and women identified as free people of color, meanwhile, would be held on a pontoon in the harbor to be deported at the first opportunity. As always, stated policy and actual practice diverged significantly. The pontoon, meant to serve as a temporary prison for French free people of

[66] Kindelán to Someruelos, August 15, 1803, with enclosed "Testimonio de los autos obrados sobre la arribada que han hecho a este Pto. de Stgo de Cuba 5 Goletas y una balandara francesas...con varias familias de la misma nación pidiendo hospitalidad," in AGI, Cuba, leg. 1537A.

[67] For discussions about what policy to follow with people of color, see especially Someruelos to Kindelán, July 15, 1803, in Hispanic Society of America, Cuban and Haitian Collection, MS-HC 427/7; and the correspondence between Someruelos and Pedro Cevallos between September 1803 and March 1804, in ANC, Cuba, leg. 1733.

[68] See Minuta, Someruelos to Kindelán, October 11, 1804, and Kidelán to Someruelos, November 13, 1804, both in AGI, Cuba, leg. 1538B.

color, was quickly rendered inadequate. Santiago's governor complained that it was "in such bad shape that there was no heart capable of steeling itself against the compassion its prisoners inspired." It often flooded; it had little protection against rain or sun. People of all ages and sexes were mixed, and hunger was par for the course. Conditions were such that some of the detainees were allowed off the floating prison into town, where many appear to have remained. A year later, in September 1805, Kindelán was posting public notices around town giving French free people of color notice that they had forty days to leave the island, even as he confessed to the captain general that he knew they would not all leave. An 1808 census of Santiago put the number of French free people of color at 2,341 and the number of those enslaved at 2,457.[69]

Whatever the precise number of people of color who boarded vessels in Saint-Domingue in 1803, all of them were legally French citizens. The 1793 abolition by colonial authorities, the 1794 decree by the National Convention, and the evacuation of the slaveholding British from the South in 1798, meant that, even with Toussaint's 1801 Constitution rescinded by Napoleon, there was no legal slavery in French Saint-Domingue. But just as the Leclerc expedition had profoundly challenged that truth, so too did the seaboard journey to Cuba render freedom acutely fragile.[70]

In many cases, people identified ambiguously as servants or domestics on their departure from Saint-Domingue became in Cuba the legal property of others. Some were identified as slaves by ship captains, fellow passengers, or putative owners. Some identified themselves that way. In June 1803, when one vessel unloaded a group of people of color, thirteen of the men and eleven of the women were described as slaves of French masters. When they themselves were questioned, they allegedly identified themselves as enslaved and declared that during the evacuation, "they [had] flung themselves on the vessels in pursuit of their masters, from whom they did not wish to separate." At about the same time, another French vessel arrived in Juraguá, on the coast east of Santiago, with eight

---

[69] See Archivo Histórico Provincial de Santiago de Cuba (AHPSC), Protocolos Notariales, Escribanía del Cabildo, Protocolos 2 and 3; Kindelán to Someruelos, July 28, August 15, August 27, and September 15, 1804, all in AGI, Cuba, leg. 1538B; and March 19, 1806, in AGI, Cuba, leg. 1540A. The census information appears in Juan Pérez de la Riva, "La implantación francesa en la cuenca superior del Cauto," in *El barracón y otros ensayos*, citing ANC, AP, leg. 142, exp. 86. There is some uncertainty about whether the category "French slaves" referred to enslaved individuals brought from Saint-Domingue to Cuba by putative masters, or to people – including recently enslaved Africans – purchased by French residents once in Cuba. See Renault, *D'une île rebelle*, 116.

[70] See R. Scott and Hébrard, *Freedom Papers*, chap. 3.

people of color. A passenger on the ship, Francisco Olivares, a native of Maracaibo who had been living in Jérémie for eleven years, identified the eight individuals as slaves of various French people also arriving at the time. But when authorities questioned them, at least some of their answers suggested otherwise. Two declared that they were slaves belonging to Olivares himself; three said they belonged to a mulatta woman named Susana de Bono; another three said they were of free origin, or *libre de origen.*[71]

The answers given by the black men and women serve, of course, to raise a host of unanswerable questions. For example, might the use of the term "free origin" have been meant to insist on a long-standing, and therefore more secure, freedom than the recent, now very fragile freedom won in revolution? Did its use on arrival in Cuba represent an effort to protect against the possibility of enslavement in new territory? Or did it reflect the reemergence of old distinctions between free and freed – and even free and enslaved – in Saint-Domingue itself? And for those who identified themselves as slaves, did that identification reveal something about social relations in southern Saint-Domingue in 1803? The statements of these black men and women remind us not only of the instability of legal status in the journey from one society to another. They remind us as well of how little we know about the lived experience of freedom (or reenslavement) in Saint-Domingue itself in the critical moments of 1803. In other words, at issue is not only a potential change in condition across jurisdictions, but also the instability of free status even in the jurisdiction of origin, in which legal freedom theoretically reigned, but where reality was certainly infinitely less clear and where years of war, occupation, and migration had made status very difficult to fix.

Among the white French entering Santiago in the summer of 1803 were, in fact, people who had lived there once before. The majority were from southern and western Saint-Domingue, from regions such as Jérémie and Les Abricots, which were occupied by the British from 1793 to 1798, and where the abolitions decreed by Saint-Domingue governors in 1793 and by the French National Convention in 1794 were not initially implemented. Indeed, as David Geggus has shown, the number of enslaved people in the region during British occupation was around 70,000, and in some specific regions, there were more slaves in, say, 1795 than there

[71] See Kindelán to Someruelos, June 30, 1803, in AGI, Cuba, leg. 1537A, and attached testimonies.

had been before the revolution. Emancipation arrived in the south only after the British evacuation in 1798.[72] In part to avoid that new reality, some planters immediately abandoned the colony for Jamaica, the United States, and Cuba, in almost all cases striving to take with them at least some of the people they held as slaves. For those "masters" and "slaves" who left southern Saint-Domingue with the British evacuation, it is unclear that they experienced any profound transformation in the social relations of slavery.

In spring 1802, as Leclerc briefly consolidated control of Saint-Domingue, some of the white refugees returned to their former homes in the French colony. But little more than a year later they were on their way back to Cuba, their prospects of restoring their fortunes in Saint-Domingue gone. Thus, among the lists of passengers entering Santiago in the second half of 1803 appear people who had already been registered as residents of Santiago in 1799 and 1800. Jean Biron, from Les Abricots, who left Santiago alone in 1802, returned from Saint-Domingue in June 1803 with thirteen presumed slaves, including six children. The Rapp family, who in 1800 had registered just one slave, reentered Santiago in 1803 with nine, including seven children. A member of the Preval family, who had originally arrived in Santiago in 1798 from the Artibonite, now entered with twelve men and women listed as slaves.[73]

These records do not tell us how these people came to reenter Cuba with "slaves" in 1803. But the fact that the refugees appear to have arrived in Cuba in 1803 with more supposed slaves than they had departed with in 1802 might suggest that they had somehow acquired people during their 1802–3 sojourn in Saint-Domingue. We cannot know for sure, but scattered evidence does point to the possible reemergence of some of the social relations of slavery in Saint-Domingue, despite Leclerc's protestations about permanent liberty and despite the fact that no legal measures had formally reversed emancipation. Indeed, shortly after Rochambeau's assumption of power, some old practices of enslavement reemerged: the reinstitution of the chain gang, the return of fugitive slaves to foreign masters, the use of the terms *nègres* and *maîtres* for slaves and masters. And on January 1, 1803, Rochambeau actually proposed the immediate

---

[72] On the geographic origins of the Saint-Domingue refugees in Santiago, see Renault, *D'une île rebelle*, 174–178. On slavery in the regions occupied by the British, see David Geggus, *Slavery, War, and Revolution*, chaps. 10 and 11. On the application of abolition in the immediate aftermath of the British withdrawal, see Fick, *The Making of Haiti*, 198–199.

[73] Renault, *D'une île rebelle*, 91, 102.

restoration of slavery in Saint-Domingue. The reemergence of manumission there in 1802 and 1803 may have been a way for some to protect against this imminent reality. Thus, the category of free person – which would have legally applied to everyone in Saint-Domingue – was already, in that moment and place, under intense pressure. And the people encompassed in the category were newly vulnerable to emancipation's undoing, whether through the accumulation of individual reversals or a more general reenslavement.[74]

This ambiguous betrayal of revolutionary emancipation echoed clearly in Cuba. We have already seen evidence of Cuban slave traders traveling to Saint-Domingue in 1802 and 1803 to purchase people as slaves. Records of financial transactions by refugees provide random glimpses into what might have been such a market: a young Aline purchased in Le Cap in 1803, freed shortly after in Santiago, for instance.[75] At the same time, however, there were regular cases of Saint-Domingue people of color – black and mulatto – claiming their freedom, whether on the basis of long-standing free status, a recent manumission, or the revolutionary decrees of the 1790s. Traces remain of some of these individuals: Rosalie Vincent and Adélaïde Métayer, recently examined by Rebecca Scott and Jean Hébrard; or Lalit and Romain dit Louis Hervé, examined by French historian Agnès Renault.[76] With this profound uncertainty about the fate of freedom in general and about the status of particular individuals, it may not be as surprising as on first glance to see individuals arriving in Santiago in 1803 identifying themselves and others with terms such as "of free origin" or "slaves."

The uncertainties about legal status in Saint-Domingue notwithstanding, one thing is very clear. By late 1803, the journey from Saint-Domingue to Cuba meant above all leaving a society in which legal slavery was now definitively defeated for one where it was prospering and growing. For those who had just lost property, the possibility of making some money by selling a fellow traveler may have been tempting.

[74] Girard, *Slaves*, 224–225; Scott and Hébrard, *Freedom Papers*, chap. 3.
[75] Case is cited by Renault, *D'une île rebelle*, 205.
[76] The case of Rosalie Vincent is the subject of R. Scott and Hébrard, *Freedom Papers*. The case of Adélaïde Métayer is the subject of current research by Scott; see "Paper Thin." Lalit and Romain dit Louis Hervé are discussed briefly in Renault, *D'une île rebelle*, 182–183. For former Saint-Domingue people of color claiming freedom generally, see *Actas de sesiones de la Junta de Gobierno del Real Consulado*, November 17, 1802, in ANC, RCJF, Libro 165, ff. 255–256; and Someruelos to Rafael Gómez Robaud, July 30, 1804, ANC, AP, leg. 9, exp. 1.

An aide-de-camp to General Noailles, for example, kept the unnamed twelve-year-old boy entrusted to him by the free woman of color Marie-Louise Didier of Saint-Marc during the evacuation, registered him as his own property, and eventually sold him in Havana.[77] Changes underway in Cuba, together with the desperation of the refugees, provided incentive to interpret ambiguities about status – whether they originated in the profound uncertainty of Saint-Domingue itself or whether they emerged as a result of the journey to Cuba – in a particular way.

The Santiago that greeted the evacuees in the fall of 1803 was one in which slavery was growing at a significant pace, largely due to the influx of those very Saint-Domingue refugees. Already, in the period of 1798–1802, a community of Saint-Domingue refugees had settled in Santiago, and a subset of them was critical in expanding the place of commercial agriculture and trade in the region. One in particular, Prudencio Casamayor, was instrumental in that takeoff. He had arrived in Baracoa in 1797 and, with his brother, became involved in foreign trade there. In 1800, he moved to Santiago, set up a trading company and became perhaps the richest man in town. He armed privateers, owned vessels, and traded in slaves and Saint-Domingue coffee – which by 1801 had recovered to 57 percent of prerevolutionary levels. He worked closely with Santiago governor Kindelán, serving as official translator and informant on all things Saint-Domingue. He was "the general agent, business man, counselor and undoubtedly the banker of most of the French settlers."[78]

By the time of the massive influx of refugees in 1803, the source of Casamayor's power and prestige was wealth in land. He appears to have used the fortune he made in privateering and commerce to buy large tracts of land starting in 1802. From the Royal Treasury, he purchased former state lands (*realengos*) around El Cobre and Barajaguas; from private individuals, he bought more tracts in Hongolosongo and Dos Palmas, and together with other rich Saint-Domingue refugees, he bought huge

77 Renault, *D'une île rebelle*, 183.
78 Quote is from Gabriel Debien, "Les colons de Saint-Domingue réfugiés à Cuba," 585. On Prudencio Casamayor's activities, see Francisco Pérez de la Riva, *El café: Historia de su cultivo y explotación en Cuba* (Havana: Jesús Montero, 1944), chap. 3; Juan Pérez de la Riva, "La implantación francesa;" M.E. Orozco Melgar, "La implantación francesa en Santiago de Cuba" and Olga Portuondo Zúñiga, "Santiago de Cuba, los colonos franceses, y el fomento cafetalero," in Lamore, *Les Français*; Laura Cruz Ríos, *Flujos inmigratorios franceses en Santiago de Cuba (1800–1868)*, (Santiago: Editorial Oriente, 2006), 39–65 and Appendix 3; and AGI, Estado, leg. 2, exps. 3 and 24.

expanses of land in Santa Catalina near Guantánamo. In 1803 he owned a total of some 2,500 *caballerías* (approximately 26,000 *carreaux*, or 33,550 hectares). In some areas, he then divided the large expanses of land into small plots of 10 or 20 *caballerías* (104–208 *carreaux* or 134–168 hectares) and sold or rented them to people arriving with the deluge of vessels coming from Saint-Domingue.[79]

For those arriving with some resources the possibility of breaking into coffee production in Cuba was welcome. The price of land in the region was but a tiny fraction of what it had cost in Saint-Domingue, when the French could still buy land, and it was significantly cheaper than land in the booming Havana hinterland. Labor, on the other hand, was scarcer and dearer. Refugees who purchased land for coffee (and to a lesser extent indigo and cotton) appear to have relied on several sources of enslaved labor. Some retained access to putative slaves from Saint-Domingue who had made the journey with them, or whom they had purchased from other recent arrivals. Almost all supplemented their labor force with people newly purchased. Here, again, Casamayor appears to have lent his services, using his experience in that trade and his involvement in French privateering to help provide access to slave labor. He was, in the words of one Cuban historian, eastern Cuba's "great promoter of slave-based plantation capitalism," comparable perhaps to Francisco Arango in Havana.[80] Casamayor thus laid the groundwork, and Santiago governor Kindelán cooperated, condoning the presence of so-called French "slaves" to an extent that undermined his mandate to deport all but the absolutely necessary. It probably did not hurt that Casamayor had given Kindelán his own coffee estate, the *Santa Ana* in Gran Piedra.[81]

By standard measures, the strategy was hugely successful. Before the 1803 influx of Saint-Domingue refugees, eastern Cuba had a total of eight coffee farms. In 1804 alone, fifty-six new ones were started.[82] The physical and economic scale was not as large as that of the Havana boom. Growing coffee, after all, required less land, fewer hands, and

[79] Gabriel Debien, "Les colons de Saint-Domingue réfugiés à Cuba"; J. Pérez de la Riva. "La implantación francesa"; and O. Portuondo, "Santiago de Cuba."

[80] On Casamayor and the provision of slave labor, see J. Pérez de la Riva, "La implantación francesa" (quote is from p. 378), and Cruz Ríos, *Flujos inmigratorios*.

[81] María Elena Orozco Melgar, "Cuba et les îles sous le vent: La course comme facteur identitaire...," in Christian Lerat, ed., *Le monde caraïbe: Échanges transatlantiques et horizons post-coloniaux* (Bordeaux: Pessac, 2003), 97–116.

[82] M.E. Orozco Melgar, "La implantación francesa"; F. Pérez de la Riva, *El café*, chap. 3; and ANC, RCJF, leg. 92, exp. 3929.

little capital outlay compared to that necessary to grow sugar.[83] But the
coffee boom wrought by the French arrivals brought large-scale, slave-
based commercial agriculture to eastern Cuba for the first time.

Thus, precisely at the moment when the French were militarily defeated
in Saint-Domingue, and as the black victors, former slaves, declared independence and reaffirmed emancipation, a reactionary order – of coffee,
slave trading, and slavery – emerged in Santiago. People who would have
remained free in Saint-Domingue/Haiti became slaves once more in Cuba,
joined by new captives from Africa or other parts of the Caribbean. And
planters who had shipped coffee to the United States from southern Saint-
Domingue now grew it and shipped it from eastern Cuba.

When plotting the downfall of Toussaint and the revolution of Saint-
Domingue, Napoleon had looked to the Spanish in Cuba as an ally in
his counterrevolution, one that would provide material aid because of a
shared commitment to slavery and European rule. In the final months of
1803, as the failure of Napoleon's project became clear, Cuba served as
a source of a different kind of assistance. It provided a space – literally
and figuratively – where something like the old Saint-Domingue could be
sustained for the time being, where masters and slaves would once again
be masters and slaves, and where coffee planters could continue to try to
approximate the fortunes of prerevolutionary Saint-Domingue. In Cuba,
French planters could keep their sights on Saint-Domingue and profitably
weather a crisis that even after thirteen years they believed might still be
reversible. They made their Cuban fortunes, but they still enumerated
property – in land and in people – in the place they refused to call Haiti.[84]
And French authorities explicitly discussed the usefulness of this nucleus
of French planters in Cuba, who might serve as an important resource
should France recoup Saint-Domingue or should Cuban territory ever
come under French rule.[85] Eastern Cuba functioned as a kind of alternative space, where planters defeated by the Haitian Revolution could start
anew and thus partially undo the revolution that had almost destroyed
them.

---

[83] Importantly, of the Havana sugar mills with the ten largest harvests in 1804, eight had
been constructed by French technicians. See Moreno Fraginals, *El ingenio*, 1:75.

[84] This is clearly evident in notarial records in Santiago. See, for example, the individual
entries in Escribanía del Cabildo, Protocolos 2, and Escribanía Raúl Manuel Caminero
Ferrer, Protocolos 58 and 59 in AHPSC.

[85] In 1806, for instance, a rumor circulated in French circles that Spain was preparing to
trade former Santo Domingo for part of Cuba. Debien, "Les colons de Saint-Domingue
réfugiés à Cuba," 589–591.

Napoleon's project in Saint-Domingue had been defeated, but its remnants took root elsewhere. On France's evacuation of Saint-Domingue, the former Spanish part of the island, Santo Domingo, became a space of military counterrevolution. From there French officials challenged Haitian sovereignty and kept alive the threat of a French reconquest.[86] Eastern Cuba became a space of economic counterrevolution. This was another way in which the Haitian Revolution helped propel Cuban slavery and plantation society. The presence of the refugees, then, served both as a tangible reminder of black victory in Haiti and as evidence of the flexibility and resilience of the system just defeated in Saint-Domingue.

Black Leadership Again

Of course, in Saint-Domingue itself, black men and women challenged and ultimately defeated the French campaign to undo revolution and emancipation. In Cuba, proximity to the revolution and long-standing patterns of communication ensured that people encountered perspectives very different from those represented by the expansion of coffee slavery around Santiago. Indeed, as the French in Saint-Domingue approached their defeat, Cubans heard and read the words and ideas of an emerging and completely unprecedented class of black political leaders in the New World. So as the Santiago governor and his deputies collected the statements of thousands of refugees who explicitly cast themselves as the victims of black violence, they also received eloquent testimonies to the contrary.

In September 1803, for example, Governor Kindelán received a letter from Nicolas Geffrard, who had lived in Santiago after the War of the South and was among the contingent of free people of color who had returned to Saint-Domingue early in the Leclerc expedition. Originally an ally of Leclerc, in the fall of 1802 he was one of many defectors to the rebel cause; indeed, by the War of Independence, he commanded all the rebel forces of the south. In 1803, his letter to Kindelán was an eloquent and brutal condemnation of the comportment of the French army and government in Saint-Domingue. He spoke from personal experience, having witnessed and escaped Leclerc's last desperate measures in October 1802, when French forces in Le Cap rounded up and drowned thousands of black and colored members of the colonial army.[87] Geffrard vividly

---

[86] See Chapter 5.
[87] Girard, *Slaves*, 209–217.

recounted the atrocities for Cuban authorities, casting black and mulatto rebels as the rightful bearers of justice and humanity, the white French as its barbaric usurpers. His letter to the Cuban governor is worth quoting at length:

> The French Generals sent to Saint-Domingue have made themselves guilty before justice and humanity.... You are too close to this island not to know that they have repaid the constancy of our affection and our loyalty to the Metropolis with gallows, by tossing and drowning us in the depths of the sea, with executions.... Every day in Le Cap they had dogs taught to live off human blood devour three or four of our brothers. You must have hesitated to believe that these cannibal dogs were cared for by the Captain-General's Honor Guard.... Inspired by a temper deeper than that of Nero, Caligula, and Heliogabalus, Rochambeau forced our daughters and sisters in Port-au-Prince to dance in a salon in his house ... decorated with heads and bones of the dead, lit by the frightening light of a Sepulchral lamp. Yes, Governor, these terrible events are exceedingly true; more than 15,000 of us have perished.... Was it not enough to rob us of our liberty so solemnly proclaimed?... [France] wanted more: our properties, our lives![88]

Geffrard asked – perhaps rhetorically – about the disbelief and horror with which the Cuban governor might have read his account of French atrocities against men of color. Yet Cuban authorities were already well aware of much of what he mentioned. They had received accounts of the drownings and of men gassed to death with sulfur in the holds of French ships. And they certainly knew about dogs trained to devour black men, for it was the colonial state in Cuba that had provided them free of charge.[89] All that was now past, concluded Geffrard. Foreshadowing what would soon appear in Haiti's Declaration of Independence, he added:

> After having demonstrated a patience never before seen in history, we have risen up against our assassins, and made strong by the justice of our cause ... we have taken all of the countryside. We have battled against those reptiles arrived from Europe, we have vanquished them.... Expelling the monsters from this

---

[88] Kindelán to Someruelos, September 15, 1803, enclosing Geffrard to Someruelos, 27 Fructidor An 11 [sic], in AGI, Estado, leg. 2, exp. 59; and Kindelán to Someruelos, November 14, 1803, in AGI, Cuba, leg. 1537B. On rebel leaders' overtures to the British in Jamaica in 1803, see Julia Gaffield, "Haiti and Jamaica in the Remaking of the Early Nineteenth-Century Atlantic World, *William & Mary Quarterly*, 69, 3 (2012): 583–614.

[89] See Kindelán to Someruelos, November 30, 1802, in AGI, Cuba, leg. 1536B.

territory, we promise never to disturb the peace of our neighbors. Masters today of ourselves... our hearts dictate that we treat our neighbors as we ask them to treat us.[90]

He closed with an offer to open up Haitian ports to Spanish trade.

Kindelán never replied. Instead, he set about discovering the channels by which the letter traveled from Geffrard in Saint-Domingue to Kindelán, interrogating several local residents who had received and passed on the letter. The process he uncovered suggests, among other things, that an explicit defense of black independence and emancipation and a condemnation of French brutality entered the same public sphere in which sensational stories of black violence and white flight already had the status of routine knowledge and common sense.

In fact, an important purveyor of the insurgents' vision of freedom was the readily available *Gaceta de Madrid*, which had dedicated considerable space to covering the Leclerc expedition and its aftermath. Given the news it was publishing, Cuban authorities came to see the newspaper as a serious problem. Someruelos wrote to the Minister of State to urge that the government use more restraint in what it chose to publish. He explained that the newspaper was "sold to the public, and everyone buys it, and it circulates well among the blacks," who, he added, read it, discussed it, and analyzed its contents "with considerable spirit [*viveza*]."[91]

Thus it was that in this state-sponsored newspaper, people in Cuba encountered not only gripping accounts of black military victories but also public expressions of the ideals of freedom elaborated by Haitian rebels. Indeed, it published the very words of the black leaders fighting the French. The issue of the gazette that had prompted the Cuban captain-general to complain to Madrid contained two proclamations by black Haitian leaders, both dated November 29, 1803. One was signed by Dessalines, regarding the evacuation of Le Cap, and another was signed by Dessalines, Henri Christophe, and Agustin Clervaux declaring independence from France. In both documents, the black leaders invited refugees who had fled the colony to return and live peacefully under

[90] Kindelán to Someruelos, September 15, 1803, enclosing Geffrard to Someruelos, 27 Fructidor An 11 [sic], in AGI, Estado, leg. 2, exp. 59; and Kindelán to Someruelos, November 14, 1803, in AGI, Cuba, leg. 1537B.
[91] Someruelos to Sec. de Estado, May 25, 1804, in AHN, Estado, leg. 6366, exp. 78. A transcription of the letter also appears in Someruelos to Sec. de Estado, August 13, 1809, in AGI, Estado, leg. 12, exp. 50.

the new system being erected. But their invitation also entailed a clear threat.

> The God who protects us, the God of free men, commands us to extend our victorious arms towards [the refugees]. But those who, intoxicated with a foolish pride.... still think that they alone form the essence of human nature and who pretend to think that they are destined by heaven to be our owners and our tyrants [can] never come near the island of Santo Domingo, because if they do, they will find only chains and deportation.[92]

This was the proclamation that had so worried Someruelos – a proclamation in which was manifest the power of new black leaders, who forbade the return of Saint-Domingue to its colonial ruler.

Just one week after Someruelos penned his attack on the publication of this document, a new proclamation appeared in the pages of the gazette. This time it was the official Haitian Declaration of Independence, signed by Dessalines on January 1, 1804, and published in the gazette six months later on June 1.[93] We know that other copies of the Haitian Declaration of Independence had already arrived in Cuba, aboard French ships, for example, and that authorities on the island had done their best to have them confiscated.[94] But despite their attempts to limit its circulation, by June the declaration was translated into Spanish and published in a newspaper that circulated among Cuban blacks. Thus were people of color in Cuba able to read or hear the Haitian Declaration of Independence, a proclamation of former slaves who had vanquished their masters by force of arms.

What Cubans would have encountered in that printed, translated version of the declaration was not only a confirmation of black military victory, but also powerful evidence of the black leaders' participation in contemporary political and intellectual arguments about freedom, race, and rights. The principal aim of the document was to publicly sever ties with France and to establish and name a new state, Haiti. "Independence

---

[92] *GM*, March 23, 1804, 267–268. Only recently has this proclamation been regarded as an authentic, first declaration of independence. See Leslie Manigat, "Une brève analyse-commentaire critique d'un document historique," *Revue de la Société Haïtienne d'Histoire et de Géographie*, 221 (2005): 44–56; Jenson, *Beyond the Slave Narrative*, chaps. 2 and 3; and David Geggus, "Haiti's Declaration of Independence," and Patrick Tardieu, "The Debate Surrounding the Printing of the Haitian Declaration of Independence," both in Julia Gaffield, ed., *The Haitian Declaration of Independence*, forthcoming.

[93] *GM*, June 1, 1804.

[94] Someruelos to Cevallos, March 14, 1804, in AHN, Estado, leg. 6366, exp. 70.

or death!" was its rallying cry. In this it echoed the first American Declaration of Independence a few decades earlier, whose signatories pledged
their lives to independence. But in almost every other regard, the Haitian
document was *sui generis*. It was a work of critical, sometimes subversive engagement with the assumptions that underlay the proclamations
of the two preceding Atlantic revolutions. Against the well-worn claim
that the black rebels of Saint-Domingue were directed by white manipu-
lators stood the statement, "We dared to be free when we were not [free],
for ourselves and by ourselves," which explicitly cast them as agents of
their own history and their own liberty.[95] Against the familiar accusations of black savagery stood instead the attribution of that savagery to
France and Europe: "barbarians who for ages have stained [our country]
with blood," "assassins – tigers still covered in the blood [of our] wives,
husbands, brothers, sisters." French commitment to liberty, meanwhile,
was a sham. France held up a "phantom of liberty" before the eyes and
ears of the blacks and tried to conquer them, not just through physical
violence, but also with the "piteous eloquence of their agents' proclamations." Readers of the printed Declaration of Independence would have
thus encountered a powerful reversal of standard racist fare. Here, black
men and women fought against the savage, deceitful French to "ensure
the empire of liberty," "this territory of liberty" in Haiti.[96]

The final phase of the Haitian Revolution constituted a war between
revolutionary emancipationism and a counterrevolution of slavery and
racism. If the French evacuation appeared to signal a victory for the
former, in a world still very much invested in slavery's regime, that victory could well prove insubstantial. The new Haitian state might seek to
project its voice and vision of antislavery, black solidarity, and Haitian
sovereignty. But its leaders understood the obstacles. They knew the question was: Who would listen and how?

In Cuba – as elsewhere – men with power and men with slaves defied
Haiti's challenge through the most effective means possible. They refused
to acknowledge it at any level. They continued to write about the place
that had become Haiti as a "foreign colony" named "Santo Domingo,"
Spanish, of course, for Saint-Domingue. And Spain, like every power
of the age, withheld recognition. Second, they continued to rely on the

[95] *GM*, June 1, 1804.
[96] Julia Gaffield found the first known surviving copy of the printed Declaration of
Independence in TNA, CO, 137/111/1. It is available on the TNA website at http://
nationalarchives.gov.uk/documentsonline/haiti.asp. For a translation, see Dubois and
Garrigus, eds., *Slave Revolution*, 188–191.

institutions of slavery and colonialism and the assumptions of racial superiority. In Havana, when the *cabildo* and the Real Consulado met in the
first months of 1804, members did not even mention Haitian independence. Neither was the Declaration of Independence noted in the Santiago *cabildo*. All three institutions, meanwhile, did celebrate when, a
few months later, on April 22, 1804, the king of Spain, for the "good of
the Nation and the prosperity of [his] dominions" extended the "free"
slave trade for another twelve years for Spanish traders and six years for
foreign ones. Haiti's challenge aside, slavery would stand.

Still, even the confident extension of the slave trade in Spanish territories seemed to contain the traces of other possibilities made more
imaginable as a result of the Haitian Revolution. Thus, the king's Royal
Cédula reaffirmed (once more) the "absolute prohibition" against the
introduction of creole or *ladino* slaves, reflecting the widely held belief
that it was creole slaves who were most responsible for dangerous ideas
and acts. On the same day, the king issued a companion decree specifically for Cuba. It called for the introduction of female slaves as a way to
increase the labor force at more modest expense. Importantly, the decree
was issued in secret, to avoid the "*incovenientes*" that would result if
the enslaved learned of it and demanded its immediate implementation.
Thus, as Haiti began its life as an independent nation, in nearby Cuba,
the king made policy that sought to consolidate the boom in slave-based
plantation production, while at the same time nodding to the emerging
threat posed by the enslaved themselves.[97] The battle between freedom
and slavery that engulfed late revolutionary Saint-Domingue would continue to reverberate beyond its borders.

---

[97] Real Cédula, April 22, 1804, in ANC, Reales Ordenes (hereafter RO), leg. 40, exp.
56, another copy of which appears in BNJM, CM Morales, libro 80, no. 11; Cabildo
ordinario, August 23, 1804, in AHOHCH, AC, vol. 60, f. 132v; and José Antonio Saco,
*Historia de la esclavitud de la raza africana en el nuevo mundo y en especial en los países
Américo-Hispanos*, (Havana: Ministerio de Educación, 1960–1963), 3: 53.

5

"Masters of All"

Echoes of Haitian Independence in Cuba

On January 1, 1804, Jean-Jacques Dessalines became the first head of state of the new country of Haiti. A former slave, possibly African born, unable to read or write, he took the reins of power vowing no return to slavery or French rule. Newspapers of the day hinted at the portent of the rupture: "The Negroes have substituted for St. Domingo, *Haiti*, the name which the island originally bore," with that word symbolically erasing European dominion.[1] What the rupture would entail in practice, no one knew. In France and England, in the United States, in Jamaica, Cuba, and in Haiti itself, people struggled to apprehend what Haiti's existence would mean: A doomed experiment to wait out in anticipation of the return of Europe and slavery? A model of black capacity that abolitionists could tout? An African maroon state writ large? A new kind of power poised to extend militant antislavery across the hemisphere?

In the January 1 Declaration of Independence, which circulated widely across the Atlantic world, people of many stations listened and read for clues. In it, Haitian leaders offered a public and formal promise of non-intervention, much like the one they had delivered unofficially to Cuban authorities in the final months of 1803. The 1804 declaration announced, "Let our neighbors live in peace . . . let us not, as revolutionary firebrands, declare ourselves legislators of the Antilles, nor let our glory consist in troubling the peace of neighboring islands."[2]

---

[1] *Daily Advertiser* (New York), March 5, 1804 (XX, 5909, p. 3). On the question of whether Dessalines was African born, see Deborah Jenson, "Jean-Jacques Dessalines and the African Character of the Haitian Revolution," *William and Mary Quarterly*, 69, 3 (July 2012): 615–638; Geggus, *Haitian Revolutionary Studies*, 208.

[2] Haiti, Declaration of Independence, TNA, CO, 137/111/1, available at: http://nationalarchives.gov.uk/documentsonline/haiti.asp. For the 1803 promise to Cuban

It is unlikely, however, that governors and planters in the region would have felt reassurance at the promise, especially given other things intimated in the text itself. "Peace to our neighbors, but anathema to the French name! Eternal hatred of France! Such are our principles." But what did Dessalines mean when in the midst of his vehement denunciation of France, he exhorted, "Let us frighten all those who would dare try to take [liberty] from us again; let us *begin* with the French"? Contemporary newspapers sometimes ended their published extracts of the declaration precisely with that line, as if to persuade readers that the story had not ended with the Declaration of Independence.[3]

Indeed, in the first days and months of the new year – Year 1 in the Haitian Revolutionary calendar, still Year 12 in the French – day-to-day life unfolded against a backdrop that may have felt less like the achievement of a definitive independence than like an uncertain reprieve in a long, drawn-out war. The effects of this war – subdued and low-grade by comparison to what came before – were palpable around the region. In Spain, and especially in its territories close to Haiti, the idea that black leaders would target Spanish interests and even Spanish people was not new. During the Revolution, when France and Spain had been at war, Spanish military leaders in Hispaniola had continually predicted that when the black army tired of fighting the French, it would target the Spanish. After that war, Spain became France's ally and provided significant military and financial support to France in its futile attempt to retain control of Saint-Domingue. So when Haitian leaders announced that they were "begin[ning] with the French," Spanish authorities in Cuba, as allies of France and just miles from Haiti, felt particularly exposed.

In Cuba, where the revolution's runoff had arrived almost immediately, much remained unchanged. The slave trade continued; indeed, in April 1804, the "free" trade in African captives was reaffirmed and strengthened.[4] Still, as the Cuban captain-general reported to his superiors in Spain, zealous vigilance was needed in order to "find out the progress of that new government, its political and military maxims, its land and naval forces, Dessalines's views of the Spanish government, and anything else that would be useful for the precaution of our Colonies" (Figure 5.1).[5]

---

authorities, see Geffrard to Someruelos, 27 Fructidor An 11 [sic], in AGI, Estado, leg. 2, exp. 59.

[3] Ibid (emphasis added), and *Evening Post* (New York), March 7, 1804.

[4] Murray, *Odious Commerce*, chap. 1.

[5] Someruelos to Cevallos, August 20, 1804, in AHN, Estado, leg. 6366, exp. 89.

Coronacion de Juan Santiago Desalines primer
Emperador de Hayti

FIGURE 5.1. Emperor Jean-Jacques Dessalines, 1805. Courtesy of the John Carter Brown Library at Brown University.

As the Haitian state materialized from the long, tumultuous revolution, Spanish authorities in Cuba soon found themselves confronting aggressive Haitian attacks on their shipping and plausible reports of Haitian state agents infiltrating Spanish territory. On the ground, on plantations, and in the countryside, local authorities witnessed the emergence of self-styled Haitian agents – enslaved men, born in Saint-Domingue, or Africa, or Jamaica, or Cuba, vowing to do as the Haitians had done.

Years ago, Eugene Genovese argued that the Haitian Revolution propelled a parallel revolution in black consciousness, as slaves and people of color across the Atlantic world fixed on the example of revolution in Saint-Domingue as inspiration and model.[6] But independence itself also made a difference. For now, ostensibly, the story had an outcome: the once-enslaved had won; they had taken the land and become masters of all. As masters, they had set about creating a national state, one with an army, a navy, and with leaders who strove to project its new voice. Though neighboring authorities did not use the term "foreign policy" to describe the way that the new state would deal with its neighbors, in Cuba they did wonder: Is our system in its sights? They knew already that Haiti was in the sights of the growing black and enslaved population living under their rule.

Haitian Independence as Fact and Fiction

Haiti's Declaration of Independence was the second in the hemisphere. The first and more famous one, the U.S. Declaration of Independence, signed on July 4, 1776, boldly signaled the North American colonists' intention to form a new state and society. But the North American revolutionary war would not end for another six years. In Haiti, the January 1, 1804, Declaration of Independence came at the end of the war, after the signing of the Articles of Capitulation by Rochambeau and after the evacuation of the French army from the cities of the former Saint-Domingue. Yet not a single neighboring government recognized Haitian independence; all continued technically to consider it a colony of France in rebellion. France, meanwhile, refused to give up its claim to the territory. Indeed, French statesmen hoped to use the eastern part of the island, former Spanish Santo Domingo, a French possession since the 1795 Treaty of Basel, as a launching pad from which to organize the reconquest of Saint-Domingue/Haiti. France's governor there, Marie-Louis Ferrand,

---

[6] Genovese, *From Rebellion to Revolution*, 96.

recruited French refugees in places such as Cuba for the purpose of making war on Haiti. He published declarations against Dessalines and the Haitian army, whom he continued to call "brigands." He issued prohibitions on trading with the ports under Haitian control, aggressively challenging the very fact of Haitian independence.[7] As Deborah Jenson has argued, in 1804 Ferrand launched a campaign to assert France's sovereignty over all of Hispaniola – a sovereignty, she adds, "exerted with the single goal of marginalizing, not governing, Haiti."[8] From just across an always-porous border, France waged economic, political, and intellectual war on Haiti.

Not surprisingly, then, the new Haitian government immediately assumed a defensive position. In the first year of its existence, the new state bolstered its naval forces, and by the end of the year it counted, said reports, on "50 gunboats, a schooner and a brigantine with 14 cannons."[9] Confident that the Haitian army's strength against the French consisted in maintaining mountain strongholds, Dessalines ordered the fortification of the interior and vowed that in case of an attack, the coastal towns would be destroyed and the country defended from the mountains. Cannons were moved from the coasts. Every citizen, without regard to color, was required to do the physical labor of moving the heavy equipment into the mountains. The loads (at least in theory) were proportioned according to the individual's strength, and residents were prohibited from hiring anyone to do the labor for them. The work of fortifying the interior was soon enshrined in the country's first constitution in 1805, the last article of which declared that "at the first sound of the alarm cannon, the towns will disappear and the nation rise." It was fitting, then, that new nation's name was Haiti, "land of tall mountains."[10]

---

[7] On Ferrand, see Fernando Pico, *One Frenchman, Four Revolutions: General Ferrand and the Peoples of the Caribbean* (Princeton, N.J.: Markus Wienner, 2011), and Graham Nessler, "A Failed Emancipation? The Struggle for Freedom in Hispaniola during the Haitian Revolution," PhD diss., University of Michigan, 2011. For responses in Cuba to his attempts to recruit French refugees, see Someruelos to Ferrand, March 31, 1804, in AGI, Cuba, leg. 1707.

[8] Jenson, *Beyond the Slave Narrative*, 113.

[9] "D. Domingo de Grandallana traslada a D. Francisco de Borja lo que comunicó el 29 de Diciembre el Comandante de la Marina de la Coruña sobre las atrocidades que cometen los negros de la Ysla de Santo Domingo contra las embarcaciones españolas," January 9, 1805, in AMN, Departamento de Cartagena. mss 2238, doc. 69, ff. 242–43.

[10] On the policy of fortifying the interior, see Girard, *Slaves*, 317. For examples of journalistic coverage of the policies, see *Commercial Advertiser* (New York), April 10, 1804; *Alexandria Advertiser*, May 16, 1804. The Haitian Constitution, General Measures,

Whether in preparation for further war or to consolidate a victory already won, the new Haitian state took other steps, none more controversial than the preemptive elimination of potential enemies, identified for the most part on the basis of national and racial origin. In the tense and uncertain first weeks of independence, rumors circulated about the imminent destruction of the white French population in Haiti. The January 1 Declaration of Independence had already suggested such a path.

The French name still haunts our land.... When will we tire of breathing the air that they breathe.... They are not our brothers, that they will never be, and if they find refuge among us, they will plot again to trouble and divide us.... Look for your children, your suckling infants, what have they become? I shudder to say it... the prey of these vultures.... What are you waiting for before appeasing their spirits?... Will you descend into their tombs without having avenged them? No! Their bones would reject yours.

Then, on February 22, Dessalines published a proclamation that launched publicly the campaign of executions. Issued at Gonaïves, the document ordered the arrest and execution of all persons known to have participated in any way in the massacres carried out by Leclerc and Rochambeau's governments. It also cast that campaign in the language of justice, government procedure, and national consolidation. Article 3 ordered the publication of the full names of all those executed, "to warn all the nations that while we give refuge and protection to those who act toward us with good faith and friendship, nothing will deter our vengeance against the assassins who have taken pleasure in bathing in the blood of the innocent children of Haiti." Dessalines personally traveled from city to city, sometimes overseeing the selection of those to be executed and those to be saved. All in all, most of the remaining white French residents were killed, their goods confiscated for the new state.[11]

The news circulated at lightning speed. All spring and into summer, foreign newspapers published riveting accounts under such headlines as "Massacre of All the Whites of St. Domingo."[12] News of early massacres in Les Cayes began circulating in March, with many of the victims

---

Article 28 is available on Constitutions of the World Online, http://www.modern-constitutions.de/nbu.php?page_id=02a1b5a86ff13947rcob1c57f23ac196&show_doc=HT-00-1805-05-20-fr. On the naming of Haiti, see Geggus, *Haitian Revolutionary Studies*, chap. 13.

[11] The February 22 proclamation appears in Jean-Jacques Dessalines, *Lois et actes sous le règne de Jean-Jacques Dessalines* (Port-au-Prince: Éditions Presses Nationales d'Haïti, 2006), 21–22.

[12] *Philadelphia Evening Post*, June 3, 1804.

identified by name and sometimes by profession: Gatreau, interpreter; Laboissiere, merchant; Toirac, doctor; and others, among them a host of planters. Forty-five unnamed men belonging "to a privateer of St. Yago [Santiago] de Cuba" were hanged on February 15 at sunrise, "and 150 more killed, whose names are not known."[13] Stories published far and wide publicized accounts of massacres across Haitian territory: Les Cayes, Jacmel, Jérémie, Port-au-Prince, Gonaïves, and Le Cap. Such accounts often echoed the sensationalism of revolutionary-era narratives about the misfortune of innocent victims, the hellish cruelties of the avengers, and the unspeakability of the acts committed.[14]

As was often the case, other, very different interpretations of the events also circulated at the time, to be mostly forgotten later. Dessalines's February justifications for the policies were widely published and discussed abroad. On April 28, as the massacres ended, Dessalines issued a new proclamation, proudly and famously announcing that he had "avenged America."

> At last the hour of vengeance has arrived and the implacable enemies of the rights of man have suffered the punishment due their crimes.... Thus perish all tyrants over innocence, all oppressors of mankind!... We have rendered to these true cannibals war for war, crime for crime, outrage for outrage.[15]

Together, Dessalines's proclamations of January 1, February 22, and April 28, 1804, cast vengeance as a necessary foundation for the new state. It represented, on the one hand, a reconciliation with ancestors and fellow citizens achieved through violent, final retribution, and, on the other, the consolidation of the state by the physical removal of the most visible internal opposition.

Copies of the April 28 proclamation explaining the massacres appeared (like the other two) in international newspapers. Sometimes, newspapers printed correspondence between Haitian government officials and private individuals, relating the scale and depths of French atrocities in 1802–3, in part to make Haitian retaliation seem tempered in comparison, to educate an international public about the horrors of French rule, and to

---

[13] *Daily Advertiser* (New York), March 5, 1804, and *Philadelphia Evening Post*, April 18, 1804.

[14] For a few examples, *Connecticut Herald*, May 1, 1804, *Philadelphia Evening Post*, June 3, 1804; *United States Gazette* (Philadelphia), May 1, 1804; *Alexandria Daily Advertiser*, May 16, 1804; *Charleston Courrier*, May 29, 1804; *The Balance and Columbian Repository*, (Hudson, NY), June 12, 1804.

[15] Dessalines, *Lois et actes*, 27–31. A copy appeared in *The Balance and Columbian Repository*, June 19, 1804.

help seal the moral legitimacy of the new state that had emerged in opposition to it. But as Deborah Jenson has pointed out, the Haitians may have "misinterpreted...the degree to which Americans could be reassured by the notion of a carefully targeted rather than random execution of whites."[16]

In Cuba, the press did not give much coverage to the massacres. The *Gaceta de Madrid* appears to have published just one story about an alleged census of whites conducted by Dessalines just before he ordered the execution of the men and put the women to labor on public works. Unlike the U.S. press, Spanish and Cuban newspapers did not publish extensive accounts of the spring campaign or Dessalines's proclamations about them. After complaints from the captain general in Cuba about the publication of Haitian proclamations, the minister of state had instructed the newspaper's editor to stop printing articles about black victories in the errant colony. The articles, he argued, posed a risk to the security of white and European rule.[17]

But news, as always, was accessible in other ways. During the revolutionary period itself, people seeking to escape unrest in Saint-Domingue had made for nearby Cuban shores. So too in this period did people furtively sail or row to Baracoa, Guantánamo, and Santiago, in hopes of escaping the massacres.[18] In Le Cap, Christophe issued a proclamation forbidding ship captains from transporting French residents out of the country; in such cases, vessels and cargo would be confiscated and the shipmaster executed. According to press reports, Haitian schooners and row boats patrolled the waters, and officers boarded every vessel leaving Haitian ports in search of French passengers trying to escape.[19] Christophe's decree notwithstanding, it seems that some officials tolerated the departures. On March 31, authorities in Les Cayes approved the departure of a Madame Latapier aboard the sloop *Saint-Joseph*,

[16] Jenson, *Beyond the Slave Narrative*, 140.

[17] Marqués de Someruelos to D. Pedro Cevallos, March 14, 1804, in AHN, Estado, leg. 6366, exp. 70; Cevallos to Someruelos, July 19, 1804, in AGI, Cuba, 1733.

[18] For news of arrivals in the months during the massacres, see, for example: Kindelán to Comandante de la Compañía de Cazadores, March 2, 1804 in ANC, CCG, leg. 66, exp. 2; Kindelán to Someruelos, March 10, 1804, in ANC, CCG, leg. 66, exp. 5; Martín Flores Quijano to Kindelán, June 24, 1804 (three letters on same date regarding different arrivals); Carlos de Cobian [?] to Kindelán, June 25 or 29, 1804; and Kindelán to Someruelos, June 29, 1804, all in ANC, CCG, leg. 67, exp. 1. For a general discussion of the challenges raised by this new wave of refugees, see Baracoa cabildo minutes, May 11, 1804, enclosed in Kindelan to Someruelos, June 9, 1804, in AGI, Cuba, leg. 1693.

[19] *Commercial Adverstiser* (New York), April 10, 1804.

captained by Felix Saint-Jean, himself Haitian and black. Before leaving Les Cayes Saint-Jean presented himself to the port registry office to give notification of the journey, list his crew members and their salaries, and agree to observe Haitian laws of navigation and commerce. He also appeared before customs officials in Les Cayes and received permission to carry Madame Latapier's belongings to Cuba. He received approvals from both offices, under seals that read *Liberté ou la Mort, Isle d'Ayty, Anne 1 de l'Independence* [sic], which Cuban authorities quoted verbatim and then described, as they might have years earlier, as documents issued by "rebel blacks in said colony."[20]

Importantly, Spanish vessels helped transport people fleeing Haiti, thus exposing their captains and crews to punishment by the new state. Haitian corsairs captured the *Niño de la Humildad* and held its captain, Miguel Chaparro, and the crew for thirteen days before releasing them. From prison in the southern port of Côteaux, Chaparro learned that the Haitians had captured and condemned other Spanish vessels. "The only motive they gave for these actions," he explained, "was generally that Spanish vessels were transporting white residents from Saint-Domingue to Cuba."[21] So, while people in eastern Cuba did not have access to the sometimes sensational coverage of the massacres that circulated in U.S. newspapers, they did get to hear directly from men such as Chaparro or passengers such as Latapier.

News of Haitian happenings also arrived from towns in the former Spanish colony of Santo Domingo, contested between Dessalines and Ferrand. In early 1804, the border town of Montecristi, and further east, Santiago and Cotui, had come under the control of Dessalines, who appointed José Campos Tavares, a Spanish man of color, as his local commander. It was here in May 1804 that Ferrand waged armed war against the new Haitian state, sending French detachments to dislodge Campos Tavares and assert French authority.[22] Dessalines issued his first proclamation to the Spanish residents of Santo Domingo on May 8, 1804. In it,

[20] "Testimonio de los Autos obrados sobre el permiso pedido por la Dama francesa Latapie para la venta de una balandra Francesa nombrada San José procedente de los Cayos de San Luis a Fernando Muñoz con que arribó a este Puerto," in AGI, Cuba, 1538B.

[21] Testimony of Captain Miguel Chaparro, enclosed in Kindelán to Someruelos, March 31, 1804, in ANC, CCG, leg. 66, exp. 2.

[22] Emilio Cordero Michel, "Dessalines en Saint-Domingue Espagnol" in Alain Yacou, ed., *Saint-Domingue espagnol et la révolution nègre d'Haïti*, (Paris: Karthala, 2007); Gaspar Arredondo y Pichardo, "Memoria de mi salida de la isla de Santo Domingo el 28 de Abril de 1805," in Rodríguez Demorizi, *Invasiones Haitianas*; Sara Johnson, *The "Fear of French Negroes,"* chap. 2; and Nessler, "A Failed Emancipation?"

he stressed his benevolence toward the Spanish – up until that point – and then gave a glimpse of what awaited them should they support the French:

I have repressed until now the vehement ardor of my soldiers.... Know that my soldiers, impatient, await but a signal.... A few more instants and I will crush the rest of the French under the weight of my power. Spaniards! You, whom I address only because I wish to save you; you who have hesitated... I give you fifteen days from this proclamation to notify me of your intentions and embrace my cause. In a word, you know that I can do everything I intend; think of your salvation.[23]

The actions of Ferrand and Dessalines and the certainty of violent conflict unleashed a wave of refugees on Cuban shores. On May 8, 1804, the official date of Dessalines's proclamation, the British frigate *Tartar*, captained by John Perkins, a Jamaican-born man of color and possibly the first black commander in the British Navy, landed in Baracoa with ninety-four people fleeing from Montecristi to avoid "being slaughtered by the Blacks." Perkins returned to Montecristi and, by May 21, had transported a total of 932 refugees to Santiago. "I reflect on the happiness I felt on saving so many lives that would have otherwise been barbarously sacrificed by the brigands," he wrote.[24] On May 15, an American vessel captured by French corsairs operating out of Baracoa arrived with a smaller group of fleeing French and with copies of Dessalines' proclamations of April 28 (to the French on the massacres) and May 8 (to the Spanish threatening something similar). While the local governor confiscated the documents to prevent their circulation, the people who carried them certainly talked and conveyed what they had seen and feared.[25]

As the massacres of white French subsided, rumors swirled about Dessalines's plans to massacre people of color. The rumors led to more attempts at flight. One day in June, for example, eight canoes from Jérémie arrived in Baracoa with seventy-three passengers, the majority described as mulatto. The first week of July, another twenty-three arrived aboard three vessels. One day in August, thirty-five passengers, all of them of

---

[23] Dessalines proclamation, May 8, 1804, *Lois et actes*, 33–35.
[24] Someruelos to Pedro Cevallos, June 21, 1804, in AHN, Estado, leg. 6366, exp. 84. Perkins to Commander of Baracoa, enclosed in same. Log books of captain and master of the *Tartar* are in TNA, ADM 5/1498 and ADM 52/3703, respectively.
[25] Comandante Baracoa to Kindelán, May 15, 1804, in AHN, Estado, leg. 6366, exp. 84. On the conversations, see Arredondo, "Memoria de mi salida," in Rodríguez Demorizi, *Invasiones Haitianas*, 153. Baracoa cabildo minutes, May 11, 1804, enclosed in Kindelan to Someruelos, June 9, 1804, in AGI, Cuba, leg. 1693.

color, arrived in Santiago.[26] While the numbers cannot compare to the more than 18,000 that had arrived in Santiago in the second half of 1803, it is clear nonetheless that in the volatile first months of independence, amidst massacres actual and rumored, waves of people sought refuge on Cuban shores. The problem was significant enough to have prompted Dessalines to expand on Christophe's earlier prohibition on leaving the country. On October 22, 1804, Dessalines issued a decree aimed at curbing "the flight of men and women of color native to the country." Any captain caught transporting Haitians out of the country would be jailed for ten months and then banished, their cargo and ship confiscated. Meanwhile, "all natives found aboard foreign vessels [would] be shot in public."[27]

From massacres, to migrations, to vivid pronouncements against France, to calls to rise up in defense of liberty, the immediate postindependence period probably felt less like something entirely new than like one more chapter in a long and uncertain struggle. That Haitian leaders had the upper hand for the moment did not signal that the fight was over.

War and Trade

The French continued to wage war against their former colony, targeting in particular the new state's ability to engage in trade. In the summer of 1804, General Ferrand issued a decree fixing the physical boundaries of the territory controlled by France, and he announced that all ships trading to the west of those boundaries – that is, with Haiti – would be captured and considered fair prize. There was, in fact, significant trade to target, much of it from the United States. American ships traveled to Haitian ports loaded with flour or textiles, and purchased coffee above all. In addition to this "innocent" trade, as U.S. officials called it, there was another concurrent and well-known trade through which the Americans supplied Haiti with weapons and munitions.[28]

---

[26] Kindelán to Someruelos, June 23, 1804, in AGI, Cuba, 1549; Someruelos to Cevallos, July 21, 1804, in AHN, Estado, leg. 6366, exp. 87; Kindelán to Someruelos, July 15, 1804, and August 15, 1804, both in AGI, Cuba, 1538B.

[27] Dessalines, *Lois et actes*, 39–40.

[28] The value of U.S. exports to the French West Indies in 1805 was $7.4 million; the figure comes from John Coatsworth, "American Trade with European Colonies in the Caribbean, 1790–1812," *William & Mary Quarterly*, 24 (1967): 262. On United States–Haiti trade, see Rayford Logan, *The Diplomatic Relations of the United States with Haiti*,

Sometimes, the American ships also carried black men from Saint-Domingue who were now returning to independent Haiti. Just two weeks after independence, on January 14, 1804, Dessalines issued a proclamation explaining that because "a large number of native black and colored men suffer in the United States for lack of means to return to their country," Haiti would pay captains of American vessels forty *gourdes* for each person returned. Article 2 of the decree stated that a copy would be sent to the United States Congress. Copies were printed in several American newspapers, as well as in the *Gaceta de Madrid*, which circulated in Cuba.[29] In May 1804, the *Betsey* from Philadelphia carried guns, ammunition, and cannons; its crew was composed mostly of black sailors returning to Haiti. The *Louisiana*, also traveling out of Philadelphia at about the same time, carried munitions and about ninety "recruits."[30] The policy can be understood as evidence of the Haitian state seeking to make the freedom and sovereignty just achieved more widely accessible. But in the context of France's policy of nonrecognition, under which no sovereignty was acknowledged, the policy represented recruitment for belligerent purposes.

The French vociferously complained through diplomatic channels. But on the ground – and seas – other means were used. Ferrand did his own recruiting, issuing decrees that invited white French refugees in Cuba and elsewhere to return to his Saint-Domingue, promising housing, funds, and lands to those willing to take up arms against their black enemies.[31] While some heeded the call, it was largely through the practice of privateering that Ferrand carried out his most effective attack on the new Haitian state. He loosely licensed privateers, requiring little of them but to terrorize anyone trading with Haiti. In the first two years of Haitian independence, French privateers captured 106 American vessels traveling to or from Haiti. On February 15, 1805, Ferrand went as far as to declare that all individuals found on vessels bound to or from "any ports in Hispaniola

---

1776–1891 (Chapel Hill: UNC Press, 1941), chap. 5; and Greg Williams, *The French Assault on American Shipping, 1793–1813: A History and Comprehensive Record of Merchant Marine Losses* (Jefferson, N.C.: McFarland & Co., 2009). There was also significant British and Danish trade. See the testimony from the captain and crew of the Haitian vessel *Mainbau* in "Presa de la goleta de negros *Mainbau* de Santo Domingo por la corbeta *Desempeño*," January 22, 1805, in AGMAB, EA, leg. 37.

[29] Dessalines, *Lois et actes*, 13–14; *GM*, June 12, 1804, 522.

[30] Logan, *Diplomatic Relations*, chap. 5. The discussions of the *Betsey* and *Louisiana* appear on 162–163, 174.

[31] See Ferrand's decrees dates 26 Ventose An 12 and 6 Floreal An 13, both attached to Kindelán to Someruelos, #1490, May 27, 1805, in AGI, Cuba, 1539.

occupied by the rebels, shall suffer death." The same would hold true for those found within two leagues of any Haitian port.[32] With such acts, Ferrand actively disputed Haitian sovereignty, waging war, he insisted, against "brigands" rather than an independent nation.

However ambitious Ferrand's intentions, it was hard for him to provide a base for the privateers. British naval power around the island made it difficult for French vessels to make it back to Santo Domingo with their prizes. Even if they could make it back, there was not enough money in circulation there to make the sale of confiscated goods profitable for the privateers. So, as had happened during the revolution itself, France relied on Spanish ports for that purpose. The privateers often attacked American vessels in the Windward Passage between Baracoa and Môle Saint-Nicolas, taking their prizes to Baracoa and Santiago. The French privateers had letters of marque issued in Saint-Domingue before the French evacuation, or in Guadeloupe, or in Ferrand's Santo Domingo. Some, such as the citizen Santiago Savournin, captain of the *Adélaïde*, carried papers from Ferrand and entered regularly in Cuban ports with prize vessels, distinguishing himself, according to one historian, for his frequent capture of slaving vessels loaded with African captives.[33] Often the property was condemned *de facto* and without trial, the vessels and their (human and other) cargo sold, and duties that should have been paid to the king and state instead were divided among local Cuban officials complicit in the enterprise. In Baracoa, corruption was rampant, from the lieutenant governor, officials of the Royal Treasury, the mayor, the Coast Guard, down even to the notary.[34]

Of the 106 U.S. ships captured by French privateers, the majority, according to France's ambassador to the United States, were captured by Cuban-based French privateers targeting the Haitian–U.S. trade. The American brig *Fame*, for instance, owned and captained by James Misroon from Charleston, traveled to Le Cap to sell cloth and to buy

---

[32] On Ferrand and the privateer attacks on the Haiti–United States trade see Picó, *One Frenchman*, 46–49; Jenson, *Beyond the Slave Narrative*, 164; Williams, *French Assault*, 33.

[33] Ferrand, Comisión del Conductor de presas to Sr. Santos Savourrin, capitán del pilote bote nombrado *Argonaute*, October 22, 1805, in AHPSC, Juzgado de Primera Instancia, leg. 375; Minuta, Someruelos to Kindelán, July 31, 1804, and Kindelán to Someruelos, December 14, 1804, in AGI, Cuba, leg. 1538B; and Cruz Ríos, *Flujos inmigratorios*, 49.

[34] Jose Repilado (Tte Gob de Baracoa, after death of Murillo) to Kindelán, February 22, 1806, and Domingo Díaz Paez to Kindelán, Cuba, September 14, 1806, both in AGI, Cuba, leg. 1648.

coffee with the proceeds. He lingered at Le Cap, not being able to sell as much for as high a price as hoped. Finally, on his way back to Charleston, he was attacked by the French privateer *L'Union* and taken to Santiago de Cuba, where the vessel and cargo were condemned without trial. The same fate awaited dozens of American ships that had traveled to Haiti for trade and ended up captured by not-always-lawful French privateers and then diverted to Cuban coasts.[35]

French privateers also did not limit their attacks to American trade. They captured Haitian vessels directly, sometimes bringing those into Cuban ports as prizes, as happened, for instance, with the "privateer felucca belonging to the Brigands" appropriately named *La Liberté*.[36] They also attacked British trade to Haiti, targeting British vessels out of Môle Saint-Nicolas, Le Cap, Jérémie, and elsewhere in Haiti. Whatever attempts Spanish authorities made to comply with neutrality laws, it is clear that Cuban coasts were full of French privateers. The questioning involved in trying to determine whether they were there with legitimate reason often merely provided the time necessary to sell the captured vessels and cargo. Privateer captains testified that they had legitimate letters of marque and that their charge was to attack shipping to the ports held by the rebels, or blacks, or brigands, in order, said one, to "annihilate" them. Excuses and denials notwithstanding, a significant and aggressive community of French privateers flourished in eastern Cuba.[37]

The Spanish colony of Cuba thus actively supported France's assault on Haiti, in particular on Haiti's ability to trade with foreign powers. Haiti was not long in retaliating. Visiting Saint-Domingue in the spring of 1803, Cuban planter and statesman Francisco Arango had predicted that the greatest threat an independent Haiti would represent to Cuba was its potential to endanger Cuban commerce by attacking local shipping. In the first months of 1804, his prediction began to materialize. As far away as La Coruña in Spain, port commanders were taking note of

35 Williams, *The French Assault*, 49, 58, 63, 88, 103, 112, 113, 126, 133, 135, 141, 178, 189, 206, 216, 231, 243, 278, 309, 323, 324, 335, 346. The case of the *Fame* appears on p. 141. The Americans believed Spanish officials to be involved in this illegitimate business. See James Madison, Official Instruction to Robert R. Livingston, March 31, 1804, in *The Writings of James Madison [1803–1807]*, edited by Gaillard Hunt (New York: Knickerbocker Press, 1807), 7: 136. See also Marqués de Irujo sobre queja de los EEUU de armarse corsarios franceses en Cuba, July 4, 1804, in AGI, Cuba, leg. 1707.
36 Fernando Murillo to Kindelán, October 24, 1804, in ANC, CCG, leg. 67, exp. 14.
37 On British complaints, see "El Marqués de Someruelos evacua el pendiente informe sobre la quexa del Ministro Británico de armarse corsarios franceses en aquella isla," September 1, 1804, in AHN, Estado, leg. 6366(2), exp. 91.

the growing maritime force of the new state, which seemed willing to go fifteen or twenty miles out to sea to capture Spanish vessels.[38] Among the first incidents to be noted was the Haitian capture of the Spanish schooner *Santa María*, declared legitimate prize by General L. Bazelais at Jérémie on March 3, 1804. In summer 1804, the polacre *San Antonio de Padua*, headed for Santiago de Cuba, was captured by Haitian forces, boarded, said reports, by twenty-five or twenty-six black men, its merchandise confiscated, and its crew imprisoned.[39] In June 1804, the Spanish brig *Buena Fé*, headed from Santander, Spain, to Veracruz, Mexico, was confiscated by Haitian vessels and taken to Port de Paix, where the ship's cargo was confiscated. Reports about the fate of the crew varied somewhat. They were captured and imprisoned; some were chained and made to labor on public works. Some reports said nine of the young ones were selected as "servants to [Haitian] officials and the rest were ordered killed." One report noted that those killed were "cruelly assassinated, cut into small pieces." If the stories that circulated reflected something of old, familiar tales of black barbarism, they also contained glimpses into the real world of politics and commerce. The Spanish boat captured by the Haitians was sold to Americans, who were actively trading with the new nation. They then loaded the emptied vessel with Haitian coffee to sell in the United States. The Americans, whom the Spanish accused of profiting from war, were even said to have purchased a few of the unfortunate Spanish sailors "as slaves."[40]

[38] See minutes of Havana cabildo meeting, July 20, 1804, in AHOHCH, AC, tomo 60, ff. 116–116v. D. Domingo de Grandallana to D. Francisco de Borja, January 9, 1805, forwarding "Comandante de la Marina de la Coruña sobre atrocidades que cometen los negros de la ysla de Santo Domingo contra las embarcaciones españolas," December 29, 1804, in AMN, Cartagena, mss. 2238, doc. 69, ff. 243–243v.

[39] Someruelos to Cevallos, November 23, 1804, in AHN, Estado, leg. 6366, exp. 100, including testimony of Spanish sailor José Large. There are several ships by the same name that leave Spain in 1804 headed to Cuba or America. See AGI, Arribadas, 439B, exp. 358; AGI, IG, leg. 2132, exp. 50 and leg. 2136, exp. 146.

[40] See Joseph Murillo to Someruelos, October 7, 1804, in AGI, Cuba, leg. 1648; Someruelos to Pedro Cevallos, October 16, 1804, in AHN, Estado, leg. 6366, exp. 95; Kindelán to Someruelos, September 30, 1804, in AGI, Cuba, leg. 1538B; and "Asuntos Particulares. La Casa de Santa Cruz e Hijo del comercio de Bilbao solicita se declare robo de mar o piratería el apresamiento hecho por los negros de Santo Domingo del Bergantín *Buena Fe*," March 20, 1805, in AGMAB, Sección Corso y Presas (CP), leg. 5240. The crew and captain of a Haitian vessel named the *Mainbau* testified about an unnamed Spanish vessel captured by the Haitians. They testified that they had seen some of the crew "working for the Americans" and that they did not know the fate or whereabouts of the rest of the crew. See "Presa de la goleta *Mainbau* de Santo Domingo," January 22, 1805, in AGMAB, EA, leg. 37.

However alarming some of the news, officials who reported on the incidents seemed to understand them as a move in a global contest over trade, recognition, and sovereignty. When Bazelais condemned the Spanish *Santa María*, he made the Haitian state's intention clear: "Consequent to the intentions of the Government clearly declared, I inform you that being the Spanish allies of France, your schooner has been confiscated with application to the State of Haiti."[41] Even Governor Someruelos conceded that Haiti's attacks on the vessels represented retaliation for Spanish support of France. He explained to the minister of state: "I attribute this conduct of the Blacks to the attacks of French privateers on American ships that trade with and take arms and other items to [Haiti]. Since these French privateers and their prizes are welcomed in the ports of his Catholic Majesty, it is said that the Blacks have declared war on Spain."[42] Someruelos was simply distilling the reports he received on Haitian captures of specific Spanish vessels, as well as general reports that Dessalines was acquiring armed vessels from the U.S. to serve hostile purposes against Spain. Even American newspapers reported "that Dessalines had declared War against Spain in mid-July [1804] and that his privateers were already starting to capture Spanish vessels."[43] Haiti and France were still at a kind of war. And the Spanish colony of Cuba found itself stuck between the violently contending claims of the two countries.

In addition to attacks on Haitian-bound vessels and crews, France waged war in another, even more violent and destructive way. On January 6, 1805, Ferrand issued a chilling decree. Aimed, it read, at "annihilating the rebellion of the blacks," "reducing its population," and "depriving [the rebels] of the means of recruiting forces," it authorized both civilians and military personnel to fan out into Haitian territory and capture people under the age of fourteen. Most of the captives would become property of their captors, but boys between ten and fourteen and girls between twelve and fourteen would be sent to Santo Domingo to be exported and sold abroad. It bears emphasizing that the decree targeted Haitian children *on Haitian soil*. Ferrand simply insisted on treating Haitian soil as rebel, rather than foreign and sovereign territory.[44] Historian Graham

[41] Gral. de Brigada Bazelais to Captain Domingo Anhellín, Comandante de la Goleta de *Santa María*, Jérémie, March 3, 1804, in AHN, Estado, leg. 6366, exp. 83.

[42] Someruelos to Cevallos, November 21, 1804, in AHN, Estado, leg. 6366, exp. 98.

[43] Kindelán to Someruelos, October 31, 1804; and translation of *Telégrafo Gazeta de Baltimore*, no. 2980, September 1, 1804, both in AHN, Estado, leg. 6366, exp. 102.

[44] Ferrand, Decree, January 6, 1805, in Rodríguez Demorizi, *Invasiones Haitianas*, 101–104. The decree was published in Haiti, *Gazette politique et comercial d'Haïti*,

Nessler has recently shown that the raids and captures authorized by Ferrand did, in fact, occur and that they received the official blessing of the French state in Santo Domingo. After issuing the decree, Ferrand charged his commandant Joseph Ruiz with producing official certificates affirming each captive's origin in so-called rebel or brigand territory. Notarial acts of slave sales in the years immediately following Ferrand's decree, for instance, identify "slaves" as having been captured in "rebel" territory, suggesting that the policy was implemented and that free young Haitians were captured and enslaved. When Ferrand issued the decree, his private instructions to Ruiz stated that, though he had said nothing in regard to adults, all Haitian men over the age of fourteen captured on Haitian soil should be shot.[45]

It is difficult to know the extent to which the part of Ferrand's decree ordering the sale of children *off* the island was implemented. American newspapers, which followed Haitian events closely, do not appear to have printed or discussed the reenslavement decree, though they did exhaustively cover Ferrand's February 15, 1805, *arrêté* condemning vessels and ordering the execution of captains trading with Haiti. The fate of American shipping was more newsworthy than the reenslavement of Haitians.[46] Of course, the absence of newspaper reports on the reenslavement decree does not mean that it was not implemented. Even before the decree, French officers had already established the practice of selling black "brigands" abroad. In December 1804, for instance, Ferrand reported the successful sale of "black brigands" from Santiago de los Caballeros to South Carolina in exchange for rice. Such a sale – and it is impossible to know if there were more – served to raise revenue for cash-strapped Santo Domingo, just as it sent people whom the French state deemed potentially dangerous to a country engaged in trade with the enemy.[47] Would Ferrand – or, for that matter, private individuals – have adopted the same practice in regard to France's allies? During the Leclerc and Rochambeau periods, French officers illegally sold black rebels to Cuba, despite Spain's alliance with France. It is not inconceivable

no. 25 (1805). Dessalines was interested in circulating its bold threat, which he cited in his second proclamation to Spanish residents of Santo Domingo, dated April 12, 1805. He wrote: "Provoked by a decree issued by Ferrand ... I resolved to go take control of an integral portion of my States and to erase there even the last vestiges of the European idol." Dessalines, *Lois et actes*, 43–48.

45 Nessler, "A Failed Emancipation?," 301–302.

46 Rodríguez Demorizi, *Invasiones haitianas*, 101–104. Dozens of U.S. newspapers published English translations of the decree. See, for example, *Aurora General Advertiser* (Philadelphia), April 15, 1805.

47 The case is discussed in Nessler, "A Failed Emancipation?," 307.

that such a trade would have revived, or even expanded, once Ferrand launched a public campaign of reenslavement and exportation.

Whether the reenslavement policies were applied domestically or abroad, one certain result was Dessalines's decision to invade Santo Domingo in February–March 1805. Though ultimately unsuccessful, the invasion was covered in the international press, and new waves of refugees and their stories took flight. In Baracoa, in the first week of March, more than 400 arrived; on one day in April, another 418 arrived, "each one a new object of misery and compassion, for one sees in them but naked-ness and hunger."[48] Importantly, though local authorities and planters in neighboring territories had often expressed concern that Haiti, once inde-pendent, might try to make other conquests in the region, public interna-tional discourse about Dessalines's march on Santo Domingo never used that frame of interpretation, casting it instead as the latest episode in the ongoing war between France and its errant colony. Dessalines likely also saw it as what he hoped would be the final battle of the war, one that would secure not the victory of "brigands" but rather the sovereignty of Haiti.

In the crucial year or two immediately after Rochambeau's evacuation of Saint-Domingue in November 1803, then, Haitian independence was not really understood as a *fait accompli* either by the main protagonists of the story or by attentive international observers. The war continued. The new French colony of Saint-Domingue – that is, eastern Hispaniola or former Spanish Santo Domingo, just miles from old Cap Français now renamed Cap Haïtien – became France's "single largest concentration of troops in the Greater Antilles," its commander bent on making war on Haitian commerce and on carrying out a violent campaign of depopu-lation, extermination, and reenslavement against Haitians.[49] Dessalines, for his part, acutely conscious of France's position, stood by his foun-dational promise: eternal hatred of France. In other words, neither man, neither state saw independence as a done deal.

Haitian Foreign Policy and Slave Resistance

While the conflict between France and its former colony clearly contin-ued, black leaders at the same time set about creating a national govern-ment, forming new institutions, seeking ties of commerce and diplomacy

---

[48] Kindelán to Someruelos, May 1, 1805, in AGI, Cuba, leg. 1693.
[49] Quote is from Girard, *Slaves*, 335.

with other governments, and consolidating a freedom from slavery that could survive, indeed repel, France's onslaught. Attentive observers saw Haiti's double role at this crossroads. On the one hand, Haiti was the first independent black and antislavery state, one which projected itself internationally in that manner. On the other, the Haitian state was a weak formation, vulnerable to armed attack by the French and to multiple maneuvers of political and economic isolation by the other powers of the region. In the aftermath of Dessalines's failed march on Santo Domingo, for example, press reports declared Haitian independence not a fact, but "a fiction," a temporary claim, reversible at any moment. Yet, just months later, the same newspapers published the text of the first Haitian Constitution in its entirety, giving space on widely read pages to the concrete expression of Haitian sovereignty and to its avowal of revolutionary antislavery:

Article 1. The people inhabiting the island formerly called St. Domingo, hereby agree to form themselves into a free state sovereign and independent of any other power in the universe, under the name of Empire of Hayti.

Article 2. Slavery is forever abolished.

Article 12. No whiteman of whatever nation he may be, shall put his foot on this territory with the title of master or proprietor, neither shall he in [the] future acquire any property therein.

Article 14. . . . The Haytians shall henceforward be known only by the generic appellation of *Blacks*.[50]

Less forcefully, the Constitution also made clear that freedom would not go beyond Haitian borders. Article 36 read:

The Emperor shall never form any enterprise with the view of making conquests, nor to disturb the peace and the interior administration of foreign colonies.

This article merely reaffirmed a policy already expressed for some time, most recently in the 1804 Declaration of Independence. But already in 1799, Toussaint had acted on a promise not yet made. In order to protect

---

[50] The full text of the Constitution was published widely in the United States. See, for example, *New York Gazette and General Advertiser*, July 15, 1805 (from which the translation here is taken); *New York Commercial Advertiser*, July 15, 1805; *Aurora General Advertiser* (Philadelphia), July 17, 1805; *The Democrat* (Boston), July 20, 1805; and *National Intelligencer* (Washington, D.C.), July 22, 1805. On the 1805 Constitution, see Fischer, *Modernity Disavowed*; Jenson, *Beyond the Slave Narrative*; Claude Moïse, *Constitutions et luttes de pouvoir en Haïti, 1804–1987*, vol. 1 (Montreal: Edition du CIDIHCA, 1990); and Julia Gaffield, "Complexities of Imagining Haiti: A Study of National Constitutions, 1801–1807," *Journal of Social History*, 41/1 (Fall 2007): 81–103.

his ability to trade with British and American merchants, he revealed to the British the existence of a French conspiracy to incite a slave rebellion in Jamaica. Now, in 1804–5, Dessalines seemed to replicate Toussaint's policy – in order to protect the interests of the Haitian state, antislavery would remain national rather than foreign policy. Slavery outside Haitian territory would be respected. In both cases, that respect derived not from an acceptance of the institution of racial slavery but from an interest in containing the hostility of neighboring powers, all of whom recognized human property.

Historians have generally been divided on the question of whether the Haitian state sought to intervene and provoke slave revolution on other islands. Despite a general lack of evidence, some have accepted and incorporated such claims of possible Haitian intervention into narratives about an unwavering Haitian commitment to an expansive New World freedom. Others, meanwhile, have dismissed such claims as spurious, products either of overactive imaginations or of loose and drunken talk. Proponents of the latter view emphasize the noninterventionist claims made in the early Haitian state documents, which renounced the idea of Haitian intervention. They argue that Haitian leaders would not have secretly supported or encouraged revolution in the Caribbean; to have done so would have been to risk provoking a maritime blockade or invasion. The very politics of survival suggest that Haiti could not – and therefore did not – pursue an activist, antislavery foreign policy.[51] Recently, however, scholars have revisited the question of whether the new Haitian state sought to intervene in regional conflicts over slavery and freedom. This emerging work encourages readers to take seriously the still-slim possibility of intervention – more flexibly defined – as a way to understand more fully the self-conception of the Haitian state and its place in the wider world.[52]

That Haiti's example circulated and that black and brown people used it to think and talk about freedom, or power, or change is undeniable.

---

[51] For examples of the first view, see St. Victor Jean-Baptiste, *Le fondateur devant l'histoire* (Port-au-Prince: Editions Presses Nationales d'Haïti, 2006 [1954]), chap. 5; and Jean Fouchard, "Quand Haïti exportait la liberté aux Antilles," *Revue de la Société Haïtienne de Histoire et de Géographie* 143 (1984): 41–47. On the second view, see especially David Geggus, "Slavery, War, and Revolution in the Greater Caribbean," in D.B. Gaspar, D. Geggus, eds., *A Turbulent Time: The French Revolution and the Greater Caribbean* (Bloomington: Indiana University Press, 1997), 1–50.

[52] Jenson, *Beyond the Slave Narrative*, and Johnson, *The "Fear of French Negroes."*

Subversive mentions of Haiti in sugar houses and on street corners, the appearance of medallions of Dessalines in Brazil in 1805 or printed images of Christophe passed hand to hand in Havana in 1811, surely suggest the circulation of Haiti, materially, culturally, and spiritually. That enslaved people and free people of color accused of conspiring or rebelling against their masters or governments regularly invoked Haiti as model does as well. Many, many people spread across the colonies and free nations of the Americas looked to Haiti, and sometimes acted as a result. The existence of such people, of course, does not necessarily suggest a Haitian state project of subversion. Still, even if Dessalines did not deputize agents to generate slave revolts abroad, that did not necessarily prevent others from trying to assume that role regardless.

The first indication of a potential Haitian project of slave rebellion emerged in territory once Spanish. Shortly before Christmas Day in 1805, on the British island of Trinidad – Spanish until 1797 – authorities claimed to have discovered a massive conspiracy among its enslaved population. Centered in the regions of Maraval and Carenage, with a significant population of French planters and their slaves, the alleged conspiracy was said to involve hundreds of enslaved men and women. According to contemporary testimonies, the conspirators had used existing organizations of "convoys" or "societies" to organize regiments. They had sworn oaths, gathered uniforms and weapons, and appointed kings and other authorities to rule after their triumph. The uprising was to take place on Christmas Day, but about a week before, authorities uncovered the plot. Their investigations led to the public hanging of three leaders: Sampson, who was king of the Macaque Regiment; Baptiste, king of the Cocorite Regiment, and Carlos, general-in-chief of the latter. A fourth captive appears to have been spared on turning "King's evidence."[53] Part of what had aroused the suspicion of British authorities was that the black market women were singing, according to one account, "The blood of the whites is good to drink, the flesh of the whites is good to eat. Long live Dessalines!" There was, then, at least a symbolic bond between the political and cultural expressions of Trinidad's enslaved and the example

[53] *Mercantile Advertiser* (New York), February 6, 1806. On the rebellion, see Michael Craton, *Testing the Chains* (Ithaca: Cornell University Press, 1982), 233–36; Hollis Liverpool, "Rituals of Power and Rebellion," PhD diss, University of Michigan, 1993, 225–227; Jenson, *Beyond the Slave Narrative*, 168–175; Lionel Fraser, *A History of Trinidad* (London: Cass, 1971 [1891]), 1: 269–271, and Roberjot Lartigue, *Rapport de la conduite qu'a tenue M. Roberjot Lartigue* (Paris: Impr. Dubray, 1815).

of a Haitian state presided over by a black man, a former slave now emperor of Haiti.[54]

Some, however, alleged that the links were more strategic than symbolic. Roberjot Lartigue, a former planter in Saint-Domingue who in 1805 served as a French agent in the Danish island of Saint-Thomas, claimed that a group of Haitian emissaries sent by Dessalines was working in the Danish colony to plot a Christmas rebellion in Martinique and Guadeloupe. His own zealousness, he argued, had led authorities to restrict trade with Haiti and to banish a group of Haitians residing in Saint-Thomas. Denied entry in the French Antilles, the agents traveled instead to the island of Trinidad to provoke slave rebellion there.[55]

At the time, key players accepted Lartigue's insistence that Haitian agents appointed by Dessalines were working to subvert order on at least three Caribbean islands. Based largely on his warnings, French authorities in Guadeloupe and Martinique began seizing Haitian vessels.[56] In France itself, the government appears to have taken seriously the plot alleged by Lartigue, especially after news of the alleged Trinidad conspiracy reached Europe. With allegations of a subversive Haitian presence in Saint-Thomas and Trinidad, French authorities began warning that the targets of Dessalines's ambitions now included nations other than France. The French chargé d'affaires in Madrid notified the Spanish government that "emissaries of Dessalines have left Saint-Domingue with the intention of organizing a slave revolt in the American establishments of European powers" and asked them not just to expel, but also to arrest all men of color arriving from Haiti. The Spanish king complied, issuing a royal decree to that effect less than two weeks later.[57]

Some of the information coming out of Trinidad did, in fact, suggest a connection not only between that island and Haiti but also between Haiti and other, unnamed islands. Miguel de Herrera, governor of the Spanish island of Margarita, received reports of the testimony of one

---

54 Both French and Kreyòl versions of the alleged chant have survived; see Lartigue, *Rapport*, 3, and Fraser, *A History of Trinidad*, 1: 271, respectively.
55 See Lartigue, *Rapport*; Jenson, *Beyond the Slave Narrative*; and Leo Elisabeth, "Les relations entre les petites Antilles françaises et Haïti," in Marcel Dorigny, ed., *Haïti, première république noire* (Société d'Histoire d'Outre Mer, 2002), 177–206.
56 Elisabeth, "Les relations," 183–184.
57 French Chargé d'Affaires in Madrid to [?], dated Madrid, September 6, 1806, in AGI, Estado, leg. 86A, exp. 21; Montes to Cevallos, Minister of State, January 22, 1806, in AHN, Estado, leg. 6375, exp. 2 Someruelos to [?], February 28, 1807, reporting receipt of Royal Order of September 14, 1806 regarding Dessalines's agents, in ANC, AP, leg. 142, exp. 34.

of the conspirators, who had begged for his life in exchange for a full confession. Taken to the Governor's house to make his revelation, the witness confessed:

that for two years in agreement with the rebels of Saint-Domingue the thing was arranged with that Island, so that every week each black put in two *reales* and they had already 400 ounces gold and elsewhere 600 *pesos*, various rifles, gunpowder and bullets so that on the designated signal they would assassinate their masters and come with their weapons to Port of Spain, where everything would be confused in the midst of burning . . . and start massacring all the whites and the mulattos who would not follow them.

Interestingly, the testimony here echoes other available descriptions of the ways in which the organization of the rebellion utilized already existing "societies" established originally for the purposes of entertainment, but among which the saving and pooling of funds were already established practices. The man ended his testimony, elaborating – whether on his own or in response to a question – that "It was not only [Trinidad] that was in communication with Haiti, because there were others." Herrera sent the report to his counterparts in Cuba, Puerto Rico, and elsewhere.[58]

The slave's testimony, if true, reveals an ambitious design, in which groups or "societies" of slaves had been in communication with Haiti roughly since independence, all that time methodically setting aside money and collecting arms for the purpose of the projected rebellion. Of course, the witness trying to produce something dramatic enough to save his life may have embellished details or even fabricated much of what he confessed. If that was his purpose, he failed; the governor condemned him to death immediately on hearing his testimony. The testimony, moreover, has come down third- or fourth-hand from someone described by Herrera only as a trustworthy person.[59]

How plausible was this damning testimony? With so many French in Trinidad – white planters, republicans of color, slaves – communication of some sort with Haiti would not have been inconceivable. Evidence of substantial slave unrest emerged even before the discovery of the plot. For example, in 1804 a widespread poisoning campaign affected the plantations owned by French planters, and the principal suspects in that

---

[58] Miguel de Herrera, Governor of Isla Margarita, to Toribio Montes, Governor of Puerto Rico, December 30, 1805, enclosed in Montes to Cevallos, Minister of State, January 22, 1806, in AHN, Estado, leg. 6375, exp. 2; and Herrera to Someruelos, December 31, 1805, in AGI, Cuba, leg. 1714.
[59] Herrera to Montes, December 30, 1805, in AHN, Estado, leg. 6375, exp. 2.

episode were French slaves.[60] Could a plan have been set in motion, whether initiated by Haitian agents or instead by local slaves, who then communicated their intentions to Haiti via a myriad of networks and ties across the Caribbean Sea? Do we have here, in other words, the briefest glimpse of a transcolonial network of agents, organizers, and recruits systematically preparing to reproduce Haiti's example?

No answer to that question was clear at the time, just as none is clear now. But authorities in neighboring territories took precautions just in case. In Cuba, authorities redoubled their efforts at vigilance. Someruelos worked with city officials in Havana to try to uncover the presence of French slaves sold illegally to area planters. In Santiago, Kindelán expanded the role of the Compañía de Cazadores de la Costa, which he had created in 1803 to guard the coasts and to prevent the movement of black people between Haiti and Cuba – in either direction. While this new force patrolled the coasts, in the interior, peace would be maintained by sending out parties – of maroon hunters, regular infantry, or the recently proposed rural legions – to patrol the countryside, apprehend runaways, and impede the formation of any kind of movement by the enslaved.[61] In Puerto Rico, Governor Toribio Montes responded to the possible threat raised by the Trinidad testimony by strengthening surveillance measures across the island. He requested lists of all the slaves and information on the security used to guard them on estates; he ordered a census of free people of color, with information on their occupations and activities; he asked for lists of former prisoners, deserters, and former soldiers; and he asked for a final list of all the arms and weapons held in private homes.[62]

Thus, by November 1806, when colonial officials received the King's Royal Order calling for the arrest of any person of color arriving from Haiti, authorities were already well aware of the possibility that Dessalines's agents were ensconced in their territories. By then, however, Dessalines was dead. "It has been learned from some American vessels that the black Dessalines who was chief of the Ethiopian army of Santo

[60] On the poisonings, see TNA, CO 295/12 and 14.
[61] Kindelán to Someruelos, May 29, 1805, in AGI, Cuba, 1539; Callejas, *Historia de Santiago de* Cuba, 57–59; "Extracto de los Varios Expedientes producidos por las ocurrencias notables de la isla de Cuba durante los años 1805 y 1806," Extracto no. 8, SHM, CGD, Roll 41, doc. 4-2-9-10; Conde de Mopox y Jaruco to Príncipe de la Paz, "Representación sobre el sistema militar de la Ysla de Cuba" in SHMM, CGD, Roll 41, doc. 4-2-9-12. See also Belmonte, *Ser esclavo en Santiago*, 313–314.
[62] Montes to Cevallos, January 22, 1806, in AHN, Estado, leg. 6375, exp. 2.

Domingo has been killed."[63] He was assassinated on October 17, 1806, in a conspiracy that included his two successors, Henri Christophe and Alexandre Pétion.

Whether anxious planters or imprisoned slaves, sources in Trinidad asserted the presence of Haitian agents and material links to the Haitian state. Unfortunately, there are few surviving records of internal government deliberations about the new state's foreign policy in the first years of independence, nor even of deliberations about the inclusion in the Constitution of the article of nonintervention in the internal affairs of neighboring colonies. It is impossible to know with any certainty whether or not Dessalines had sent agents to generate revolution in Trinidad, or Cuba, or in any of the other nearby slave societies.

Historians have long noted spikes in instances of slave rebellion and conspiracy in the 1790s in general and in 1795 in particular, as news of revolutionary emancipation in the French Caribbean became well known among the enslaved of the Atlantic World. In 1805–7 – as word of Haitian independence spread and as visual images and artifacts of Emperor Dessalines circulated in the New World – a smaller wave of conspiracy and rebellion spread across the region. In addition to the Trinidad case in 1805, authorities uncovered evidence of slave conspiracies in Cuba and in the United States in North and South Carolina, Virginia, Maryland, and New Orleans. In 1806, plots were discovered in Jamaica, Puerto Rico, Virginia, Georgia, and western Cuba; in 1807, in Demerara, Bahia (Brazil), and Mississippi.[64] Thus, while very significant doubts remain about the existence of "agents" deputized by Dessalines or by the new Haitian government, another perhaps more plausible possibility is the emergence of self-appointed agents, men and perhaps women who acted, or thought they acted, in the spirit represented by the independent state of Haiti – whether or not they were charged to do so by Dessalines or anyone else.

Cuban Slave Rebellion, 1806

In Cuba, despite physical proximity to Haiti and despite official talk of possible Haitian agents, no slave rebellion materialized in the immediate aftermath of independence in 1804. Not one has yet come to light.

---

[63] Kindelán to Someruelos, November 15, 1806, in AGI, Cuba, 1540B.

[64] Geggus, "Slavery, War, and Revolution," 46–50; García, *Conspiraciones y revueltas*; João José Reis, *Slave Rebellion in Brazil*, 40–44; Herbert Aptheker, *American Negro Slave Revolts*, 240–243.

Authorities, however, did uncover several slave conspiracies. While nothing suggests the actual presence of agents sent by the Haitian state, other recurring fears of local authorities do appear to have been on target in at least two of the conspiracies, in Bayamo in 1805 and Güines in 1806. In both, the example of black rebellion and victory in Haiti served clearly as direct inspiration for the would-be rebels. And in both cases it was foreign creole slaves – already feared and outlawed for well over a decade – who served as the principal agents of revolutionary planning. In Bayamo, it was enslaved people recently brought from Jamaica who took the lead; in Güines, it was a man born and enslaved in rural Saint-Domingue. It is highly unlikely that the leaders of either movement acted as Dessalines's recruits. Rather, they spearheaded a local effort to emulate Haiti's course on their own initiative and, especially in the case of the Güines plot, in response to an evermore brutal slave system in Cuba.[65]

In spring of 1806, in Güines, ground zero of Cuba's sugar boom, an enslaved man from Saint-Domingue plotted with other slaves of the region to rise up against their masters, kill most of the whites, take arms and horses, and establish themselves in "absolute liberty as in Gua[rico]."[66] The presence of Haiti in the testimony of slaves and the ruminations of authorities is not surprising: Haiti and the language of black freedom and racial apocalypse were in constant circulation across the Atlantic world. But in this once-remote part of Havana province at this particular moment, the reference might have had special meaning. It was spoken by a man who claimed to have taken part in the revolution, and it was discussed in the region of Cuba where the transformations that had

---

[65] The 1805 Bayamo conspiracy involved mostly Jamaican slaves. Many were recently arrived and could not speak Spanish, so some testimony was taken through an enslaved interpreter. The testimony is interesting for other reasons, as well. For example, the physical punishment of enslaved witnesses during the proceedings is noted in the records, which is rare in Cuban slave rebellion testimony from this period. Several of the slaves had not been baptized (including some owned by priests) and were allowed to take their oaths by "the god they adored" rather than by the cross. See "Testimonio de la criminalidad seguida de oficio contra el Negro Miguel, Juan Bautista, y José Antonio," 1805, AGI, Cuba, leg. 1649.

[66] "Expediente criminal contra Francisco Fuertes y demás negros... sobre levantamiento en el pueblo de Güines, 6 Mayo de 1806," in ANC, Asuntos Políticos, leg. 9, exp. 27. The original document is badly damaged. What I am here interpreting as a reference to Haiti reads: "que quedarían asolutos y livres como el Gua[broken]." Guarico, the colonial Spanish name for Le Cap, and Santo Domingo continued to be used to refer to Haiti in the immediate postindependence era. The damage to the original document also means that the corners of the pages that would normally be numbered are often missing. I will provide page numbers in brackets, but these correspond to my pagination of a printout from a microfilm copy made in the Cuban National Archives.

converted Cuba into the new Saint-Domingue were most apparent and concentrated.

Güines was a fertile region of rich red soil. About thirty miles southeast of the city of Havana, it had long been home to the island's principal enclave of tobacco farmers, by and large small-scale producers. Beginning in the late 1780s and 1790s, they had been largely (and sometimes violently) eclipsed by sugar and large-scale landholding. It was in this valley of Güines that the post-Saint-Domingue Cuban sugar industry would begin its ascent. From four sugar mills in 1784, it grew to have nine by 1792, and twenty-six by 1804, just two years before the conspiracy.[67] But the sugar revolution in Güines meant more than a multiplication of sugar estates. The region also boasted the largest and most technically advanced sugar mills, those owned by some of the most powerful men on the island. When Cuban planters gave then-incoming Governor Luis de Las Casas his very own sugar plantation in 1790, it was located in Güines. It was also in Güines that Francisco Arango owned *Ninfa*, which was for many years the largest sugar plantation in Cuba and for some of those years the largest sugar plantation in the world. Nicolás Calvo's *Nueva Holanda*, also the island's largest estate for a time and the place where Governor Someruelos was welcomed to Cuba, stood in Güines as well. In 1808, 244 enslaved men and women labored on the estate. Also in Güines were the sugar plantations of the president, the *síndico*, the *prior*, the *cónsul*, and the *conciliario* of the Real Consulado. Technicians from Saint-Domingue, men who had fled from the revolution and the collapse of their industry in the French colony, were intimately involved in the creation and operation of many of these estates.[68]

Finally, the dramatic rise of sugar in the region was accompanied by a rise in the number of enslaved people purchased to work on what were fast becoming the island's most impressive agricultural and industrial establishments. Indeed, of all the African captives entering Cuba at this point, a significant proportion was headed to the sugar-growing regions of Havana province.[69] In 1775, almost three-quarters of the population

[67] It would go on to have 47 in 1827, and 66 in 1846. The figures are from Moreno Fraginals, *El ingenio*, 1: 140. Figures provided by Levi Marrero differ slightly: 8 in 1796 and 26 in 1800. See *Cuba* 10: 141. On the sugar revolution in Güines, see Moreno Fraginals, *El ingenio*, 1: 57–62.

[68] Moreno Fraginals, *El ingenio*, 1: 58, 110. The 1808 figure for slaves on *La Ninfa* comes from "Partido de Güines. Padrón de las Haciendas con expreción del número de Esclavos, Mulas y Carretas. Alexandría," January 18, 1808, in AGI, Cuba, leg. 1689.

[69] Laird Bergad, Fe Iglesias García, and María del Carmen Barcia, *The Cuban Slave Market, 1790–1880* (Cambridge: Cambridge University Press, 1995), 27.

of Güines had been classified as white; by 1817, the majority of the population was black and enslaved, and the white population accounted for less than 38 percent of the total.[70] Güines, then, had seen sudden and far-reaching changes in the decade or two preceding the conspiracy: the rise of a modern and prosperous sugar industry, the entrenchment of slavery, and a rapid and dramatic escalation in the numbers of slaves. It was a region, moreover, where people were intimately aware of Saint-Domingue's history: its powerholders were knowledgeable men, seeking consciously to emulate prerevolutionary Saint-Domingue. Its sugar experts were men who had lived in the French colony surrounded by slaves who became rebels. And, as the outline of the conspiracy suggests, among the enslaved conspirators were people well aware of Haiti's example.

The first alleged conspirator captured by authorities was Mariano Congo, an African-born man held as a slave by Don Esteban Alfonso. One Sunday in April 1806, Mariano Congo traveled to the *ingenio Concordia* in Guara, about fifteen miles from the town of Güines, where he was to recruit three other Congo slaves, Joaquín, Marcelino, and Toribio. The three men revealed the plot to their overseer, and Mariano was captured soon after his arrival and put in the stocks. His arrest set in motion an extensive investigation into the alleged plot. The three slaves who revealed the existence of the plot were questioned. So was Mariano. And then so was almost every other slave they named.

The more than 500 manuscript pages of testimony and correspondence reveal the outlines less of a well-laid out conspiracy than of the beginnings of one. When the plot was discovered, its leaders were still attempting to identify and recruit supporters. The area that the plot's architects had identified was nonetheless a broad one. They recruited among slaves in the towns and outskirts of Guara and Melena, both towns in the jurisdiction of Güines, and they targeted Güines proper as well.[71] Indeed, the leaders apparently spoke to slave drivers and slaves on over a dozen estates and farms in an effort to make their attack matter. Among the *ingenios* in Guara where they appear to have recruited were *Nuestra Señora del*

---

[70] Marrero, *Cuba*, 9: 217, 221. See also "Resumen general de los moradores que comprehende el Partido de Guara en todo el año de 1799," in "Expediente instruido con objeto de fomentar la población blanca de esta Ysla," in ANC, RCJF, leg. 184, exp. 8324. Here the population for the district of Guara, where the conspiracy was centered, is given as: whites 304, black slaves 266, mulatto slaves 4, black free people 4, mulatto free people 6.

[71] Guara, Melena del Sur, and Güines were *términos municipales* under the jurisdiction of the *partido judicial* of Güines. See Pedro José Imbernó, *Guía geográfica y administrativa de la isla de Cuba* (Havana: La Lucha, 1891).

Rosario (owned by Agustín Ugarte with 77 slaves), *Nuestra Señora de la Ascención* (owned by Gabriel Raimundo Azcárate with 100), *Nuestra Señora del Carmen* (belonging to Ignacio Ugarte with 56) and Fernando Muñoz's *Concordia* with well over 100, where the ambitious plot was eventually undone. In Güines, the plotters targeted the ingenio *San Antonio de Aguas* and *San Julián*, owned by Pedro Ponce de León and Pedro Nolasco Garzón, respectively. They also apparently recruited on properties of other well-placed Havana residents, including the *ingenio el Navío* owned by the Countess of Buenavista and a *cafetal* (coffee farm) owned by Antonio del Valle Hernández, secretary of Havana's Real Consulado. In Melena, they tried to recruit among the slaves of Miguel Barroso, against whom their master, Esteban Alfonso, was party to a long-standing land dispute.[72] Thus, the plot's leaders had cast a wide net that extended in every direction from their home base in Melena: south to Aserradero, northwest to Guara, northeast to Güines, and straight north about twenty-five miles to Guanabacoa, right outside Havana itself (Figure 5.2).

This ambitious plan began with one conversation between two men: Francisco Fuertes and Estanislao. About a month and half before the discovery of the plot, one of their companions, a man named Bernardo, had hanged himself after being severely punished for running away. In the immediate and somber aftermath of the suicide, Estanislao had said to Francisco, "*compadre*, we can't bear the whites any longer, it is time to kill them." Francisco hesitated, pointing out that they had no weapons, to which Estanislao countered that "none of that matters because there as well [in Saint-Domingue] they had the same shortages and they knew how to fight with rocks."[73] Later that night, the two men met in the

---

[72] The names of the *ingenios* come up throughout the testimony. Note that that one of the plantations on which they recruited was owned by Gabriel Raimundo Azcárate. Just a few years earlier, in 1802, Azcárate held as a slave at least one man from Saint-Domingue, identified as "Carlos el Francés." (See Chapter 4). The number of slaves on each farm is for 1804, the closest year for which there is documentation available. See "Padrón General correspondiente al territorio que comprende el Sacramento de Guara," March 20, 1804, in AGI, Cuba, 1684. The number for *Concordia* is illegible: 61 men and either 67, 69, 57, or 59 women. On the land dispute between Alfonso and Barroso, see "Expediente de Domingo José Aciego y Esteban Alfonso, in AGI, Ultramar, leg. 25, exp. 7.

[73] "Expediente criminal contra Francisco Fuertes," ANC, AP, leg. 9, exp. 27, [20, 52–84]. The description of this conversation between Fuertes and Estanislao appears first on pp. 1–20 and then again at 52–84. In the first instance, Guarico can be read clearly but the words around it cannot. In the second description Guarico also appears clearly but around illegible text followed by the "allí tambien," thus making clear that *allí* refers to Guarico.

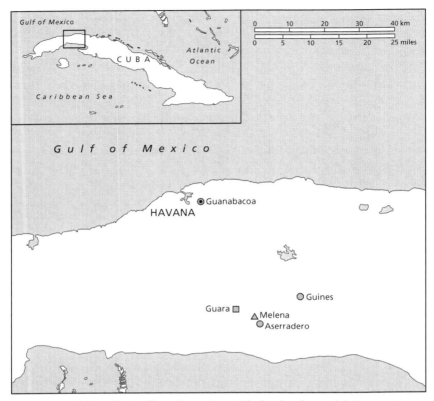

FIGURE 5.2. Map of 1806 Slave Conspiracy. The leaders focused their recruitment efforts in Melena del Sur, Guara, Asseradero, and Güines. Their plan was to march to Guanabacoa, just outside the city of Havana.

woods to continue the conversation in more depth. Other enslaved men from the estate joined them – Mariano, Mateito, Manuel, Cristóval, and Juan de Dios – and they agreed to organize a rebellion and to recruit all the blacks from neighboring sugar, coffee, and other farms, deciding who would recruit where. There was disagreement about what the immediate target should be: Should they stick to the farms around Melena and Guara, or head north to Guanabacoa? In the many conversations that ensued, the march on Guanabacoa seems to have won out. It was there that their master Esteban Alfonso served as alderman. If they could find him, they decided, they would kill him. About that they agreed.

The plot had two clear leaders and a messenger. One leader was Francisco Pantaleón, known generally as Francisco Fuertes, who though initially skeptical about their chance of success appears to have done much of the recruiting on neighboring farms. He was about twenty or twenty-one years old at the time of the conspiracy. He was creole, born to African parents in nearby San Miguel del Padrón, and he seemed to have a way with words. When he first arrived at one plantation to recruit followers, he went to the slave huts and addressed a group there, proposing:

> *compañeros*, you already know because you have been on this *ingenio* long enough, the subjection and punishment the whites give us; I come to tell you that we have recruited and have on our side all the blacks from Melena from the coffee farms and the blacks belonging to Don Pablo Esteves, the ones of Garzón, el Navío, and all the other sugar mills to attack next Monday and kill all the whites.[74]

Fuertes could also read, write, and sign his name. Indeed, he would use all those skills in the trial to draft a set of questions for his master to answer before authorities.[75]

The other leader was Estanislao. Estanislao, who first proposed the rebellion to his companion, had been born in Port-au-Prince around 1781. To his fellow slaves he appears to have bragged about having participated in the Haitian Revolution. Questioned by authorities, he spoke differently, admitting having been born there before the revolution but never having "intervened" in it at all. He explained that his master was a "*comisario francés*," who took him to Jamaica at some point in the revolution. In Jamaica, he was sold, eventually ending up in Cuba as the property of Esteban Alfonso.[76]

---

[74] Ibid., [24–26].

[75] Gloria García identifies his parents as African on the basis of baptismal records. See Gloria García, "Vertebrando la resistencia," 286.

[76] "Expediente criminal contra Francisco Fuertes," ANC, AP, leg. 9, exp. 27, [8–9]. Unfortunately, Estanislao provides no date for when he left Saint-Domingue for Jamaica nor when he was sold to his Cuban master. Asked where he was during "the invasion of Guarico," he replied: "in French Port-au-Prince and that after that he fled with his master who was a French commissioner (*comisario francés*) who took him to Jamaica and who there sold him to Don Salvador who brought him to Don Estevan Alfonso in the company of the same *negro* Mariano and another named Juan Bautista, whom his master sold." The mayoral of *Concordia*, Salvador de Artiago, is referred to as Don Salvador elsewhere in the testimony from the case. A population list from the region in 1804 lists a Salvador Artiaga, aged 20, as a *boyero* on the Concordia. If this is the same person, then his age would suggest that the trip to Jamaica in which he purchased the three men, including Estanislao from Saint-Domingue, would have occurred not too long before. Estanislao's mention of his Saint-Domingue master as a *comisario* is mysterious. Neither the Colonial Office Jamaica papers at Kew nor Gabriel Debien's lengthy index

Estanislao testified that he was sold with Mariano, the Congo slave who served as messenger and recruiter and whose capture at *Concordia* had set off the massive investigation.[77] But nothing in the testimony gives any hint about when the fates of the two men became intertwined. Had Mariano also been in Saint-Domingue, or did the two men meet when they were sold to the same master in either Jamaica or Havana? About Mariano Congo all we know is that he went to recruit other Congo slaves, Toribio, Marcelino, and Joaquín, at *Concordia*. Whether he chose or was assigned by the others to that task because of the ethnic connection, we cannot know for certain.

The three slaves most implicated in the plot thus differed from one another in at least one important respect. One was African, another was Creole, and the third was Haitian, three figures sometimes associated with different "types" of slave rebellion: African or restorationist, creole, or bourgeois revolutionary.[78] Their collaboration, in and of itself, suggests the need to look beyond such labels to discover the ways in which slave resistance and rebellion drew simultaneously on multiple sources of power and motivation.

In these turbulent times, the slaves of Güines lived and worked in a booming agricultural sector, where production was on the rise, and the demand for work and obedience grew ever more insistent. So as the alleged leaders and their fellow slaves were questioned, it was this context that they identified as the immediate cause for their conspiracy. Several testified that Estanislao, the Haitian slave, had insisted that it was time, that they were tired of working, that they couldn't take the whites anymore, that it was time to kill them. Even many of the slaves who rejected the call to rebellion testified that their work schedules were unrelenting, that they were given no time to work on provision grounds, that they

---

of Saint-Domingue arrivals in Jamaica note the arrival of a civil commissioner. Estanislao may have used the term *comisario* in a more generic sense to apply to a lower-level official, a police inspector, or a civil clerk, for instance. In the end, based on available evidence, we cannot know at exactly what point in the revolution he left. See Debien, *Les colons de Saint-Domingue passés à la Jamaïque: 1792–1835*, chap. 10–13 and appendix.

77 "Expediente criminal contra Francisco Fuertes," ANC, AP, leg. 9, exp. 27, [8–9].

78 An extensive literature on slave resistance and rebellion across New World slave societies has classified instances of slave revolt and resistance with categories such as African, restorationist, creole, and so on. Among the most important are Genovese, *From Rebellion to Revolution*; Michael Mullin, *Africa in America* (Champaign: University of Illinois Press, 1992); Craton *Testing the Chains*; and Michael Gómez, *Exchanging our Country Marks: The Transformation of African Identities in the Colonial and Antebellum South* (Chapel Hill: University of North Carolina Press, 1998).

received no religious instruction or care, and that discipline was too severe.[79]

Indeed, in the witnesses' lists of grievances, the complaint that seemed most urgent and important was the severity of corporal punishment. A coworker's suicide appears to have been the immediate trigger for the attempted revolt. Bernardo had tried to run away, and upon his capture was beaten until blood ran down his leg, after which he was placed in the stocks. The very next day he was made to work with manacles on his ankles. Exhausted, said his companions, he hanged himself from a tree. Bernardo's suicide came shortly after the deaths of other slaves on the plantation, deaths attributed as well to brutal punishment: the death of Rafael who died as a result of a punishment that in Jamaica was called Derby's dose, in which slaves were made to eat the excrement of other slaves; of María del Rosario and another unnamed black woman, one of whom was locked and killed in the hen house; of Pedro Carabalí, beaten to death with a stick and thrown in the fire; and of Joseph Mandinga and a seven-year-old "criollito," both dead as a result of unspecified punishment.[80]

The key to the plot seems to lie in the conditions and abuses amply described in the slave testimony. In fact, the authorities, while investigating the slave plot, initiated an investigation into the conduct of their master, Esteban Alfonso.[81] Fuertes himself drafted a weighty document from which his legal representative was to present questions to Alfonso. Fuertes's missive was a litany of abuses and violence – of an overseer as cruel as Nero, he wrote, who set dogs on slaves when his whipping arm got too tired, who dispensed beatings *a la ley de Bayona* (that is, tied to a chair or ladder), who cut him with a razor on his backside, who threw dirty water at the food as the workforce tried to eat it, and who buried slaves who died of punishment (and even those who had not quite yet died) in ditches without notifying authorities.[82] Indeed, when Estanislao was asked the customary question: did he not know that uprisings of "inferiors against their superiors, especially when these involved assassinations and other cruelties" were among the gravest of crimes, he replied unequivocally that he did know. But, he said, his misery, his condition, and the "treatment he suffered at the hands of his

---

[79] "Expediente criminal contra Francisco Fuertes," ANC, AP, leg. 9, exp. 27, [1–22, 52–84].
[80] Ibid., [52–84, 492–495].
[81] Ibid., [221–231, 489–490].
[82] Ibid., [492–495].

master had led him to plot such extraordinary things, to try to better his fate, and lessen the burden of his servitude." Here we are reminded of Herbert Aptheker's pithy contention that it was slavery itself that caused slave rebellion.[83]

Immediate conditions had clearly led the slaves of Güines to contemplate revolt. But Haiti – its precedent, its image, its very existence – had itself become a part of those conditions. Its name was continually spoken. Authorities suggested they had averted something like Haiti; they stressed the Haitian origins of the movement's leader; and they lamented the refusal of local landholders to abide by laws prohibiting the ownership of *negros franceses*. Haiti was spoken of even more among the enslaved. Estanislao, himself Haitian, referred to it all the time in his efforts to recruit his companions. He spoke of it as his place of origin, and he bragged to his co-conspirators about having participated in the revolution. The point of rising up, he told them, was to win freedom, like in Haiti. When they hesitated, he again invoked Haiti, urging them to not be afraid: Haitian slaves had been willing to try it. Like them, they had been without arms and resources, but they had risen up with rocks and clubs and won their freedom. Here Haiti served as something of a challenge, a dare: if French slaves had the courage to rise up, why shouldn't they? But more than a dare, Haiti was also a desired state. The uprising, they said to each other, would render them free "as in Guarico." In fact, said one of the men, they all had a long discussion about Haiti. They talked about the revolution, about the greatness of their *compañeros*, the feats that they had accomplished, and about the fact that they were now "absolute lords" of Haiti – a formulation that implicitly acknowledged Haitian sovereignty.[84]

The power of these Haitian invocations probably owed something to the fact that at least one of the men doing the invoking had himself come from that revolution. Estanislao had witnessed some of it, as he admitted even to authorities. Mariano may have done so as well, though we cannot know for sure. On other farms in the area, as well, French or Haitian slaves appear to have lived among Spanish creoles and *bozales*. Pablo Estévez, who owned one of the mills on which the conspirators attempted to recruit, insisted that all the trouble originated with *hacendados* who failed to comply with the prohibition against the importation of foreign,

---

[83] Ibid., [173–197]; and Herbert Aptheker, *American Negro Slave Revolts*, 139. See also Genovese, *From Rebellion to Revolution*, xxiv.

[84] "Expediente criminal contra Francisco Fuertes," ANC, AP, leg. 9, exp. 27, [24–27].

creole blacks.[85] The Conde de Mopox, who had spent years already advocating for a rural police force, and who owned two sugar mills and a *cafetal* around Río Blanco, on the route from Guara to Guanabacoa, declared on learning of the 1806 movement that local slaves were "on alert, observing the developments and progress . . . of those insurgents [in Haiti], much more informed and instructed by *los negros franceses* who have been introduced here and are dispersed across the entire island," including on mills where the conspiracy took shape.[86]

Clearly, when enslaved men around Guara invoked Haiti in 1806, they drew on a whole series of connections: direct contact with people who had emerged from that society, an intricate and dense web of news and rumor they had grown accustomed to hearing, an animated respect for Haitian rebels to whom they referred as their *compañeros*, and maybe, above all, the steadfast lure of freedom. But at the same time, men such as Estanislao and Francisco invoked Haiti as a way to make an argument about their own lives and immediate conditions in Cuba. The point is not to diminish or exalt the impact of Haiti and its revolution, but to stress that any potential influence developed in the context of daily life in slavery on particular plantations, in daily interactions with masters and overseers and others enslaved alongside them. References to Haiti, therefore, could be as much about quotidian and local experiences as about Atlantic revolution. If Haiti could be used by statesmen and planters to advance particular arguments – the need for a growth in the African trade, the imperative of white immigration programs, the necessity for coastal security, and so on – it could also certainly be used by slaves: to assert their worthiness, to manipulate the fears of white overlords, to express immediate and urgent grievances, or, maybe, to help imagine a place without whites or a place without slavery. In Güines in 1806, to imagine such a place was indeed revolutionary.

Marronage

If there were people from Saint-Domingue on the plantations of Havana's hinterland who produced the 1806 plot, there were surely many more in

---

[85] Ibid., [37].

[86] Conde de Mopox y Jaruco to Príncipe de la Paz, June 30, 1806, in SHMM, CGD, Microfilm Reel 41, doc. 4–2–9–12. Mopox does not elaborate on the question of which mills had a French presence, making it seem like a generalized phenomenon. One of the farms on which Estanislao and his colleagues recruited was owned by a man known to have owned at least one French slave (Azcárate). While there were surely more, there is no inventory to confirm the extent of this phenomenon.

Santiago and eastern Cuba. But, curiously, the place closest to Haiti, with the largest concentration of French people of color, slave and free, appears to have produced no slave conspiracy or rebellion, even though it, too, was witnessing a boom in slavery as a result of the Haitian Revolution. If the revolution or independence were inspiration for rebellion, how do we account for this apparent incongruity?

The settlement of Saint-Domingue refugees in eastern Cuba gave an enormous boost to the cultivation of coffee and to the regional system of plantation slavery more generally. That boom was focused on two areas: a large ring around the city of Santiago de Cuba, starting on the west in the Sierra Maestra and up and around to the zone of Gran Piedra on the east, and a smaller area to the east, north of the Bay of Guantánamo, between Tiguabos and Santa Catalina. The coffee boom that took root there turned the region into something like a southern Saint-Domingue writ small, transforming the population of the city and the landscape and activities of the countryside: from eight *cafetales* in the area before the exodus of 1803 to 138 by 1807, 120 of them owned by French *colons*.[87]

The region began to approximate Saint-Domingue in another way as well. In the first years of Haitian independence, the practice of marronage – which had been widespread in prerevolutionary Saint-Domingue – exploded in eastern Cuba. Marronage had existed in Cuba for a long time, and in eastern Cuba, with its mountainous terrain, sparse population, and absence of large-scale cultivation, communities of maroons, or *palenques*, had long survived. As French coffee planters began transforming the rural landscape and economy of the region – clearing roads, putting more and more land under cultivation, hiring overseers to discipline slaves – the two systems collided: the rising, modern coffee plantation system pioneered by the French and the longstanding practice of marronage. In the temporal and spatial overlay between the two processes we see the dramatic encounter between an ascendant slavery in the east and a growing resistance to its implantation.

That encounter happened in multiple ways. In some cases, coffee farms developed in areas relatively close to already existing maroon settlements. This was the case in the general area of the Sierra Maestra. Long-standing maroons now had the chance to interact with plantation slaves in very close proximity. Some of those slaves, including some from revolutionary Saint-Domingue, reencountered a familiar form of resistance carried out

---

[87] Orozco Melgar, "La implantación francesa"; F. Pérez de la Riva, *El café*, chap. 3; ANC, RCJF, leg. 92, exp. 3929.

in their new place and time by local Cuban slaves – some African born, some creole. A growing slave population on the new coffee farms fed existing maroon communities and on occasion revived ones that were disappearing. For example, in the mountains around El Cobre, where a community of runaway slaves of the Spanish king had lived since roughly the 1730s, winning their freedom and resettling in Cobre in 1800, new French-owned coffee estates blossomed, and with them the phenomenon of marronage. New runaways settled on old, abandoned maroon lands around El Cobre. In this way the terrain itself became a kind of palimpsest, hosting over time different examples of resistance and community building, each of which left traces for subsequent ones – remains of ceramic containers with money hidden by earlier maroons, shards of the shells that had been used as signals, weathered stakes from palisades meant to impede the advance of intruders.[88]

In other areas, both processes developed at the same time. As coffee plantation slavery became part of a landscape that had until then been very little cultivated, new maroon communities emerged. A good example is the area around the Gran Piedra. Seven of the nine new *palenques* known to have been established between 1800–19 were located there, where none had existed before. The same district was also home to well over half of all the coffee farms in the region in 1807. The historical reconstruction of the route taken by a slave hunter in 1815 shows the almost perfect confluence between the coffee and *palenque* belts north and east of Santiago (Figure 5.3).[89] Here, the rise in marronage accompanied the rise of plantation slavery itself.

The sudden development of coffee plantation slavery and maroon settlements at such close proximity sometimes resulted in violence. In May 1805, three incidents captured the attention of everyone in the region. On the 24th, a group of about twenty maroons invaded an unnamed farm owned by Juan Francisco Sánchez in Manantuaba, just two leagues from the city of Santiago, killing the overseer and injuring another man. Shortly before, in separate incidents, the same group had killed two French residents, one a free man of color working on lands rented from the coffee

[88] See, J. Pérez de la Riva, "La implantación francesa," 366; and Belmonte, *Ser esclavo en Santiago*, 282, 297; Gabino LaRosa Corzo, *Runaway Slave Settlements in Cuba: Resistance and Repression*, (Chapel Hill: University of North Carolina Press, 2003).

[89] Francisco Pérez de la Riva gives a total of 192 coffee farms in the *jurisdicción* of Santiago de Cuba, of which 109 appear to be located within the general area of Gran Piedra. See F. Pérez de la Riva, *El café*, 29. The numbers of new maroon communities is from La Rosa Corzo, *Runaway Slave Settlements*, 227.

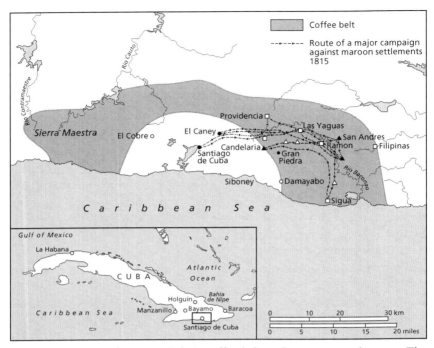

FIGURE 5.3. Map of eastern Cuba's coffee belt and runaway settlements. The route taken by government forces in the 1815 campaign to root out maroon communities of the regions illustrates the overlap between the expansion of coffee cultivation and the rise of maroon settlements on the fringes of the new coffee zones.

estate of a French widow named Piret, also in Manantuaba; the other Pierre Dufú (perhaps Dufour), a white Frenchman who rented coffee lands in Guaninicum, four leagues outside the city. The governor, who already had three parties patrolling the countryside, sent out another four squads, including the free colored militia.[90] The city council in its regular session three days after the attack, following many expressions of anxiety, called a special plenary meeting for the following day. After much discussion of the general state of alarm in the city, the members decided to raise funds to pay and reward people to annihilate the fugitives. A few weeks later, on June 7, the maroons were captured.[91]

[90] The incidents are described in Kindelán to Someruelos, May 29, 1805; June 14, 1805; and September 5, 1805, all in AGI, Cuba, 1539.
[91] Santiago Cabildo, May 27 and May 28, 1805, in AHMSC, AC, T. 17 (1804–1807), 89–92; and Kindelán to Someruelos, June 14, 1805, in AGI, Cuba, 1539.

Still, the public remained apprehensive, and, on June 23, the city council held an open session at which slaveholders and landowners were
invited to speak on the question of how to confront the alarming rise
of hostile maroon settlements. Lieutenant Coronel Antonio Vaillant,
nephew of the former governor of Santiago, the subinspector for the
free colored militia of Santiago, and himself a slaveholder and owner of a
local sugar plantation, spoke at length. Like most of the others present, he
agreed the time to act was now, to "put out in time the sparks that could
produce a voracious fire similar to the one in our neighboring colony."
What was most alarming about the recent crimes was that they had been
carried out practically at the doors to the city. In the countryside, as well,
the maroons were getting bolder. A few days earlier, he said, his slave
driver had seen a group of about thirty-five to forty maroons crossing
within sight of his *ingenio* near El Cobre. The day before, his overseer
had seen a smaller group of about seven also nearby; other neighbors
had spotted them as well. The fact that the maroons were showing themselves so openly was noteworthy. Perhaps they were "driven by hunger
rather than politics," he speculated, but even so the practice still offered
"an opportunity for our slaves to shake off their yoke and swell [the
maroons'] ranks."[92]

This new daring and the current circumstances required a response
that was more structural than simply offering prizes to slave hunters.
Vaillant argued that trade, habits, sociability even, had to be rethought.
Weapons of all kinds were sold indiscriminately; apothecaries (*boticas*)
sold drugs that could easily and silently kill people; and residents of the
countryside traded with maroons routinely, exchanging money, food, or
weapons for wax and honey. It was this behavior on the part of the
general population that needed to be reformed in order to defeat the
maroons. Vaillant speculated that it was very likely that there might be
among the maroons "some among the many arrived and brought from
Saint-Domingue, whether free, whether slaves," and thus he insisted that
on their capture, authorities should assiduously ascertain their origin and
deport any foreign creole slaves. Finally, he called for swift and brutal
punishment.[93]

On September 3, authorities hanged one of the captured maroons; six
were each given "a hundred lashes on the pillory," and three others were

---

[92] The text of Vaillant's speech is attached to Kindelán to Someruelos, September 5, 1805, in AGI, Cuba, 1539.
[93] Ibid.

sentenced to witness the hanging and whippings. Whether that punishment was swift or brutal enough to satisfy Vaillant we cannot know. But it does seem that he was correct in at least some of his speculations about the maroons. Authorities captured twenty-three maroons. Of these, seven were women and five of those were "French," that is from Saint-Domingue/Haiti. The governor insisted, however, that of the men – sixteen in total – none was French and that all were Africans or *bozales*.[94] Some historians have argued that Someruelos consistently underreported the number of free and enslaved Saint-Domingue refugees in Cuba. If he did this generally, he certainly would have had incentive to do it in this case, given that almost since 1791 one of the major fears expressed by Cuban authorities was that a connection would be established between maroons and French slaves.[95] So it was that marronage flourished in this French-dominated region, attracting at least some French slaves to the runaway ranks.

This was also true in parts of eastern Cuba where white Saint-Domingue refugees colonized the land. Among the clearest examples is the mountainous area north of Guantánamo Bay. It was in the region of Santa Catalina, a small valley at the foot of the Sierra del Saltadero de Guaso, that in 1803 Prudencio Casamayor and other refugees had collectively purchased a huge tract of land, dividing it into smaller units to lease or sell to their arriving compatriots. Soon, lands that had long been owned by old creole ranching families were transformed into profitable coffee estates worked by slaves, brought from Saint-Domingue or purchased in Cuba.[96]

Tiguabos, about ten kilometers west, was also home to a large concentration of refugees, many of whom had been coffee planters in Saint-Domingue: Lescabes, Charpentier, and Foucauld with coffee farms in Jérémie, while others had owned coffee farms in Les Cayes, Acul, and Marmelade, among other places. Some had arrived in the early 1790s, others in 1803, and by around 1810, they dominated the local economy. While the French population constituted only about a quarter of the population of Tiguabos, they held 77 percent of the area's slaves in 1811. Clearly, it was the French who led the local turn to coffee and slavery. They built and developed that system in a place that had already been

94 Kindelán to Someruelos, June 14, 1805, in AGI, Cuba, 1539.
95 Portuondo, *Entre esclavos y libres*, 76–77, 86–90.
96 On the transition from creole ranching to French coffee cultivation, see Portuondo, "Santiago de Cuba."

the site of conflict between slaves and authorities. Indeed, Tiguabos was home to colonial Cuba's most famous slave catchers, some of whom had traveled with their hunting dogs to Jamaica in 1795 to participate in the repression of the Maroon War. In 1803, it became one of the head-quarters of the newly formed Compañía de Cazadores, which patrolled coasts in part to protect against the arrival of black French. Despite the repressive machinery put in place, slave resistance in the region, fed by the expansion of slavery, continued unabated. Already in the 1790s there had been reports of a new maroon settlement; at the end of the decade maroons attacked some fishermen, commandeered their boats, and sailed toward Saint-Domingue.[97] In the first decade of the nineteenth century, after the implantation of French coffee, the area became home to the most important runaway slave settlements in eastern Cuba: in the mountains north of Guantánamo, surrounding Tiguabos, Mayarí, and Baracoa.[98]

In eastern Cuba, then, in the first decade or so of the nineteenth century, two processes converged. One was the emergence of a coffee plantation system pioneered by Saint-Domingue refugees, which in turn, expanded the local institution of slavery. The other, a direct result of that expansion, was the intensification of marronage. The first process clearly owed much to the Haitian Revolution: it was planters displaced by revolutionary events who propelled it, buying and renting lands, planting coffee trees, and bringing or purchasing slaves to work them. The relationship of the second process to the Haitian Revolution is significantly less clear. Indirectly, at least, the two were related, for the rise of marronage is generally linked to the rise or intensification of slavery, which in eastern Cuba was very much tied to the results of the Haitian Revolution.

Were there more direct ties as well? There has long been specula-tion about links between maroons in eastern Cuba and blacks in Haiti and Jamaica, and in popular culture and local folklore those ties are assumed. The 1979 Cuban film *Maluala*, for instance, opens with a scene of maroons from the *palenque* by that name meeting and trading with Haitian smugglers near the coast. Several important historians have made

---

[97] Diego Ferrer Bosch and José Sánchez Guerra, *Rebeldía y apalencamiento en Guantánamo y Baracoa*, (Guantánamo: Centro Provincial de Patrimonio Cultural), 41–46.
[98] Portuondo, "Santiago de Cuba;" La Rosa Corzo, *Runaway Slave Settlements*, 91–92, 138; Debien, "Les colons de Saint-Domingue," 600–601. On the French there in the early 1790s, see the correspondence of Santiago Governor Vaillant in ANC, CCG, leg. 43, exp. 5; on conditions there at the start of the nineteenth century, see Kindelán to Someruelos, February 18, 1805, in AGI, Cuba, 1539.

similar claims, but the principal source cited, as Gabino LaRosa Corza points out, is a local government document aimed at wresting more funds from the captain-general for the purposes of security.[99] Of course, if such a trade existed, it is not likely to have left much of a documentary trace. Maroons acquired food and guns not only as a result of attacks on local farms, but also as part of regular trade in honey and beeswax that they conducted with locals. The region generally supported substantial petty and illicit coastal trade. On the windward coasts, the governor said, landing or sailing unnoticed was more difficult, but the leeward coasts, "where there are no guards and barely any inhabitants because of the rough and uncultivated terrain," were much more difficult to patrol. In addition, in some of the small towns near the runaway settlements, including Tiguabos, there were very few officials who could be counted on to carry out the governor's orders against the *palenques*; in some cases, they could scarcely write their names, having been selected for local posts only because the others were even less qualified. It is not hard to suppose, then, that evading capture or detection was very possible, and indeed, already during the revolution, maroons had been known to escape toward Saint-Domingue. Still, there is no evidence of direct contact between Cuban maroons and Haitian individuals. Ultimately, the explosion of marronage in eastern Cuba was the direct result of local slavery and its intensification, not of Haitian independence, even if the implantation of that specific system of slavery originated in large part from the dispersal wrought by black revolution in Haiti.[100]

Other interesting parallels nonetheless emerge if we juxtapose the growth of marronage in Cuba in the period after the French evacuation of Saint-Domingue and the establishment of an independent Haitian state. In Santiago, as refugee planters sought to create a society exempt from the reach of radical antislavery and black power, as they founded their new counterrevolutionary space of coffee and slavery, that very society fed the forms of resistance endemic to the Saint-Domingue slavery from which they came. In Haiti itself, independence and the fear of another French expedition led Dessalines and other leaders to fortify mountain

99 La Rosa Corzo, *Runaway Slave Settlements*, 111–112. Among historians who assert the existence of the trade are José Luciano Franco, *Palenques de negros cimarrones*, (Havana: Colección Historia, 1973), 104; and Francisco Pérez de la Riva, "El negro y la tierra, el conuco y el palenque," *Revista Bimestre Cubana*, 58, 2–3 (1946): 108.

100 Kindelán to Someruelos, August 15, 1804, in AGI, Cuba, 1538B, and February 18, 1805, in AGI, Cuba, 1539. Ferrer Bosch and Sánchez Guerra, *Rebeldía y apalencamiento*, 41–46.

strongholds. For decades the mountains had been an effective refuge for runaways, and during the revolution they had served the black rebels well in their campaign to defeat their enemies. With independence declared, the country's new leaders looked to the mountainous interior – maroon land – as their guarantee of freedom. They transferred weapons to the mountains, eventually building impressive fortifications. The country's first Constitution enshrined the idea: "at the first sound of the alarm cannon, the towns will disappear and the nation rise."[101]

If the practice of marronage was important in the Haitian Revolution, there is a way in which independence turned the former French colony into a maroon state writ large – a sovereign *tierra de los negros*. The whites had been defeated; the blacks had taken the land. But if this was a metaphorical maroon state, it was one that departed significantly from its predecessors. First, this was a formally established state, with a constitution, for instance, and a navy. Second, it did not return newcomers to slavery.[102] Finally, it did not seek to isolate itself, but rather to engage the world and to project its power (such as it was) and its voice in the service of radical antislavery. The following decade, when Alexandre Pétion declared in Article 44 of the 1816 Constitution that all blacks (and Indians) and their descendants were Haitian – and therefore free – on stepping foot on Haitian soil, Haiti became a sovereign space of freedom, the maroon state of the Atlantic world. While this notion of a sovereign space of freedom was built on the experience and institution of marronage, it was at the same time inherently "worlded," not backward or isolated or restorationist, in the sense suggested by Eugene Genovese long ago. Indeed, Haitian statehood, if anything, inverted the standard relation between center and periphery, colony and metropole. By becoming literal free soil, a condition that had previously applied in metropoles and from which colonies had been explicitly exempted, Haiti made itself

[101] On the policy of fortifying the interior, see Girard, *Slaves*, 317. For examples of journalistic coverage of the policies, see *Commercial Advertiser* (New York), April 10, 1804; *Alexandria Advertiser*, May 16, 1804. The Haitian Constitution, General Measures, Article 28 is available on Constitutions of the World Online, http://www .modern-constitutions.de/nbu.php?page_id=02a1b5a86ff139471cob1c57f23ac196& show_doc=HT-00-1805-05-20-fr.

[102] On the protection offered by Haitian governments to fugitive slaves, see Ferrer, "Haiti, Free Soil, and the Revolutionary Atlantic" and Epilogue. While there are multiple known cases of the Haitian state protecting foreign slaves seeking freedom in Haiti, in one case, Christophe appears to have returned six fugitives from Turks Island. See B.S. Rowley to W. Croker, July 15, 1810, in TNA, ADM, 1/261. My thanks to Julia Gaffield for sharing this document.

the metaphorical metropole of the Black Atlantic, implicitly embracing a
diasporic notion of citizenship that acknowledged the reality of African
dispersion in the Americas.[103]

In the decade or so after the rash of maroon attacks of 1805, local
authorities in Santiago seemed powerless to destroy the settlements. In
1815, frustrated at the lack of progress in defeating them, Santiago governor Eusebio Escudero, without authorization from anyone, proceeded
to negotiate. Relying on the services of Crisanto Pérez, the overseer of
the Caujerí farm who had experience trading with the maroons, the governor proposed a peace. Worked out over several weeks, the deal would
have given the four principal maroon leaders their own freedom and
money. Each one would receive the title of captain, continuing to lead
his maroons, with the help of two corporals selected from among them.
The rest of group would be divided into four classes; the first class, or
the most able ones, would receive freedom after two years of service;
second-class maroons would be free after three years; and so on. Their
services would include "reducing" those maroons who were not part of
the treaty, and working on one of two estates, the first worked for their
own sustenance, the second worked as their own money-making venture.
Any labor on public defense works would be remunerated with a modest
wage.[104]

Hearing of the negotiations, the captain-general in Havana blanched.
He consulted with the Real Consulado, which predictably and passionately recommended abandoning the plan. Could a handful of three hundred blacks, they asked rhetorically, have produced this much terror in
the governor? "All this has been done with a kind of solemnity as if it
were a matter between one nation and another . . . the [maroon] *caudillos*
were represented by a Secretary as if they were Plenipotenciaries of a
recognized government, and face to face they were made offers of peace
and liberty."[105]

It is impossible to know whether the form of the negotiations – the
solemn, sovereign character described in Havana – was initiated by colonial authorities, if it was a condition for the meetings imposed by the
maroons, or if it emerged organically as a result of both parties interact-
ing and negotiating to their advantage. In any case, the deal collapsed.

[103] On Haiti and free soil, see Ferrer, "Haiti, Free Soil, and the Revolutionary Atlantic."
      For Genovese's argument, see *From Rebellion to Revolution*.
[104] F. Pérez de la Riva, "El negro y la tierra," 116–119.
[105] ANC, RCJF, leg. 141, exp. 6935, quoted extensively in ibid., 120–121.

Rejected by Escudero's higher authorities, it was soon rejected by the maroons themselves. They demanded, reported the governor, a more general freedom, "the Captains not content to enjoy it if was not also guaranteed to all, [adding] other daring and threatening expressions."[106]

The descriptions of the maroons negotiating as if they belonged to a sovereign state and their demands for a broader liberty, made in the years after Haitian independence, might have contained faint traces of Haiti as model, perhaps particularly so in a region in which some of the maroons, slaves in the surrounding countryside, and masters came from revolutionary Saint-Domingue. A contemporary once noted that African-born maroons always headed or faced east, believing that they would arrive in Africa that way. Of course, facing east on a clear day in mountainous Oriente also meant facing – sometimes literally seeing – Haiti.[107]

Haiti was not at the root of Cuban marronage in the early nineteenth century. Even if a rise in marronage in eastern Cuba coincided with the establishment of independent Haiti, it still clearly predated the Revolution. If Haiti might have served as an obvious and proximate example for maroons seeking freedom, autonomy, and distance, there were other powerful examples. The maroons of Jamaica, for instance, were well known in the region that was home to the island's most renowned slave catchers. When local maroons rejected the peace treaty finally in 1819, they invoked not the obvious example of Haiti, but the more proximate one of El Cobre, where the descendants of seventeenth-century slaves of the king refused to work as slaves, established a community that eventually numbered over one thousand members, sent emissaries to the King of Spain, and won their freedom in 1800.[108] When in Cuba – and perhaps elsewhere – slaves accused of conspiring against their masters or the state recounted conversations about their goals of taking the land or setting out for *la tierra de los negros*, they may have been referring to many things at once. Haiti, certainly, but just as often something

---

[106] ANC, CCG, leg. 138, exp. 3, quoted in ibid , 123–124.

[107] Callejas, *Historia de Santiago de Cuba*, 58. Callejas, writing in 1823, also noted that creole runaways tended to head towards the coasts, hoping to escape by sea "a las colonias." Though clearly not accurate, contemporaries did use the term *colonia* to refer to Haiti, as well as other Caribbean colonies.

[108] The case of the *cobreros* is well studied. See Jose Luciano Franco, *Las minas de Santiago del Prado y la rebelión de los cobreros* (Havana: Ciencias Sociales, 1975); María Elena Díaz, *The Virgin, the King and the Royal Slaves of El Cobre* (Stanford: Stanford University Press, 2002); and Olga Portuondo, *La virgen del Cobre* (Madrid: Agualarga, 2002).

closer – a former or current settlement, somewhere in the mountains of eastern (and sometimes even western) Cuba.

Events in the French colony of Saint-Domingue had provided a powerful example to enslaved people in Cuba since 1791. When those events produced the state of Haiti in 1804, no one knew if the power of the example would be amplified or not. Masters and authorities might, if anything, find it easier to contain the damage from a state than from a raging military confrontation. They could isolate the new state diplomatically; they could seek ties of trade from which to profit without having to compromise their commitment to slavery or white rule in their home territories. Or, while keeping an eye open and an ear attuned to developments in the new state, they could essentially ignore it. Thus, "Haiti" continued to figure in their documents as a foreign colony, as Guarico, or Santo Domingo; its heads of state as *caudillos*; its national army as brigands and rebels. Cuban authorities pretended that Haiti was a nonentity, and pretending, they hoped, would make it true.

For the enslaved, however, the opposite may well have been the case. Slave testimony suggests that slavery could represent a permanent state of low-intensity war, with the enslaved regularly talking about how to wage that war and win.[109] For the first time, what they so often talked about had happened, and this time, their people won. They had taken the land and become masters of themselves and everything around them. With that new reality in mind, the enslaved elsewhere could, if they wanted to, imagine themselves as Haiti's self-appointed agents. The appeal of that position derived certainly from Haiti's achievement, but for men such as Estanislao, it emerged also from the brutal and violent experience of slavery in Cuba.

Nothing, meanwhile, directly suggests that Haitian leaders themselves knew of any of those particular deputies, or that they did anything specific to help produce them. But that is far from signifying that Dessalines and his state were uninterested in promoting global antislavery. Cognizant that Haiti's example and Haiti's actions helped inspire a pool of ready deputies from among the ranks of enslaved workers, political acumen

---

[109] This analysis is based on the extensive judicial testimony from a range of Cuban slave conspiracies. See Ferrer, "Speaking of Haiti," and Aisha Finch, *Insurgency Interrupted: Cuban Slaves and the Resistance Movements of 1841–1844* (Chapel Hill: University of North Carolina Press, forthcoming).

might have suggested that the most strategic route was not to categorically dismiss the possibility of antislavery revolution, but rather to bide one's time and await the kind of opportunity that might help one succeed in expanding it. As it turns out, one such opportunity was not long in coming.

6

Atlantic Crucible, 1808

Cuba Between Haiti and Spain

From the start of the French and Haitian revolutions, Spanish officials had decried the instability of the present, indeed of history itself. In the early 1790s, Cuban planter Francisco Arango lamented, "I have awakened and seen that all my work was built in mid-air. . . . the peace and tranquility of my compatriots . . . hanging by a thread." Colonial governors pondered the "novel character that distinguished the present epoch from all previous ones" and worried about governing under circumstances that "of necessity change the rules prescribed in other very different times."[1] These men and others like them well understood that it was in moments such as these that they were at their most vulnerable, their world most susceptible to being undone. Political observers, and later historians, have also appreciated that basic truth. From comparative work on the history and sociology of revolutions to studies of slave rebellions across the New World, scholars have long argued that divisions at the top are key in opening up the spaces that would-be revolutionaries occupy and then expand – if not forever – then for a time. The tumult of the French Revolution in metropolitan France certainly proved to be one of those turning points for colonial Saint-Domingue, and everyone at the time knew it.

In 1808, a parallel moment arrived for Spain and its American territories. That year Napoleon's forces occupied Spain, and with the Spanish royal family captive in France, Napoleon installed his brother Joseph on

---

[1] Arango, "Discurso sobre la agricultura," in *Obras*, 1: 170–171; Las Casas, Bando, February 25, 1796, in "Expediente relativo a las precauciones y seguridad" in ANC, RCJF, leg. 209, exp. 8993; and Joaquín García to Conde de Campo de Alange, November 25, 1791, in AGS, SGU, leg. 7150.

the Spanish throne. In cities and towns across the Spanish peninsula, the population dramatically resisted the imposition. They refused to recognize the "intruder" king, and they proclaimed their loyalty to Fernando VII. Provincial juntas emerged to rule in the absence of a rightful king, and rebellion and war against France broke out not only in Madrid, but from the French border on the north to Andalucía in the south.

In the context of this turmoil, the colonial or American question quickly became a further source of tension and instability. Many towns across Spanish America founded their own juntas, which, while loyal to the deposed king, were essentially autonomous units with a fundamentally unclear relationship to any governing body in Spain. As the Spanish opposition organized, giving rise first to the Junta Suprema Central (or Junta Central) in September 1808 and eventually to the Consejo de Regencia (Regency) in 1810, the Latin American juntas generally withheld recognition, in effect declaring provisional independence from Spain – from the Spain ruled by Napoleon and the Spain established in defiance to that rule in Sevilla and eventually Cádiz.

It was in the southern coastal city of Cádiz, long the center of Spain's American trade, that the country's first sovereign national assembly would gather, bringing together peninsular and colonial delegates to draft Spain's first constitution. Delegates convened to discuss and legislate as the legitimately constituted representatives of a sovereign nation. Everything was at stake, as all the transcendental questions of the Age of Revolution were suddenly thrown open for public discussion: the place of overseas territories in the nation, the racial boundaries of citizenship, the fate of slavery.

These were, of course, the very questions that had also emerged during the French Revolution. That fact was not lost on the Cuban planter class and its allies, who did everything in their power to have the most "sensitive" conversations conducted in Cádiz sealed away from public view. But if they understood the perils of the moment, so, too, did others. In Haiti, leaders took almost immediate advantage of the crisis to help expel France from neighboring Santo Domingo. In Cuba, people of all stations used the spaces opened by the crisis to push against the limits of traditional politics. For planters, the crisis provided a perfect opportunity to wrest concessions from a weak metropole and to further the project they had embarked on almost three decades earlier. For some of the enslaved, meanwhile, the war against the French was an opportunity to resist French masters on coffee plantations. For some free men of color, it provided a chance to push for rights in the militia or for independence.

Across the island, it opened the possibility of talking about politics in a new way. And as uncertainty and unrest deepened across Spanish America, as speech became revolution in one after another Spanish territory, the question in Cuba became: How far will it go, and where will it end?

1808, Havana

In early July 1808, residents of Havana worried about rumors of trouble in Spain. But officially, at least, no one knew that Fernando had been deposed by Napoleon. Indeed, they did not even know that Fernando was king, for his father, Carlos IV, had still been on the throne when the last news had arrived. Then, on July 17, a ship from Cádiz entered Havana harbor with a new intendant and a large bundle of papers. The papers contained news of a popular uprising in March that had forced King Carlos IV to abdicate in favor of his son Fernando. Then Napoleon, whose forces were ostensibly in the Iberian Peninsula to defeat the British in Portugal, had invited most of the Spanish royal family to Bayonne to broker a reconciliation between Carlos, Fernando, and the unpopular Príncipe de la Paz, Manuel Godoy. At the time of the papers' arrival, the royal family was still in Bayonne, essentially captive, and Napoleon's brother Joseph I had been placed on the Spanish throne.

The news was momentous, but it was just the beginning. As Someruelos kept reading, he learned that the majority of Spaniards were refusing to recognize the "usurper king." Warfare had broken out in the center of the kingdom in Madrid and in other parts of the peninsula. Cities, refusing the authority of the French Joseph, formed juntas to govern in defense and in the absence of Fernando VII, *el deseado*.[2]

In Havana, Someruelos quickly called a meeting of the most important military, economic, and political authorities. Making the initial decision was not hard. They, too, refused to recognize French rule, proclaimed Fernando VII king, and, like their compatriots, vowed war against France. The very same day, the governor published a proclamation to the island's residents. It began matter-of-factly: "Know that I have received just today some manifestos, proclamations, and edicts." But when he summarized the information contained in the papers, he let loose the language of passion and exhortation. The papers described, he said, "an act of treachery

---

[2] "Extract of a Letter from Havana, July 20," in *Poulson's Daily Advertiser* (Philadelphia), August 5, 1808.

more vile than any seen or heard in centuries." Everywhere he invoked the metaphor of slavery, imposed by France on Spain and all of Europe, resisted now by heroic Spaniards who refused its yoke. Despite the exalted language, he called on the public to contain its passions: to act patiently, tolerate the French among them, and give generously for their brethren in the peninsula.[3] Even before the statement hit the street, the whole city was on edge, eager for news, and exchanging rumors. People with access to the government palace flooded the halls, galleries, and stairwells, awaiting the governor's resolution. The news of the cabinet's decision to stand by Fernando and against the French was greeted, accounts tell us, by cries of "Long live Fernando, long live the governor, and death to the French!"[4]

That unanimous resolve, however, did not last long, and it buckled first at the very center of power in Havana. Just two days after the arrival of the news, planter-statesman Francisco Arango proposed that Havana establish its own junta, like the provincial ones created across Spain in spring and summer 1808 to defy the French, to proclaim adherence to Fernando VII, and to rule in the name of the absent king. In support of Arango's project for a junta were the men most allied with the modernizing project of plantation agriculture, who may have seen the proposed institution as a space for autonomous reform. A junta might, for example, allow them to expand free trade provisions or reduce the taxes they paid to the church. Opposed were those allied with church and military. The military officer Francisco Montalvo, who in 1794 had defended Frenchmen against Jean-François's massacre at Bayajá and who in 1803 had hosted officers and soldiers from the evacuating French army in Cuba, was the most vocally opposed. He interrupted Arango midspeech, slammed his fist on the table, and announced that there would be no junta while he was still alive and carried a sword. Even before a final decision was taken,

---

[3] "Proclama. Habitantes de Cuba, Hijos dignos de la generosa nación española," July 18, 1808, in AHN, Estado (Junta Central Suprema Gubernativa del Reino), 59A. A printed copy is available in *Demostración de la lealtad española: colección de proclamas, bandos, órdenes, discursos, estados de exército . . . : publicadas por las juntas de gobierno, ó por algunos particulares en las actuales circunstancias . . .* (Madrid: Imprenta Repullés, 1808).

[4] Jacobo de la Pezuela, *Historia de la Isla de Cuba*, (Madrid: C. Bailly-Baillière, 1878), 3: 381–382; and Sigfrido Vázquez Cienfuegos, "Cuba ante la crisis de 1808: El proyecto juntista de La Habana," in Serrano Mangas, Fernando, et al., eds., *IX Congreso Internacional de Historia de América*, 2 Toms., Mérida (Badajoz): Editora Regional de Extremadura, 2002, 1: 263–269.

anonymous handbills in the city condemned the project as "tyrannous and independent." No junta was established in Havana.[5]

To say that these were precarious times is an understatement. There was no central governing body in Spain recognized in the Americas (or, for that matter, in Spain, as the Junta Central would not be established until later in the year). The most powerful people in Havana quickly began fighting amongst themselves about what political course to follow. The *situado*, the regular silver subsidy from Mexico, had stopped arriving. Sugar and coffee rotted for lack of ships to take them. There was also precious little access to official news, not just for the irregularity of communication in wartime, but also because it was uncertain from what "officials" such information would have arrived. In this climate of uncertainty, "daily and for many hours crowds amassed in the Plaza de Armas, at the docks, and even in the governor's palace to find out what neither Someruelos nor anyone else could tell them."[6]

It was not just talk that agitated the public, but also writings, publications, and the circulation of papers. Since the French Revolution, the Spanish king and his officers in America had tried to limit the circulation of dangerous political news and "seditious papers." They had even prohibited public talk of controversial news. Now, in 1808, as a result of the French invasion of Spain, such talk and writing exploded across the Americas. Suddenly, political papers were everywhere: handwritten handbills (*pasquines*) nailed to doors; new newspapers trying to fill an insatiable demand for information; pamphlets with transcribed text from public speeches, masses, and meetings; manuscripts with dialogues, songs, and poems; printed or hand-drawn cartoons; even patriotic word games. Everywhere, exuberant political speech occupied public space.[7] As

[5] Pezuela, *Historio de la Isla de Cuba*, 3: 382–385; Francisco Ponte Domínguez, *La junta de la Habana en 1808* (Havana: Editorial Guerrero, 1947). On the handbills (*pasquines*), Levi Marrero, *Cuba*, 15: 12–13. See also S. Johnson, "From Authority to Impotence," 197–203; and Michael Zeuske, "Las Capitanías Generales de Cuba y Puerto Rico en el gran Caribe, 1808–1812," in Manuel Chust and Ivana Fresquet, *Los colores de las independencias iberoamericanas: Liberalismo, etnía y raza* (Madrid: CSIC, 2009), 21–48.
[6] Pezuela, *Historia de la Isla de Cuba*, 3: 386.
[7] For examples, see "Legajo que contiene papeles anónimos señalados con los no. 1 hasta el 19," in AGI, Cuba, 1778B; "America. Cuba. Anónimos de Ciudadanos Cubanos," and "America. Cuba. Comunicaciones sobre la lealtad de la Ciudad de la Habana a Fernando VII," both in AHN, Estado (Junta Central Suprema Gubernativa del Reino), 59L and 59K, respectively. Joaquín Llaverías, "Unas décimas políticas," in *Archivos del Folklore*, 1 (1924): 52–62. On the explosion of writing and speech in the context of 1808 in Spain and Spanish America, see François-Xavier Guerra, "'Voces del pueblo': Redes

historian François-Xavier Guerra has noted, the proliferation of speech, writing, and ritual that emerged with the crisis of 1808 represented less the expression of opinion than of values: an impassioned defense of the Spanish king and an absolute refusal of the French one. The register was uniformly combative, the tone "unanamist" (*unanimista*).[8]

As in the very first proclamation of the Cuban captain-general, in much of the new patriotic writing the metaphor of slavery predominated: Napoleon sought to turn the Spanish into slaves; the supporters of the French were all vile slaves. The *Semanario Patriótico,* one of the most important peninsular newspapers of the period and one that appears to have circulated in the Americas, regularly and passionately invoked such metaphors. One article described the French army as barbarous and inhuman spillers of blood; "we fight them," said another, "because we do not want to be slaves."[9] Invocations of armies of slaves or battles for freedom were, of course, standard rhetoric of the period; slavery here was a central metaphor in the condemnation of political tyranny. But in an Age of Revolution that saw the rise of Haiti and of international abolitonism, "slavery" as fighting word gained other, equally powerful valences. In the Caribbean, that metaphor had always been particularly charged, in recent years even more so.

As patriotic speech and papers flourished, Napoleon tried to broadcast his own message. After the abdication of Fernando VII, Napoleon saw to it that those vessels heading to Spanish America carried an ample supply of papers, letters, and proclamations to give to prospective allies. French foreign minister Jean-Baptiste de Nompère de Champagny sent missives to Spanish colonial governors promising prosperity and peace, and he enclosed dozens of public documents to emphasize his point, simply expressed: that King Joseph I "wanted nothing but to give liberty to a people enslaved for many years."[10] Even in the midst of war and between opposing sides, there was a certain unanimity of discourse and metaphors. Both sides were doing determined battle against something they called slavery.

---

de comunicación y orígenes de la opinión pública en el mundo hispano (1808–1814), *Revista de Indias*, 62, 225 (2002): 357–384.

[8] Guerra, "'Voces del pueblo,'" 359.

[9] *Semanario Patriótico* (Cádiz), November 17, 1808, and May 25, 1809.

[10] "Correspondencia interceptada a Miguel José de Azanza, encargado de la cartera de Asuntos Exteriores con José I, relativa al envío de varios comisionados para fomentar la sedición en América," in AHN, Estado (Junta Central Suprema Gubernativa del Reino), leg. 54G; Someruelos to Kindelán, March 15, 1810, in ANC, AP, leg. 211, exp. 55.

The effort of persuading Spanish Americans to accept the rule of Spain's French monarch was led by the *afrancesados*, Spaniards who supported the French and became part of Joseph I's government in Madrid. Miguel de José Azanza, former viceroy of New Spain, now foreign minister of French-occupied Spain, wrote to Spanish American authorities emphasizing the "happiness, advancements, and improvements" that would come with Joseph's rule. Indeed according to Napoleon's Spanish Ambassador to the United States, French agents were everywhere in the Americas. One report received in Havana warned that Napoleon had fifty agents in Baltimore ready to fan out into Spanish territory in the Americas. In Cuba there were at least a dozen: several in Havana, two each in Santiago and Puerto Príncipe, one each in Trinidad, Sancti-Spíritus, Santa Clara, Remedios, Holguín, and Baracoa. The agents went with instructions to spread the word that recent changes in Spain would be advantageous to the colonies.[11]

It is unclear whether the papers written and sent by Joseph actually circulated widely in the Americas. In November 1808, when the governor of Havana received the Bayonne constitution drafted by Joseph I for Spain the previous July, he and the city council staged a public burning of the unopened charter by one of the city's official executioners. Here, even the act of *not* reading became a public patriotic ritual.[12] Still, it is hard to imagine that Napoleon's concerted effort – the number of vessels and agents and sheer pages – vanished into thin air without notice. When one of Napoleon's agents was caught in Havana, he had in his possession thirty-three letters to Spanish American authorities, pencil drawings of fortresses and cities, four manuscript notebooks with biographical and

---

[11] Miguel Artola, "Los afrancesados y América," in *Revista de Indias*, 15 (1949), 541–567; and Isidro Fabela, *Los precursores de la diplomacia mexicana* (Mexico, D.F.: Secretaría de Relaciones Exteriores, 1926), 156–166.

[12] A description of the public burning of the Constitution in Havana is included in "Juicio de Residencia de Sebastián Kindelán," in AHN, Consejos, 21130, ff. 154v–155. Several copies of the Constitution arrived in Cuba, and it is unclear whether all were burned. One was forwarded by Ferrand in Santo Domingo, together with a letter refusing to accept Spanish colonial declarations of war against the French. Ferrand asked: "With what reason then can the Spanish colonies, which are bound to obey the mother country, arrogate to themselves a right to declare war in their own name, without the previous authority of their legitimate sovereign?" While the letter was official correspondence between two government officers, it was published in translation, along with Napoleon's Constitution, in U.S. newspapers, suggesting there were multiple ways to access forbidden texts. See, for example, *Poulson's American Daily Advertiser*, January 11, 1809.

heroic episodes of the lives of Napoleon's generals, and more.[13] Among the agent's papers was also a personal letter from one of Napoleon's French officers in Spain to Cuban planter Francisco Arango. The two men had met in Saint-Domingue when Arango traveled there in 1803, and they had spent time together again later that year when the French evacuation of Saint-Domingue brought hundreds of French officers and troops to Havana. The letter to Arango was an enumeration of all the commercial and political advantages that Napoleon would rain on the colonies and a request that Arango use his great influence to propagate this information. Someruelos published a manifesto summarizing the case against the accused agent. In it he provided a description of the papers carried by the spy. But with crowds across the city clamoring for justice against against France's collaborators and with Arango already publicly associated with the unpopular attempt to create a junta in Havana, Someruelos decided to make no mention of the missive to Arango. The emissary was not so lucky: he was hanged in public on June 30, 1810. The papers he had brought with him for Mexico, Caracas, Puerto Rico, and elsewhere were publicly burned at the foot of the gallows. The ones addressed to people in Cuba, as the public manifesto curiously specified, were put in a closed and sealed packet to be kept in government offices.[14]

Among the *afrancesados* of Joseph's government in Spain were several important creoles from Havana. One was Gonzalo O'Farrill, born in Cuba to one of the oldest sugar families on the island. He had a prominent military career in Spain, where he was in close contact with other resident creoles, Francisco Arango among them in the 1790s. Though in Spain, O'Farrill still maintained links with Havana, owning property and communicating with nine brothers and sisters back on the island. In the fateful

---

[13] The agent's name was Manuel Rodríguez Alemán y Peña. "El Gobernador de la Havana instruye de las noticias correspondentes sobre el Emisario Manuel Rodríguez Alemán y Peña," August 30, 1810, in AGI, Ultramar, leg. 84; and Francisco Filomeno, *Manifiesto de la causa seguida a Manuel Rodríguez Alemán y Peña* (Havana, 1810), especially 4, 5–6, 13–14, 19–20, and 23.

[14] Filomeno, *Manifiesto*. It is interesting that the publication made explicit mention of secret documents, saved in sealed packets in government offices. With this kind of information in public circulation, it is not entirely surprising that conspirators would soon plot to enter and search government offices for secret orders regarding abolition. The man who wrote the letter to Arango was Sebastian Thouvenot. He was indeed in Le Cap during Arango's mission there in 1803, and he appears to have been granting passports that allowed people to leave Saint-Domingue with their "servants." For some examples, see the Barbot Family Papers, South Carolina Historical Society, 11/66/1.

year of 1808, he became Fernando VII's minister of war. When the Spanish royal family was sequestered by Napoleon, O'Farrill decided to heed Fernando's call for obedience to the new King José (Joseph) I. Months later he would emerge as one of Joseph's most important ministers, a member of the Council of State, Minister of War, and interim Minister of State, the Indies, and the Treasury. In exile years later, he was said to host prominent Cuban visitors and to keep abreast of technological advances to share with his compatriots.[15]

Another Cuban member of Joseph's government in Spain was the Marqués de Casa Calvo, former commander of Spanish-occupied Fort-Dauphin (Bayajá) in 1794, where he had kept a fragile peace among the black auxiliaries after the famous massacre there. During the French occupation of Spain, he served as lieutenant general and held several other positions in Joseph's government. He had extensive contacts in Havana, where he owned two sugar plantations, both of which were confiscated as a result of his alliance with Napoleon.[16]

Both men were part of dense creole networks on the island, personally acquainted with its governor and other officials, as well as with some of the most important members of sugar society. It is difficult to imagine that the men in Cuba who pondered issues such as the creation of an independent junta or whether or not to swear loyalty to an absent king would have missed the fact that O'Farrill was one of the signatories of the constitution they made such a show of burning. By virtue of the identity of some of Joseph's officers, because of Napoleon's welcome promises of free trade and legal equality between peninsular and American Spaniards, and perhaps also because men such as Arango had a long history of seeking maximum room for negotiation and autonomy, words, offers, and signals sent from occupied Spain certainly reached – and perhaps even appealed

[15] María Dolores González-Ripoll, "Entre la adhesión y el exilio: trayectoria de dos cubanos en una España segmentada," in Piqueras, José Antonio, ed., *Las Antillas en la era de las luces* (Madrid: Siglo XXI, 2005); Dominique Goncalvès, "Havana's Aristocrats in the Spanish War of Independence, 1808–1814," in Christophe Belaubre, Jordana Dym, and John Savage, eds., *Napoleon's Atlantic: The Impact of Napoleonic Empire in the Atlantic World* (Leiden: Brill, 2010), 81–95; Juan Mercader Riba, *José Bonaparte: Rey de España* (Madrid: CSIC, 1983), 63n; Andres Muriel, *Notice sur D. Gonzalo O'Farrill, lieutenant-général des armées de S.M. le Roi d'Espagne* (Paris: Bure Frères, 1835), 78–79; and Miguel José de Azanza y Gonzalo O'Farrill, *Memoria de D. Miguel José de Azanza y D. Gonzalo O'Farrill, sobre los hechos que justifican su conducta política. Desde marzo de 1808 hasta abril de 1814,* (Paris: Imp. de P.N. Rougeron, 1815), 291; Moreno Fraginals, *El ingenio*, 1: 29.
[16] Mercader Riba, *José Bonaparte*, 186. Calcagno, *Diccionario*, 149–150, 458–468.

in – Cuba, even if not with the intensity of those produced by the patriots battling the French.[17]

Whatever the attempts of Napoleon's Spanish state to make inroads in the Americas, in no territory was he successful. Instead, some cities established juntas to rule in the name of Fernando VII; others refrained from establishing them and subordinated themselves to the Junta Central in Sevilla. But one or another decision produced no sense of stability or security. They were at war with France; they had no king, and absolutely nothing was certain. As people rushed to speak, reason, persuade, and lament, the public itself expanded and forms of expression multiplied. In the process, even seemingly unanimous patriotic fervor sometimes betrayed conflicting visions of history and the present.

In the explosion of speech and writing that occurred in Cuba starting in 1808, the vast majority of writers and speakers defended the king and excoriated the French. But along the way, they often did much more. They discussed war and bloodshed, political representation and legitimacy, freedom and slavery – if mostly metaphorically in the case of the last two. In the process, all kinds of inconvenient tropes, images, and words invigorated an emerging public sphere.

One anonymous poem (*décima*) that circulated around Havana (and possibly Santiago) was a vivid defense of Fernando VII and a scathing attack on the French – standard fare across the Americas in 1808. But in this case the author also invoked other recent history.

Twenty five Generals	*Veinte y cinco Generales*
Beginning with the fierce Sonthonax	*Desde el fiero Sonthonax*
have made without disguise	*les han hecho sin disfraz*
a war against the natives.	*la guerra a los naturales*
They were the cause	*Ellos fueron los causales*
of their greatest misery,	*de su desdicha mayor*
and with so much heartache	*y con tanto sinsabor*
you want people still to love	*quieres que amen todavia*

---

[17] The extensive literature on the peninsular crisis and independence in the Americas has devoted relatively little attention to the relationship between the Napoleonic government in the metropole and Spanish territories overseas. That scholarship traditionally emphasized the rupture between Spain and America. More recent work, which views independence as a more contingent outcome and which devotes more attention to political and intellectual links between the Spanish and Spanish American movements, tends not to focus on the Napoleonic state in Spain. Thus, it does not sufficiently consider how a truly contingent account of the crisis and of independence would have to take seriously the American overtures made by Joseph I and the American responses to them. An important recent move in that direction is Belaubre, et al., eds., *Napoleon's Atlantic*. See also Adelman, *Sovereignty and Revolution*, 178–179, 186–187.

the same tyranny	*a la misma tiranía*
that caused them so much horror?	*que le causó tanto horror?*
They saw themselves robbed	*Ellos se vieron saqueados*
under the name of protection	*con nombre de protección*
by the barbarous oppression	*por la bárbara opresión*
of some horrendous soldiers.	*de unos horrendos soldados*
Their homes, spared	*sus hogares perdonados*
by their insurgent slaves,	*por sus siervos insurgentes,*
were roughly seized	*fueron presas inclementes*
by voracious Poles	*de Poloneses voraces*
more vile and rapacious	*mas ladrones y rapaces*
than Toussaint and his agents.	*que Toussaint y sus agentes.*[18]

This vision of Saint-Domingue shared something with ones that had long prevailed in Cuba, in particular the notion that the French had caused their own downfall. But now that portrayal – with mentions of Toussaint, the insurgent slaves, and the Polish legions sent to Saint-Domingue by Napoleon in 1802 – was incorporated into a public defense of their own government. The Haitian Revolution thus entered the *public* repertoire of political debate at one of the tensest times in Cuban history.

What is especially striking, however, is how inclusive that public was sometimes thought to be. Just one day after the arrival of first news in Havana and the publication of the governor's *proclama*, an anonymous exhortation appeared in manuscript form, signed simply J.M.P.M. and cleverly titled "What would you have done (asked the fool to the wiseman) if you were God? The same thing (replied the wiseman) that God has done."[19] The document was an appeal for unity and courage addressed to the broad population of Spaniards in the four corners of the earth (Europe, America, Africa, and Asia). Even closer to home, the anonymous piece reached broadly. One paragraph began with the declaration "most loyal blacks and mulattoes of this island, we always count on your patriotic zeal," and then quickly broadened it to include people of color in the formerly Spanish part of Hispaniola:

Spanish Island of Santo Domingo, people of color: remember what you owe to faithful Spain, that none of those who passed through there went unattended and that our kings, magistrates, and communities favored you; now remember

---

[18] Llaverías, "Unas décimas políticas."

[19] "¿Qué hubieras hecho tu (preguntó un necio a un sabio) si fueras Dios? Lo mismo (respondió el sabio) que Dios ha hecho," in "America. Cuba. Anónimos de Ciudadanos Cubanos," in AHN, Estado (Junta Central Suprema Gubernativa del Reino), 59L. See also Sigfrido Vázquez Cienfuegos, "Anónimos en la Habana durante el verano de 1808: Un ejemplo de pensamiento conservador," *Araucaria. Revista Iberoamericana de Filosofía, Política y Humanidades*, 13, 26 (2011): 226–245.

the cruel and barbarous treatment that France gave you. Don't forget either the inconsistency of Napoleon, who first declared you free and then slaves. If you trust him, he will sacrifice you with impunity out of hate that you denied him a third of your properties and your neck for the shackles. France intends to make itself master of the world, ending with you by blood and fire. Unite, unite with honorable Spaniards who will give you commerce and protection.

The paragraph is rife with contradictions. It contains a condemnation of the French for restoring slavery in Santo Domingo in 1802, yet it completely glosses over the continued existence of slavery in Cuba and Spanish America more generally. Certainly *pardos* and *morenos* in Cuba had plenty of opportunity to see their "necks for the shackles." This was not the author's only mention of the Haitian Revolution; he also specifically alluded to the defeat of the French by "a handful of Ethiopians without weapons" and reminded them of what they had seen with their own eyes: "Did you not see yesterday [France's] defeated remains with General Lavalette?" It is a curious mention, aimed surely at presenting the French as militarily weak. But some readers or listeners may have wondered: If the French had been defeated by a handful of unarmed blacks, and the Spanish were currently losing to the French, did that mean that the Spanish were also vulnerable to the kind of defeat the French had suffered at Saint-Domingue? Whatever the document's internal contradictions, two things are clear. First, the author treated recent, detailed episodes from the Haitian Revolution – the arrival of a defeated Lavalette in Havana, for instance – as something he could reach for in making a public argument. Second, the derogatory references to unarmed Ethiopians notwithstanding, the author addressed people of color as part of a public now confronting a grave political crisis.

At least some black residents of the city appear to have felt the same way. One Sunday shortly after the arrival of the first news from Spain, a man named Monfundi Siliman, king of a Congo *cabildo de nación* (African-based fraternal society), apparently gave an impassioned speech before a large gathering in support of the deposed Spanish king. The speech was published in bilingual format, with one column in Spanish and the other "in their own native dialect."[20] Though ostensibly

---

[20] "Proclama que en un cabildo de negros congos de la ciudad de la Habana pronunció su presidente rey Monfundi Siliman, un domingo por la tarde con motivo de la llegada de Cádiz del navío San Justo," in BNJM, manuscript, R/60378 (35), 1–2. Literary and linguistic scholars have raised questions about the authenticity of the text. On the one hand, the creole or pidgin version is suspiciously similar to imitations of *bozal* speech that would appear in later decades. On the other, certain linguistic elements of the text can be verified against other authenticated examples of "Afro-Hispanic language,"

pronounced at a meeting of a Congo *cabildo*, King Siliman's speech
addressed a host of people identified collectively as his kinfolk (*parientes*),
friends, and shipmates, as well as others identified by African ethnicity:
Congos, Luangos, Carabalí, Lucumí, Arará, and so on.[21] The speech
was a fervent, vernacular denunciation of the evil French (described var-
iously as dogs, robbers, Jews, and devils) and a celebration of the popular Madrid rebellion against them. Describing Havana on receiving the
news from Spain, the *cabildo* king asked his audience: "Haven't you
seen . . . what the whites did the other day when everything seemed crazi-
ness and drunkenness? I, who came to Havana in the time of the Governor
named Unzaga, have never seen such a thing. How people ran! How they
yelled, and sang and danced because the Spanish had killed the French
like so many ants."[22]

While he described the reactions of white *habaneros*, the Congo king
explicitly sought black responses to the current political crisis. At key
moments in the speech, he asked his audience: "What do you say about
all that? Speak, tell me."[23] In this manner, he created, at least symbolically, the space for black opinion and speech. And that opinion and speech
would likely have different sources than that of Havana's white residents.
For instance, to hammer home his point about the evil of the French, Siliman asked: "Don't you see, kinfolk, all the mischief the wretched French

making it difficult to discard as caricature. John Lipski, *A History of Afro-Hispanic Language*, 147–149; Juan Pérez de la Riva, "Cuadro sinóptico de la esclavitud en Cuba y de la cultura Occidental," in *Actas del Folklore* (Havana), 1, 5 (1961). See also Sigfrido Vázquez Cienfuegos, "Reacción de la población de color de la Habana ante los sucesos de 1808," in Manuela Cristina García Bernal and Sandra Olivero Guidobono, eds., *El municipio indiano: relaciones interétnicas, económicas y sociales*, (Sevilla: Universidad de Sevilla, 2009), 351–368; Carmen Barcia, *Los ilustres apellidos: negros en la Habana colonial* (Havana: Ediciones Boloña, 2009), 82–84.

[21] "Proclama que en un cabildo de negros congos de la ciudad de la Habana pronunció su presidente rey Monfundi Siliman," in BNJM, manuscript, R/60378 (35), 1–2. Shipmates in the dialect version is *carabela*, defined in the brief glossary at the end of the document as "all those who have come on the same ship." Some evidence suggests that the use of term *carabela* (in English, caravel, a light sailing ship originally used by the Spanish and Portuguese in the fifteenth and sixteenth centuries) was used beyond this one example. For example, *carabela* was used for shipmate in the testimony of slaves following the Bayamo 1805 conspiracy mentioned in Chapter 5. Assuming the term was not unusual at the time, it is interesting that the Spanish version of the text uses the translation *compañeros*, instead of *carabela*, making invisible the violent trade that necessarily preceded the existence of this black public on that Sunday morning.

[22] Ibid. Luis de Unzaga y Amezaga, was governor of Havana from 1782 to 1785.

[23] "Proclama que en un cabildo de negros congos de la ciudad de la Habana pronunció su presidente rey Monfundi Siliman," 3.

have done with us in Santo Domingo, killing some, frying others, castrating others like overseers do with pigs? Oh, kinfolk!" In one sentence, he invoked both the history of the Haitian Revolution and the violence of slavery: see what they have done with *us* there. In public, an African *cabildo* king expressed a powerful solidarity between blacks in Cuba and those in Saint-Domingue.

In his praise of the Spanish, the African king did something similar, judging Spain's benevolence (like France's malevolence) with specific reference to its black subjects. He reserved special praise for Governor Someruelos. Look at the way the governor treats us, he said, "making us officers, giving us flags, drums, rifles, and sabers just like the whites. We have money, horses, farms, houses, all that we want because we are free." Someruelos incorporated and promoted; the French, meanwhile, enslaved them. So, he asked, "Do you want to be slaves of that Sir *Cachorraso*?[24] No, relatives, better to die hanged." The decision before them, then, was simple: to die if necessary defending Havana against the French. In very tense and uncertain times, it was a call to arms, loyalist and in defense of the king, but also one that publicly and clearly invoked the powerful image of armed black men committed to freedom.

Thus the rapid proliferation of patriotic speech and writing, even if relatively unanimous in tone and allegiance, helped create a new kind of public – one that allowed Africans to speak publicly of politics and war. Of course, their voices carried little if any political weight – speaking was not the same as being heard. But given how many unexpected people spoke and how sometimes undisciplined were their interventions, the effect was one of a cacophony of voices and accents.

In this context, the challenges for local authorities were many: governing in the midst of war and in an almost total political vacuum, keeping control of a diverse and highly restive population eager to show their devotion to the king, and containing the significant anti-French fervor inflamed by war. Local newspapers published impassioned accounts of events in Spain, not just of military confrontations, but of other less official, sometimes violent, encounters. Stories of French "spies" dragged into the streets and bludgeoned to death by Spaniards in Madrid circulated widely in a local context in which tens of thousands of French had settled peaceably, to that point. Someruelos rightly feared that this

[24] *Cachorraso* is a colloquial term that combines *cachorro* (puppy or young person) with the augmentative suffix *-aso* (*-azo*), for something large or overgrown. Preceded by the title *señor* (sir or mister) it appears to convey derision.

could change at any moment. Authorities' eagerness to protect naturalized French residents had several sources, not the least of which was the protection of property. Indeed, the junta in Spain had called for the expulsion of the French and the confiscation of their goods many months earlier, but Someruelos in Cuba had instead called for tolerance combined with vigilance. As passions flared and the public called for retaliation against the French, Someruelos concluded that keeping the peace would require the expulsion of the French. Thus, on March 12, 1809, he ordered the departure of all French residents of Cuba not yet naturalized as Spanish.[25]

For some, the measure came too late. Just days after the expulsions began, violence erupted in the city. On March 21, two French carpenters who lived in the countryside and were traveling into the city of Havana were stopped by an officer who sought to bring them before authorities for questioning. As they made their way to the government house, they were accosted by a crowd, composed mostly of "kids of color." The multitude grew as the young men were joined by "many others, older, vagrants, and ne'er-do-wells" ready to take advantage of the fact of war against France. Tempers flared; insults and rocks were hurled. Soon the crowd began attacking other French along the way, and looting their homes and businesses. In the confrontations, three people were killed.[26]

With the city on alert, the disorder quickly spread to the surrounding countryside. South of Havana was a new and booming coffee district. From fewer than ten *cafetales* in 1790, it came to have almost 800 by 1817.[27] As in the east, it was French refugees who were primarily responsible for the takeoff, and so the district had a substantial population of people now viewed by many as enemies. Captain Manuel Abreu, writing from the rural town of San Marcos, reported, "there is not one coffee farm which has not been looted under the pretext of expelling the French, nor

---

[25] Marqués de Someruelos, *Proclama de 12 de marzo de 1809.* AHOHCH, AC. Libro 76, Folios 107–113v.

[26] Someruelos, "Comisión por el tumulto," Havana, March 23, 1809, in AGI, Cuba, 1719. See also the description in Pezuela, *Historia de la Isla de Cuba*, 3: 395–396; Juan de Dios Molina, "Noticia de las personas y casas que fueron asaltadas en los días 21 y 22 del corriente [Marzo] en este barrio extramuros de Guadalupe a mi cargo," in AGI, Cuba, 1703. For a recent analysis of the "riots," see Matt Childs, " 'The Revolution against the French': Race and Patriotism in the 1809 Riot in Havana," in Belaubre, et al., eds., *Napoleon's Atlantic*, 119–138.

[27] On slavery in the western coffee districts, see William Van Norman, *Shade-Grown Slavery: The Lives of Slaves on Coffee Plantations in Cuba* (Nashville: Vanderbilt University Press, 2013); Rolando Álvarez Estévez, *Huellas francesas en el Occidente de Cuba*, chap. 6. Figures are from Pérez de la Riva, *El café*, 50.

is there a person of that nation who has not been insulted and affronted." It did not escape authorities' notice that every one of those coffee farms was worked primarily by enslaved laborers, on average around forty per farm. So Abreu was quick to warn that the attacks on the French and their *cafetales*, committed "in plain sight of our blacks, will have fatal consequences if not suppressed in time."[28]

Indeed, some consequences were already visible. In Alquízar, one of the richest coffee districts in western Cuba, men and women held as slaves by French proprietors took the opportunity to escape from their now-absent French owners and roam the countryside freely, engaging in attacks of all kinds. On the coffee farm of the Marquis d'Espinville, slaves were "full of insubordination and implicated in the looting of [the master's] house. . . . They have said with the greatest audacity and resolve that in the event of returning to the dominion of their master or another Frenchman, they would take his life." A day later, "people of color had arrived on [local] estates to persuade the blacks that with everything that had happened they were now free."[29] The official in charge of subduing the rebellious slaves was Antonio María de la Torre y Cárdenas, a veteran of the Saint-Domingue war of 1793 who had also traveled with his father, José María, to Cádiz in 1804, where he met with and purchased at least two slaves from Jean-François. The Marquis d'Espinville, meanwhile, had helped in the negotiations between the Spanish and black insurgent leaders Jean-François and Biassou on the border between Spanish Santo Domingo and French Saint-Domingue in 1793. Thus, the current moment of upheaval, of slaves rebelling on French-owned plantations, very likely conjured up on Cuban soil a direct and powerful memory of the Haitian Revolution.[30] Across the region and into the emerging coffee areas of Guamacaro in Matanzas, authorities decided that every French-owned farm with more than six slaves had to have a Spanish overseer, so as to keep control and

---

[28] Manuel Abreu, Capitán de Partido de San Marcos, to Someruelos, March 23, 1809, in AGI, Cuba, 1702. This *legajo* is full of similar complaints in the regular reports and letters from captains in Alquízar, Guatao, San Marcos, and elsewhere from March and April 1809.

[29] Antonio de la Torre to Someruelos, April 18, 1809, and Cayetano de Campo to Someruelos, March 25, 26, and 28, all in AGI, Cuba, 1702.

[30] On de la Torre in Santo Domingo and Haiti, see Chapter 3. On the Marquis d'Espinville's participation in the negotiations on the French-Spanish border in Hispaniola in 1793, see Jacques Nicolas Léger, *Haiti and Her Detractors* (New York: Neale Publishing Company, 1907), chap. 6. On the memory of the Haitian Revolution in moments of rural unrest in Cuba in a later period, M. Iglesias, "Los Despaigne en Saint-Domingue y Cuba."

avoid tempting the enslaved to attack their day-to-day overlords, now seen as representatives of Spain's enemy.[31]

The chaos provoked by the profound political crisis of 1808 in Spain created dangerous and volatile space in Cuba. This was true, of course, across Latin America. But in Cuba, the very significant presence of French residents, tied in the minds of most to a recent past of violent revolutionary upheaval, gave the tensions a particular cast. There, the presence of so many French, as the lines between Spain and France became harder and starker in the context of war, created new opportunities for day-to-day conflict. The French were despised enemies, and Cubans hurled all manner of verbal and physical vitriol at them. But the French were also slaveholders. And now their Frenchness made them highly vulnerable to attack, by neighbors and by the people they held as slaves. Like the city itself, the countryside was on edge: roaming bands of people refusing to serve French masters, French masters fled or expelled, their slaves left living freely. This was, of course, the kind of division and uncertainty that created openings. Authorities understood that well, and they worried.

1808, Santiago

In Santiago, with roughly ten thousand French residents in 1808, the situation was even more explosive. In July, as soon as news of events in Spain arrived, local residents began burning houses belonging to French refugees. It was only the archbishop's public prayer for peace and calm that had quieted spirits.[32] But the lull proved brief, and the threat of violence hung over the city and its environs.

As in Havana, political speech – printed and whispered – burst forth seemingly from everywhere. Public prayers were organized not just by the church officials but by ordinary residents as well. Nicolasa Angula, a former slave who was heard publicly and hysterically lamenting the disappearance of the king, held a nine-day prayer (*novena*) for the Virgin of Pilar in honor of the king and the Spaniards under attack in Europe.[33] Across the city, incendiary papers appeared, posted on church doors,

---

[31] On the decision to use Spanish overseers, see Cayetano del Campo, March 24, 25, 26, 1809; and Junta de Vigilancia del Sumidero de Guamacaro, April 10, 1809, in AGI, Cuba, 1702.

[32] Kindelán to Someruelos, August 30, 1808, in AGI, Cuba, 1549. The figure of 40 for the average labor force comes from Álvarez Estévez, *Huellas francesas en el Occidente de Cuba*, 56.

[33] "Diligencias obradas sobre lo ocurrido la noche del día 15 de diciembre [1808] acerca de la mulata Nicolasa Angulo," in AGI, Cuba, 1778B.

thrown in the windows of government offices, dropped on streets for passersby to find. Most of these papers attacked the French and accused local officials of protecting them. One, which appeared on August 6, 1808, gave the governor five days to deal with the French, "and if some resolution is not taken you will see a night of judgment against these brigands."[34] Another, nailed to the door of a *mulata francesa*, predicted bloodshed more inscrutably: "the clouds that sustain the master of the army under the power of our beloved monarch are about to unleash a flood that will be universal and bloody."[35] The papers reflected the tension and uncertainty of the day. But full of threats and incendiary language, they also clearly added to the climate of speculation and fear, becoming part of the crisis itself.

On the night of September 18, 1808, word spread that enemy ships were gathering off the harbor and that on that very night the French in town were going to put all the Spaniards "to the sword" and "behead" them. Hearing this, a free man of color and member of the *pardo* militia, José Dolores Arredondo, started urging people to arm themselves and head down to the wharf to stop any movement of the French.[36] While all this was going on – rumors and warnings flying, people gathering to ascertain things for themselves – an anonymous paper appeared, found by a young enslaved girl and eventually turned over to Governor Kindelán. It was Kindelán, as much as the French themselves, who was the paper's principal target. Why, asked the broadside, did the governor so favor the French?

Why do we not disarm these men who have always given proof of their perfidy and signs of being revolutionaries? Don't you know that they have sworn allegiance to Napoleon and to his brother Joseph as King of Spain? Do you not know that they have had parties to celebrate the success they think has been achieved against the Spanish? Don't you know that they have a proclamation that encourages slaves, mulattoes, and the white French, the first to shake off the yoke of slavery, the others their submission to our laws and Government?[37]

In the proliferation of talk, rumor, and accusation, the possibility of violence was not just considered but also explicitly spoken, not only

---

[34] Anónimo # 1 in "Legajo que contiene papeles anónimos señalados con los no. 1 hasta el 19," in AGI, Cuba, 1778B.

[35] Anónimo # 12 in "Legajo que contiene papeles anónimos" in AGI, Cuba, 1778B.

[36] "Testimonio del expediente sobre la averiguación de los alborotos causados la noche de ayer 18 de septiembre [1808] por José Dolores Arredondo y socios," in AGI, Cuba, leg. 1778B.

[37] The handbill is transcribed in "Testimonio del expediente sobre la averiguación de los alborotos causados la noche de ayer 18 de septiembre" and "Legajo que contiene papeles anónimos," both in AGI, Cuba, leg. 1778B.

among authorities or planters but in papers publicly and visibly circulated, posted, and discussed.

Soon the rumors began pointing to independence: "there is a rumor circulated that no more *situados* will arrive in this Plaza because authorities already know that the district of [Santiago de] Cuba will rise up and proclaim its independence."[38] The idea of independence entered the public sphere explicitly, as people of all stations interpreted the events of 1808 to determine where everything might lead. Here, the option of independence, while not inevitable, was certainly not unimaginable, and to draw conclusions, the historical lessons were close at hand, in Haiti, in the United States.[39]

People talked of uprisings and brigands, of slaves undoing their enslavement, and of locals proclaiming independence. Images invoked bloody and universal confrontations on Cuban soil. Such talk – in the context of war, amidst intensified animosity against Saint-Domingue refugees, in a setting whose recent history was so marked by the Haitian Revolution – animated and gave urgency to speculation of "another Haiti" materializing in Cuba.

In that context rumors about slavery and freedom emerged almost immediately. In Santiago, public papers mentioned a French proclamation

[38] February 26, 1809, in "Diario muy reservado que lleba esta Sría. de Gobierno desde el momento que empezaron a conocerse en esta Plaza las diferencias entre España y Francia en el mes de julio de 1808," in AGI, Cuba, 1782B.

[39] Important recent work on Latin American independence has argued forcefully that creoles did not envision seeking independence in 1808. In this view, creole elites initially sought "voice" rather than "exit." While this revisionist perspective is useful in its more contingent understanding of independence, it may go too far in overlooking the ways in which independence may have already been imaginable as an outcome as early as 1808–1809. François-Xavier Guerra has argued that after U.S. independence, the Spanish state began imagining Latin American independence as highly probable; it is curious, then, that he gives so little consideration to the possibility of parallel notions of imagined futures developing in Latin America itself. If we allow for a much wider gamut of possibilities in the political imagination, we might better understand the brutal reaction of the Spanish authorities against the junta members and the moderate position that creoles did take in the end, a position they took in part in response to real and imagined threats from non-elite actors. For examples of the revisionist work, see François-Xavier Guerra, *Modernidad e independencias: Ensayos sobre las revoluciones hispánicas* (Madrid: MAPFRE, 1992); François-Xavier Guerra "Lógicas y ritmos de las revoluciones hispánicas," in *Las revoluciones hispánicas: independencias americanas y liberalismo español*, 13–47; Jeremy Adelman, "Iberian Passages: Continuity and Change in the South Atlantic" in David Armitage and Sanjay Subrahmanyam, eds., *The Age of Revolutions in Global Context*, 50–82; and José M. Portillo Valdés, *Crisis Atlántica: Autonomía e independencia en la crisis de la monarquía hispana* (Madrid: Marcial Pons, 2006), chap. 1.

urging slaves to shake off the yoke of slavery; in Havana, people of color insisted that recent events rendered the slaves of French planters free. It is unclear what the precise sources of these rumors were. It is possible that the rumors were vague distillations of French public documents – theoretically banned, publicly burned, but clearly discussed – that the new king "wanted nothing but to give liberty to an enslaved People." One source for the rumors, then, might simply have been the voluminous and contradictory surplus of unverified information. The fact that the government admitted to secreting papers in its offices, as had been done with the documents carried by the Mexican spy hanged in Havana, likely also contributed to the proliferation of rumors. Another possibility is that the rumors were the result of purposeful – either hopeful or scheming – interpretations of all that speech and writing. One man in Havana, just three months before the uprisings against the French, insisted that rumors of freedom and slave rebellion were rampant. The source, he said, was the French themselves, who, attacked or insulted by Spanish neighbors, began "threatening an insurrection of [their] slaves, promising them freedom in the event that these residents insult them through some recklessness, a suggestion that has spread and, by mention alone, frightens."[40]

If the exact sources of the rumors are vague, one thing was becoming eminently clear: the moment was ripe for unrest. The metropole was at war and in turmoil; the ties of colonial control and governance severely eroded; political legitimacy elusive and illusory. At home, elites were divided – church, military, government, planters. Official proclamations and plebeian rumors talked of slavery and freedom, independence and bloodshed. Episodic violence erupted. It was scenes such as this that had provided the opportunity for enslaved men and women in Saint-Domingue to take action eighteen years earlier, and there were plenty of men and women in Cuba who knew in their bones where it all could lead.

Haiti and 1808

The parallels, such as they were, were not lost on Haitian leaders. Already in 1806, creole patriot Francisco Miranda had traveled to Haiti on his way to launch a war of independence against the Spanish in Caracas. In a meeting between the two men, accounts of which may well be apocryphal,

---

[40] Conde de Casa Barreto [to Junta], Havana, December 14, 1808, in AHN, Estado (Junta Central Suprema Gubernativa del Reino), 59K.

Dessalines asked Miranda how exactly he planned to achieve independence. When Miranda responded with talk of assemblies, proclamations, and manifestos, Dessalines (so the story goes) laughed: "I see you hanged or shot." Revolutions, he explained, were not made with paper and ink: "Know, sir, that to make a revolution, to succeed at it, one needs to do only two things: cut heads and burn houses [*Coupé têtes, brûlé cazes*]."[41] Given the depth of the Spanish crisis two years later in 1808, and with it a better likelihood of success, it is possible that had Dessalines been at the helm of the Haitian state in 1808, a more interventionist and aggressive anticolonial and antislavery foreign policy might have developed at that juncture.

By 1808, however, Dessalines had been killed, and there were two Haitian heads of state: Henri Christophe, president of the State of Haiti in the north, and Alexandre Pétion, president of the Republic of Haiti in the south. Well aware of recent events in Spain and their potential repercussions closer to home, both men acted immediately to take advantage of the crisis. In many ways, they had the upper hand.

Christophe learned of events in Spain and the resistance to French rule from news arriving in Le Cap from London in the fall of 1808. He immediately informed Spanish residents across the border, still under French rule. On the border, commerce and communication were reestablished, and Haitian provisions alleviated some of the scarcities suffered by the Spanish. But Christophe cast his net wider, writing almost immediately to authorities in Havana to make clear that Haiti (or his Haiti, at least) recognized only Fernando VII as Spain's legitimate monarch. There were practical matters to raise, as well: should authorities in Cuba be interested, a mutually beneficial trade might be established between the ports under his command and Santiago, Baracoa, and other Cuban ports. What he wanted above all, he said, was for peace and union to reign between Haiti and Spain, his neighbor. He wrote as a "very humble and very obedient servant" of his interlocutors, expressing only the greatest admiration for the heroism that the Spanish were displaying in fighting the French. Despite the deferential tone of his address, the portrait he painted of Spanish action contained an implicit assertion of Haitian power:

The Spanish nation has shown itself in all its glory by its love for its King Fernando VII and by the valor with which it has vanquished the invincible soldiers of

[41] Ardouin, *Etudes sur l'histoire d'Haïti*, 6: 241–242; Clément Thibaud, "'Coupé têtes, brûlé cazes': Peurs et désirs d'Haïti dans l'Amérique de Bolivar," in *Annales*, 58, 2 (2003): 305–332.

Bonaparte. It has given other nations an example of what the energy of a truly courageous people can do.[42]

Haiti, of course, had defeated the "invincible" French already. If defeating the French made Spain an example to the world, then in that they were surely following Haiti, now in Year 5 of Independence, according to the letter's heading. The Cuban governor did not respond. Not to be deterred, Christophe sent the same letter a month later, addressing it to the Comandante de la Marina in Havana. This was a curious choice of correspondent, for the commander was a vocal and powerful detractor of the governor. Christophe clearly wanted to give his proposal the greatest chance of being heard and considered.[43]

While pursuing connections in Havana, Christophe also worked elsewhere to make inroads with the Spanish. He made contacts across the border, with Spanish residents who had declared war on Ferrand's French regime in Santo Domingo. He communicated with the governor of Puerto Rico and the leader of the Spanish movement, Juan Sánchez Ramírez, and agreed to send three hundred men, as well as shipments of arms and munitions. In part with Christophe's help, Spain's crisis of 1808 accomplished what Dessalines had not achieved in 1805: the expulsion of the French from Hispaniola forever.[44] Having helped the Spanish defeat the French in Santo Domingo, Christophe then used that as currency to gain favor with Spain. His agent in Philadelphia took letters to the Spanish consul, detailing the aid he had provided in Santo Domingo and proposing a "treaty of alliance and commerce" that would give Spain most-favored-nation status in Haiti.[45]

[42] Christophe to Someruelos, Le Cap, November 1, 1808, in AGI, Estado, leg. 12, exp. 57.
[43] Christophe to Juan Villavicencio, Comandante General de la Marina de la Habana, December 2, 1808, in AHN, Estado (Junta Central Suprema Gubernativa del Reino), leg. 59B. For more on the conflicts between Someruelos and Villavicencio see Juan Villavicencio to Junta, July 21, 1808, in the same legajo; and Pezuela, *Historia de la Isla de Cuba*, 3: 381–386.
[44] César Cuevas Pérez and Guillermo Díaz Bidó, *Presencia francesa en Santo Domingo, 1802–1809* (Santo Domingo: Editora Nacional, 2008); and ANC, AP, leg. 297, exp. 52. After the restoration of Spanish rule in 1809, Christophe was in communication with and provided aid to various anti-Spanish, proindependence (and possibly pro-Haitian) conspirators in 1809–1810, and possibly later. See Anne Eller, "'All would be equal in the effort': Santo Domingo's 'Italian Revolution,' Independence, and Haiti, 1809–1822," *Journal of Early American History* 1, 2 (2011): 105–141. There is some indication that Pétion may also have supplied arms to the Spanish in exchange for cattle in 1809; see Nessler, "A Failed Emancipation?," 348–358.
[45] See copy of unsigned letter presented by Christophe agent Joseph Bunell Blancan to D. José Ignacio de Viar, in AGI, Estado, leg. 12, exp. 54.

In Havana, Governor Someruelos vehemently opposed Christophe's project of alliance with Spain. While he did not reply to Christophe's offer of friendship, he did forward the letter to authorities in Spain. From them, he received a surprising reply: a Royal Order instructing him "to reply to Henri Christophe that it has given the Junta Suprema great pleasure to hear the sentiments he expresses toward the Spanish nation, and it is the Royal Will that you cultivate relations of friendship with said black chief by sending a person in your confidence to his residence."[46]

The order notwithstanding, Someruelos was unwilling to imagine an official emissary from Cuba to Haiti. The last time he had sent someone to Le Cap, it was still French, and his delegate had been Francisco Arango, hardly an appropriate choice in 1808. Finding a suitable person was, of course, the least of Someruelos's problems. In the interim between receiving Christophe's letter and the Junta Central's order, Someruelos also received a missive from Alexandre Pétion, president of the Haitian republic in the south, currently at war with Christophe. Pétion sent a ship to begin picking up "all the Haitians in Cuba who desire to return to their homes," for he wanted to "restore to their country the poor souls who generally do not owe their exile to anything other than the misfortunes of the civil war that happened here in the time of the French." To curry favor, the letter closed with a reference to the harmony and coordination that existed between his government and the Spanish newly in Santo Domingo. It was to no effect. Santiago governor Kindelán did not let Pétion's men off the ship and made them wait for a reply out in the harbor. When that reply came, it was negative and cursory. He had no power to receive vessels or enter into agreements with "foreign colonies," he said. His very choice of words, of course, ignored the fact that Pétion's letter identified the people he wrote about as Haitians, the "time of the French" as past, and current historical time as Year 6 of Independence.[47]

While Someruelos refused Pétion's request, he did put the request to good use, as an argument against sending an emissary to Christophe. Spain could not send one to Christophe, he argued, because to do so, when Pétion was also seeking friendship, would be to put Spain in the middle of the war between the two Haitian states. He could not accept Chrisophe's delegate and not accede to Pétion request for the same representation.

---

[46] Junta to Someruelos, Real Orden, February 18, 1809, in AGI, Estado, leg. 12, exp. 57.

[47] Pétion to Kindelán and Pétion to Someruelos, both dated January 14, 1809; and Kindelán to Someruelos, January 23, 1809, all in ANC, AP, leg. 244, exp. 144. An extensive file with more of the correspondence among Spanish authorities in Spain and Cuba is in AGI, Estado, leg. 12, exp. 54.

Someruelos gave another reason as well. If he sent an emissary to Christophe, then Christophe might want to send one to him, and that emissary would be a black man. The arrival of Haitian representatives and communication with Haiti more generally, he insisted, would only serve to spread "doctrines contrary to servitude" among Cuban blacks. Relying on such arguments, he made a decision and informed his superiors in Spain: "I have considered it appropriate to suspend for now compliance with this sovereign resolution."[48]

Someruelos's refusal prompted an interesting discussion among authorities in Spain. The secretary of state and members of the Junta Central conceded that difficulties might arise from establishing more formal relations with Christophe. In addition to the question of the rivalry between the two Haitian leaders, they acknowledged a more fundamental issue:

It is well known that the colonial system is completely opposed to the principles of liberty proclaimed in Haiti, and that an imprudent and open communication between that island and ours could be the origin of a political upheaval, for in the end the example can be very tempting and the idea of independence is easily received in the minds even of those men who, according to some, are destined for slavery.

On one level this was standard talk of contagion; on the other, it was an unusual (if still cursory) recognition of Haiti's political presence. Haiti's power here had two sources. First, Haiti was "a people of color that declares itself free in the middle of the Greater Antilles...the Republic of Haiti: a free people and consequently opposed to the slavery of the blacks." Second, amidst profound unrest in Spanish America, Haiti could pursue alliances that might prove deadly for Spain's interests in the New World. That very danger, however, was only more reason to send a representative to Christophe – to enter into some form of relationship and to watch closely, the better to manage the risk. The British were doing it, and in this moment of grave crisis Spain had even more at stake.

So, on September 10, 1809, the secretary of state re-sent – this time in triplicate – the original Royal Order asking Someruelos to appoint a representative to Haiti. New instructions merely added that Someruelos should be careful to appoint someone with the tact and judgment requisite

---

[48] Someruelos to Secretario de Estado, July 28, 1810, in AGI, Estado, leg. 12, exp. 51.

for so sensitive a mission. Still, the Cuban governor did not budge. "I already explained," he wrote on November 10, 1809:

I have considered it appropriate to suspend the dispatch of a person of my confidence to Haiti with the stated purpose of cultivating friendly relations with that Government. And since the obstacles [*inconvenientes*] today remain the same, I hope that with knowledge of them you will communicate to me His Majesty's ruling on this matter, leaving said suspension in effect in the meantime, and communicating to you that my opinion will always be that I believe it prejudicial to the peace of this island, in which there are large numbers of slaves and people of color, to establish correspondence with the black and mulatto *caudillos* of Santo Domingo, be they of one color or the other or both.[49]

The promise to wait for further instructions and clarification notwithstanding, his refusal was effectively absolute. Havana would not seek friendship with Haiti; he would not court black presidents or their representatives, nor would they be received in Havana. Not even war would alter the priorities of Havana's power elite. Meanwhile, every day hundreds of freshly arrived Africans continued to be announced for sale: 95 or 290 or 800 at a time, at the "accustomed hour," in one of several accustomed places.[50]

We have no direct evidence of how Christophe (or Pétion) reacted to the Cuban governor's rebuff. But in 1810–11, Christophe began intercepting some of the slave ships arriving regularly in Havana. His navy brought the vessels to Haitian ports, the human cargo disembarked as legally free persons, and the vessels with crew were sent on their way. Such was the fate of at least three ships: an unnamed Portuguese ship, intercepted in November–December 1810 while en route from Rio to Havana with 440 captive Africans; the *Santa Ana*, whose shipment of 205 slaves was liberated and taken by Christophe's forces to the port of Gonaïves sometime in April–May 1811; and the *Nueva Gerona*, intercepted in September 1811. In addition, the Havana *consulado* referred to the capture of "various slave ships" prior to the interception of these three, news of which, they said, was circulating in Havana.[51] Cuban

49 Ministro de Estado to Someruelos, September 1, 1809, in AGI, Estado, leg. 12, exp. 54; and Someruelos to Ministro de Estado, November 10, 1809, in AGI, Estado, leg. 12, exp. 49.
50 For examples of auction announcements, see "Loose Sheets re. Slave Trade," in Harvard, Houghton, Escoto Papers, Supplement, MS Span 52.1, box 3, no. 9.
51 On these three examples, see Junta Consular to Capitán General, February 23, 1811, and June 26, 1811, in BNJM, CM Morales, Tomo 79, nos. 23 and 26, respectively; Claudio Martínez Pinillos to Real Consulado, March 24, 1812, in ANC, AP, leg. 106, exp. 21; and Pedro Sánchez Griñán to Suarez de Urbina, April 21, 1811, in ANC, CCG, leg.

planters and authorities, unwilling to believe that Christophe could be doing this on his own account, laid the blame on the British. Yet the British themselves worried about the fate of their own ships and about Christophe's growing naval power. He acquired a frigate in May 1811, declared a blockade on those ports held by Pétion, and in one instance fired on and killed three crew members aboard a British vessel believed to be violating the blockade. There was ample evidence of Christophe's growing power and boldness and no indication that he captured Cuban slave vessels at anyone's directive.[52] In addition to bringing captives to free soil in Haiti, Christophe's government also worked to free Haitian citizens held captive in Cuba, including children stolen by Spanish privateers from fishing boats off the Haitian coast.[53] Whether Christophe was motivated in part by Someruelos's rebuff, by the desire to project Haitian antislavery and Haitian power internationally, by the desire to increase his population and labor force, or some combination of these, we cannot know.[54]

In Havana in 1810, empty slavers were thus arriving with news of Haitian attacks and of captives liberated on Haitian soil. Meanwhile, from South America, news arrived of war and declarations of independence against Spain: Caracas on April 19, Santa Fe de Bogotá on July 20, Cartagena on August 16, New Spain on September 16. From Pétion's Haiti came news that André Rigaud had returned in December, had set himself up as leader of the South, and from there, at Bonaparte's behest, was working to foment revolution in Cuba.[55] In Spain, the French had

94, exp. 2. Haitian interception of slave ships is discussed briefly in Franco, *Comercio clandestino de esclavos*, 106–107 and Franco, *Revoluciones y conflictos internacionales*, 97. The fate of the *Santa Ana*, which was taken to the port of Gonaïves, may be linked to the history of the famous village and ritual center of Souvenance, a few miles from that city. In oral and popular history, the origins of the place are associated with a slave ship whose human cargo was liberated and taken to that area in roughly this period. Personal communication, Patrick Tardieu, November 2006; and Jean Casimir, February 2007.

[52] See TNA, War Office (WO) 1/75, esp. ff. 279, 283–285, 329–331; and TNA, WO 1/76, ff. 25–107, 121–123, 179–188, 207–217, 269–285.

[53] Comte de Limonade to Captain General of Cuba (Apodaca), January 19, 1813 in ANC, CCG, leg. 102, exp. 2, reproduced in Franco, *Documentos*, 165. While the complaint is dated January 1813, it appears that some of the episodes had happened significantly earlier: one of the adults so captured was jailed for eight months and then spent time working on the island after he was freed.

[54] On Haitian maritime strength in this period and examples of attacks on British shipping, see the extensive correspondence in TNA, WO 1/75 and 1/76 and ADM, 1/262.

[55] See Pedro Sánchez Griñán to Suarez de Urbina, April 21, 1811; and Sánchez Griñán to Someruelos, in ANC, AP, leg. 213, exps. 41 and 125, respectively.

advanced on Andalucía; Sevilla, the seat of the Junta Central for over a year, had fallen, and its leaders had been forced to flee to a small island off the coast of Cádiz. There, the Junta Central dissolved itself and established in its place the Consejo de Regencia, or Regency, which soon thereafter convened the Cortes of Cádiz. This was, without doubt, a defining moment: one where profound division and uncertainty created unprecedented peril, or opportunity.

Conspiracies and Constitutions

It must all have weighed heavily on the governor of Cuba, responsible for keeping order amidst so many invitations to disorder. On the night of October 4, 1810, however, he sat before the coffin of his only daughter, a father perhaps uninterested in politics. Yet, even on that night, politics intruded, as the quiet wake was interrupted by news that a conspiracy was afoot. Scheduled to begin in three days' time, it sought nothing short of independence from Spain. Havana was to join the ranks of Spanish American cities breaking with the motherland. Word was already spreading around the city, and the public was anxious and restive. An investigation ensued with lightning speed: suspects were captured; they were questioned without lawyers; standard judicial procedure was abandoned in favor of proceedings by an ad hoc junta that answered only to the governor.[56]

The investigation purported to have uncovered an extensive conspiracy, involving individuals from prominent families in the city, freemasons with links to the United States and France, members of the city's black and mulatto battalions, and some slaves. One leader was Román de la Luz, a freemason whom the governor described as a distinguished person closely linked by blood to the first families of Havana. Whatever his provenance, in the weeks before his capture he had dedicated himself to the organizational work of the conspiracy, in particular to publicizing and distributing seditious papers. Another leader was Luis Fernando Bassave, also from a distinguished Havana family and a captain in the Havana Cavalry Regiment. According to the governor, his principal role in the conspiracy appears to have been to recruit and incite black and

[56] Franco, *Las conspiraciones de 1810 y 1812*, 38. For a discussion of the limitations of the available sources from the conspiracy, see Carmen Barcia, "Otra vuelta de tuerca a la conspiración de Román de la Luz y los avatares de Joaquín Infante," published online at http://www.academiahistoria.cu/index.php/Bitacora/Discursos-de-entrada-de-los-Academicos/Otra-vuelta-de-tuerca-a-la-conspiracion-de-Roman-de-la-Luz-y-a-los-avatares-de-Joaquin-Infante.

mulatto residents of the city to rise up and rebel under his leadership.[57] A third white leader, Joaquín Infante, was never caught. He escaped to the United States and from there to Venezuela, where he participated in the war against Spain (earning the nickname "the second Robespierre") and where he also wrote and published a constitution for Cuba.[58] All three men, in 1809, had signed a letter in opposition to a disposition of the governor that limited trade with the United States, suggesting that they were, like many of their compatriots, strong advocates of free trade. Not surprisingly, then, the constitution associated with the movement abolished many of the most onerous taxes imposed by the metropolitan government.

The conspiracy also made inroads in the city's free black militia. Unfortunately, whatever testimony was taken from them has not survived, so we do not know what particular role any of these men might have had, nor can we judge the credibility of the charges against them. It is also impossible to know what it was about the movement that might have attracted them to the effort. Nothing in the discussion of the conspiracy in 1810 suggests that it was antislavery or antiracist. Infante's constitution maintained slavery. It maintained white privilege, while defining white in a way that could include indigenous people, *mestizos*, and descendants of Africans four generations removed. Free people of color may have interpreted such proposals as an expansion of *gracias al sacar*, making available without charge the practice by which people of color were allowed to "free themselves of their status as colored" (*librarse de su condición de pardo*) in order to practice professions reserved for whites by law.[59] It was a different article of Infante's constitution, however, that might have most appealed to members of the free colored militias.

[57] "Expediente de la causa formada en 1810 en la Habana sobre intento de sublevación y francomasonería en la que se hallaban comprendidos Joaquín Infante, Luis Basave, Román de la Luz... tramitados por la Vía Reservada," in AGI, Ultramar, leg. 113. The file is partially transcribed in Franco, *Conspiraciones de 1810 y 1812*, 37–75.

[58] "Expediente de la causa formada en 1810," AGI, Ultramar, 113; Franco, *Conspiraciones de 1810 y 1812*, 72–73; and Joaquín Infante, *Proyecto de Constitución para la Isla de Cuba* (1811), http://biblio.juridicas.unam.mx/libros/2/808/10.pdf. For recent work on Infante and his constitution, see Leida Fernández Prieto, "Joaquín Infante en el ideario político independentista americano: de lo local a lo continental," in Diana Soto Arango y Miguel Ángel Puig-Samper, eds., *Discursos políticos de criollos ilustrados en las independencias americanas* (Madrid: Doce Calles, forthcoming).

[59] Applications for *gracias al sacar* had been on the rise since the last decades of the eighteenth century. See Ann Twinam, *Public Lives, Private Secrets: Gender, Honor, Sexuality, and Illegitimacy in Colonial Spanish America* (Stanford: Stanford University Press, 1999). See also the 1807 petition of would-be notary José de Salas, in ANC, AP, leg. 138, exp. 58.

Article 23 stated that "The white deputy inspectors... of the black militias will be abolished, and [the colored militias] will be subject immediately, like the white militias, to the Estado Mayor."[60] The proposed article
brought the organizational structure of the colored militias more in line
with that of the white ones, by removing the former from the purview of
an intermediate set of subinspectors. The measure would have had considerable appeal among colored militia members, who often suffered all
manner of public humiliation at the hands of the white subinspectors.[61]
The movement for them might thus have represented an opportunity to
eliminate a racial barrier and to make the dignity and honor of their
uniforms more meaningful.

Whether it was that particular feature of the movement, or the more
general call for independence, some black members of the militia appear
to have heeded it. Unfortunately for them, it may have been precisely their
adherence that doomed it. Luis Bassave, charged with recruiting among
people of color, grew worried about their participation and betrayed the
plot to the governor, characterizing it as a black riot. Thus four members
of the colonial black militia– Ramón Espinosa (first sergeant), Juan José
González (second sergeant), Buenaventura Cervantes (first corporal), and
Carlos de Flores (soldier) – were all sentenced to ten years in prison and
to be chained by the ankle. In addition, two enslaved men – Juan Ignacio
González and Laureano Infante (coachman to Joaquín Infante) – were
also judged guilty and sentenced to eight years in jail and 200 lashes in
public – 150 through the streets and 50 in the pillory.[62] One suspected
conspirator went unpunished: a free black carpenter and retired black
militia member named José Antonio Aponte, whose taste for conspiracy
would soon prove to be undiminished.

Bassave and the others arrived in Cádiz to serve out their sentences in
the fall of 1810, precisely as the Cortes convened for the first time and
began raising, by very different means, some of the questions that had
been central to the conspiracy: sovereignty, colonialism, citizenship, slavery, and rights. The first decree of the Cortes, dated September 24, 1810,
proclaimed the principle of national sovereignty, represented now by the
Cortes itself. The new institution would soon establish freedom of the
press, prohibit torture, and abolish seigniorial jurisdictions, tithes, trade
monopolies, and the colonial labor systems of *mita* and *repartimiento*.

[60] Infante, *Proyecto de Constitución*, Title V, Article 23.
[61] On complaints against white subinspectors made by the colored battalions, see Carmen
Barcia, *Los ilustres apellidos*, 270–272.
[62] "Expediente de la causa formada en 1810," AGI, Ultramar, leg. 113.

It also established equality of representation and equality of political, economic, and juridical rights among all Spaniards, both European and American.[63]

Cuba sent two delegates to the Cortes, one from Havana, the other from Santiago. Havana's member was Andrés de Jaúregui, a prominent sugar planter, slaveholder, and a close associate of Francsico Arango's. He arrived in Cádiz on February 11, 1811, with a secretary, two slaves, and three servants. Sworn in at the end of the month, his first important intervention came on March 26, when José Miguel Guridi y Alcocer, a priest from Tlaxcala, Mexico, presented an eight-part public proposal for the gradual abolition of slavery, starting with the immediate abolition of the slave trade, the freedom of all future children born to enslaved mothers, the payment of a salary to enslaved workers, and equality of treatment between free servants and slaves. There can be no doubt that Jaúregui vigorously opposed the proposal, but when he rose to speak he did not say that. Instead, he insisted that to speak of the issue publicly was to invite catastrophe on his island. His proposal that the matter be considered in secret passed unanimously.[64]

A week later, on April 2, Agustín de Arguelles, delegate for Oviedo in northern Spain, made a new proposal.[65] He began in a different vein, calling for the abolition of torture generally. His second point raised the issue of the slave trade. He proposed:

that without lingering on the protests of those who have an interest in the continued importation of African slaves in America, Congress decree abolished forever such a vile traffic and that, from the date of the publication of the decree, it

[63] Cortes de Cádiz, *Colección de los decretos y órdenes de las Cortes Generales y Extraordinarias en 24 de septiembre 1810 hasta igual fecha en 1811* (Madrid: Imprenta Nacional, 1813), vol. 1 (see decrees 1, 5, 9, 20, 42, 61, 82). The question of whether Indians and Africans would be considered Spanish citizens was, of course, a critical one. The Cádiz constitution gave automatic citizenship to Native Americans or Indians born in Spanish territory; but denied it to the African descended. Free people of African descent had to follow the more difficult path of naturalization. The relevant articles in the Constitution are 1, 5, 10, 18–22.

[64] Accordingly, the *Diario* for the March 26 session reported only that the Mexican delegate "presented some proposals regarding the well-being of America, which were ordered sent to the Constitutional commission." See *Diario de sesiones de las Cortes Generales y Extraordinarias*, no. 178. Sesión del día 26 de marzo de 1811. The *Diario* is available online at http://www.congreso.es/portal/page/portal/Congreso/Congreso/Hist_Normas/200. The description of Jaúregui's response comes from "Copias de la Junta del Real Consulado y Sociedad Patriótica sobre las proposiciones relativas a la manusmisión de los esclavos y los graves peligros que podrían resultar a esta isla," May 23, 1811, in Harvard, Houghton, Escoto Papers, MS Span 52, Box 19, no. 18.

[65] Both interventions are reproduced in Arango, *Obras*, 2: 85–87.

prohibit in all of the possessions that comprise the Monarchy in both hemispheres the introduction or sale of African slaves.

When he finished, one of his colleagues rose: "It is unseemly for the Congress not to approve this moment the first of those propositions," referring to the abolition of torture. A second delegate spoke: "I ask that this point not be discussed but rather that we immediately proceed to a vote on the abolition of torture." Then a third: "To attempt a discussion of this matter is to degrade human understanding."[66]

Jáuregui listened to the ardent interventions and immediately thought of the French National Convention's abolition of slavery, without opposition or debate, in a similarly dramatic and passionate moment in February 1794. He waited no longer and rose to speak. First, he applauded the principles and sentiments that motivated the proposal, which he claimed to share. But he insisted, again, that no good could come of a public discussion of so sensitive an issue.

The island of Cuba, and in particular Havana, which I represent, is the most interested in this affair. That vast territory enjoys today profound tranquility. With the news that this matter is under consideration, and without a resolution that reconciles the many interests at stake, the peace that happily reigns in a territory so advantageous in all regards could well be compromised. Disastrous movements, known to you, are agitating a large part of the Americas. Will we risk disturbing the interior peace of one of the most precious portions of overseas Spain? . . . Let us not rush things; let us treat them with the order that prudence requires. Recall the imprudent conduct of the French National Assembly and the sad, most fatal consequences it produced. . . . I therefore conclude by proposing formally that the matter be taken up by whomever His Majesty desires but that it be done precisely in secret session to avoid the consequence we would otherwise have to fear . . . and that the discussion not be included in the *Diario de las Cortes*.

Jáuregui famously won the war: the Cortes did not abolish either slavery or the slave trade. But he lost the battle. The proposal and the full discussion was published in the *Diario* and to it was appended Guridi Alcocer's original proposal, initially kept secret but now published for everyone to see.[67]

When news of the proposals arrived in Havana, the alarm among Arango's coterie was almost frenzied. Years before, Arango had confessed that his vision of Cuba's happiness and prosperity hung by a

[66] Arguelles's proposal and the discussion that followed were published in *Diario de sesiones de las Cortes Generales y Extraordinarias*, no. 185. Sesión del día 2 de abril de 1811.
[67] Ibid.

thread, dependent above all on the submission of hundreds of thousands of enslaved Africans. Now the thread might further fray as a result of a distant congress and deputies with good intentions and precious little understanding of his reality. This was precisely the kind of thing that had destroyed Saint-Domingue: public and ill-advised talk of freedom, among planters new desires for independence precisely to avoid that freedom, and a profound loss of certainty in which the wrong people had found opportunity.

Everywhere in the city, said the governor, all people talked about was the abolitionist proposals before the Cortes. Rumors in city and countryside suggested that freedom had already been proclaimed by the legislature. One priest walked the streets telling every black person he saw that the Cortes had given them freedom effective in ten years. "Great, sir," said Someruelos, "is the sensation caused among these inhabitants and very sad the notions being whispered."[68] The governor, the city council, the Real Consulado, and the Sociedad Patriótica all mobilized immediately, quickly dispatching letters, reports, complaints, and all manner of argument to Cádiz. "It is a question of our very lives, our fortunes, and that of our descendants," began the city of Havana's memorial to the Cortes. The lengthy missive, penned by Arango himself, refuted point by point the arguments made by the deputies in favor of abolition. To the charge that the laws of all civilized nations had already abolished it, he countered that only "in the frenetic pages of the French Revolution and its guillotinizing laws [*guillotinadoras leyes*] had slavery been abolished." England and the United States carefully considered the abolition of the trade for two decades before acting. He compared the number of slaves in Cuba to that in other colonies to show that Cuba was far from having the requisite number for its enterprises. To cut off the supply now, he argued, would only increase the physical burdens on those slaves already in Cuba. The brief mention of the welfare of slaves notwithstanding, his concerns lay elsewhere: such brash action would violate the rights of property and endanger the prosperity of the island.[69]

---

[68] "Representación que por encargo del Ayuntamiento, Consulado, y Sociedad Patriótica de la Habana hizo Francisco Arango y Parreño y se elevó a las Cortes por los expresados grupos" in Arango, *Obras*, 2: 19; and Someruelos to Ignacio de Pezuela, May 27, 1811, in *Documentos de que hasta ahora se compone el expediente que principiaron las Cortes Extraordinarias sobre el tráfico y esclavitud de negros* (Madrid: Imp. de Repulles, 1814), document 5.

[69] "Representación de la Ciudad de la Habana a las Cortes, el 20 de Julio de 1811," in Arango, *Obras*, 2: 45.

Arango argued that the most immediate threat was the one to public order and the safety of the island's white inhabitants. To raise hopes of imminent freedom among slaves, said Arango, "is to open the door to their dangerous reflections . . . it is surely to excite them if not to insubordination then at least to indocility." And in a stunning reflection of the planters' view of their world, he added: "In the stupidity of the black [man] and in the solitude of our estates, subordination is indispensable, and most frightening, therefore, anything that loosens this singular recourse, this principal defender of the existence of whites who live among so many blacks."[70]

In signaling this grave risk, however, Arango and his compatriots were far from submissive or pleading. Indeed, his tone was quite the opposite. Throughout, he made clear that the threat to him and his class was also a threat to Spain. First, if slaves destroyed the island's wealth, Spain would lose a valuable possession. But was the rebellion of slaves the only risk facing Spain? In that moment, in which much of Spanish America had revolted against Spain, was there not also the risk of alienating the local creole elite, who would decide whether to follow the path of, say, Venezuela, or instead remain a loyal and integral part of the Spanish monarchy? The very tone of Arango's text raised the specter of disloyalty. For example, it explicitly questioned the depth of legitimacy of the Cortes, as well as its ability to arrive at wise legislation. "The great majority of this sovereign nation . . . has not made sacred deposit of its supreme authority in a complete and legitimate way. . . . Forgive us for reminding you, with the most profound submission, that an absolute majority of votes only rarely, most rarely, produces good laws." Legal historian Reinaldo Suárez Suárez has commented that this was the kind of language and argument that had preceded many of the contemporaneous breaks with Spain.[71]

In the Cuban case, there was the further complicating factor of the United States. When the news of the abolition proposals arrived in Havana, William Shaler, U.S. consul in the city, decided to seize the advantage. He met regularly with prominent creoles, discussed with them the possibility of Cuba's annexation to the United States, and even handed out copies of the U.S. Constitution, a document which, of course, protected the institution of slavery. In July, an essay Shaler had written detailing the potential value of Cuba to the United States was

---

[70] Ibid., 2: 47.
[71] Ibid., 2: 23–24; and Reinaldo Suárez Suárez, "Repercusiones de la Constitución de Cádiz: Guridi y Alcocer y la esclavitud en Cuba," in *Anuario Mexicano de Historia del Derecho*, 22 (2010): 339–365.

apparently circulating in Havana. The American option could not, natu-rally, be mentioned in the city's memorial to Spain. But the document's tone, together with the reality of insurgency elsewhere and of growing U.S. power nearby, was not lost on metropolitan authorities. Current circumstances were already giving Cuban sugar interests the power to maneuver. As the captain-general reminded the minister of state, the issues of slavery and freedom demanded the utmost caution and secrecy, "so as not to lose this important island."[72]

Much was at stake. Creole patricians talked bluntly about the risks of rebellion from their slaves, but the way they wrote left little doubt that they, too, might be perfectly capable of disloyalty. In that key moment, a major feature of nineteenth-century Cuban politics came into sharp relief. Cuban loyalty was conditional. It would have a price, and at the top of the bill was the protection of slavery.

In the city's response to the abolitionist proposals of 1811, a second feature of nineteenth-century Cuban politics also came into focus: the usefulness of Haiti. Its image, successfully manipulated, could quiet offi-cial talk of abolition. And so Haiti was everywhere in Arango's memorial. It was the Haiti of 1791, in which the enslaved rose up, killed masters, covered the world's richest colony in blood, and turned it into a mountain of ashes. Such was the language of the memorial, as it argued that it was precisely this fate that the actions of the Cortes had potentially opened for Cuba. Slaves believing rumors of freedom would in the end take matters into their own hands and repeat Haitian scenes on Cuban soil.[73]

But conjured in the responses of Havana's elite was also the Haiti of 1811:

of the barbarous King of Haiti, who already threatens us with forces superior to ours by land and sea, who already insults our flag [*pabellón*] and who finds black recruits on our own vessels; who with his finger shows us the path by which he can bring to his flag all of Africa; that even without going that far, in Jamaica he will find 400,000 captives [*encadenados*]. What a horrifying prospect![74]

[72] Ibid; J.C.A. Stagg, "The Political Essays of William Shaler," in *William and Mary Quar-terly*, 59 (2002); and Someruelos to Ignacio de Pezuela, May 27, 1811, in *Documentos de que hasta ahora se compone el expediente que principiaron las Cortes Extraordinarias sobre el tráfico y esclavitud de negros*, document 5.
[73] "Representación de la Ciudad de la Habana a las Cortes, el 20 de Julio de 1811," in Arango, *Obras*, 2: 19–52; "Copias de la Junta del Real Consulado y Sociedad Patriótica sobre las proposiciones relativas a la manumisión de los esclavos y los graves peligros que podrían resultar a esta isla," May 23, 1811, in Harvard, Houghton, Escoto Papers, MS Span 52, Box 19, no. 18.
[74] "Representación de la Ciudad de la Habana a las Cortes, el 20 de Julio de 1811," in Arango, *Obras*, 2: 43.

The actions of the Cortes encouraged the insubordination of slaves, who in 1811 had as ally and potential leader a proximate black king. The combination was deadly.

In Arango's hands, the invocation of Haiti was clearly flexible. In 1791, he had insisted that there was nothing to fear from revolution in Saint-Domingue and that the expansion of the slave trade could continue. In 1811, there was everything to fear, and abolition had to be postponed. In both cases, the outcome was clear: the continued expansion of slavery in Cuba. But what of Haiti itself? Could the northern kingdom, or for that matter Pétion's republic, really pose the threat that Arango invoked in 1811? Did Christophe have the power, as Arango said, to point with his finger and usher in the destruction of slavery by the enslaved themselves? In 1805–1806, even as Haitian agents purportedly incited conspiracies from Trinidad to Cuba, the Haitian state does not appear to have organized or seconded such efforts, apparently abiding by their constitutional promises of nonintervention. The decision to hold back may have been strategic in that it spared the new state the retaliation of its neighbors. But it may have been strategic in another sense as well. In 1805–1806, there was no particular reason to think that a slave rebellion anywhere would succeed. In 1811, however, conditions were very different. Risk and opportunity are of necessity defined contextually, and the context of 1808–1811 was as fertile and treacherous as any that people could imagine.

7

A Black Kingdom of This World

History and Revolution in Havana, 1812

In January 1812, Jean-François – one of the first leaders of the slave revolution of Saint-Domingue, former slave and maroon turned general and admiral, commander of the black auxiliaries, erstwhile defender of France's Louis XVI and Spain's Carlos IV – showed up in Havana. He had been there before, in December 1795, following the evacuation of Bayajá (Fort-Dauphin). That time, Havana authorities had confined him to his ship for fear that even the sight of him – black, decorated, proud – would give local people dangerous ideas. Then he was exiled to Cádiz. Still, people in Havana had seen him and his companions, and printed images of him had circulated from hand to hand. There had been ungrounded rumors of his return before. Now, in 1812, Jean-François was back, walking the streets of Havana freely. Dark in color and small in stature, he wore his uniform, a blue jacket with gold buttons decorated with anchors and eagles. He told one black resident of Havana that he wanted to be seen and recognized as an important subject, and he dressed the part, going out of his way to change into his uniform before meetings he deemed important. He visited the homes of free people of color in the city; he gathered with slaves and others in plazas and on street corners; he even saw some old acquaintances "from his *tierra*."[1]

On March 14, he left Havana for its hinterland, accompanied by two local men – Estanislao Aguilar, a free mulatto artisan known to forge passes for slaves who wanted to travel between city and country, and

---

[1] On Jean-François's trip to Havana in 1795, see Chapter 3. On 1811–1812, see testimony of Clemente Chacón in ANC, AP, leg. 12, exp. 14, f. 61/B70, and testimony of Estanislao Aguilar in ANC, AP, leg. 12, exp. 18.

Juan Bautista Lisundia, a free black man who often played drums with enslaved Congos. After leaving the city, the men stopped at the *ingenio Trinidad*, owned by Nicolás Peñalver, esteemed member of the Havana city council, *caballero* of the Royal and Distinguished Order of Charles III, and master to perhaps one hundred enslaved men and women.[2] There Jean-François and his companions sought out the slave huts. Dressed in his blue uniform, Jean-François told a small group of enslaved men that he was a general, there by order of his king to bring them freedom. He showed them the papers, read out loud from them in French, and Lisundia summarized in Spanish. Everyone gathered in the hut, toasted with *aguardiente*, and swore to fight for freedom. Then Lisundia played the drums, and Jean-François danced.[3] The Haitian general had returned, this time with orders from a black king to lead them in revolution.

From the *Trinidad* plantation, the now larger group went on to *Peñas Altas*, owned by an army officer named Juan de Santa Cruz. There the revolution would seem to start in earnest. Jean-François and Lisundia gathered the slaves and explained their mission, again reading the freedom papers from the king. The leaders put a guard at the bell tower so as to avert a summons for help. Then they set fire to most of the plantation: the residential buildings, the boiling house, the bagasse house, the slave huts, and, of course, the sugar cane. Behind the curing house, Lisundia killed the first white man; on Jean-François's orders, Tomás and Esteban from *Trinidad* and three unnamed slaves from *Peñas Altas* killed another. Then they took their machetes to a woman and two children.[4] Some of the rebels were able to take horses, and the group got ready to head out to the next plantation, *Santa Ana*. Amidst the fire and confusion, Alonso Santa Cruz Congo asked the leaders where they were taking "the blacks."

[2] ANC, Intendencia, leg. 899, exp. 12. I am grateful to Gloria García for sharing this source with me.

[3] Testimony of Clemente Chacón in ANC, AP, leg. 12, exp. 14, f. 61/B70; Estanislao Aguilar in ANC, AP, leg. 12, exp. 18; Gabriel Peñalver and Tiburcio Peñalver in ANC, AP, leg. 13, exp. 1, ff. 185–187, 187v–88.

[4] The description of the events on *Trinidad* and *Peñas Altas* is taken from the testimony of witnesses, most of them enslaved, from those two plantations (Tiburcio, Baltasar, Gabriel, Tadeo, and Raymundo Peñalver on *Trinidad*; and from *Peñas Altas*: Antonio Cao, José María Santa Cruz, Alonso Santa Cruz Congo, Antonio María Santa Cruz Macuá, José Trinidad Carabalí, and Andrés Santa Cruz), all in ANC, AP, leg. 13, exp. 1. There are contradictions in the descriptions of the events of that night, even on something as basic as the order in which they attacked plantations. It is clear that Jean-François, Lisundia, and Aguilar went to *Trinidad* first and recruited a group to go with them to *Peñas Altas*, where the main attack occurred. They appeared to have burnt cane fields on *Trinidad*, but it is unclear whether that was before or after the attack on *Peñas Altas*.

Lisundia replied, holding his unsheathed machete, "that if he asked him one more word, he would wring his neck [*le arrancaba el pescuezo*]." Everyone obeyed. Revolution, as Dessalines had once allegedly insisted, required discipline, and violence.[5]

Still, even those were not enough. Neither was the leadership of the man whom everyone called the black general from Guarico. At *Santa Ana*, the rebels were defeated, and over the next weeks and months, authorities jailed and punished more than fifty rebels and suspects in Havana, publicly executing and brutally displaying the remains of fourteen of them. Jean-François was hanged, his head severed and put on a stake at the entrance to *Peñas Altas*, where a few weeks earlier he had arrived heralding freedom and revolution – an ignominious end for a decorated black general, whose name, the governor had once said, resonated in Havana like that of a conqueror and hero.

When Jean-François was arrested and questioned, however, one of the first things he said was, essentially, I am not that man. He was emphatic: he was not and did not want to be called Jean-François. His name was Juan Barbier. The many other witnesses, of course, did not hear this, and so they continued testifying about the presence of the Haitian Jean-François (referred to in Spanish as Juan Fransuá), who wore a general's uniform, read to them from French papers, and promised them freedom in the name of his king. Faced with such declarations and to avoid potential confusion, the scribe occasionally followed witnesses' mentions of Jean-François with the parenthetical notation: "(*es Barbier*)."[6]

The liberator, it turned out, was an imposter. The real Jean-François, who had left Havana for Cádiz in January 1796, had died in the Spanish port city in 1805. The man who promised to lead the enslaved to freedom in Havana in 1812 was someone else entirely. Said by various people to be a native of Africa or of Saint-Domingue; a veteran of the Haitian Revolution; a former resident of Charleston, South Carolina; and self-identified as North American, the man Barbier/Jean-François was an almost total mystery. We do not know when he arrived in Havana or from where. If he lived in Charleston, no evidence of that residence appears to have survived. He identified as from "his land" a Havana woman held as a slave by a nun of the Santa Clara convent, a Santo Domingo order that had

---

[5] This episode appears in the testimony of Alonso Santa Cruz Congo, in ANC, AP, leg. 13, exp. 1, ff. 95v–98. On Dessalines's advice to Miranda, Thibaud, "'Coupé têtes, brûlé cazes.'"

[6] Testimony of Juan Barbier, in ANC, AP, leg. 12, exp. 16; and testimony of Tiburcio Peñalver in ANC, AP, leg. 13, exp. 1, ff. 187v–188.

evacuated to Havana in 1795.[7] The papers with which he announced
freedom to the enslaved workforce of *Trinidad* and *Peñas Altas* were
likewise false. Rather than a king's order of liberation, one was simply
a letter written in French by what appears to be a small slaveholder (or
leaser) in San José Buenavista (Matanzas) complaining about a sick slave.
The other was an ad in English for William Young Birch, publisher and
stationer in Philadelphia. Whether the documents Barbier carried were
random, or whether they hold some kind of clue, is impossible to know.[8]
Whatever else remains a mystery, it seems irrefutable that the liberation
orders sent by a black king were a sham, and that the man reading them
in the slave huts of western Cuba was not who everyone said he was.

    Those strange facts notwithstanding, the movement in which the fig-
ure of Jean-François played a vital role remains among the most ambitious and important in the history of the Black Atlantic. Authorities –
and later historians – identified the plot's mastermind as José Antonio
Aponte, a free man of color, a carpenter and artist, a veteran of the free
black militia, perhaps a priest in the Afro-Cuban religion of Santería.
Aponte, working closely with other men such as himself, had devised
a plan. First, they would (and did) target the rich sugar plantations on
the outskirts of Havana. With the sugar mills burning, Aponte and his
companions would then strike at the heart of the heavily fortified capital city. Each of the leaders would launch separate attacks on the city's
fortresses and armories, seizing weapons with which to arm the 400 men
who, Aponte said, were organized and waiting to rise and follow when
called. According to some contemporary accounts, the Havana plot was
linked to other nearly contemporaneous ones in eastern Cuba, in Puerto
Príncipe, Bayamo, and Holguín. Some have even posited possible links

---

[7] Childs describes Barbier as African-born and a former resident of Saint-Domingue and
Charleston; see Matt Childs, *The 1812 Aponte Rebellion in Cuba amd the Struggle
Against Atlantic Slavery* (Chapel Hill: University of North Carolina Press, 2006), 21.
Authorities identified Barbier as "de nación congo que ha sido vecino de Charleston,"
but it is unclear how they know this. See testimony of Gil Narciso, Juan Luis Santillán,
José Fantacia Gastón, and Isidro Pluttón, in ANC, AP, leg. 12, exp. 16. An examination
of records from Charleston – directories of free people of color; rental records of low-cost,
sometimes transient housing run by Saint Michael's Church; sacramental records; arrival
records; and so on – have yielded no person by that name. SCHS, Saint Michael's Church
Records, and City Directories for Charleston, South Carolina, for the years 1803, 1806,
1807, 1809, and 1813. The reference to the woman from his land appears in Barbier's
testimony, in ANC, AP, leg. 12, exp. 14, f. 79v.

[8] See the translations of the two documents in ANC, AP, leg. 12, exp. 18. They are also
transcribed in Franco, *Conspiraciones*, 187–189.

with the United States, Jamaica, Santo Domingo, and Brazil.[9] Leaving aside the question of the movement's geographic reach and connections, in Havana itself its designs and goals were expansive. Months of planning had linked free people of color and enslaved, countryside and city. Recruits' names were kept in a book of adherents to the cause. Aponte dictated a public proclamation, later nailed to the door of the government palace. The men even had flags ready to post at their camps. The plot's ambitiousness, however, came less from the these preparations than from its explicit goal, simply expressed: freedom for the slaves.[10]

In a revolutionary age that saw the radical repudiation of slavery in the Haitian Revolution and the destruction of the hemisphere's oldest colonial power in places such as Mexico and Peru, this unusual movement – with assumed names and false papers – may have been as close as Havana got to revolution.[11] Though it was violently defeated, Aponte's movement provides invaluable insight into the Age of the Revolution, a creole Age of Revolution that was Cuban and Haitian, Caribbean and Black Atlantic, Spanish and Spanish American, English and French, West African and Ethiopian. Aponte drew on New World, European, and African intellectual and political currents to craft a revolutionary movement that would make real the era's promise of meaningful transformation. For these revolutionaries, making that promise real meant, without a doubt, ending slavery and, very likely, ending colonial rule. Anthropologist Stephan Palmié has perceptively suggested that the "ambiguities, ruptures, and seeming aporia" of Aponte's testimony should call into question easy conclusions and "manufactured certainties" about the nature of the movement and about Aponte's complicity in it.[12] Indeed, we might say the same about all easy conclusions. Yet a careful engagement with the extensive documentary record for the 1812 movement – including thousands of pages of judicial testimony taken in Havana in 1812 and extended testimony about

[9] On links between Havana and the east, see M. Childs, *The 1812 Aponte Rebellion*, 147–150; on possible connections beyond Cuba, see Franco, *Conspiraciones*, 15–16.
[10] For mentions of freedom as goal of movement, see, for example, the testimony of: José Carmen Peñalver, José Trinidad Carabalí, Tiburcio Peñalver, Francisco Xavier Pacheco, ANC, AP, leg. 13, exp. 1, f. 10, 43v, 141v, 187v–188, 290; Salvador Ternero in ANC, AP, leg. 12, exp. 14, ff. 81/B90; Cristobal de Sola, Jorge Gangá, Fernando Mandinga, in ANC, AP, leg. 12, exp. 13, f. 3, 11, 12v; Juan Reguiferos, Juan (*calesero*), and *careo* between Joaquín and Juan, in ANC, AP, leg. 12, exp. 26.
[11] The masonic conspiracy of 1823, Soles y Rayos de Bolívar, was another important attempt.
[12] Palmié, *Wizards*, 82–98. Quotes appear on 94.

a picture book that Aponte created and discussed with his fellow conspirators – in fact renders more persuasive the claim that Aponte was
indeed a revolutionary. In that record, Aponte emerges as a historian,
strategist, and theorist who visualized history, including the history of his
own time and his own people, in order to imagine a radical, subversive
world beyond the revolution: the next black kingdom of their world.[13]

Aponte's Present: Atlantic Havana, 1811–1812

Four things happened in 1811 that would profoundly shape Aponte's
revolution. In May of that year, news arrived in Havana of the motion
for the abolition of the slave trade and slavery in the Cortes of Cádiz.
The proposals and debate published in the *Diario de Sesiones* circulated
widely, and people everywhere talked about them. On plantations, in the
city, and across most of the island, rumors circulated not just that the
Cortes had broached the topic of slave trade abolition, but that they had
in fact already declared slaves free. Though the rumor of freedom was
false, the stir it caused was real. "Great, sir," said the captain-general,
"is the sensation caused [by the news] and most sad the notions that are
everywhere whispered."[14]

Of course, the Spanish Cortes was not the only one acting against
the slave trade in that moment. On May 14, 1811, the British Parliament passed the Slave Trade Felony Act, which made punishable with a
fourteen-year sentence the participation of any British subject in the slave
trade. The principal targets of the new law were those British traders, captains, seamen, factors, and underwriters who had met the challenge of the
1807 abolition of the British slave trade by transferring their resources,
experience, and savvy to the Spanish and Portuguese trade. The 1811 Act
thus sought to achieve a more substantive enforcement of the slave trade
ban. In the same year, moreover, the Royal Navy began in earnest its

---

[13] The last clause alludes to Alejo Carpentier, *The Kingdom of This World*, translated by
Harriet de Onis (New York: Noonday Press, 1989).

[14] On the circulation of and reaction to the news from Cádiz, see Chapter 6. The quote is
from Someruelos to Ignacio de Pezuela, May 27, 1811, in *Documentos que hasta ahora*,
document 5. In Puerto Príncipe, rumors of abolition decreed by the Cortes and concealed
by Cuban authorities were a major factor in the outbreak of a significant rebellion in
January 1812. See "1ª Pieza de los Autos Seguidos Sobre Subleba [Broken] Negros
Esclabos de la Va. de Pto. Príncipe," AGI, Cuba, 1780; Tte Gob Sedano to Someruelos,
January 4 and February, 1812, both in AGI, Cuba, 1640; Ignacio de la Pezuela to [?],
February 14, 1812, in AGI, Ultramar, 84; and M. Childs, *The 1812 Aponte Rebellion*,
122–127.

campaign to suppress the trade on the high seas, targeting vessels flying Spanish flags, which were often owned by British subjects and manned in part by British crews. The discussion and passing of the bill in Parliament was amply covered in the international press, but in Atlantic port cities such as Havana, news of England's new campaign against Spanish slavers arrived firsthand and made palpable the growing power of Atlantic antislavery.[15]

As abolitionist news from Europe made the rounds in Havana, another event much closer to home would soon give people even more to talk about. On June 2, 1811, after months of preparation, Henri Christophe in northern Haiti had himself crowned King Henri I and Haiti declared a kingdom. Days of festivities in Le Cap saw dances, musical performances, the public recitation of poems, and invocations of Greek and Roman gods: Apollo, Neptune, Mars, Minerva, Clio, and l'Empire des Fées. All culminated with the coronation of Christophe and his wife, Marie-Louise. News of the coronation of a black king in Haiti spread like wildfire, covered extensively, for example, in the North American press (Figure 7.1).[16] Though no articles on the event appear to have been published in Cuba, the news was everywhere talked about. In Remedios, in central Cuba, a lawyer defended a free black man from charges of conspiracy by insisting that all the accused man had done was talk "with other blacks about the political state of those of his class on the island of Santo Domingo and the coronation of King Christophe." "What is so strange," asked the lawyer, "about the fact that he talked about events so worthy of calling attention to themselves by their rarity? Do not the whites speak of them without any reserve and ponder aloud their causes and effects?"[17]

In Havana, there may have been even more talk of the coronation. Among the leaders of Aponte's movement, everyone talked about the Haitian king. Aponte showed a portrait of Christophe that he had drawn from memory after closely studying one shown to him by an unnamed

---

[15] Murray, *Odious Commerce*, chaps. 2 and 3; Ferrer, "Cuban Slavery and Atlantic Antislavery." The Spanish complained vigorously, arguing that British law did not prohibit the Spanish slave trade. See, for example, Apodaca to Wellesley, May 23, 1811, in TNA, Foreign Office (FO), 72/117; Duque del Infantado to Marq. Wellesley, December 19, 1811, in TNA, FO, 72/119; Copy of a Dispatch to Mr. Wellesley, May 7, 1811, TNA, FO, 72/108.

[16] The festivities are described in Julien Prévost, Comte de Limonade, *Relation des glorieux événements qui ont porté leurs Majestés Royales sur la trône d'Hayti* (Cap-Henry: Chez P. Roux, 1811).

[17] "Consulta de los Autos seguidos...contra varios negros por sublevación," April 30, 1812, in ANC, AP, leg. 12, exp. 27, ff. 12v–14v.

Christophe crowned king of Hayti.

FIGURE 7.1. Christophe's coronation as King of Haiti in 1811. Wood engraving, American, nineteenth century. Credit: Granger Collection, New York.

black man he had talked to at the cavalry dock in Havana harbor. Presumably that unnamed man showed the image to others, and once Aponte had his own drawing ready, he shared it with many – presenting it at his house, receiving visitors who had heard about it and wanted to see it, lending it out to members of the black militia. Shortly after, an image of Christophe appeared, minutely folded, and either discarded or forgotten along a corridor of the fortress where the suspects in the movement were imprisoned. Clearly, Christophe – now King Henri I – was known in Havana, by name, by title, by countenance.[18]

Then in December of that year, something else happened, something that may have made men such as Aponte, who actively talked and thought about freedom and black sovereignty, contemplate whether the time had

---

[18] *Careo* (face-to-face meeting before legal authorities in the courtroom) between Aponte and Melchor Chirinos, in ANC, AP, leg. 12, exp. 17, ff. 88–89; testimony of Domingo Calderón and José Antonio Mas, in ANC, AP, leg. 12, exp. 18, ff. 128v–129v.

come to act in pursuit of both. A group of about twenty people, six heads of family and their dependents, arrived in Havana. The heads of household were all black men, and all had been officers in the rebel army of Saint-Domingue, serving under Jean-François himself. They had allied with the Spanish government against the French Republic, and when Spain lost to France in 1795, they were evacuated, first to Havana (where black *cabildos* allegedly prepared celebrations in their honor) and then promptly, in the case of these particular men, to Central America. Now, in late 1811, they were in Havana once more, staying again in Casa Blanca, a maritime settlement across Havana harbor. But this time the black auxiliaries were heading home, as it were, to Santo Domingo, to the once-again Spanish portion of Hispaniola wrested from France in 1809 with the help of Henri Christophe. And these men were not imposters, but real veterans of the Haitian Revolution.

With Santo Domingo once more Spanish, authorities in the peninsula had issued orders – printed in Havana's *Papel Periódico* – for the return of those who had left following the colony's cession to France.[19] In Cádiz, home to the bulk of the former auxiliary forces, local authorities began considering petitions and granting passports for return. In November 1809, among those who received permission to travel to Havana en route to Santo Domingo was Francisco Agapito – born in Plaisance in former Saint-Domingue, named captain among the black rebels just three days into the Haitian Revolution, promoted to lieutenant colonel in 1792 after receiving a bullet to his left side, a veteran of campaigns in Les Cayes, Limbe, Port Margot, Borgne, Dondon, Marmelade, Gonaïves, San Rafael, San Miguel, and Hincha, and by 1809 head of all the black auxiliaries in Cádiz. Like Agapito, other black men and women receive permits to travel to Havana from Cádiz. Among them were other black auxiliaries, as well as veterans of Havana's black militia who had been banished to Cádiz for their participation in the independence conspiracy of 1810.[20] It is not clear how many of those who received such permission actually

[19] Real Orden, January 10, 1810, and Someruelos Decree, April 26, 1810, ordering publication in Havana, both in ANC, RO, leg. 43, exp. 6.

[20] The Royal Orders and other correspondence regarding Agapito's travel to Cuba and later Puerto Rico and Santo Domingo from 1809–1815, see "Expediente de Francisco Agapito," all in AGI, SD, leg. 964, and AGI, Ultramar, leg. 328, exps. 17 and 36. For the permissions to return to Havana from Cádiz that were issued to black militia members implicated in the Román de la Luz conspiracy in Havana in 1810 (Ramón Espinosa, Juan José Gonzáles, Carlos de Flores, and Buenaventura Cervantes), see AGI, IG, leg. 2141, exps. 13 and 27.

traveled to Havana. At least three times, imminent departures of the men were delayed. Sugar planter Andrés de Jaúregui, as Havana's deputy to the Cortes, worked behind the scenes to keep any from embarking, meeting with the governor of Cádiz and other officials to impress upon them how dangerous it would be to send the famous black auxiliaries to Cuba.[21]

The twenty from Central America had not had to deal with the resistance of the Cuban planter class and its representatives, so they did make it to Havana and were now biding their time in Casa Blanca. The heads of family had been decorated officers under General Jean-François; they had lived as free men for decades; and they continued to identify themselves by their military titles: Brigadier Gil Narciso, Lieutenant Isidro Plutón, to name just two. Their arrival in Havana prompted a frenzy of speculation, rumor, and wishful thinking. Black residents of the city found reasons to make the quick journey to Casa Blanca to see the men for themselves, to ask them questions: From whence did they come and where were they headed? Who had sent them to Havana and what was the purpose of their visit? Who were they? Brigadiers? Admirals? Could they please see their military uniforms? At first, explained a captain among them, they entertained the questions and showed the visitors their uniforms. But apparently the requests to see the uniforms had become so frequent and insistent that the officers had stopped showing them.[22] One of Aponte's colleagues in the plot was Salvador Ternero, a free African-born man, a member of the 5th Company of the black battalion of Havana, and captain of an African (Mina) *cabildo*, who in March 1809 had been arrested for taking part in the attacks on French residents of Havana. Ternero was one of those people who made repeated visits to

---

[21] Andrés de Jaúregui to Muy Ylustre Ayuntamento [de la Habana], July 27, 1811, in SN-AHN, Almodóvar, C. 36, D. 1. Jaúregui also complained about the unnamed slave who had traveled to Cadiz with Román de la Luz in his banishment from Cuba. The slave, hearing all kinds of news and debate in Cádiz, was refusing to serve his master because "the Cortes had declared all men equal and there were no longer slaves nor distinctions at all [*diferencia alguna*]." Jaúregui spoke to authorities in Cádiz, had the slave arrested, and was working to have him banished to Ceuta or Islas Baleares; the latter, he believed, was also a good destination for the black auxiliaries of the late Jean-François. Jaúregui reported all this to his friends, family, and colleagues in Havana. It is likely that the men about whom he complained had their own networks of communication and support. It is not inconceivable, then, that people knew about the possible return to Havana of black auxiliaries and former suspects in the 1810 conspiracy.

[22] Testimony of José Fantacia Gastón, in ANC, AP, leg. 12, exp. 16.

see the famed black officers. Indeed, he went to Casa Blanca on three separate occasions, each time taking a different companion, even exchanging medicinal advice with the brigadier himself.[23]

Authorities soon realized that the presence of Jean-François's troops in Havana – at a moment when a man who called himself Jean-François had traveled to plantations to read alleged declarations of freedom and to lead slaves in revolution – was too powerful an invitation to disorder. The same day the Haitian veterans were questioned in connection with the plot, authorities decided that they needed to be put on vessels and sent on their way.[24] The city was too agitated, and black *habaneros* were too keenly aware of the presence in their city of black veterans of the Haitian Revolution.

Each of these very specific events – the arrival of news of abolition proposals at Cádiz, England's 1811 Felony Act and the escalation of the naval campaign against the slave trade, the coronation of Henri Christophe in Haiti, and the return to Havana of some of the famed *negros auxiliares* of Jean-François – was present in the conception, organization, and operation of the dissident movement of 1811–12. Each in its own way signaled impending change and the possible extension to Cuba of recent moves toward freedom and equality: a more militant abolitionism in England willing to target the Cuban slave trade; the appearance of new government forms in Spain apparently willing to tackle the question of slavery; the crowning of a black king in what had recently been the capital of brutal slavery; and the sudden appearance of famed black military officers in Havana itself. Surely, Aponte and his companions may have reasoned, the world was becoming new, and this new present might be just the time to make their own change, to make their own history in Cuba.

As plotters and recruits discussed the potential rebellion, they confessed to one another – as many others had done before them – that they could no longer tolerate the existence of slavery. But rather than express only a general sentiment, such a claim now had clear political and historical referents. Said a free black man to an enslaved one whom he sought to recruit for the rebellion: "we will form a junta of negros to rise up because

---

[23] Testimony of Salvador Ternero, in ANC, AP, leg. 12, exp. 14, f. 81 (B90). On his militia service, see María del Carmen Barcia, "Los Batallones de Pardos y Morenos en Cuba (1600–1868), in *Anales de Desclasificación*, 1, 2: 8 On his leadership role in the cabildo, see M. Childs, *The 1812 Aponte Rebellion*, 97–99.

[24] Juan Ignacio Rendón, March 24, 1812, in ANC, leg. 12, exp. 14, f. 88.

it just cannot be that [you/we] remain slaves."[25] This was probably in
January 1812, by which time that conviction appeared to have clear
international backing. The same slave, Cristobal de Solas, said he had
overheard multiple discussions among other black coachmen such as
himself about how "in no other place but here, speaking of this Island,
is slavery tolerated or known."[26] If not exactly correct, the assertion
among the black coachmen clearly echoed the arguments made in Cádiz –
published in the *Diario de Sesiones*, read and discussed in Cuba – that
slavery was "already outlawed by the laws of civilized nations."[27] Thus,
when the conspirators met in their *cabildos* or at Aponte's house, or
on street corners and plazas in the city, this seemingly propitious world
context could not but have buoyed them. They spoke to each other,
supremely conscious of their place in the world and eager to assume the
historic role that the era seemed to signal for them.

But something very different also provided impetus: the seeming imper-
meability of Havana to these transformations. For if changes in the outside world seemed to foretell change, in Havana scenes of slavery and
racism did the opposite. It was not just that the period of the Haitian
Revolution and its aftermath coincided with the rapid escalation of slavery in Cuba in general terms. As Aponte and his friends weighed the
possibility of antislavery rebellion, they were also witnessing a particularly dramatic and violent rise in slavery's local significance. The passage
of slave trade abolition in England and the United States had eliminated
Cuba's main suppliers of African labor. From imports of around 3,200
captives a year through the transatlantic trade in, for example, 1806, the
supply dwindled to a paltry 528 in the first year of the ban in 1808. That
massive decline, however, proved to be just temporary. British and American traders worked with Spanish and Cuban interests to circumvent the
law, and under cover of Spanish flags, more and more slaving vessels
that combined Spanish and English (and American) capital, people, and

---

[25] The quote is: "trataban de hacer una junta de negros para lebantarse porque no podia
ser que estuberran [sic] siendo esclabos [sic]." The use of the third person by the scribe
makes it impossible to know whether the free black recruiter, unnamed in the testimony,
was himself referring to slaves in the third person, or using the first person plural to
signal a collective black intolerance for slavery. The testimony, by Cristobal de Solas,
appears in "5ª Pieza Contra los morenos Cristóbal de Sola, Pablo José Valdes y otros
sobre sublevación," March 9, 1812, in ANC, AP, leg. 12, exp. 13.

[26] Ibid.

[27] Proposal of José Miguel Guridi y Alcocer, March 25, 1811, published in *Diario de
Sesiones*, April 2, 1811.

equipment arrived in Cuban ports with human cargo to sell. In 1810, just two years after the enactment of the slave trade ban, almost 6,300 Africans disembarked in the port of Havana as slaves – a nearly twelve-fold increase in two years. Expressed another way, arrivals of Africans jumped from 44 a month to 523. The numbers for 1811 itself are only slightly smaller, close to 5,700 for the year.[28]

The increase was not lost on the population of Havana. The port was significantly busier; the warehouses where captives were sold were full, even as there always seemed to be room for more. On a single day in October 1811, 800 men, women, and children who had arrived from the African coast aboard the *Montezuma* were offered for sale at Warehouses 6 and 7. A few buildings down, at 10, another 290 from the *Volador* were offered on the same day "at the usual hour."[29] One of the doctors in charge of overseeing the vaccination of the new arrivals described his horror on seeing the sickly condition in which many arrived and hearing about the large numbers lost at sea in the middle passage. No sensible heart could see this without deploring the atrocity; no wonder, he concluded, the abolitionists at Cádiz found attentive audiences.[30]

This was Aponte's present; this was Aponte's place. It was one on the cusp of two worlds, caught in an extended and erratic passage between slavery and freedom. One of those worlds was populated by abolitionists and black kings and generals, the other by a growing number of Africans arriving in miserable condition to become chattel slaves. This metaphorical hinge between the age of slavery and the age of abolition – or between the first and second slaveries – was, however, more than a structural transformation or abstract passage. It was something lived palpably from day to day. Black men and women read or heard Spanish proposals that from this day forward, no human being could be bought or sold as a slave;

---

[28] http://slavevoyages.org/tast/database/search.faces?yearFrom=1808&yearTo=1808& mjslptimp=31312; http://slavevoyages.org/tast/database/search.faces?yearFrom=1810& yearTo=1810&mjslptimp=31312; http://slavevoyages.org/tast/database/search.faces? yearFrom=1811&yearTo=1811&mjslptimp=31312.

[29] *Diario de la Habana*, October 22 and 23, 1811, in Harvard, Houghton Library, Escoto Papers, Supplement, MS Span 52.1, box 3, no. 9. Both sales were advertised for October 23.

[30] Tomás Romay to President, Real Consulado, July 12, 1811, in ANC, RCJF, leg. 150, exp. 7409. The Transatlantic Slave Trade Database shows the *Montezuma* arriving in Havana on October 13, 1811, with 820 captives (http://slavevoyages.org/tast/database/search .faces?yearFrom=1810&yearTo=1815&shipname=montezuma); the database does not show an 1811 entry for *Volador*.

they held in their hands images of a black king in Haiti, a land where
blacks had conquered the whites. And at the same time they watched the
unloading of slaving vessels and read announcements of the sale of thousands of human beings. It was the act of bearing witness to this second
set of events that helped give meaning to the first, the painful distance
between the two perhaps giving a group of black men named Aponte,
Chacón, Lisundia, Barbier, Peñalver, and others the decisive incentive to
plot their bid.

Yet, if freedom was foremost in the minds of these dissidents, the first
reports of the outbreak of their rebellion – and thus the first archival
instance of the revolution – gave no indication of that goal. "I have
just been informed that at the ingenio Peñas Altas something unpleasant
has occurred this morning," wrote Governor Someruelos.[31] Still, even the
confused initial dispatches hint at the beginnings of something potentially
major in form. Authorities worried about the presence of *franceses* among
the rebels and about the proximity of the rebels' targets to the coasts. They
noted also that the rebels headed east toward Matanzas along the north
coast, a route that was dangerously underpopulated, "or better said, with
no white population," reported a brigadier from Guanabacoa.[32] This was
what Arango had called the "solitude of our sugar plantations," where
so few white men lived among so many blacks.

Fittingly, it was at a plantation called "solitude" – *Soledad* – that
the rebels reportedly set one of the first fires of the rebellion. *Soledad*
was a thoroughly modern sugar plantation located in Guanabo, about
twenty miles east of Havana. The attack on *Soledad* does not appear to
be mentioned in the voluminous judicial documentation in Havana, and
because historians have generally constructed the story of the movement
from those records, the attack, if it happened, has also disappeared from
historical narratives of the 1812 rebellion. The story of what was said
to have happened has thus been written omitting a critical action that
revealed something immensely important about the insurgents' political
and intellectual project. For the *Soledad* that the rebels attacked belonged
to someone who had recently enjoyed some notoriety in Havana: Andrés
de Jáuregui, the city's deputy to the Cortes of Cádiz, the man who had
worked so diligently – and publicly – to defeat proposals for the abolition

[31] Someruelos to Martín de Arostegui, March 16, 1812, in SN-AHN, Almodóvar, C. 36,
D. 1.
[32] Brigadier Martín Ugarte to Someruelos, March 16 and March 17, 1812, in SN-AHN,
Almodóvar, C. 36, D. 1.

of slavery and the slave trade in the Spanish world.[33] Jaúregui's *Soledad* was a fitting target indeed for these enemies of slavery.

Propaganda and the Plot

The 1812 plot expressly used recent Atlantic developments – abolition debates in Cádiz, for example, or the coronation of King Christophe – to give moral legitimacy and political urgency to the movement. More than merely "background," these events were critically important history, which was, Aponte knew, what made them such potent propaganda as well. They provided powerful material for him to shape into a rousing message, indeed into a political imperative.

The figure of Juan Barbier is emblematic. He was the not-so-tall black man, of uncertain origin – Congo, *negro francés* from former Saint-Domingue, resident of Charleston – dressed in a military uniform, who read papers of freedom at the plantations where the rebellion began on March 14–15. He was the one whom everyone called Jean-François, after the powerful black general who had fought against the French in Saint-Domingue, who had briefly come to Havana in December 1795, and who had died in Cádiz just seven years earlier. When Barbier later testified, he made it seem as though the name had been thrust upon him by others, but after his capture, that version of events was also the more convenient one. For some reason, authorities do not appear to have asked him how he got this name, nor even when and why he had come to Havana.

Still, the testimony does provide insight into how the conspirators talked about and viewed the ostensibly famous Jean-François. One morning Aponte arrived at the house of free black militia member and tavern keeper Clemente Chacón with Barbier in tow. Aponte introduced Barbier as Jean-François (Juan Fransuá), an "*Admiral* who served under the orders of the *negro Cristoval Rey de Santo Domingo* and who came with dispatches to entice free blacks and the slaves of this island to achieve the independence of the latter, conquering this land, in addition to others

---

[33] References to the attack on *Soledad* appear several times in the dispatches produced in the first day or two after the initial outbreak. As one of the authors of the reports himself says, rumors were rampant in the immediate aftermath of the first assaults. The fact that the attack on Jaúregui's estate is not mentioned in the later documentation might suggest that it never happened. Alternatively, authorities may have decided not to draw attention to the insurgents' attack on a plantation owned by a very vocal proslavery Cuban deputy to the Spanish Cortes. Mentions of the attack on *Soledad* appear in Ugarte to Someruelos, March 17, 1812 (two letters with same date); Someruelos to General de la Marina, March 16, 1812, all in SN-AHN, Almodóvar, C. 36, D. 1.

already taken." And then Aponte had Barbier show Chacón the papers he had to that effect.[34] That scene was repeated with only minor modification at almost every important instance of recruitment, with different conspirators taking on the role that Aponte had played at Chacón's house. On the plantations, it was Juan Bautista Lisundia, Chacón's son, who performed the introduction, presenting Barbier/Fransuá as a "general who by orders of his King was giving freedom to the slaves." After Barbier read aloud the papers in French, Lisundia summarized them in Spanish. When the rebellion began, the king's orders were again invoked – the king had ordered everything burned, the whites killed.[35]

Whether at Aponte's house in the city or in a slave hut in the countryside, the desire for freedom and the call to arms were given material form, embodied by a man calling himself Jean-François and legitimated through the written documents – freedom papers – he held in his hands. For Aponte, an artist who crafted images and stories for a living, the scene – a Haitian general returned with orders to give freedom to the slaves and lead them in battle – was surely a potent and persuasive one. For the enslaved men and women being recruited, the scene may have seemed both powerful and frightening. Had the time really come? This was clearly not a question of the usual chatter of all the other years.[36] This time, the war was really starting. This time, there stood before them a uniformed black man representing a real black king, reading them papers granting freedom.

But part of the reason Barbier's performance seemed to work was that recent events made the performance entirely plausible. That he was Jean-François was surely supported, people may have surmised, by the presence in Havana of Jean-François's troops, who spoke with local people of color and who identified themselves by military title and their association with Jean-François. In this context, it was not hard for people to assimilate Barbier – uniformed, discussing plots of freedom – to the return of Jean-François's men to Havana. He was Jean-François plotting in the city, recruiting slaves, his men waiting at Casa Blanca to help lead the fight. We do not know if people in Havana were aware of Jean-François's death in Cádiz in 1805. In Haiti, of course, the much-talked-about return of

---

34 Testimony of Clemente Chacón, March 19, 1812, in ANC, AP, leg. 12, exp. 14, starting at f. 61 (B70). Emphasis in original.
35 See, for example, testimony of Alonso Santa Cruz Congo, José Trinidad Carabalí, Tiburcio Peñalver in ANC, AP, leg. 13, exp. 1, ff. 95v–98, 124v–27, 187v–88.
36 See Ferrer, "Speaking of Haiti"; for an important discussion of fear as something felt by people of color, rather than as something they inspired, see Sara Johnson, *The "Fear of French Negroes."*

Mackandal (who had been executed by the French in 1758 for leading a massive poisoning campaign) to lead them in the battles of 1791 had been a key source of inspiration and power for the revolution's adherents.

Barbier's performance was also made plausible, of course, by a more proximate Haitian connection: the coronation of King Christophe in Le Cap just a few months earlier. There was indeed a black king not that far away, and he reigned over a land in which there was no slavery and in which black men controlled the state. This was not fantasy anymore; it was now their present. Reading the king's order of freedom, Barbier became in that moment the king's emissary, Christophe's emissary – that category of person that Cuban governor Someruelos had so viscerally opposed over the last few years.[37]

Barbier's reading of Christophe's freedom orders worked, however, not just because King Christophe existed, but also because Barbier's audience found the notion of Christophe's solidarity with foreign slaves believable. Numerous witnesses recounted rumors of material assistance from Haiti. In one story that came up several times in testimony, Haiti had sent men (5,000 by one count) who were waiting in the "mountains" or "hills of Monserrate" to join in the struggle for freedom. Monserrate was the name of a street that paralleled the city walls and also the name of one of the entrances into the city, but it was not particularly hilly, nor conducive to hiding large groups of soldiers. Monserrate may have referred instead to a hilly area on the island's north coast, outside the city of Matanzas and, coincidentally, just off the path the rebels were said to have taken from Jaúregui's *Soledad* to Matanzas. Whatever place the rebels meant, there is no documentary trace of Haitian men waiting near Havana to do battle against slavery. Importantly, one of the recruiters said that among the Haitians were men from Havana who had gone to Haiti to join Christophe's army and had returned with it now to liberate Cuba. One key witness testified that he even knew the names of the generals at the head of the group, "being sons of Havana who had gone to Guarico to join the army of King Christophe."[38] It is a fascinating assertion, one that echoes Francisco Arango's earlier complaint that Haiti's king was finding black recruits on Spanish vessels. British and

---

[37] On that opposition, see Chapter 6. Word of the possibility of Cuba and Haiti exchanging agents or emissaries may have been circulated by slaves and servants of high officials. Someruelos's own coach driver, Luis Mandinga, was questioned in the investigation of the plot. See his testimony at ANC, AP, leg. 12, exp. 13, ff. 14v–16v.

[38] *Careo* between Aponte and Chacón in ANC, AP, leg. 12, exp. 14; and *careo* between Aponte and Ternero, ANC, AP, leg. 12, exp. 18.

American officials regularly complained about black sailors finding refuge and staying in Haiti. It is, of course, not inconceivable that some from Cuba would have done the same.[39]

More than an abstract order of freedom, Christophe's alleged directive was also an apparent offer of material aid, and thus a near guarantee that freedom would come. Witnesses' faith in Christophe's solidarity was grounded in an interpretation of recent history. First, Christophe's assistance in the recent fight against the French in Santo Domingo was well known. He had sent arms to the rebels there, and the rebels had won. Second, and more important, people seemed to believe that Christophe had already been recognized as a legitimate king by foreign powers who supported the rise of antislavery. Conspirators and their recruits suggested, for instance, that Haiti's king had been recognized by Spain and England.[40] The plotters may have assumed Spain's recognition as emerging from the new antislavery convictions emanating from Cádiz, or perhaps from the circulation of talk about the metropolitan government's order to Someruelos to send an official agent to Christophe. England's recognition, though also factually inaccurate, seemed the natural result of its role as a global antislavery power. In one version of the rumor, England – an ally of Spain in the current war against Napoleonic France – had ordered the end of slavery in Cuba and threatened to invade Havana (as in 1762) if the order was not executed. The claim was, of course, false, but it likely built on pieces of news then circulating in Havana – about England's escalating naval campaign against slavery as of 1811, or widespread discussion of a condemnation of Cuban slavery published in London that, said the governor, was in the hands of everyone on the island.[41]

One of the more interesting claims made during the investigation was that England was working directly with Haiti to end slavery in Cuba. Aponte apparently told at least one recruit that "the English arrested ships that came loaded with blacks because they did not want there to be

39 Arango, "Representación," 1811, in *Documentos que hasta ahora* ... (1814), 62. On sailors escaping to and staying in Haiti, see Ferrer, "Haiti, Free Soil, and Atlantic Antislavery"; Jeffrey Bolster, *Black Jacks: African American Seamen in the Age of Sail* (Cambridge, Mass.: Harvard University Press, 1997), chap. 5.
40 See testimony of Francisco Xavier Pacheco, in ANC, AP, leg. 13, exp. 1, f. 291.
41 See testimony of Francisco Xavier Pacheco, in ANC, AP, leg. 13, exp. 1, f. 291; ANC, AP, leg. 12, exp. 13, f. 14; testimony of Fernando Mandinga, in ANC, AP, leg. 12, exp. 13, f. 12v. On the Governor's claim about the English abolitionist article, see M. Childs, *The 1812 Aponte Rebellion*, 160.

slavery," a reference surely to recent achievements of British abolitionism in 1807 and 1811. But once the British captured and condemned the vessels, the human cargo was sent to Haiti "to be governed by the Black King." While there seems to be no evidence of England sending freed captives to Haiti, in Havana in 1811 people would surely have heard of other recent and dramatic episodes.[42] Since late 1810, Christophe's navy had intercepted several slave ships bound for Cuba and liberated the Africans on board, bringing them to Haitian soil as free men and women and sending the crews and empty ships on to Havana.[43]

It was in this world that slaves and free people of color recruiting and being recruited for rebellion might have imagined Christophe's commitment to their own freedom – a world where men and women who would have been enslaved alongside them had reached, through the intervention of Christophe, free soil in Haiti.[44] In this light, the hopeful mentions of aid coming from Haiti were less evidence of misapprehension or folly than an optimistic reading of contemporary politics. They were, in other words, a powerful expression of the intellectual and political engagement of the rebels and conspirators of 1811–12. Aponte pushed that engagement to the fore, using recent history – the coronation of Christophe, the arrival of Jean-François's troops, the escalation of England's naval campaign against the slave trade, the abolitionist proposals at Cádiz – to craft a powerful message about his movement. The world was with him; aid was certain; victory was within sight. Recent events made that message plausible, if not exactly true.

Did Aponte himself believe in the truth of what he told others? Did he think 5,000 men waited in not-so-distant hills to help them win freedom? Did he believe that Christophe, or for that matter the Cortes of Cádiz or the king of England, had sent actual orders to end slavery in Cuba? Did he believe Barbier, or the men at Casa Blanca, had been sent by Christophe for that purpose as well?

The judicial testimony reveals Aponte as a strategist, willing to sacrifice what some saw as truth for what he saw as justice. But that may be a

---

[42] Testimony of Francisco Xavier Pacheco, in ANC, AP, leg. 13, exp. 1, f. 291. On lack of evidence regarding the British freeing captives to Haiti, Roseanne Adderley, personal communication, June 20, 2011.

[43] On these three examples, see Junta Consular to Capitán General, February 23 and June 26, 1811, in BNJM, CM Morales, Tomo 79, nos. 23 and 26, respectively; and Claudio Martínez Pinillos to Real Consulado, March 24, 1812, in ANC, AP, leg. 106, exp. 21.

[44] On the notion of postindependence Haiti as "free soil," see Ferrer, "Haiti, Free Soil, and Atlantic Antislavery."

thorny proposition. The rebels may have resurrected the name and figure of Jean-François as a strategy of mobilization. But to think of that move only as a rational strategy, as anthropologist Stephan Palmié reminds us, is to lose sight of the profound slippage between instrumental and symbolic practices in revolutionary politics generally. "Given his chance," Palmié writes, "Barbier might, in fact, have turned into a Jean Francois [sic]."[45] Perhaps; but equally important is that Barbier's metamorphosis into Jean-François could well have transformed the very figure of Jean-François – a man who had, in fact, been allied with slaveholding Spain against the French Republic, who had been defeated in that war, who sold people into slavery while he fought the French, and who continued to hold and possibly sell slaves even as late as 1804 in Cádiz – into a liberator, a man who announced and fought for general liberty. Barbier, in other words, might have reformed Jean-François.

Whatever pitfalls may surround the question of Barbier's identity, the broader question of the conspirators' political strategy remains very relevant. Even if we set it aside in considering Barbier's reincarnation of Jean-François, it quickly resurfaces in light of the fact that the conspirators, mostly free men of color, had to decide how to convince slaves to join them. Aponte sent Barbier/Jean-François to do that; he appointed the free black man Juan Bautista Lisundia as his guide, and he approved the document that would be read on the plantations by the man meant to be Jean-François, sent by his king.

We do not know exactly what Barbier read to the slaves of *Trinidad* and *Peñas Altas* the night of the rebellion. Testimony describing the events is agreed that he read documents in a foreign language and that Lisundia summarized them in Spanish as being "for" or "about" freedom. Yet the letter that Aponte allegedly approved and ordered read was in Spanish, and it was hardly an order of freedom from a king. Written about a week before the rebellion, it read like this:

Your Excellency Mr. Secretary. Dear Sir, after having greeted with you with due respect, and with your permission, I will declare my sentiments because my will is ready to spill my last drop of blood for God and my faith in Jesus Christ and for our liberty. We only repeat that I want above all that you deign to treat me

---

45 Palmié, *Wizards*, 133–135. This analysis was informed by comparisons to the Andean insurrections in the 1780s, which produced figures such as Tomás Katari, Tupac Amaru, and Tupaj Katari, all of whom assumed new identities, names, and personas as rebel leaders. See Sergio Serulnikov, *Revolution in the Andes: The Age of Tupac Amaru* (Durham: Duke University Press, 2013). My thanks to Sinclair Thomson for sharing thoughts on the issue of impersonation and revolutionary leadership.

[*curarme*] so that neither bullets nor sabers can injure me ... if possible [broken] that there be so many that they serve me for everything, for fortune, to have money, to obtain the highest ladies, even the woman who owns me [*mi propia ama*], but that they not take from me the service [*oficio*] of Christians, nor of hearing mass, or of confession. Finally, I await only a response.[46]

The letter was certainly about freedom; after all, its author offered to spill his last drop of blood to achieve it. But the letter invoked freedom in a way that appeared to have little to do with the antislavery currents of the Age of Revolution. Here the path to freedom, the practical means of achieving it, explicitly included spiritual power. Written in the spirit of preparation for war, the letter requested protection from death and injury. It also elaborated on the goal of the rebellion, on what a newly achieved freedom might entail. Yet here again, the aims overlap little with those that leaders may have encountered, for example, in British antislavery articles or the proposals from Cádiz. Rebels fought for freedom and faith, the letter said, but also hoped to receive other favors. First was money; second was women, but not just any women: elite ladies, perhaps even their own mistresses.

It was this letter that the man who has come down in history as the leader of the rebellion – José Antonio Aponte – allegedly ordered to be read aloud on the plantations to console and encourage the slaves. Scholars of the Aponte rebellion have generally avoided talking about the letter. The Cuban historian José Luciano Franco does not discuss it in his voluminous work on the movement. Matt Childs refers to it as a letter "describing the plan for the rebellion." Cultural work on the movement has also neglected to mention the letter.[47] This evasion is not entirely surprising, as the rebels' petition fits awkwardly at best within straightforward narratives about liberation struggles and antislavery. Yet clearly the document was important to the men who led the movement and who deemed it appropriate to read at the launching of the rebellion.

It is curious that though the letter was apparently intended to be read to enslaved recruits on the plantations, it was addressed explicitly to someone identified as "Your Excellency Mr. Secretary." There is reason to speculate that this secretary may have been one of the black auxiliaries, formerly in the troops of the real Jean-François, who were then staying

[46] The letter was found on Barbier/Jean-François when he was arrested. See ANC, AP, leg. 12, exp. 13, ff. 26–26v. Parts of the text are illegible. For testimony about the letter, see ANC, AP, leg. 12, exp. 13, ff. 14v–42.
[47] M. Childs, *The 1812 Aponte Rebellion*, 140.

in Casa Blanca. When in March 1812, authorities questioned the black auxiliaries, they asked the men repeatedly if their leader, Brigadier Gil Narciso, had a secretary. He did: Isidro Pluton, one of the auxiliaries, served in the capacity of secretary to Narciso while in Cuba. With the exception of the letter, the only times the historical record mentions a "secretary" is in reference to one among the black auxiliaries. The letter's reference to healing and cures is also noteworthy, especially given that some conspirators confessed to discussing medicines and home remedies with the auxiliaries in Casa Blanca. The revolutionaries' enigmatic letter, then, may have been evidence of an attempt to forge – or to further – potentially subversive links with the veterans of the Haitian Revolution then on Cuban soil.[48]

Whoever the letter's intended recipient, its author was an enslaved man named Pablo José Valdés, who closed the letter with his signature. We know a little about him from the court testimony. He was the enslaved coach driver for a white man named Melchor Valdés y Pedroso, a former municipal magistrate in Havana. Because he was literate, Pablo regularly helped others compose and read documents. Since at least February, he and his enslaved companions had been talking about an order of freedom that the governor was hiding or ignoring. Finally, he appears to have been questioned in connection with the investigation into the 1810 Román de la Luz conspiracy.[49] Valdés penned the letter addressed to the secretary, then allegedly gave it to a man named Benito, who allegedly gave it to Juan Barbier/Jean-François, who then gave it to Aponte. Aponte then read the letter aloud before a group of the conspirators and gave it to Barbier to "take it to the countryside to console the blacks from the sugar mills."[50]

It is interesting that in this movement so dominated by free men of color, leaders decided to use this letter, penned by an enslaved man, to share with plantation slaves. Perhaps they imagined an affinity of goals or feeling that could serve the purpose of the movement. Importantly, the letter echoed other public or semipublic conversations between the free black plotters and enslaved people. According to several witnesses, a free black man, probably Clemente Chacón, reassured an enslaved man

---

[48] "Autos sobre la averiguación de los cómplices en la conspiración de los negros . . . para inquirir si los negros depositados en Casa Blanca estaban comprendidos" in ANC, AP, leg. 12, exp. 16; and testimony of Salvador Ternero, ANC, AP, leg. 12, exp. 14, f. 81.

[49] ANC, AP, leg. 12, exp. 13, ff. 14, 24–38, 40.

[50] Ibid., ff. 24–26, 37v–40. Aponte denies having ordered the letter read; Barbier, Chacón, and Lisundia all testify that he did.

speaking at a tavern about being punished by his master. Chacón said "not to have any worries, that a few days from now they would all be free." Others among the group joined in, one adding that he was going to marry a local countess and live in an important house in Havana.[51]

The conversation, like the letter, was first and foremost notice of a bid for freedom. In one, the coming of freedom within days was announced; in the other, help was sought to succeed in the struggle. The other things – money or white women or luxurious houses – were tangible symbols of the overturning of slavery, figurative references for everything forbidden to them in colonial Cuba. Victory would thus entail partaking in the most closely guarded privileges of a white, colonial, slaveholding society. Yet Aponte and his companions were well aware of the rise of black emperors and kings from slavery, of the establishment of a black court and nobility, and of the power of black generals, admirals, and brigadiers in Haiti. The victory they imagined in Havana in 1812, then, involved not only inverting the hierarchies of colonial society – of turning the world upside down – but also extending privileges being won by black men elsewhere to their own lives. Still, the question of how goals such as attending mass, or marrying white women, fit into the broader ideological currents of antislavery, if we ask it, is our question, not theirs. As Winthrop Jordan has written in the context of a different conspiracy, "the reality of [rebels'] intentions had its own self-justifying independence. . . . Why *explain* such intention when it carried its own justification in the circumstances of their lives? Freedom, after all, was freedom."[52]

Shortly before the rebels met to discuss the letter, they gathered to confer about another document. This one had been dictated by Aponte and transcribed by Francisco Xavier Pacheco, a free black man, a member of the free black militia, and a carpenter who had learned his trade from Aponte and who now specialized in the repair of carriages. Once the letter was finished, a fellow plotter took it and nailed it to the door of the governor's residence and seat of government. This was a public document.

If historians barely mention the letter to the slaves, this public decla-ration has received significantly more attention. Childs described it as a

---

[51] See testimony of D. Francisco Victoria, D. Blas Peña, and Clemente Chacón (who denies making the statements), in ANC, AP, leg. 12, exp. 14, ff. 7 (B9), 8 (B10), and 12v (B14v). The countess was identified as the Condesa de Lagunillas.

[52] Winthrop Jordan, *Tumult and Silence at Second Creek: An Inquiry into a Civil War Conspiracy* (Baton Rouge: Louisiana State University Press, 1995), 162. Emphasis in original.

"political manifesto" with a "powerful message," which, though "not a formal political document composed by a congress or junta . . . should be regarded as a declaration for Cuban independence." In this he followed a powerful historiographical tradition that characterized the movement as a whole not only as antislavery but also as anticolonial, starting as early as 1877, when Juan Arnao, the emigré revolutionary writing from Brooklyn, called Aponte the "first Cuban to dream the beautiful inspiration of rebelling against Spanish dominion in a practical way."[53]

Let us turn to the proclamation. (See Figure 7.2). In Spanish, the spelling is almost entirely phonetic; there is no punctuation; words and syllables are separated or joined in the wrong places – all familiar features of texts written by newly lettered writers. A nearly literal translation in English would be:

the time of our unfortunate or fortunate venture has come. My wishes are with your happiness. You will make me happy; for this I need the union of your good harmony, of peace among those of the class, good faith, religion and fear of God; in that way we will achieve good success according to our intentions; it is for this that I ask for unity, respect of the elder for the younger [*del mayor al menor*] and I order you at the sound of the drum and trumpet to be ready and without fear to destroy this empire of tyranny and this way we will vanquish the arrogance of these enemies and so I ask you to have no fear, I say to you that with your help we will achieve happiness, all invoke in the first place María Santísima who is the standard of our Remedio and pray to God for your chief who will do the same for you.[54]

The proclamation was found on March 15, just as the rebellion was starting on the plantations. It was meant thus as an announcement of the imminent launching of the urban phase of the revolution. When the city council members read the document, they concluded that it demonstrated a plan to reenact the scenes of Saint-Domingue. The authors may well have had those scenes in mind, and they may have assumed that their audiences did as well. But there is nothing in the document itself to suggest anything like that. There is no explicit mention of Haiti, and the only possible invocation of race consists of the phrase *los de la clase* (those of the class), perhaps shorthand for people of color, as in the commonly used descriptor *la clase de color*. There is no mention of ending slavery or of killing whites. The most bellicose statement was this: "at the

---

53 M. Childs, *The 1812 Aponte Rebellion*, 156; Franco, *Ensayos históricos*, 145.

54 ANC, AP, leg. 12, exp. 14, f. 33. The first three words in the proclamation are illegible. They may have been written over other words that were erased, and hence are even harder to read. They look most like "Adelante Abaneros Compatriotas." I have added some punctuation to make the document more legible. See Figure 7.2 for a copy of the original.

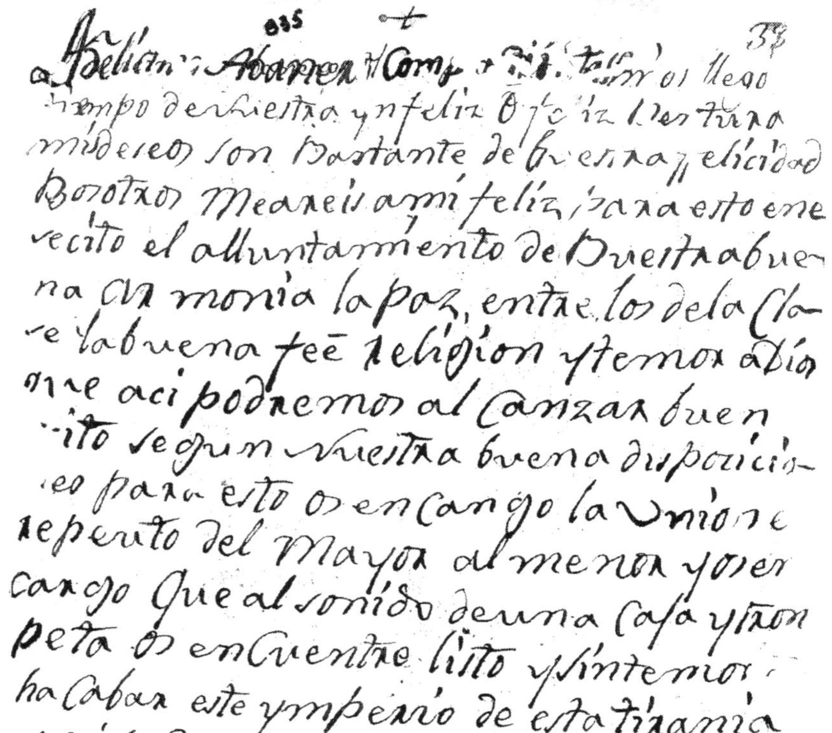

FIGURE 7.2. Proclamation allegedly dictated by José Antonio Aponte to be posted on the doors of the governor's headquarters on the launching of the rebellion on March 14–15, 1812. Archivo Nacional de Cuba, Asuntos Políticos, leg. 12, exp. 14. Courtesy of the Archivo Nacional de Cuba, Havana.

sound of the drum and trumpet to be ready and without fear to destroy this empire of tyranny, and this way we will vanquish the arrogance of these enemies." But "this empire of tyranny" and the "arrogance of these enemies" could have referred to many things – the rule of a particular governor and his allies, the still-hostile French, the Spaniards, whites, slavery and slaveholders. Nothing in the document itself suggests that the author was thinking in terms of a state or nation or independence. Instead, the bulk of the piece elaborated on other things: peace, harmony, and godliness. It would seem, then, that interpretations of the *pasquín* as a clear and powerful proclamation of independence might be guilty of molding the enigmatic evidence from Aponte's movement into something significantly less ambiguous – nationalist, antislavery, antiracist, even, in one formulation, pro-worker.[55]

Both the proclamation and the letter that Aponte ordered read to the slaves framed the coming struggle in religious language. The plantation letter proposed a fight for freedom and faith, a formulation that was also very present in the testimony of Aponte's fellow rebels and conspirators. The letter's final plea was about the importance of Christian faith, confession, and mass. The public proclamation, meanwhile, invoked faith and the fear of God as aids in the fight, and the figure of the Virgin Mary, in particular the Virgen de los Remedios, as the rebels' standard and protector. It makes sense, then, that among the things found by authorities in Aponte's house was an image of the Virgin, along with the fabric and decoration with which the conspirators were to make a flag. The figure of the Virgen de los Remedios carried a longstanding association with armed battle. During the conquest of Mexico, she had served as a kind of patron for the Spanish against the Aztecs. In 1762, the colonial state in Mexico had organized prayers to her image in support of Havana's battle against the British, a battle that loomed in the imaginary of Havana's community of free black militia members. In Aponte's own lifetime, the Virgen de los Remedios, dressed as a general according to some accounts, was the patron saint of the royalist forces in Mexico, doing battle against proindependence (and antislavery) forces led by the priests Miguel Hidalgo and José María Morelos, whose own patron was the Virgin of Guadalupe.[56] The Virgin chosen by Aponte was thus a multivalent figure: a protector of men such as Aponte's grandfather who

55 See Franco, *Ensayos históricos*, 145.

56 Testimony of Francisco Xavier Pacheco, ANC, AP, leg. 13, exp. 1, f. 47; José Antonio Aponte, leg. 12, exp. 14, f. 72; and report on the items found in Aponte's house, in ANC, AP, leg. 12, exp. 17. On the Virgen de los Remedios, see Silvia Chávez, "Cientos veneran a la Virgen de los Remedios," *La Jornada* (Mexico), September 2, 2013. According to

had battled the British decades earlier and an enemy of the patron saint of the popular forces fighting for an end to slavery and Spanish rule in Mexico.

Other equally complex religious references appear elsewhere in the historical record – as vague mentions in the testimony of suspects and as physical artifacts recovered among the belongings of the accused. Years ago, José Luciano Franco suggested that Aponte was a priest of Changó and that he presided over an African *lucumí* (Yoruba) *cabildo* called Changó-Teddún, or Santa Bárbara. As Stephan Palmié and others have observed, Franco cites no evidence for these claims. For other assertions about Aponte's background – for example, that he participated in the American Revolution – Franco cites "popular legend." Popular accounts of Aponte and his movement could have survived from the early nineteenth century into the twentieth and reached the ears of Franco, a working-class autodidact, grandson of an enslaved woman, former cigar worker, port worker, and street cleaner who later became one of the most prolific historians on the island. While a fascinating possibility, this does little to clarify the accuracy of the claim about Aponte's religious role in his community.[57] Other elements of the testimony and investigation, however, clearly suggest the significance of African-derived religious beliefs and practices in the organization of the revolt. For example, that Aponte was a practitioner might be implied by the testimony of Juan Barbier/Jean-François, who explained that in one of his visits to Aponte's house, Aponte had led him out to a yard, where he showed him some stones that he had gathered on the beach. Aponte asked Barbier to observe how he had placed them in the shapes of serpents and snakes. The authorities, naturally, did not ask Barbier to elaborate, nor did they ask Aponte about the meaning or significance of the encounter during his own testimony. Franco, who surely read the voluminous testimony many times, may have been referring precisely to testimony such as this in portraying Aponte as a man with a public spiritual role in his community.[58]

Franco, Aponte had recently carved a statue of the Virgen de Guadalupe for a local church. See Franco, *Ensayos históricos*, 146.

[57] Franco, *Ensayos históricos*, 147–150; Palmié, *Wizards*, 90. The biographical information on Franco is from Oscar Ferrer Carbonell, "José Luciano Franco: Historiador paradigmatico," in *Periódico Cubarte*, December 13, 2011, available at http://www.cubarte.cult.cu/periodico/opinion/jose-luciano-franco-historiador-paradigmatico/20809.html.

[58] See Barbier's testimony in ANC, AP, leg. 12, exp. 14, starting at f. 79v. *Otanes* (or stones) in Santería are often kept in a yard of the house (as Aponte appears to have done), but they are usually kept in tureens or pots, and not arranged in shapes (as they seemed to be in this case). Finally, they would not have been shown to a non-initiate (which they

Several other conspirators appear to have practiced Afro-Cuban religions. During the investigation of Clemente Chacón and Juan Bautista Lisundia, father and son, authorities searched the house the men shared, which served as a tavern, boarding house, and meeting place for the conspirators. The items authorities found there suggest recourse to different sources of power and inspiration. First were items linked to the immediate plot: a crudely drawn picture of the fortress of Atarés (one of the rebels' targets), seven rifle rounds, some gunpowder. Another, very different kind of artifact also surely alarmed the uniformed men who found it: a proclamation by Henri Christophe. Finally, there were "two plumes of rooster feathers with heads apparently made of rags and ribbons . . . in a trunk various feathers also of rooster . . . [and] in a wooden box some trinkets for what they call witchcraft [*brujería*]."[59]

These last items, said Chacón, belonged to his son Juan Bautista Lisundia. Both father and son were free men. Chacón was a member of the black militia, while Lisundia was one of the few among the free black conspirators who was not. Indeed, it is not clear that he had any occupation at all, or none that was ever mentioned in the testimony. Lisundia, a creole, also identified himself as Congo. He played the drums regularly with Congos, and was described by his father and others as having close ties to slaves and *bozales* both in the city and countryside. It may have been this association that prompted Aponte to designate him as Jean-François/Barbier's guide in the countryside, where on arriving at the slave quarters he helped Barbier communicate his message of freedom, played the drum, and then led in the killing and burning. It is perilous, of course, to read human emotion into sparse judicial testimony, but one gets a hint, perhaps, of the pride Chacón might have felt for his son, who despite not having followed his father into the militia was now playing a central role in what might be the event of their lifetimes. Chacón apparently bragged of the feats of his now important son, who, he said, had recruited and readied twenty-two *ingenios* for the rebellion. "He was a lion," the father

appear to have been here). In the end, the brief allusion to the encounter in the testimony is inconclusive, and it might signal different Afro-Cuban religions, including Santería practices from Lucumí (Yoruba) or Arará (Fon) traditions, or *palo monte* associated with Congo traditions.

59 The contents are described in ANC, AP, leg. 12, exp. 14, ff. 10v (B12v), 32–32v (B34–34v). Also found was a letter signed Santa Cruz "en que le anuncia que las ideas se le han varajado." Santa Cruz was the last name of the owner of the *Peñas Altas* plantation, where the rebellion occurred, and presumably of some of the people he held as slaves.

added, "and he would destroy much."[60] But things turned out otherwise. Chacón later recounted his first meeting with his son after the events at *Peñas Altas*. The two men met at about nine o'clock that night at the small plaza at Aponte's house. Lisundia explained to his father "that they had set fire to the *ingenio* of Lieutenant Colonel Santa Cruz [*Peñas Altas*]... killing various people from there." Then, with more emotion, Lisundia told his father that "he was going to where Jesus Christ [is]," and he asked for his father's "blessing because he was lost." All his father could do, however, was give him eight coins (*reales*).[61] The sense of helplessness or frustration in the elder Chacón may help explain the manner in which he described his son's belongings to authorities. Repeatedly asked to explain their significance, he grew weary. He doesn't know, he said; there is nothing bad about them, he insisted more defensively; and, finally, they were only meant to "scare off flies."[62]

On the one hand, one can almost hear the defeat and disappointment in his voice. Arrested, soon to hang, he may indeed have wondered about the usefulness any of these things – proclamations of their own or by Christophe, African religious artifacts, or Marian images. On the other hand, perhaps the response itself betrayed a sliver of defiance. Were authorities, like the flies he mentioned offhandedly, also scared of the African religious artifacts? Might his answer have been a play on the old Roman phrase commonly used in Cuba, "the eagle does not hunt flies," widely used to challenge and mock the self-importance of authorities? In any event, whether the interrogators believed Chacón or not, his response seemed to say: I will never tell you, and you will never know. And because he never told them, we will never know either.

History and the Mystery of the Book

Chacón's gesture – whether of defiance or frustration – is echoed in Aponte's own testimony. The search of Aponte's house, like that of Chacón's, produced an odd collection of documents and artifacts: published laws on the colored battalions and on religious brotherhoods, images of the Virgin Mary and the Haitian king, copies of *Don Quijote*, guides to Havana and Rome, manuals of grammar and art, compendiums of the history of the world. Also in his house, hidden deep

---

[60] See *careo* between Chacón and Aponte, in ANC, AP, leg. 12, exp. 14, starting at 67v.
[61] Testimony of Clemente Chacón in ANC, AP, leg. 12, exp. 14, f. 61 (B70).
[62] Ibid, f. 10v (B12v).

inside a trunk full of clothes, was a pine box with a sliding top, and
inside this smaller box was another book, authored by Aponte himself.
It was Aponte's so-called *libro de pinturas*, or book of drawings. Like
the other items confiscated from his (or Chacón's) house, the book's
contents were a confounding mix of materials and images: hand-drawn
pictures and maps, pasted-on scenes cut out from fans and prints, and
occasional handwritten or printed words. In the pages of the book, moreover, Aponte represented a dizzying array of subjects: Greek, Roman,
and Egyptian gods; biblical figures and allegories; popes and kings across
ages and continents; Havana sugar mills and fortresses; distant and local
armies.[63]

The fact that Aponte had hidden the book suggests that he was aware
that its contents might be read as subversive or dangerous. Indeed, the
book had an important place in the conspiracy, for as the plotting for
the rebellion proceeded, Aponte showed the book to his co-conspirators,
explaining some of its images as a way to help prepare for the coming
revolution. To understand the ways in which these would-be revolutionaries imagined their role in history, and how they theorized their own
present and future, the book is thus an invaluable resource – a rare find
for the project of writing a new kind of intellectual history of the Age of
Revolution.[64]

We confront, however, a major obstacle: Aponte's book of pictures is
missing. After authorities discovered it in his house, it became key evidence in the investigation. But what happened to the book after that is
impossible to know. According to Matt Childs, Someruelos asked to see
some of the documentation from the case, in particular Aponte's and others' last confessions before their execution. In 1844, when another major
conspiracy shook the island, authorities asked to see some of the materials
from the 1812 trials.[65] Perhaps Aponte's book of drawings was among

---

[63] The information on the discovery of the book and other items in Aponte's house appears
in ANC, AP, leg. 12, exp. 17. There may be an interesting overlap with the Tailor's
Conspiracy in Bahia in 1798, during which one of the recruiters, Luis Gonzaga, a militia
member like Aponte, was found to have kept a notebook of his own making, in addition
to items such as published laws on the militia, Marian images, and books on the history
of the world. See Gregory Childs, "Seditious Spaces: The 1798 Tailor's Conspiracy and
the Public Politics of Freedom in Bahia, Brazil," book manuscript in progress.

[64] On new conceptions of intellectual history, see Dubois, "An Enslaved Enlightenment";
Trouillot, *Silencing the Past*; and Anthony Bogues, "And What About the Human?
Freedom, Human Emancipation, and the Radical Imagination," *Boundary* 2, 39, 3
(2012): 29–46.

[65] M. Childs, *The 1812 Aponte Rebellion*, 153, 177.

the documents given to Someruelos in April 1812 or to investigators in 1844, and it was lost in the process.

Thus, for this revolution that never quite came to pass, perhaps the most important source is a book that no modern scholar has ever seen. While the book is lost, another fascinating document has survived: Aponte's court testimony about it. Over the course of three days, Aponte sat with judicial official José María Nerey and described the images in the book one by one, for a total of seventy-two. Nerey followed up on most of Aponte's initial descriptions with demands for clarification. How forceful those demands were we do not know, but there is no obvious indication of physical torture in the proceedings.[66] What follows is an analysis of the transcript of that testimony that focuses on the book's negative presence to explore in more depth the possible intellectual histories of Aponte's revolutionary movement.

Looking at the book and listening to Aponte, interrogator Nerey was soon struck by the fact that so many of the human figures in the book were painted as black. Literary critic Juan Antonio Hernández has evocatively wondered about the reactions of fellow conspirators to whom Aponte showed this book full of powerful black men. He likens the experience to the profound amazement of Ti Noël, the fictional protagonist of Alejo Carpentier's *The Kingdom of This World*. During Henri Christophe's reign, Ti Noël returned to Haiti from Cuba and encountered this uncharted world of black majesty: where, in a black king's palace, the ministers, the chef, the hussars, the actors, everyone was black, even "the Immaculate Conception standing above the high altar of the chapel, smiling sweetly upon the Negro musicians who were practicing a *Salve*."[67]

As in Christophe's kingdom, so too in Aponte's picture book did black men wear crowns and sit on thrones. Black ambassadors were respected, black priests celebrated Mass, black scholars advised the pope, black men

---

[66] This is always difficult to assess. The testimony of Aponte's interrogations about the book sometimes used the verb *reconvenir* (to reprimand or reproach) to describe the interrogator's follow-up questions in cases where he was skeptical of Aponte's description. The testimony does not, however, use the term *apremiar* (to compel or constrain), which might imply the application of more force or coercion and which was used in other testimony taken from enslaved people in other instances of rebellion or conspiracy in Cuba in this period. See, for example, the testimony taken in the 1805 slave conspiracy in Bayamo in 1805, in AGI, Cuba, leg. 1649.

[67] Juan Antonio Hernández, "Hacia una historia de lo imposible: La revolución haitiana y el libro de pinturas de José Antonio Aponte," PhD diss., University of Pittsburg, 2005, 170–171; Alejo Carpentier, *The Kingdom of this World*, translated by Harriet de Onis (New York: Noonday Press, 1989), 114–115.

led the cavalry, black armies vanquished white ones, white kings were beheaded for blasphemy. A black Virgin was venerated and defended by black men, a sign near her bearing the biblical inscription, "I am black, but the most beautiful."[68] Thus, Aponte showed his companions a wondrous world where the faces of political, spiritual, and military power were almost always black.

If Aponte's companions were amazed, then surely the investigators responded with their own surprise and puzzlement at the world revealed to them by this uncommon black carpenter. And so they pushed him for answers that would provide understanding. Why were there so many black priests? Why was the cavalry black? Who was this important-looking black man? They were so confused at times that the tables turned, and Aponte became the expert, enlightening them on matters of history and religion. Discussing the picture numbered 37, for example, Aponte explained that it showed Pope Clement XI with his black librarian and a black cardinal. Nerey wondered if all this was true. "When and why were these black men cardinal and librarian to the pontiff?" he asked Aponte. Elsewhere in the same picture Aponte had drawn Pope Pius IV and three black priests at the door of the temple at Santa María di Populo in Rome. Again, Nerey wondered what was true and what might have been fable or fancy invented by Aponte. "Why," asked Nerey, "were these men painted with such vestments, and did such men [really] exist in Rome?" Aponte seemed to answer patiently, each time providing the titles of the books where he had read the specific story, or naming his source of oral information. In his responses about this particular image, for example, he cited a book on the life of San Antonio Abad and one on the city of Rome, in addition to oral accounts of a long-ago visit to Rome by two Havana priests, who had there seen a black priest celebrating Mass.[69] In this encounter between inquisitioner and accused, it was the latter who became the knowledgeable and patient teacher.

Was Nerey himself aware of the reversal as it happened, and could that have been why the grammar of his questions to Aponte changed over the course of the interrogation? Instead of asking questions about whether specific things in the book had really happened in history, he began asking instead, "how do you know about this?" It was a safer kind of question;

68 ANC, AP, leg. 12, exp. 17, passim. The beheading of the white king and the veneration of the black virgin appear in the same image (45–46) at ff. 62–63; the biblical passage is from Song of Songs (Solomon), 1:5.
69 ANC, AP, leg. 12, exp. 17, ff. 53–55.

it did not concede Nerey's own ignorance, nor grant Aponte the upper hand. Thus, in their discussion of picture 44b–45, which according to Aponte showed the invasion of Tarragona by the black King Tarraco and his black troops, Nerey asked "how he knew that there existed a King Tarraco who conquered Tarragona." Aponte replied that he knew it from the "the book of San Antonio Abad which he had read" and from "noticias de la Historia universal." The sources must have seemed legitimate to Nerey, so taking Aponte's word that there was some factual basis for the story, he proceeded to delve deeper into the image. Why had he combined the story of King Tarraco with the biblical story of Sennacherib? Aponte's answer was that he did it "for Reason of History, like everything else in the book."[70]

Aponte's answer sounds more consequential than Chacón's insistence that the things authorities uncovered in his house were for scaring flies. Still, there is something similar in the responses: unscripted gestures of defiance that suggested to the interrogators that *they*, black men, were privy to a knowledge that they would not share or clarify beyond a certain point. Nerey's ignorance would stand, Aponte seemed to say. *He* understood how history rendered these images coherent, even if Nerey could not.[71]

But what was this history to which Aponte referred? Clearly, it was a history of the world reconceived, a new universal history in which black men ruled. And in this pictorial history of the world, Aponte gave Ethiopia pride of place. Indeed, when one conspirator was asked how Aponte had explained the book to him, he said that the only description

---

[70] ANC, AP, leg. 12, exp. 17, ff. 59–60. Tarraco, or Taharqa, is mentioned in several contemporary histories of Spain as a black king (sometimes Egyptian, sometimes Ethiopian) who invades the Iberian peninsula. See, for example, "Tratado de cronología para la historia de España" which was published in *Memorias de la Real Academia de Historia* (Madrid; Sancha, 1796), and Juan Francisco Masdeu, *Historia crítica de España y de la cultura española*, a twenty-volume work published between 1783 and 1805. Individual volumes were reviewed in the press, and a review that appeared in the Madrid newspaper *Espíritu de los mejores diarios que se publican en Europa*, no. 133 (June 16, 1788), specifically mentioned the alleged invasion of Spain by the Egyptian King Tarraco. The story of Sennacherib defeated by an angel, meanwhile, appears in Lord Byron's 1815 poem "The Destruction of Sennacherib," suggesting that it was a tale with some currency in Aponte's age. Though Nerey is puzzled by Aponte's pairing of the story of Tarraco and Sennacherib, in fact, the Bible (2 Kings 19) describes an alliance between "Tirhakah King of Ethiopia" and Hezekiah, King of Israel, against the Assyrian king Sennacherib.

[71] A similar feeling, in a very different context, comes across powerfully in Carolyn Kay Steedman, *Landscape for a Good Woman* (New Brunswick: Rutgers University Press, 1987), 144.

Aponte had offered was that the "blacks and Kings painted in it were from Abyssinia." In that moment of complicity between two conspirators, Abyssinia, or Ethiopia, became the essence of the book. So, it is worth pausing to consider what Ethiopia might have meant for the revolution that Aponte and the others were trying to make in 1812.[72]

The Ethiopia that Aponte drew was a majestic and powerful one. It was a sovereign state and Christian kingdom ruled by a black king. In Aponte's book, Ethiopian armies repelled attacks on Jerusalem; Ethiopian ambassadors were regaled in Europe; Ethiopian priests celebrated Mass in Rome; Ethiopian emperors even controlled nature, causing floods and droughts by closing and opening sluice gates at will.[73] If Aponte's inquisitioners doubted the truth of the scenes Aponte painted, the scenes in fact reflected knowledge of Ethiopia long in wide circulation. In the fourteenth and fifteenth centuries, Ethiopian rulers had launched a concerted effort to establish the country as an international power. Numerous Ethiopian missions traveled to Europe to seek alliances with Christian kingdoms. Ethiopian monks began a tradition of pilgrimage to Rome, most of the sojourners staying – as Aponte had explained in his description of Image 37 – at a religious complex called Santo Stefano degli Abissini. If these men embodied Ethiopia's spiritual power, others embodied the power of the Ethiopian state. On their return from a mission to King Alfonso V of Aragón in Spain, two Ethiopian ambassadors carried Alfonso's offer to marry his daughter to the Ethiopian emperor Yeshaq and his son to an Ethiopian princess.[74]

It was this Ethiopia that appeared in the pages of Aponte's book, populated as it was by black kings and priests whose power was widely recognized. About that Ethiopia, Aponte had numerous sources. Between the search of his house and his replies to Nerey during the discussion of the book, we know about some of them. Aponte mentioned, for instance, the 1610 *Historia eclesiástica, política, natural y moral de los grandes y remotos reynos de la Etiopía, monarchía del emperador, llamado Preste*

---

[72] *Careo* between Melchor Chirinos and Salvador Ternero, in ANC, AP, leg. 12, exp. 17, f. 81. On Ethiopia in Aponte's book, see Hernández, "Hacia una historia de lo imposible," 181–207; and Jorge Pavez Ojeda, "Lecturas de un códice afrocubano: Naturalismo, etiopismo y universalismo en el libro de José Antonio Aponte (La Habana, circa 1760–1812)," *Historia Crítica* (Bogotá), 45 (September–December 2011): 56–85.

[73] For some examples, see Aponte's descriptions of images 6–7, 14–15, 16–17, 29, 37, 44a, 44b–45, and 46, in ANC, AP, leg. 12, exp. 17.

[74] On Ethiopian–European relations, see Matteo Salvadore, "The Ethiopian Age of Exploration: Prester John's Discovery of Europe, 1306–1458," *Journal of World History*, 21, 4 (2011): 593–627. See also Aponte's description of the Roman residence for Ethiopian priests in his discussion of Plate 37, in ANC, AP, leg. 12, exp. 17.

Juan de las Indias, by Luis de Urreta, a priest and professor of theology in Valencia. In that book Aponte would have encountered not only vivid descriptions of Ethiopia, but also accounts of the visits of Ethiopian monks and ambassadors to Rome and Europe. Aponte shared this particular book with others, including his apprentice, Trinidad Núñez, who then shared it with a black woman from Guanabacoa named Catalina Gavilán, suggesting a world in which such images and texts circulated among urban blacks.[75]

Another book that came up repeatedly in the testimony was probably *Fundación, vida y regla de la grande orden militar y monástica de los cavalleros y monges del glorioso Padre San Anton Abad, en la Etiopía*, published in Valencia, Spain, in 1609, about the Ethiopian religious order, the Caballeros de San Antonio Abad, which had been established in the fourth century. The alleged author, Juan de Baltasar Abisino, was himself Ethiopian and a member of the order of Saint Anthony. In his account, Baltasar highlighted the Caballeros' dual source of power, for the monks were also soldiers, having taken vows both religious and military, and their leader, Prester John, was a powerful black priest–king. (See Figure 7.3). For Aponte and his companions who wrote letters, penned proclamations, and offered testimony about fighting for liberty *and* their faith, the character of this fighting force likely resonated.[76] It is possible, then, to find evidence for some of Aponte's accounts of Ethiopia in works such as these and perhaps even to suggest affinities between those works and Aponte's vision – the attraction of black state power, the significance of spiritual authority.

But to do only that would be to miss an opportunity to explore the link between Aponte's vision and other currents of imagination; it would be to bypass an important episode in the intellectual history of the Black

[75] Luis de Urreta, *Historia eclesiástica, política, natural y moral de los grandes y remotos reynos de Etiopía* (Valencia: Pedro Patricio Mey, 1610); Antoine Bouba Kidakou, *África negra en los libros de viajes españoles del Siglo de Oro: La imagen del Negro en la España del Siglo de Oro* (Madrid: Editorial Académica Española, 2012), 69–77. On the circulation of the book, see testimony of José Trinidad Nunes, in ANC, AP, leg. 12, exp. 17, f. 96v–97.

[76] Juan de Baltazar Abissino, *Fundación, vida y regla de la grande orden militar y monástica de los caualleros y monges del glorioso Padre San Anton Abad, en la Etiopía, monarchia del Preste Juan de las Indias compuesta por don Juan de Baltazar Abissino* (Valencia, 1609), available on Google Books. Bouba Kidakou, *África negra*, 81–91. Because neither Aponte nor the house inspectors gave full titles or publication information, it is possible that the book he mentioned was another one, though many subsequent ones on the order of San Antonio Abad used the Baltazar book as a foundation. See the discussion in Palmié, *Wizards*, 293, and Jorge Pavez Ojeda, "Expediente contra José Antonio Aponte, La Habana, 1812," in *Anales de Desclasificación*, 1, 2 (2006): 757–758.

IL PRETEIANNI, RE.D'
ETHIOPIA

Rome Kal: Mar: 1599   IoannicOrla: formis.

FIGURE 7.3. Portrait of Prester John, King of Ethiopia, by Luca Ciamberlano, c. 1599. Credit: AGE Fotostock America.

Atlantic. Aponte may have relied on seventeenth-century Spanish texts to develop his vision of a faraway black kingdom, but he did so at the dawn of the nineteenth century, precisely at the same time that black men and women elsewhere were doing something analogous, for Ethiopia was already in the Americas when Aponte started drawing it.

In the still new United States, black abolitionists and ministers spoke of the greatness of Ethiopia. New black churches called themselves Ethiopian and Abyssinian – the first in Savannah, the African Baptist Church, in 1773, and perhaps the most famous, the Abyssinian Baptist Church (today in Harlem) in 1808. In Jamaica, where Ethiopianism would develop with great force in the late nineteenth and early twentieth centuries, a former slave named George Liele, who was one of the founding members of the Savannah congregation, founded the island's first Baptist church, the Ethiopian Baptist Church, in 1784. In these circles, it appears to have been biblical Ethiopia that was most consistently invoked. It was the Ethiopia of Psalm 68, Verse 31: "Princes shall come out of Egypt; Ethiopia shall soon stretch out her hands unto God." The fact that the invocation was biblical did not mean that it was not also political. Recall the case of the battalion of enslaved soldiers in Virginia who fought for England against the patriots; they called themselves the Ethiopian Regiment and wore a sash across their uniforms that read "Liberty to Slaves."[77] Famous black freemason Prince Hall explicitly linked the biblical prophecy of Ethiopia with real-world struggles for black freedom. In 1797, before his Masonic brothers in Boston, he cast blacks in revolutionary Saint-Domingue as the embodiment of Ethiopia's prophetic promise:

My brethren, let us remember what a dark day it was with our African brethren, six years ago, in the French West Indies. Nothing but the snap of the whip was heard from morning to evening; hanging, broken on the wheel, burning, and all manner of tortures inflicted on those unhappy people, for nothing else but to gratify their masters' pride, wantonness and cruelty. But blessed be God, the scene is changed; they now confess that God hath no respect of persons, and therefore receive them as their friends, and treat them as brothers. Thus doth

---

[77] See James Sidbury, *Becoming African in America: Race and Nation in the Early Black Atlantic* (Oxford: Oxford University Press, 2009); Sylvia Frey, *Water from the Rock: Black Resistance in a Revolutionary Age* (Princeton: Princeton University Press, 1992), chap. 2; Douglas Egerton, *Death or Liberty: African Americans and Revolutionary America* (New York: Oxford University Press, 2009), 71; Laurie Maffly-Kipp, *Setting Down the Sacred Past: African American Race Histories* (Cambridge: Harvard University Press, 2010); Leonard Barrett, *The Rastafarians: Sounds of Cultural Dissonance* (Boston: Beacon Press, 1977), 40, 76.

Ethiopia begin to stretch forth her hand, from a sink of slavery to freedom and
equality.[78]

If the presence of Ethiopia in Black Atlantic texts and institutions was
already established in the last decades of the eighteenth century, those
mentions acquired new meaning and force with the establishment in 1804
of an actual existing black state in the New World. Like Ethiopia, but
immediate in time and space, Haiti had black emperors and kings and
victorious black armies. Might Haiti then be a sign of a new age on
the horizon? Writers in Haiti certainly said so. Black victory in Haiti
was the beginning of redemption, Haitians the "regenerators of Africa."
Haitian intellectuals invoked Ethiopia (and Egypt) to make a larger point
about race. Theories of racial inferiority, they argued, were false justifications for slavery and colonialism. In fact, Africa was the cradle of
civilization.[79] Haitians elaborated this critique of European racism not
just amongst themselves but internationally. For example, Prince Saunders, an African American educator, worked closely with Christophe's
government to publish a collection of "Haytian Papers" for circulation
in England and the United States. The Africa argument served almost to
close the last piece in the volume: "Our traducers pretend to have forgotten what the Egyptians and Ethiopians, our ancestors were: the Tharaca
of Scripture [Tarraco in Aponte's testimony], that mighty monarch who
was the dread of the Assyrians, came from the interior of Africa, as
far as the columns of Hercules." Was Saunders imagining a response
of incredulity when he added, "the records that attest their works still
remain: the testimony of Herodotus, of Strabo, and of other historians of
antiquity, confirm these facts"?[80]

When Aponte told his own tales of African power and might – first in
pictures, then in judicial testimony – authorities did doubt his account.
Yet black people in Haiti, the United States, Jamaica, and elsewhere were
telling similar stories, and like Aponte and Saunders, they cited their
sources to anticipate potential cynics. We do not know if Aponte had
direct access to those other Black Atlantic stories of Ethiopia, but the fact

---

[78] Prince Hall, *A Charge Delivered to the African Lodge, June 24, 1797 at Menotomy*
(Boston: African Lodge, 1797), 11–12.
[79] Some of the writers who made this kind of argument included Noël Colombel, Baron
de Vastey, Boisrond Tonnerre, and Juste Chanlatte. For a summary, see Nicholls, *From
Dessalines*, 41–46.
[80] Prince Saunders, *Haytian Papers*, 219.

that they all flourished at the same time might suggest their circulation, even without direct evidence.[81]

There is another important if perhaps more mundane way in which Ethiopia circulated in Aponte's world, and that is in everyday speech, as a synonym for black. Just as black preachers and writers and artists used the term, so too did European authors and governors and slaveholders. They spoke of the propensities of the "Ethiopian race," and they used "Ethiopian" when speaking of black people in the present. But there may have been important distinctions in the way the designation was applied. When speaking of slaves, rarely, I think, did authors or authorities use *Ethiopian* or its plural form. Those people were *negros* or *nègres*; the labor force as a whole the plantation's *negrada*. The term "Ethiopian," meanwhile, seemed to be used more when white speakers or writers wanted to call up a notion of an embodied threat. Thus, they wrote in 1791 of the "evil inclinations of descendants of Ethiopia" in Cuba, who would certainly ally with Haitian rebels if given the opportunity. In 1800 authorities wrote of Cuban slaves who would join Toussaint to achieve liberty and "honorific posts among the Ethiopian troops." Frequently they referred to the Haitian rebels themselves as Ethiopians: Toussaint was a "sanguinary Ethiope," the black fighters were "Ethiopian troops," Georges Biassou marched with "other Ethiopian chiefs," and so on. Thus, while the label Ethiopian was a synonym for black at the turn of the nineteenth century, it is imperative to note that it may not have been deployed randomly for "anyone black," as some have suggested.[82] It seems to have been used as a selective synonym for *black*, when white speakers sought to convey a certain power or autonomy in the black

---

[81] A biography of Phillis Wheatley was found among the papers of a Jamaican free man of color in Havana in 1835. See Romy Sánchez, "Enjeux politiques d'une circulation américaine des savoirs: la 'bibliothèque' abolitionniste de Jorge Davidson," forthcoming.

[82] For Ethiopian as a synonym for black, see Stephen Howe, *Afrocentrism: Mythical Pasts and Imagined Homes* (London: Verso, 1998), ix, 32; and Wendy Laura Belcher, *Abyssinia's Samuel Johnson: Ethiopian Thought in the Making of an English Author* (Oxford: Oxford University Press, 2012), 19–20. On the use of the term in day-to-day documents of empire, see, for example, AHOHCH, AC, September 9, 1791; García to Pedro Acuña, April 22, 1793, in AGS, SGU, leg. 7157; García to Lleonart, September 19, 1794, in AGI, Cuba, leg. 170A; Lleonart to Conde de Campo de Alange, February 22, 1795, in AGI, SGU, leg. 6855; Kindelán to Someruelos, September 15, 1800, in AGI, Cuba, leg. 1549; Barba to Kindelán, February 3, 1801, and Kindelán to Someruelos, Febraury 15, 1801, both in AGI, Cuba, leg. 1535; Barba to Kindelán, January 15, 1801, in ANC, AP, leg. 8, exp. 28. The rebels themselves, in at least one instance, appear to have used the term "Ethiopian" to refer to enslaved people in Cuba, see Salvador Ternero quoted in M. Childs, *The 1812 Aponte Rebellion*, 104.

subjects about which they wrote – in other words, when they wrote not about "a slave," but about what they feared a slave was capable of becoming.

In a world in which black soldiers in Virginia donned the label Ethiopian, in which white governors spoke grudgingly of the achievements of Ethiopian armies in Haiti, in which black churches established themselves as Abyssinian or Ethiopian, and in which an enslaved black poet was known as "the Ethiopian poetess," Aponte invoked Ethiopia in pictures and words. Doing so helped him, and others around him, imagine a victorious black revolution in Havana in 1812. The invocation allowed him to make the case that his revolution had two powerful precedents: a remote, prophetic one in Ethiopia and a proximate one in Haiti. But the Ethiopia conjured in Aponte's book was a model in very specific ways. It was, first, a demonstration of a black power that was at once military, political, and spiritual. The victorious armies of Ethiopia defended their kingdom at least in part for religion, a formulation that was very much present in the testimony from Aponte and his companions, who said they fought not only for freedom from slavery but also for their faith in Jesus Christ. Here we glimpse the revolutionaries caught not only between the age of slavery and the age of emancipation, but also more immediately between the secular time of political and personal freedom and the nonsecular time of faith and eternal deliverance.

Ethiopia served as a model in another way as well. It was a sovereign nation, ruled by a black king. No European country controlled it, and its leaders traveled the world as legitimate and respected envoys. The fact that Haiti had recently come into existence – thanks to the power of men to whom the world referred as Ethiopian – likely made it seem like the once-remote African model had new currency. Except in one regard. Unlike Ethiopia, Haiti was not recognized across the globe, and its emissaries were not welcomed by European dignitaries. In Havana just two years earlier, the possibility of having to receive a Haitian diplomat prompted the governor to disobey and denounce royal orders. By showing the reception given to Ethiopian officials, Aponte provided an image of black sovereignty while also perhaps elaborating an implicit critique of the world's hostile response to Haitian independence.

Aponte's rendering of Ethiopia represented his efforts to think through the possibilities of black sovereignty in the age of Haiti. Here was a most powerful story: a land ruled by a black sovereign with military, political, and spiritual power, a black army that vanquished all its enemies, black Christians whose piousness made Ethiopia a prized ally of European states bent on containing the power of Islam. It was these true histories of black state power that Aponte showed to his co-organizers. He turned to these images to reinforce his points; he explained their meaning to men plotting to overthrow slavery by force. The facticity of the images helped make them persuasive. Maybe it was this that made the book an appealing tool for recruitment for the rebellion. With it, Aponte was able to show his companions a possible world, possible not just in fables but in history as well. Combined with other elements of the conspiracy, the centrality of Aponte's Ethiopia might suggest that the horizon of his movement may indeed have been anticolonial. Not for nothing had Aponte spoken to his companions about becoming king.[83]

While Ethiopia is a critical presence in Aponte's book, an honest examination would concede that this story, however powerful, is not the only one. Ethiopia shared the pages, sometimes even the same page, with many other things: Apollo and Neptune, Mars and Gemini; Spanish politicians and kings; black colonial militia members in Havana; ancient philosophers and Catholic saints; rivers and mountains and palaces. We are left then with a question perhaps not that different than the one Nerey himself asked: What was everything else in the book? Why were images of black power pictured together with so many other things seemingly unconnected? What, in the end, did Apollo's carriage or Neptune's mother have to do with black kings or black armies? If Aponte's pictures ranged broadly across seemingly distant and disparate subjects, and they did so, as he said, for the sake of history, what history was he talking about? Some have read Aponte's book as a window into the thought of an unusual, erudite, self-taught black artisan comparable, say, to Menocchio, the sixteenth-century Italian miller so appealingly studied by historian Carlo Ginzburg.[84] While the comparison is instructive, it is imperative to remember that Aponte's book was also a document of rebellion. The man who authored it, and the ones who saw it, connected its contents to their own revolution and to their own entry into history. How, then, can we connect those images to the history Aponte himself was trying to make in that moment? How might we read Aponte's *libro de pinturas* – in all its unruly and inscrutable heterodoxy – alongside the ambitious if ultimately failed movement he led?

---

[83] See testimony of Clemente Chacón, in ANC, AP, leg. 12, exp. 14, starting at f. 61 (B70).

[84] Carlo Ginzburg, *The Cheese and the Worms* (Baltimore: Johns Hopkins University Press, 1992); Palmié, *Wizards*, 114.

To restore the book to the historical process requires that we embrace its impenetrability and center its inherent and strategic flexibility. In some sense, Aponte's missing pictures (and the testimony that surrounds them) demand a reading perhaps reminiscent of those intrinsic to practices with which the revolutionaries themselves might have been familiar. In communities of Santería (or freemasonry, which some have connected to Aponte's movement), for example, ascending levels of initiation produce greater and deeper knowledge, understanding, and access.[85] To situate Aponte's contradictory and resistant descriptions of the images in the context of the other voluminous testimony from the movement allows us to begin to glimpse the many layers of possible meaning that allowed Aponte to tell different stories to different people. Sometimes the fact that he did so emerges clearly from the testimony; other times we can only infer it. Still, the analysis makes clear not only – as Aponte said – that he drew what and how he did "for reasons of History," but also that he chose History for a reason.

History for a Reason: Reading Words about Pictures

Let us turn in detail, then, to specific images in Aponte's book to explore the layers of meaning and the subversive flexibility inherent in many of them. This discussion is necessarily incomplete: of seventy-two images I analyze a half dozen in depth and a few more in passing.[86] Left out will be fascinating pictures: 24–25, for example, which might be understood as a kind of visual autobiography of Aponte himself, with allusions to his childhood, his trade as carpenter, and his militia service in the Bahamas; or Image 26, which combines into a single story that unfolds on a desolate beach the Greek philosopher Diogenes, the Egyptian goddess Isis, and the Spanish king Rodrigo. In the following I focus on several images that allow us to understand Aponte's role as a leader and historian, and the ways he might have imagined the connections between history as he saw

[85] On Aponte and freemasonry, Fischer, *Modernity Disavowed*, 51–52; Palmié, *Wizards*, 130–131. I am grateful to Julie Skurski for the observation about the ascending levels of knowledge in Santería and freemasonry.

[86] Many thematic questions will also be left unasked. Particularly worthy of further analysis is the question of the possible connections between the allegories pictured and commonplace political commentary of the period. Apollo in an opera performed in this period in Havana represented former Spanish Prime Minister Manuel Godoy. What other equivalences might be here undetected by us today? Spanish "emblem books" might be a particularly fruitful place to explore these potential connections. See http://www.bidiso.es/EmblematicaHispanica/.

it, the conspiracy as he planned it, and the future of his world as he wanted it to be.

In the eyes of Spanish prosecutors, perhaps the most damning picture in the book was the one numbered 6–7. The things that made it potentially subversive, however, would not have been at all apparent in Aponte's initial description of it. Aponte began by pointing to the image of Mars pulled by two horses going up a hill, with a scorpion converted to a rooster. Mars, he explained, influences war, and it is a war scene that dominated the image. Prester John of the Christian Kingdom of Ethiopia led the Caballeros de San Antonio Abad in a battle against the Moors.

The interrogators looked at the picture and immediately noted some things that Aponte had conveniently failed to mention. First, Nerey observed not only that the soldiers were all dressed in black, but that the men themselves also appeared to be black. Why was that, he wanted to know. Aponte replied straightforwardly, "because they are *naturales de Abisinia*." Once Nerey's questions made the men's blackness part of the spoken record, Aponte felt the need to add unprompted, "because the Portuguese had discovered or conquered said part of the Globe, the two groups joined together for the Battle indicated." But the response did not make sense to Nerey. To him it seemed that the Portuguese, or the whites, were being attacked – and defeated – by the black army. Indeed, as he pointed out, the picture included two black men on horseback who carried the severed and bloody heads of what appeared to be two white (not Moorish) men. Here, Nerey seemed to suggest, was a clear depiction of what had long been referred to as "race war."[87]

Among the most curious things in Aponte's response was the fact that he volunteered the description of the Portuguese as the "discoverers or conquerors" of the region and as allies of the black army. Some have noted that Aponte may have drawn a parallel between the Moorish invasion of the Iberian peninsula and the contemporary struggle against the French invasion of the same territory.[88] While that is certainly plausible, it is conceivable that Aponte was also implicitly invoking recent Haitian history. Aponte's picture of two armies – one black, one white – as allies might have prompted, among the black conspirators who pondered the image, discussions of the alliance of Jean-François's black army and the once-conquering Spanish, an invocation perhaps made more relevant by the presence of Jean-François's troops in Havana. On the other hand,

[87] See ANC, AP, leg. 12, exp. 17, ff. 23–25.
[88] Hernández, "Hacia una historia," 253.

Aponte's insistence on the alliance between the black and white armies in the picture might have been an attempt at deflection, an attempt to explain away the image of a black army defeating the army of the white colonizer. That, of course, would have constituted an easy visual invocation of the Haitian Revolution, perhaps especially of the final, anticolonial stage of the revolution in which the black armies battled the French for independence and freedom. It is unclear whether Aponte thought these things when he drew the pictures. But his companions, like Nerey himself, could have easily seen in the image a straightforward representation of a black army defeating a white one.

Other pictures in Aponte's book permit a more direct comparison of how Aponte described the images to authorities and how he described them to his companions. In most cases, when his companions were questioned about the images in the book, they denied knowing their meaning, averring either that Aponte showed them without explanation, or saying simply that they did not understand or could not remember what Aponte had said. Shown the image of the black army defeating a white one, for example, Chacón insisted that Aponte had not explained it, and that the image was beyond his own understanding. But occasionally he and the others elaborated, allowing us to listen – if imperfectly – to how Aponte himself might have talked about the images with fellow travelers. And it is precisely in the difference between the two modes of description – to authorities in the context of an investigation and to companions in the course of organizing the movement – that we gain insight into the possible connections between the book and the conspiracy, and between the conspiracy and history.

Take, for example, Image 37. According to Aponte's description, it featured black ecclesiastical figures in Rome and two vessels, one that had brought the black priests to Rome, and the other that had transported imprisoned Moors. Aponte testified that the images presented were historical; he read about them in history books, and they were what he said they were: pictures of real black men in positions of spiritual power.

This is very likely the image Chacón discussed in his testimony when he was asked about the meaning of a picture (authorities did not provide the number) that showed two vessels, some black men dressed as ecclesiastics, perhaps an archbishop, and "a black man with signs of superiority." While Chacón insisted that he did not understand the image, he volunteered an important detail that contradicted Aponte's insistence that the picture was Rome, or *only* Rome. Chacón, in fact, testified that Henri Christophe appeared in the picture, "signaling with his left hand, a saber in his right, and a sign at his feet that said: *Cúmplase lo mandado,*" or "Execute what is ordered."[89] "*Cúmplase lo mandado*" or "*Cumple lo mandado*" was a standard phrase added at the closing of Spanish royal and ministerial orders. Given that Aponte pasted images and writings into his book, he might have cut and pasted the phrase from some unknown document, or he might simply have written it. One of the principal reasons cited for the plot was the fact that local authorities were refusing to execute a supposed order for the freedom of slaves. In the words of one enslaved man in Puerto Príncipe, "the aim of the insurrection was nothing other than liberty and it was primarily against the *cavalleros* of the City because they did not want to *execute what was ordered* in this regard."[90] In Havana, of course, the plot's leaders propagated the idea that the order of freedom had come from Henri Christophe himself. Based on Chacón's description, then, Aponte's drawing was the perfect pictorial representation of the rumor of liberation ordered by Haiti's black king.

We can ask ourselves, then, whether this was Rome, as Aponte said to authorities, or the Caribbean, or somewhere else entirely. But that question will not get us very far. The images in the book were strategically ambiguous. They could refer to a contemporary world that had given rise to men like Dessalines and Christophe. They could denote the present and immediate future, in which black men would do battle for freedom right there in Havana. Or they could represent something completely different. Black armies defeating white ones could be explained by reference to long-ago and faraway history; so too could the existence of very powerful black men. And so, when Aponte – artist and teacher – explained the images, he could tell different stories depending on the circumstance and the audience. History here was strategic; it provided a cover and an explanation for potentially subversive futures.

Aponte vowed that the images were representations of history and described them as such. Authorities suspected they were preparation for war. Stephan Palmié has criticized historians for too readily believing the version offered by Aponte's executioners because that version fits more neatly within narratives of popular resistance.[91] If the criticism has clear merit, it is also true that a careful consideration of Aponte's assertions about the innocence of the images, when placed alongside the testimony

---

[89] Testimony of Clemente Chacón, ANC, AP, leg 12, exp. 17, f. 14.
[90] Testimony of Juan Manuel Suares, in "Primera Pieza de los Autos seguidos sobre [sublevación] de Negros Esclabos de la Villa de Puerto Prícipe," January 11, 1812, in AGI, Cuba, leg. 1780, ff. 3v–5. Emphasis mine.
[91] Palmié, *Wizards*, 83–98.

offered by his companions, suggest that authorities may in fact have been on to something. This was clearly the case with the image in which a portrait of blacks in Rome fused with a portrait of a contemporary black king issuing freedom orders that had to be obeyed. But there are other important examples as well.

Aponte's book contains several pictures representing the free black battalion of Havana, of which his grandfather, father, and he himself had been members. The images numbered 18 and 19, for example, portrayed Aponte's grandfather, Captain Joaquín de Aponte, and Havana's black battalion defeating six hundred English troops who entered the city at Marianao during the 1762 British attack on Havana. In the picture, the black troops escort white prisoners, and two black soldiers stand over a dead white officer, described by Aponte as a *milor*, milord or English nobleman. Here, as in the other image, a strict historical reading is possible. In this vein, the picture of blacks battling whites straightforwardly represents a historical episode in which the colored militias were deployed in defense of Havana and Spain.[92] But Aponte's fellow conspirators would have seen the image as something more – as an emblem of black heroism, as the basis of a demand for black rights in the present, and perhaps as an indication that their own black army might be up to the challenge of defeating a white one in the proximate future.

Another image of the black militias makes clear the layers of meaning that Aponte and his co-conspirators might have attached to the pictures. Image 32–33 again portrayed the black militia defending the city against the British in 1762. But the picture is not so straightforward. First, time and history are collapsed: José Ovando, the first black captain when the militia was established in 1701, is figured in front of all the troops. Yet sharing the page are the black militia members of 1762, as if they were all protagonists in a single history. Near the Punta, or Campo de Zamora, a woman appears, representing the city of Havana and acknowledging the black troops who defended her. Authorities focused in particular on Aponte's depiction and placement of the black troops in the picture. Why, they queried, had Aponte painted military camps belonging only to the

---

[92] ANC, AP, leg. 12, exp. 17, ff. 34–36. Service record for Joaquín Aponte is in AGI, SD, 2093. There was a British attack on Marianao on June 23, in which the black militias appear to have been deployed. See César García del Pino, *La Toma de La Habana por los ingleses y sus antecedentes* (Havana: Ciencias Sociales, 2002) 93; and Schneider, *The Occupation of Havana*. On the significance of militia service for the conspirators, see M. Childs, *The 1812 Aponte Rebellion*, 78–100.

black forces, including both infantry and cavalry camps? Aponte replied that the infantry camp was that of his grandfather and black militia captain, Joaquín Aponte; the other was the cavalry camp of the white troops, "as none exists for blacks." But, as authorities quickly noted, Aponte's description did not seem to match the image before them. They pressed on, pointing out a glaring inconsistency: there were no whites in the camp that he said was the white cavalry camp. Indeed, the only people there were three black officers on horseback and a few sentries, also black. How exactly was this the white cavalry camp?[93]

Whatever the contradictory image may have portrayed about the black (and white) militias in 1762, Aponte used the image in another context to visualize what should happen in 1812. During the planning of the rebellion, Aponte showed this particular image to several of his co-conspirators: Clemente Chacón, Salvador Ternero, Francisco Xavier Pacheco, and Francisco Maroto. Perhaps when he did so he said something about the campaign of 1762. But what stuck in the minds of his companions was something else entirely. Aponte showed them the image as they discussed the details of how to organize their current rebellion, using the picture to illustrate how military camps should be organized and how each should have its own flag and guard.[94] In that moment, then, it is hard to say whether the men were consciously viewing a visual representation of an historical event or of something they themselves were about to do, or both.[95]

There are other images that suggest that Aponte's book, whatever else it may have done, served as a kind of pictorial representation of the men's current efforts. For example, Aponte's book contained several images of *campanarios*, or bell towers. The testimony from the rebellion on the plantations consistently makes references to the leaders putting guards at the *campanarios* to prevent people from ringing the bells for help.[96]

[93] ANC, AP, leg. 12, exp. 17, ff. 44v–47v.

[94] ANC, AP, leg. 13, exp. 1, f. A47.

[95] The question of whether and how Aponte might have changed or inflected the history of the British invasion of Havana is a fascinating one. Most of that history has been written with very little attention paid to the participation of people of color. (Elena Schneider, personal communication, March 23, 2013). It is, therefore, difficult to compare Aponte's account with written ones. Still, that project would be a worthwhile one, a means of approaching subterranean accounts of what is generally seen as a pivotal national (and international) episode.

[96] Images 19 and 22 described in ANC, AP, leg. 12, exp. 17, ff. 36, 38. For testimony mentioning the guard at the bell, see testimony of Alonso Santa Cruz and Tiburcio

Did Aponte use those images to impress on his recruits the importance of that particular action? Authorities did not ask. They did ask, repeatedly, about the book's many maps and drawings of the city: why did he draw this particular structure, or the route from x to y, or the entrances into and out of the city, and so on. It is difficult not to notice, as authorities surely did, the great overlap between the places depicted in Aponte's book and the places mentioned as targets in the testimony of the conspirators. The conspirators' testimony, for example, mentioned plans to attack the barracks and the Castillo de Atarés, all of which were figured in Aponte's drawings, shown very precisely in relation to other buildings and roads. The overlap might have been without meaning or purpose. Aponte himself, when asked why he had drawn those things, replied simply, "with the idea of amusing himself . . . without any other intention at all." And it is natural, after all, that there would be overlap between maps of the city and the plans of the rebels to attack it.[97] Still, the fact that Aponte used other images to explain the planning for the rebellion suggests that he may have done the same for the maps. Also pictured alongside the fortresses, armories, and barracks were other significant nonmilitary landmarks: the meeting house of the Real Consulado, Francisco Arango's residence, the Customs House, and so on. Whether these were included as potential targets or simply as part of the cityscape, we cannot know.[98]

Other images in the book suggest histories and messages even more buried and much less discernible to the investigator's naked eye. Aponte mentioned Egypt and Ethiopia, Rome and Havana, yet sometimes what he said seemed to function as a cover for what he did not say. When he described the scene that looked like a race war (Image 6–7), he failed to note that the victorious army he drew was a black one; he admitted that only when asked directly by the interrogator. Surely the interrogator did not pick up on every potentially interesting connection or observation, and Aponte would not have volunteered potentially subversive connections and readings. Yet their traces are there.

Peñalver, as well as the summary of the testimony of José Espinosa, all in ANC, AP, leg. 13, exp. 1, ff. 95–105, 187–188.

[97] ANC, AP, leg. 12, exp. 17, ff. 38–40.

[98] The maps often included the immediate countryside as well, which of course was also the target of the rebellion of 1812. The road taken by Barbier and Lisundia may appear in image 23, which shows the road from Regla to Guanabacoa; the men took a road to the *ingenios* through Guanabacoa. Without the maps in the book, it is difficult to tell how far east the images went; that is, did they include the plantations in the Guanabo area where the insurrection occurred? See testimony of Estanislao Aguilar, March 25, 1812, in ANC, AP, leg. 12, exp. 18, f. 97v.

Image 16–17, for example, was a typically inscrutable picture. In it appeared the black Prester John, the black queen Candace, the evangelist Phillip baptizing a figure known as the Ethiopian eunuch (thus initiating the African Catholic Church), King Solomon, the Queen of Sheba, their son, and a statue with no arms representing Justice. Justice had no arms, Aponte explained, "so as not to receive anything." Authorities could not have known what to make of the image, nor of Aponte's seemingly convoluted description of it. They did not even bother to ask what it meant; it did not seem significant enough to them and certainly not as interesting as other images of black armies.

Yet the picture featured the Ethiopian eunuch seated in a carriage reading a book. Aponte identified the book as the biblical prophesies of Isaiah. Aponte did not volunteer that Isaiah's prophesies included four poems, later known as the Songs of the Servant, that were powerful meditations on justice for the downtrodden. The first poem reads in part:

Here is my servant, whom I uphold... I will put my Spirit on him, and he will bring justice to the nations. He will not shout or cry out, or raise his voice in the streets. A bruised reed he will not break, and a smoldering wick he will not snuff out. In faithfulness he will bring forth justice; he will not falter or be discouraged till he establishes justice on earth. In his teaching the islands will put their hope.[99]

Justice is invoked three times in close succession in the biblical passage. The idea of justice is thus represented not just in the figure of the statue, or in the black Prester John, as one critic has suggested, but also in the unspoken subject of the open book that Aponte chose to picture in his own.[100] Assuming that Aponte was aware of those verses, he might have identified readily with the figure of the servant bringing justice – and faith – to the islands. Yet this potential visual representation of a black struggle for justice and redemption appears to have gone undetected by Aponte's inquisitioner.

Image 21 is based on more recent local history. It depicts the blessing of Havana's then-new cemetery, the Campo Santo or Espada Cemetery, which was inaugurated in 1806, at about the time Aponte claims to have started working on the book. The image shows two coffins, one of a Havana governor who died in 1766, the other of a Havana bishop who died in 1801. Both coffins were exhumed in 1806, and transferred and reburied in the new cemetery with a solemn ceremony and blessing,

[99] Isaiah, 42:1–4. The biblical story (in Acts, 8:26–35) has Philip reading the Book of Isaiah in the carriage, but he is reading Isaiah, 53:7–8.
[100] Hernández, "Hacia una historia," 187, 203, 250, 253.

which Aponte himself may well have witnessed and certainly would have heard about. Aponte's description makes no mention of the fact that both men had died of yellow fever. People in Havana, of course, knew all about yellow fever, and they knew also of the role it had played in the Haitian Revolution. They had read the regular accounts in the *Gaceta de Madrid* of the decimation of the French army in 1802–03, in part by yellow fever. They had seen the arrival of many sick French soldiers and troops, some of whom were housed and died in the San Lázaro hospital, pictured in several of Aponte's maps.[101] In this particular image, then, Aponte represented the death by yellow fever of two powerful white men from Havana. The allusion to the disease may have been coincidental. Or the picture may have served to suggest that the would-be rebels, like their earlier counterparts in Saint-Domingue, had a potential ally in nature, one they might use strategically if and when the time came to do so.

Image 8–9 is a surprising and complex allegory about greed and commerce. Aponte testified that the picture depicted the planet "Mercury of Gemini" in a carriage pulled by two large, rapacious birds. There was a green star and a *caduceo*, a staff signifying the progress of commerce. In the picture, a guard attempts to stop contraband and instead encounters death, either because he is personally unable to stop it, or because contraband cannot be stopped generally. A launch from the ship approaches; avarice jumps on the dock and also meets death.[102]

The story so far is general; it could be an allegory about colonial, indeed maritime, commerce anywhere. But Aponte clearly set the scene in Havana harbor in 1807–08. The carriage, importantly, had a picture of Manuel Godoy, Spain's controversial prime minister, favorite of the king, lover of the queen, enemy of the heir. He was pictured, said Aponte, at the height of his power. While some have taken this to mean after he received the title of Príncipe de la Paz in 1795, it is clear that the picture alluded to his 1807 elevation to the newly created position of Admiral of Spain and the Indies and Protector of Maritime Commerce. In 1807, Godoy had established the Almirantazgo, or Admiralty, a reform aimed at revitalizing the Spanish Navy after its defeat against the British at Trafalgar in 1805 and following British attacks on Spanish shipping in the Río de la Plata in 1806. With the reform Godoy, gained supreme

---

[101] ANC, AP, leg. 12, exp. 17, ff. 38–40. On the *Gaceta de Madrid*'s coverage of the yellow fever deaths, see Ferrer "Talk About Haiti: The Archive and the Atlantic's Haitian Revolution." On the arrival of sick soldiers, see Chapter 4.

[102] ANC, AP, leg. 12, exp. 17, ff. 25–26v.

control of the Navy and the authority to provide "passports" to all ships flying Spanish flags and all foreign ships visiting Spanish ports.[103]

News of the reform arrived in Havana in March 1807, and Aponte explicitly referred to its arrival in his description of the image, noting that the vessel shown in the picture was the one that brought the news of the Almirantazgo to Havana. In honor of Godoy and the reform, the Real Consulado paid for the Alameda, the city's maritime boulevard, to be lit and decorated. In September, an opera titled *Apolo y América* – with Apollo symbolizing Godoy – opened in Havana. Later that month, a grand party was organized in the Real Factoría de Tabacos. The building and its surroundings were festooned for the occasion, complete with newly commissioned frescoes by an Italian artist. The Real Consulado also published a color engraving for the occasion, depicting some of the celebrations in Havana. Though no copies appear to have survived, it was said to include an image of the house of Conde O'Reilly, lavishly decorated with lights and the *caduceo*.[104] Aponte would have seen the house, centrally located within the city walls, just as he would have seen or heard about the feast at the Real Factoría de Tabacos, not too far from his own home. With no surviving images from Aponte's book or the 1807 celebrations, no direct comparison is possible. Still, even on the basis of the short descriptions available, Aponte's image emerges as a critical engagement with the news and visual representations then circulating in Havana.

Aponte's picture, he insisted to authorities, lauded the progress of commerce. Yet his own description of it suggested otherwise. The picture, he testified, included a falling feather to symbolize the fall of Godoy from power, presumably during the crisis of 1808. In Aponte's vision, then, the author of commerce's imputed progress met his downfall. Based on this and other elements of the image, authorities were openly skeptical of Aponte's claim that the picture celebrated commerce. How, they asked, could the picture be about the progress of commerce when death is figured so prominently and even holds the *caduceo* in its hand? Death, Aponte countered, destroys only avarice, not commerce. Authorities appear to have taken him at his word, failing to note other inconsistencies. Death

[103] Royal Order, Aranjuez, February 27, 1807, published March 11, 1807, in Madrid, 8, 21, and available at https://www.play.google.com/store/books/details?id=Zxgm15f9QCwC. See also Sigfrido Vázquez Cienfuegos, "El Almirantazgo Español de 1807: La última reforma de Manuel Godoy," in *Hispania* 72 (2012): 475–500.
[104] Sigfrido Vázquez Cienfuegos, "*Omnia Vanitas*: Festejos en honor de Godoy en la Habana en 1807," in *Ibero-Americana Pragensia*, 25 Supplement (2009): 115–138.

appeared in the picture twice, both times associated with Spanish shipping or Spanish commerce. The first time it defeated the *guarda del comercio* in charge of stopping contraband; the second time (with the commerce staff in its hand), death met "avarice" as the latter landed on the dock from a Spanish vessel.

Did Aponte mean to depict the death of Spanish commerce, or perhaps of a particular Spanish commerce? Importantly, Aponte's picture included "*un negro*" pictured near the Spanish ship. That is all he says about the figure, and authorities did not ask him about it. Was he a sailor, a slave, a militia member? We cannot know. But it is perhaps important that the figure is the only one associated with the Spanish ship who did not encounter death. Whether death killed avarice or commerce, he spared the black man. The allegory, then, was perhaps less about commerce in general than about the commerce in black men and women: the commerce was destroyed, the people not – a fitting image for the age that saw the beginning of England's naval campaign against the slave trade.

But the story takes an even more historical turn with the inclusion in the same picture of a second large vessel, the warship *San Lorenzo*, about which Aponte was not asked and did not elaborate. The real *San Lorenzo* had a long history in the Caribbean. During the war between Spain and France in 1793–5, it had been part of the Spanish squadron that led the naval siege on Saint-Domingue's Fort-Dauphin, which gave Spanish forces control of Bayajá. After the siege, the *San Lorenzo* was one of the vessels that transported French prisoners of all colors to Cuba. In December 1795, it transported the remains of Christopher Columbus to Havana. On that same trip, it carried the former slave and then general Georges Biassou and other black auxiliaries and their families to Havana after Spain's defeat in Santo Domingo. Indeed, Aponte drew the vessel near Casa Blanca, where the black auxiliaries had stayed in 1795–6 and again in 1811–12. Later, as news of the Almirantazgo arrived and as Aponte began his book, the *San Lorenzo* was normally in Havana harbor, cruising within sight of the port. In 1810, it was in Cádiz, transporting French prisoners, and briefly under consideration as the mode of transportation for black auxiliaries returning to Santo Domingo via Havana. The *San Lorenzo*, then, carried a rich history, known to many in Havana.[105]

---

[105] The history of the *San Lorenzo*'s activities is recreated from "Extracto de las ocurrencias diarias de la Esquadra del Mando del Teniente General D. Gabriel de Aristizabal . . . desde Febrero de 1793," in AMN, 304, ms. 595; "Estados de guerra y vida" from

Indeed, for some of the men involved in Aponte's movement, the connection to the *San Lorenzo* was much more personal. It was on that very vessel that some members of the black militia who conspired with Aponte had done guard duty. The creole black militiaman José del Carmen Peñalver, who was centrally involved in the planning of the conspiracy and who wrote the forged passes that Barbier and Lisundia used to go the countryside on March 14 to begin the rebellion, had served on the *San Lorenzo* when it was in Havana. Another free black militia member, Hilario Santa Cruz, who played an unknown role in the conspiracy but served a four-year sentence as a result of the investigation, also testified that he had served aboard the *San Lorenzo*.[106]

With this history and association in mind, the picture that Aponte described as an allegory about the progress of commerce emerges as something much more complex. Death met those associated with Spanish commerce, perhaps including the slave trade, while in another part of the picture, the *San Lorenzo* – a ship that had spent time in revolutionary Saint-Domingue, that had brought decorated black heroes from the Haitian Revolution to Havana, and on which some of Aponte's own companions had served – stood impervious to harm. Here, then, was a trace of an alternative allegory. Aponte's testimony to authorities rendered that element of the drawing faint and elusive, buried, like so many other pictures in the volume, not just by the subsequent loss of the book but also by Aponte himself, by his strategic evasions and deflections, by the disavowals he himself was forced to effect in the courtroom.[107] But in another context, before a different audience, the picture would easily have recalled the men's own memories and experiences aboard a vessel with so much history relevant to their own.

1793–1794, 1806, and 1809 in AGMAB, Sección Buques, leg. 2235/41; and AGMAB, EA, leg. 39, carp. 1, doc. 18 and leg. 45, carp. 12, doc. 74. See also "Buques de Guerra que ha tenido la Marina Real de España desde principios del siglo," in AMN, ms. 2215; on the ship's use to transport black auxiliaries to Havana in 1795–1796, see Las Casas to Príncipe de la Paz (Godoy), January 8, 1796, in AGI, Estado, leg. 5A, exp. 24. On its possible use to transport them in 1810, see Ministro de Marina to Secretario del Despacho de Hacienda y de Indias, April 21, 1810, in AGI, SD, leg. 1062.

[106] Testimony of Hilario Santa Cruz, in ANC, AP, leg. 13, exp. 1, f. 361.

[107] Sibylle Fischer uses "disavowal" to describe the process by which certain kinds of radical imaginations and possibilities were suppressed. Part of the violence of the process, I would add, is the ways in which people such as Aponte were themselves forced, by violence or its threat, to participate in the disavowal, by having to deny or to lie in the (vain) hope of surviving. Thus Fischer's phrase in relation to Hegel (and Haiti) might also apply to Aponte himself. "Disavowal itself becomes productive, generating further stories, further screens that hide from view that which must not be seen." Fischer, *Modernity Disavowed*, 32.

This particular portrait is but one example of many, for other pictures, as well, undoubtedly contained elements that would have been obscure to Nerey but that evoked different histories, memories, and resources for the conspirators. Thus, the glorious black history pictured in Aponte's book and so visible to the eyes of all who saw it – of black kings and cardinals and generals and emperors in Ethiopia, Egypt, Rome, or Spain – was accompanied by another black history, more subterranean and potentially more subversive. It included a Spanish warship that linked Cuban conspirators to Haitian fighters; a 1762 military camp that was a model for what the men planned in 1812; a glorious black man in Rome who was also Henri Christophe. This history would have been barely, if at all, visible to Nerey, and Aponte did nothing to bring it into focus for him. But to Aponte and his companions – who shared a history as black militia members in Havana during the era of the Haitian Revolution – this other history was easily called forth by talking, looking at the pictures, and plotting how to make themselves masters of that history and the future they thought it pointed to.

Nerey, the judge Juan Ignacio Rendón, and the state they represented had, of course, no interest in that history and no desire to see that future. While it is possible (albeit unlikely) that the government destroyed the book that initially occupied so much of its attention, it is certain that authorities did not hesitate to destroy the man who created it. On April 7, in one of his last acts as governor of Havana and captain-general of Cuba, Someruelos issued a statement announcing the public execution of the rebels and plotters two days later.

The arc of Someruelos's rule as governor was perfectly emblematic of the complex history of Cuba in the Age of the Haitian Revolution. He arrived in Havana by way of one of the most impressive sugar plantations in the world at the time, Nicolás Calvo's *Nueva Holanda*. He left having just violently defeated men who sought to ally with the enslaved on plantations such as that one to make an antislavery revolution.

The public declaration that Someruelos issued to announce Aponte's sentence was profoundly violent. It described the physical punishment that awaited the convicts, and it dismissed the project as "a miserable and ridiculous farce" with origins only in the "fatuous and heated brain of the black man José Antonio Aponte." With the executions, Someruelos announced, the danger was over: "the contagion that might have been caused by revolutionary ideas, which are embraced by a very small number of people, will disappear." Any surviving sympathizers, he announced, would understand "the fate that awaits them if they try like [the accused] to disturb the the public order . . . for the resources that the government can use to annihilate in a single moment the reckless fools are incalculable."[108]

Someruelos was wrong about the origins of the plot. However much he might attribute it to Aponte's fanciful thinking, the plot was very much a product of its time and place. While clearly bearing the imprint of Aponte's imagination, it built on and made connections between the present and history, between Cuba and Haiti, Africa and Europe. It scoured the history of Ethiopia for models, and it engaged contemporary realities, from the reconquest of Santo Domingo by Spain, to the antislavery potential of the Cortes of Cádiz, to the escalation of the slave trade to Cuba in the context of British slave trade abolition, to the presence of black heroes from the Haitian Revolution in their very own city, to the coronation of King Henri I in Haiti. Aponte's plot read all these developments in light of his own world and sought to build on them to write a more expansive and immediate history of freedom in the Black Atlantic.

About other things, however, Someruelos was correct. The danger seemed contained. On the morning of April 9, 1812, exactly three weeks after Aponte's arrest, the punishment was meted out before an applauding crowd. Aponte was hanged, his head severed from his body, attached to a pole, and placed inside a steel cage. The cage was then strategically located in his neighborhood on the corner of what is now Belascoaín and Carlos III. That morning his closest companions in the movement met the same fate, though their heads were placed elsewhere: Juan Barbier or Jean-François, Clemente Chacón, and his son Juan Bautista Lisundia.[109] Though the men did indeed make history, it was not the history they had chosen.

Several weeks after José Antonio Aponte and his companions were hanged from the gallows in Havana, two other black men – their names omitted in the document that briefly records their existence – were marched into a public plaza in Havana for execution. Governor Someruelos had already returned to Spain, his tenure as the island's supreme commander over. It was his successor, Juan Ruiz de Apodaca, who continued

---

[108] Someruelos, *impreso*, April 7, 1812, in AGI, Santo Domingo, leg. 1284.
[109] ANC, AP, leg. 13, exp. 1, ff. 190–198.

the investigation into Aponte's movement and who oversaw the execution of these two supposed accomplices. Many had gathered for the public ritual, not only because of the general state of agitation that the plot had produced, but also because this particular execution would put on display the efficient and modern power of the state. The liberal government in Spain had just outlawed the use of gallows for hanging and ordered that a new, more humane and modern system, the garrote, take its place. In Cuba it was to be used the first time on these two men, and many thought they wanted to see it in action. But either the new machine was faulty, or the executioner misjudged how to work it, for when he finished the operation, the first condemned man was not dead but rather slowly and painfully suffocating. The governor, aware of the unusually large crowd and the tension in the air, ordered that the man be shot while seated on the bench of the garrote. The same thing was then done with the second man.[110] Facing unforeseen circumstances, the new governor did as his predecessors had done. He improvised to assure the supremacy of the order he was charged with guarding. Whatever world the executed men had imagined they might bring into being, in Cuba slavery and colonialism would survive the Age of Revolution.

The same was not true everywhere. As Aponte hanged and others were suffocated and shot, Spain's once-new world was convulsed in violence. In Mexico, the Spanish army besieged the town of Cautla against the forces of independence leader José María Morelos. His predecessor, Miguel Hidalgo, had been gruesomely executed in much the same manner as Aponte. In Caracas, clashes between royalist and patriot forces would soon kill more than 80,000 residents, or almost 20 percent of the population, the majority in the period between 1813 and 1814. The island of Cuba was spared that violence, its peace built precisely on the kind of terror visited upon Aponte that April morning, and the coercion visited every day on thousands of Africans arriving at its ports and laboring on its plantations. Instead of facilitating upheaval in Cuba, the crucible of revolution and independence in Haiti, Spain, and Latin America became, in the political arguments of the colonial elite a reason – one more reason – to intensify white control and discipline, that "principal defense of

---

[110] Apodaca to Ignacio Pezuela, May 22, 1812, in AGI, Ultramar, 84; and "Real Orden de la Secretaría del Despacho de Gracia y Justicia por la que se comunica un Decreto de las Cortes que dispone la abolición de la pena de horca y la sustituye por la de garrote," AHN, Consejos, leg. 13561, exp. 4.

the existence of whites that live among so many blacks ... in the solitude of [their] estates."[111]

Throughout the period of the Haitian Revolution – and later amidst the threat posed by Aponte and his colleagues in 1812 and the wave of violent confrontations in Spain's mainland colonies – the planter elite in Cuba remained confident in their ability to control their fate. As Spain's territories in the hemisphere became independent nations, Cuba's economic leaders grew firm rather than timorous. At that crossroads, they understood several things. First, Spain's losses elsewhere made their own project more important and more worthy of concessions from a beleaguered metropole. Second, their project, a latecomer in the international business of sugar and slavery, remained dependent on a slave trade increasingly under attack by England. And so Cuban planters did as they were wont to do. They calculated, and they improvised. They did not sever ties with Spain, whose leaders were now obligated by geopolitical circumstances to maintain the slave trade in order to retain Cuba. Nor did they alter their course of making Cuba a colony worth a kingdom, and of profiting handsomely as a result.

But, as Arango himself had said in 1791, everything hung by a thread, everything depended on the shaky subservience of enslaved laborers, something few would easily take for granted after 1791. So the survival of their system required violence and repression; it required that the state act quickly at any credible hint of potential subversion. For their part, enslaved men and women continued to labor, imagining other possible worlds in Africa, in Haiti, in the sovereign space of a mountain in eastern Cuba, or even in a new black state to be erected on the remnants of colonial fortresses in Havana. Many among them seemed often to talk of those other worlds, and sometimes that talk begat something further: a more heated conversation, a melancholy that became silence or suicide, a resolute deferral, and occasionally the beginnings of a real plot. Still, every plot uncovered in Cuba in the era and aftermath of the Haitian Revolution failed, and certainly none resulted in the end of slavery. The accused, the plotters, the insurgents were hanged, shot, flogged, and banished. In this, the plots of a post-Haiti Cuba were not that different than the ones discovered before 1791. In Cuba, slavery and colonialism would stand, Haiti notwithstanding.

[111] "Representación ... a las Cortes," in Arango, *Obras*, 2: 47.

The stories told here, however, make clear that they would stand as if haunted, not by the specter of Haiti, but by the possibilities that a real Haiti – with, among other things, a real navy and a real black king – had made urgently thinkable for real people like Aponte or Lisundia, or the creole Francisco Fuertes or the Haitian Estanislao, or the unidentified man held as a slave by Francisco Rodríguez, one of many who claimed his freedom on the basis of revolutionary emancipation in Saint-Domingue, or even the marvelous Ti Noël.

Epilogue

Haiti, Cuba, and History: Antislavery and the Afterlives of Revolution

On Christmas Day 1817, the brig *Dos Unidos*, which also went by the name *Yuyú*, left the port of Cádiz, Spain. By then the project of the Cortes that had convened in that city had been defeated, and Ferdinand VII, whose restoration had been so fervently awaited, had returned to the throne. Almost immediately, he abolished the liberal Constitution of 1812. Sovereignty once more rested exclusively in the person of the king. The Cortes's brief experiment with national sovereignty had not eradicated the practice of trafficking in human beings. So the *Dos Unidos* set sail for the coast of Africa to engage precisely in that trade. Its initial authorization for the journey was signed and dated the same week, and by the same minister, as the treaty with England that obligated Spain to end its slave trade. Neither the treaty nor this particular voyage, however, produced their intended outcome.

Forty-eight days after leaving Cádiz, the *Dos Unidos* arrived at the port of Bonny on the Bight of Biafra. By March 13, 1818, the captain had loaded 297 captive men, women, and children, and five days later, the vessel set sail for Cuba, where, calculated the captain, his human cargo might fetch upwards of one hundred thousand *pesos fuertes*. On the way, however, severe illness among the crew and captives forced a long stop at São Tomé. On April 29, they set sail again, planning to enter Caribbean waters at the passage between the islands of Martinique and Dominica and then make their way northwest to Havana. But on June 17–18, near the port of Les Cayes, Haiti (with only 171 of the original 297 captives still alive on board), a ship named the *Wilberforce* approached and fired. Though the vessel's name was clearly English, the corvette belonged to the Republic of Haiti, one of several similarly named vessels: the *Abolition de la Traite*, the *Philanthrope*. The Haitian captain, his name perhaps hispanized in the Spanish record as Esteban Morete, made his intentions clear: he was taking the *Dos Unidos* to Port-au-Prince, because he had orders from his government – the southern Republic of Haiti – "to detain and seize any vessels carrying shipments of slaves."[1]

The Spanish captain protested, showing papers that he insisted made his journey and his commerce legal. He complained before the Haitian captain, before the Haitian Admiralty Court, before lawyers, and even several times before the president, Jean-Pierre Boyer, who had taken office just three months earlier on the death of Alexandre Pétion. But none of it worked. The captive Africans were disembarked, prompting great joy in the city of Port-au-Prince, and they were baptized, with Boyer serving as godfather to all. The most able men were incorporated into his guard; the rest, together with the women and children, were assigned to the principal families of the city as servants and moral charges. According to Haitian historian Beaubrun Ardouin, most became industrious citizens and small proprietors. "Observe the result of the difference between Liberty and Slavery: in Cuba they would have been but wretched souls bowed under the iron rod of the colonists who purchased them; in Haiti, they became persons useful to society."[2]

The state based its expropriation, said Boyer, on the Haitian Constitution of 1816. According to the Spanish captain, the Haitian officials who refused to return the captives cited multiple articles of the Constitution: Article 1, which stated categorically that there could be no slaves in the territory of the Republic; Article 3, which granted the right of asylum; and Article 44, which stated that all blacks and Indians who set foot on Haitian soil were Haitian, and therefore free. Realizing the futility of his demand for the return of the people, the captain pushed for payment of an indemnity for the value of the captives. But he had apparently overlooked the fact that Haitian officials also invoked Article 2 of the Constitution, which canceled forever all debt contracted for the acquisition of human beings. This clause would have made it impossible for the government of Haiti to "owe" the captain money for the 171 Africans now juridically

---

[1] The chronology of the *Dos Unidos* trip is reconstructed from the testimony of its captain, Juan Manuel de María, in "Bergantín Los Dos Unidos," AGMAB, CP, leg. 5240. See also AHN, Estado, leg. 8020, exp. 5. On the names of the Haitian state vessels, Ardouin, *Etudes sur l'histoire d'Haiti*, 8: 40n5.

[2] On the complaints, see "Bergantín Los Dos Unidos," AGMAB, CP, leg. 5240; on the reception of the vessel and liberated Africans in Port-au-Prince, Ardouin *Etudes sur l'histoire d'Haiti*, 8: 83n4.

free on Haitian soil. Almost a month after the encounter between the *Wilberforce* and the Cuban-bound slaver, Haitian authorities demanded that the captain appear at court on July 14 to bear witness to the unequivocal application of Haitian law and "to hear it declared that these men can never be claimed by those who took them from their country."[3]

A few weeks later the captain quit Haiti, without his vessel, without the captives, and without any idemnification. Authorities in Havana, on order from Madrid, petitioned Boyer for restitution. Andrés de Jaúregui, former representative to the Cortes of Cádiz and staunch opponent of the abolitionist reforms proposed there, was a signatory to some of the appeals. But the Cuban arguments did not stand a chance. Boyer replied, invoking Haitian law, civilization, and common sense. With the vessel clearly in Haiti's jurisdiction, what, he asked, was the Haitian captain to do? "Could he fail to liberate those poor souls held aboard the vessel, when the Constitution of his country solemnly proclaimed that no slavery at all could exist anywhere in the territory of the Republic of Haiti?" The government's actions would stand; no restitution was possible. "The Constitution, which is my north star," explained Boyer, "has not allowed me to do anything other than what I have done."[4]

Though the case of the *Dos Unidos* is little known, it was not exceptional. In 1816 in the kingdom of the north, even without the backing of the republican Constitution, Christophe had seized an American-owned vessel, flying under Portuguese colors, headed to Cuba. The kingdom confiscated the vessel and freed its 145 captives, who were received in Le Cap, said one newspaper, as brothers and compatriots. Before that capture, as early as 1810 Christophe's navy had intercepted at least three Cuban-bound slave ships and liberated the captives on board.[5]

In Pétion's, and later Boyer's, republic, the Constitution of 1816 justified not just the liberation of captive Africans on slavers, but also the granting of asylum to slaves who traveled to Haiti of their own volition. Three months after the publication of the Constitution, seven enslaved sailors in Jamaica commandeered the vessel on which they worked and made for Haiti. When their supposed master showed up to claim them, Pétion himself explained that Article 44 rendered the sailors Haitian upon setting foot in the republic; Article 1, meanwhile, made unambiguously

---

[3] "Bergantín Los Dos Unidos," AGMAB, CP, leg. 5240.
[4] Boyer to Juan María Echeverri, Captain-General of Cuba, January 24, 1821, in AGI, Estado, leg. 12, exp. 2.
[5] The October 1817 case is discussed in Ardouin, *Etudes sur l'histoire d'Haïti*, 8: 296–297. The earlier cases are discussed in Chapter 6.

clear that no slaves could exist in Haitian territory. The fugitives would not be returned, as they were by law free and Haitian. No number of appeals by British masters and officials changed that decision. Indeed, even authorities in London conceded "that the laws of Hayti much resemble those of Great Britain, so far as not to permit persons who have once landed in that island to be considered or treated as slaves."[6]

Shortly after the case of the Jamaican sailors, the crew on a Havana-based slaver named *San Francisco de Paula*, also known as *El Africano*, rose up, commandeered the vessel, and took it to Port-au-Prince. Spanish authorities appealed and petitioned for the return of the vessel and crew, but to no avail. Pétion informed them that the ship had been lawfully condemned by Haiti's Admiralty Court on the basis of "piracy committed at sea by the vessel and the trade in unfortunate Africans, a shameful commerce condemned by civilized nations."[7] In contrast to the cases heard before British Admiralty courts in the same period, there is no known collection of cases heard before their Haitian equivalent. So we cannot know for certain what the judges meant by piracy on the high seas; nor can we learn anything about the crew members who stole away to Haiti just months after the new Constitution promised them citizenship, asylum, and freedom. But one thing at least is clear: the Haitian government publicly brandished antislavery as a standard of civilization, and found Spain wanting.

The fact that in several of these cases the Haitian court based its condemnation of the vessels on their participation in the slave trade is also of supreme importance. The presidents, first Pétion and then Boyer, articulated a daring policy: the Haitian state had the right and authority to condemn ships involved in human trafficking, a trade still legal by the laws of the nation whose ships they had confiscated. No Haitian law stated that right explicitly, yet both men stood by the implication of their nation's free soil principle. And people at the time took note. Indeed, shortly after the publication of the Constitution, privateers were already warning each other to steer clear of Haitian

---

6 The quote is from Henry Goulburn to John Wilson Croker, Esq., Jamaica Assembly, *A Report of a Committee of the Honourable House of Assembly of Jamaica Presented to the House, December 10, 1817* (London, 1818), 53. See Ferrer, "Haiti, Free Soil."

7 Pétion to Pablo Arnaud (agent for ship owner José Matías Acebal), April 8, 1817, quoted in Boyer to Kindelán (governor of Santo Domingo), September 19, 1819, in AGI, Estado, leg. 12, exp. 8. The file contains no reference to captives aboard the vessel, which may suggest that the crew commandeered the vessel en route to the African coast rather than on its way back.

coasts, for "General Pétion will confiscate the Africans in the interest of their liberty, to increase his population, and to develop agriculture in his territory."[8]

Pétion, however, extended the physical reach of Haitian free soil policies well beyond Haitian territorial waters, into the Caribbean and Atlantic seas. He famously provided moral and material assistance to Simón Bolívar in the latter's fight for independence against Spain. That aid, however, was conditional. First, Bolívar had to agree to abolish slavery in the country he liberated from Spain; second, he had to pledge that any captive Africans taken from slave-trading vessels by insurgent privateers would not be sold into slavery. Instead, they would be brought to Haitian territory, where they would be freed. As the slave trade to Spanish and Portuguese territories flourished, and as insurgent seamen plied American waters, there was considerable opportunity to seize human cargo.[9]

When the Spanish captain, and Cuban and Spanish authorities, complained about these captures and condemnations, they too found themselves forced to invoke Haitian law. They cited the Haitian Declaration of Independence, which established the state presided over by a former slave, and they cited the Haitian Constitution of 1816, which promised asylum and freedom to people they were seeking to enslave on Cuban soil. From the first document, they quoted the passage: "Let our neighbors live in peace," and asked that it be observed. From the second, they paraphrased Article 5 (though they mistakenly identified it as 15), which repeated the state's foundational promise "never to trouble the peace and internal order of foreign states or islands."[10] Thus it was that the slaveholding Atlantic confronted Haiti. Cuban slaveholders and traders quoted its foundational documents; a British Minister likened its laws to

[8] ANC, AP, leg. 124, exp. 66.
[9] On Bolívar and Haiti, see Verna, *Pétion y Bolívar*; 337–342; Sibylle Fischer, "Bolívar in Haiti" in Raphael Dalleo, Luis Duno-Gottberg, Carla Calarge, and Clevis Headley, eds., *Haiti and the Americas: Histories, Cultures, Imaginations* (Oxford, MS, forthcoming, 2012); John Lynch, *Simón Bolívar: A Life* (New Haven, Conn.: Yale University Press, 2006), 159–181. On insurgent corsairs and the Haitian Revolution, see Edgardo Pérez Morales, *El gran diablo hecho barco: Corsarios, esclavos y revolución en Cartagena y el Gran Caribe* (Bucaramanga, Colombia: Universidad Industrial de Santander, 2012), chaps. 4–5. See also "Expediente sobre que el Real Consulado de la Habana acredita el apresamiento de 127 embarcaciones mercantes españolas por buques insurgentes, piratas y otros desde el año 1801 hasta el de 1819" in ANC, AP, leg. 8, exp. 39; and Governor of Santiago to Min. de Estado, June 7, 1816 in ANC, AP, leg. 124, exp. 48.
[10] "Bergantín Los Dos Unidos," AGMAB, CP, leg. 5240.

well-regarded English ones. In all these cases, the Haitians' own interpretation prevailed.

The promise of nonintervention in 1804, and again in 1816, did not keep Haitian leaders from projecting their power, voice, and authority in the service of radical antislavery. Haitian law elevated the new nation as a potent example of freedom and citizenship for any black person – no matter his or her location or status – who could make it to Haitian territory. The state's flexibility in defining the limits of that territory, its apparent willingness to offer that asylum and freedom to men and women on slaving vessels headed elsewhere, stretched the reach of Haitian antislavery even further.

Haitian law and its application here represented an engagement with and participation in the major moral and political questions of the Age of Revolution: the fate of slavery, the relationship between rights of property and rights of liberty, and the boundaries of nationality and citizenship. In their engagement with emerging notions of rights, and in their development of real-world policies informed by them, Haitian leaders made these rights something other than what they were originally meant to be. Thus, the abstract right of liberty proclaimed elsewhere was transformed into a concrete prohibition of slavery, including the explicit cancellation of all debt ever contracted for the purchase of human beings (Article 2). The right to property, so fundamental to liberal constitutions, was also proclaimed (Article 10), but in its Haitian instantiation it encompassed the right to the property of one's own person. The sovereign nation, as elsewhere, was imagined as a "space of citizenship in which rights would be accorded and protected." But Articles 10 and 44, and the particular applications they were given, represented a robust redefinition of a space of rights that until then had been essentially national in conception. In Haiti, the space of citizenship – made available to nonwhite and enslaved foreigners – was expressly international, even diasporic. Haitian law thus gave the promise of Haiti's radical antislavery a more robust life and international projection in an age and place where neighboring states remained very much invested in the regime of slavery. Here, then, was a forceful and expansive antislavery position.[11]

However powerful in its enunciation and application, Haiti's postindependence antislavery has historically garnered relatively little attention. The annals of antislavery record, for instance, the famous Somerset case,

---

[11] Ferrer, "Haiti, Free Soil." Quote is from Samuel Moyn, *The Last Utopia: Human Rights in History* (Cambridge, Mass.:Harvard University Press, 2010), 13.

which established free soil in England in 1772, and with which the British minister in 1817 implicitly compared the Haitian Constitution. Individual petitions for freedom on the basis of free soil in England, France, Holland, Spain, and elsewhere are scattered across municipal and national archives in Europe. The papers of the British courts of admiralty and vice-admiralty, which heard hundreds of cases on captured slavers and (after 1808) liberated many a human cargo, comprise a vast, well-known, and widely used repository in the British national archives, with its catalog easily searchable online. Yet nothing comparable exists for Haiti's admiralty courts, which did the same, albeit on a smaller scale.

Perhaps one reason why Haiti's postrevolutionary interventions in an Atlantic politics of slavery and antislavery have been underestimated is that the outcome of that struggle is taken as a foregone conclusion. With England and the United States formally committed to ending the slave trade after 1807–8, and with British naval suppression gaining force, Haitian efforts seem to matter little by comparison. The decisive actors were others, the outcomes of their actions already seemingly inevitable in the long run.

Yet that narrative arc is one that rests on a linear, and predominantly Anglophone, conception of the rise and fall of slavery. In the United States and the British colonies, the end of the slave trade was momentous. A rough count from the beginning of the trade through 1807 yields over 2.2 million captives arriving in the two regions combined. After that, the number dwindles to less than 26,000.[12] Clearly, the abolition of the trade was a watershed.

Using the same temporal parameters for Spanish, Portuguese, and French territories, however, yields a very different picture. Before slave trade abolition in 1807, during the almost 300 years that the trade existed before England's steps against it, close to 3 million African captives had been landed on the shores of Spanish, Portuguese, and French American

---

[12] To 1807, see *Voyages*, http://slavevoyages.org/tast/database/search.faces?yearFrom= 1514&yearTo=1807&mjslptimp=10400.20100.20300.20400.20500.20600.20800 .20900.21000.21100.21200.21300.21400.33200.33400.33500.33600.33700.34200 .35100.35200.35300.35400.35500 and http://slavevoyages.org/tast/database/search .faces?yearFrom=1763&yearTo=1807&mjslptimp=33800.34300.34400. For the period after 1807, see http://slavevoyages.org/tast/database/search.faces?yearFrom=1808 &yearTo=1866&mjslptimp=10400.20100.20300.20400.20500.20600.20800.20900 .21000.21100.21200.21300.21400.21600.33200.33400.33500.33600.33700.33800 .34200.34300.34400.34500.34600.35100.35200.35300.35400.35500.

territory. In the short sixty-year span that followed, however, transatlantic enslavement in those territories claimed another 2.2 million souls.[13]
The impact of England's intervention registers, but in the sheer numbers
of those who continued to be enslaved, it was no watershed. Indeed, in
many of those territories, the pace of arrivals quickened intensively rather
than fading definitively.

In Cuba, Britain's legislation transformed the trade, creating the impetus for the development of a Spanish–Cuban transatlantic slave trade.
But it did little to stem the tide of captive Africans landing on its shores.
Some 92,000 had arrived between the early sixteenth century and 1807.
From 1808 until the end of the trade, however, nearly 609,000 more
would arrive on the island. Writing in 1819, King Christophe confided
to a British abolitionist that it was "only with the greatest grief that [he
could] bear to see Spanish vessels engaged in the slave trade within sights
of [Haitian] coasts."[14] This was what the Atlantic looked like from Haiti.
Indeed, from that vantage point, and even with the British aggressively
extending the reach of their new convictions, reasons for grief were not
visibly abating.

In 1817, under increasing pressure, Spain agreed on paper to end the
slave trade by 1820. The frenzy to capture and import Africans before
the treaty took effect ushered in what Cuban historian Manuel Moreno
Fraginals called the "most tragic era" of the Cuban slave trade. Reports
from the doctors assigned to vaccinate and examine incoming Africans
give a sense of the conditions on board Cuban slavers of this period. In
1818, a ship called *Amistad* (not its subsequent famous namesake) left
the port of Luanda in Angola with 733 Africans; 52 days later, it arrived
in Havana with just 188.[15]

Even after the Anglo-Spanish treaty took effect in 1820, the trade
continued to flourish. It did so illegally, with the violation of the law a

13 *Voyages*, http://slavevoyages.org/tast/database/search.faces?yearFrom=1514&yearTo=
1807&mjslptimp=10100.10200.10700.31100.31200.31300.31400.36100.36200
.36300.36400.36500.40000.50000 and http://slavevoyages.org/tast/database/search
.faces?yearFrom=1808&yearTo=1866&mjslptimp=10100.10200.10700.31100.31200
.31300.31400.36100.36200.36300.36400.36500.40000.50000.
14 *Voyages*, http://slavevoyages.org/tast/database/search.faces?yearFrom=1514&yearTo=
1807&mjslptimp=31300 and http://slavevoyages.org/tast/database/search.faces?
yearFrom=1808&yearTo=1867&mjslptimp=31300. Griggs and Prator, eds., *Henry
Christophe and Thomas Clarkson*, 128, 115–117.
15 Moreno, *El ingenio*, 1: 264; and ANC, RCJF, leg. 150, exp. 7409. The mortality
rate is significantly lower in *Voyages*, http://slavevoyages.org/tast/database/search.faces?
yearFrom=1817&yearTo=1820&shipname=amistad.

foundational feature of its day-to-day operation. As before, slavers continued to arrive at night, but now they employed new layers of deceit. Sometimes they stopped first in Puerto Rico, where there was less vigilance. There they might obtain a passport to make it seem that the captives on board had been purchased in another Spanish territory rather than on the now-prohibited African coast. Another common ruse was to arrive and disembark slaves outside Havana on some stretch of deserted coast, and then march the Africans into Havana in broad daylight as if they were the slave force of a sugar mill "in liquidation." Such subterfuges would not have worked if authorities had pressed even minimally, but they rarely did. In Cuba, the protection of the illegal slave trade became a key function of the colonial state, shaping the local practices of rule.[16]

In the 1830s, the Cuban slave trade received another major impetus with the construction of the first railroad in Cuba, built expressly to meet the needs of the sugar industry and to enable rapid transport of sugar cane to mills and of processed sugar to ports. With the capacity to open more and more land to new sugar production, the slave trade to Cuba underwent another violent period of growth. It was not until the late 1860s, sixty years after British slave trade abolition, that the journeys of enslaved Africans to Cuban coasts ended.

Viewing slave trade abolition from Havana confirms the insufficiency of examining such events from a purely national or imperial focus. The 1807–8 laws may have ended the importation of Africans to British or U.S. territory, but they did not spell the death knell of the trade more generally. Like the Haitian Revolution, the legislation of 1807 represented a major assault on slavery. Part of its effect, however, was the emergence of new actors and new zones of slavery and the slave trade.

Seen in this light, the 1807 watershed appears as a very partial one. If 1807 marks the end of an era – the one by which the fate of slavery was definitively sealed – then the actions of post-revolutionary Haiti might seem to matter little. If, on the other hand, we understand 1807 and its aftermath as less than universal in implication, then the slavery that continued as a major force in much of the hemisphere matters more. In this light, the law and policy of antislavery that emerged in Haiti after 1804 take on a far greater importance. The actions of the Haitian government – its decrees and constitutions, its naval actions, its overtures

---

[16] Ferrer, "Cuban Slavery and Atlantic Antislavery."

to foreign governments and merchants, its welcome of enslaved fugitives
or mariners, its liberation of the men and women in the holds of slave
ships – were not a footnote to the European antislavery embodied in the
British and American slave trade bans of 1807–8 or in the British naval
campaign against the trade. They were rather an insistent, largely legal
and peaceful attack on the continued power of slavery all around them.
Early Haitian governments did not become firebrands mobilizing armed
revolution among the enslaved elsewhere. But that should not be our only
measure of importance.

After 1804, Haiti stood not only as a symbol of liberty, but literally
as free soil – a place in which freedom, enshrined in the law, could be
real for black persons in their own lifetimes. Whether the people in question were enslaved fugitive sailors from Jamaica or hundreds of Africans
held captive on a vessel about to deliver them as slaves, their freedom
now found institutional and philosophical support in the constitution
of a sovereign and antislavery black state. That state elaborated laws
and pursued policies that reworked and reimagined notions of property,
territory, freedom, and citizenship. Far from being a backward-looking,
"restorationist" polity, the Haitian state engaged the weighty questions
of its age and projected a powerful antislavery that reached beyond its
borders.[17] In a world in which slavery and colonialism held powerful
sway, Haitian leaders crafted political and intellectual positions designed
to extend the promise of radical antislavery despite the very real con-
straints imposed upon them by the refusal of political recognition from
neighboring states and by the continued power of slavery in the region.

If Haiti became the epicenter of Black Atlantic freedom after 1804, Cuba
became its antithesis. The destruction of Saint-Domingue's plantation
world and the eventual rise of a peasant one on the same ground facili-
tated the hegemony of slavery, sugar, and the plantation on the neighboring island. Eager to preserve the privileges won with Saint-Domingue's
collapse and confronted with the fact of Haitian independence, authorities and planters in Cuba mobilized images of racial apocalypse to suppress any threat to their power. Such arguments predominated in the
nineteenth century, becoming one of Spain's standard defenses against
the rise of Cuban nationalism in the decades following Latin American
independence. Cuba, said authorities, would be Spanish, or it would be

[17] Eugene Genovese characterized the postrevolutionary Haitian state as backward-looking
and "restorationist." See *From Rebellion to Revolution.*

African or Haitian. Part of the afterlife of the Haitian Revolution in Cuba then was the ever-useful specter of "another Haiti."[18]

But there were many and arguably more important Haitis than that spectral and reactionary invocation. One of those other afterlives of the Haitian Revolution dwelt not in the planters' nightmare, but in the Haiti conjured in the conversations of slaves, who spoke of a place where their counterparts had taken the land and become masters of themselves. We have glimpsed that Haiti in these pages. It was the Haiti imagined by enslaved workers in Puerto Príncipe in 1795, and Bayamo in 1805, and Guara in 1806, as they plotted to make Haitian freedom their own reality on their own ground. It was the Haiti imagined by José Antonio Aponte and his companions when they looked at images of Henri Christophe and Prester John and plotted to create their own black kingdom in a Cuba without slavery. Of course, imagining a future in Haiti's image was only in part about Haiti itself. It was also about their own world in that moment and place – whether that world was a dock teeming with revolutionary news and slavers unloading Africans, or a plantation where dozens or hundreds of enslaved people made sugar, grew provisions, and negotiated daily the burdens of their servitude and the lure of other futures.[19]

At the same time, the Haiti imagined in Cuba by enslaved and free people of color was also forged out of movement back and forth between the two places, and by the actions of enslaved people from former Saint-Domingue, of black sailors and soldiers of the revolution, and of a new Haitian state that publicized its message of freedom beyond its borders. There was then a subterranean – or, to use Kamau Brathwaite's term, submarine – Haiti that materialized out of encounters between real people and that nourished imaginings of further encounters and exchanges. This too was an afterlife of the Haitian Revolution, one that served as an anchor of solidarities not just during the revolution but for a long time after.[20]

[18] Elsewhere I have examined the ways that specter was mobilized by the Spanish colonial state and its allies, and challenged by a powerful independence movement and armed insurgency; see Ada Ferrer, *Insurgent Cuba: Race, Nation, and Revolution, 1868–1898* (Chapel Hill: University of North Carolina Press, 1999).

[19] The phrase "burden of their servitude" is taken from the testimony of Saint-Domingue-born Estanislao, accused of conspiring against slavery in Cuba in 1806. "Expediente criminal contra Francisco Fuertes y demás negros...sobre levantamiento en el pueblo de Güines, 6 Mayo de 1806," in ANC, Asuntos Políticos, leg. 9, exp. 27.

[20] Kamau Brathwaite quoted in Lara Putnam, "To Study the Fragments/Whole: Microhistory and the Atlantic World." *Journal of Social History*, 39, 3 (2006): 615.

This Haiti existed in the messages spread by a black Baracoa sailor in 1823, who told others of his class of the system erected in the Haiti he had just visited; or in the Haitian flag placed on a Spanish government building in Puerto Príncipe in 1842, or in the well-worn Haitian newspapers that authorities warned were circulating in Cuba that same year. It existed, perhaps, in many whispered conversations aboard the steamships that began offering regular service between Santiago, Kingston, and Port-au-Prince in 1863, and in the plotting of enslaved people – for slavery still existed then in Cuba and Puerto Rico – who absconded to Haiti aboard them and other vessels. Haiti might have enjoyed a special place in the memories and dreams of enslaved conspirators in El Cobre in 1864, who, when questioned by authorities, testified in the only language they said they spoke, Haitian Kreyòl.[21]

The launching of an armed independence movement in Cuba in 1868 gave new meaning to potential solidarities with Haiti. The Haitian government gave refuge to insurgents and their agents, and rural Cubans sang verses praising Haitian independence.[22] It was this Haiti that attracted men and women working to end Spain's rule in Cuba. Antonio Maceo, the famed mulatto general of the Cuban wars of independence, made several important trips there between the wars. Before that, in March 1878 at the end of the first war, he publicly explained his refusal to surrender to Spain by invoking Haiti: "With our policy of granting liberty to the slaves . . . we should form a new republic assimilated to our sister of Santo Domingo and Haiti."[23] It was this Haiti, not the Spaniards' or the planters' specter, that José Martí remembered when he wrote in his diary of his visit to hinterlands of old Fort-Dauphin (Bayajá) and mentioned a young man who refused payment for having helped him and instead requested the book in Martí's pocket, the second scientific compendium of French zoologist Paul Bert. Martí invoked this Haiti before a large audience in New York when "he spoke at length about the books and the men of Haiti, which has men and books." And it was surely this Haiti that he had in mind during his meetings with Haitian intellectuals such as Anténor

---

21 The 1823 story appears in ANC, AP, leg. 113, exp. 104; 1842: in ANC, AP, leg. 137, exp. 17, and AHN, Ultramar, leg. 4614, exp. 11; 1863: AHN, Ultramar, leg. 4686, exp. 104, and leg. 4714, exp., 43.

22 AHN, Ultramar, leg. 4750, exp. 5; and Ferrer, *Insurgent Cuba*, 107.

23 Antonio Maceo, "A los habitantes del Departamento Oriental," March 25, 1878, in Antonio Maceo, *Ideología Política: Cartas y otros documentos* (Havana: SCEHI, 1950), 1: 101–102.

Firmin, statesman and author of *De l'égalité des races humaines*, one of the most important treatises against racism of its age.[24]

As in politics, so too in literature and art was Haiti at the center of international effervescence around questions of culture, race, and sovereignty. To catalogue or do justice to that Haiti here would be impossible. Still, it is worth momentarily peering forward to glimpse it. Writing shortly after the January 2010 earthquake, Jamaican historian Matthew Smith painted a vivid picture of mid-century Port-au-Prince, a "centrifuge of a black literary world" that welcomed some of the most important intellectual and cultural figures of the time: Langston Hughes, Aimé Césaire, W.E.B. DuBois, André Breton, Zora Neal Hurston, Katherine Dunham, among many others.[25] Some of the most important figures of Cuban culture visited then as well: Teodoro Ramos Blanco, Roberto Diago, Wifredo Lam, Nicolás Guillén, Alejo Carpentier. Black poet Nicolás Guillén spent time there in 1942, traveling, in part, as the representative of Cuba's Anti-Fascist National Front.[26] Wifredo Lam, one of Cuba's most important painters of mid-century, also spent time there in the 1940s. Lam's *Haitian Jungle* serves as an emblem – beautiful and lasting – of the vibrant and historic link between the two places. Later in life, Wifredo Lam talked about returning to Cuba after spending time in Paris and about encountering Haiti and his own sense of history and belonging as a black man. He mused about his role: "I could act as a Trojan horse that would spew forth hallucinating figures with the power to surprise, to disturb the dreams of the exploiters." His painting, full of surprising figures, evokes Bois Caïman, the mythic-historic place of origin for Black Atlantic revolution (Figure E.1).[27]

This, then, was another Haiti, not the specter of Spanish governors or Cuban planters. It was a Haiti also imagined, but for a different purpose. This was, as Matthew Smith suggests, the Caribbean's

---

[24] On Martí's time in Haiti, see José Martí, "Diario de Montecristi a Cabo Haitiano," in *Obras Completas* (Havana: Editorial Ciencias Sociales, 1975), 9: 198–199; and Martí quoted in Herbert Ramiro Pérez Concepción, "Haití en José Martí," *Ciencia en su PC*, 4 (2010): 61–72.

[25] Matthew Smith, "Port-au-Prince, I Love You," in *Haiti Rising: Haitian History, Culture, and the Earthquake of 2010* (Liverpool: Liverpool University Press, 2010), 186–194, quote at 190.

[26] Emilio Jorge Rodríguez, *Haiti and Trans-Caribbean Literary Identity* (Philipsburg, Saint-Martin: Jouse of Nehesi Publishers, 2011), 77–88.

[27] Max-Pol Fouchet, *Wifredo Lam* (Barcelona: Ediciones Polígrafa, 1976), quote is at 188–189; on his visit to Haiti, see Helena Benítez, *Wilfredo and Helena: My Life with Wifredo Lam* (Lausanne: Acatos, 1999), 127–145.

FIGURE E.1. Wifredo Lam, *Haitian Jungle*, 1945. © 2014 Artists Rights Society (ARS), New York / ADAGP, Paris. Photo courtesy of Eskil Lam.

Haiti, a Black Atlantic Haiti. And for those who challenged colonial or slaveholding power in the nineteenth century, or those who challenged the sway of empire and racism in the twentieth, in politics as in culture, this Haiti was a potent ally and vital inspiration.

Another visitor to Haiti in this period was Alejo Carpentier, who would later become Cuba's most famous novelist. Inspired by his visit in 1943, Carpentier wrote one of the most important novels about the Haitian Revolution, *The Kingdom of This World* (1949). In an article that figured as the preface to the novel's second edition, Carpentier coined the term *real maravilloso*, the marvelous real, to call for a literary technique capable of matching the extraordinary dimensions of New World history. Pushing against the exoticism of surrealism, rooted in layers of local history, steeped in lived faith, the *real maravilloso* was at once marvelous *and* real; it emerged from "an unusual illumination . . . of the inadvertent riches of reality." Lam's paintings, Carpentier said, captured it perfectly.[28] And he and Lam, both from Cuba, experienced this historical, aesthetic, and humanistic revelation in a Haiti that continued to offer subjects and visions for a mid-twentieth-century Caribbean.

The notion of the marvelous real emerged for Carpentier, he explained, as he walked in the ruins of the kingdom of Henri Christophe, "monarch of incredible undertakings, much more surprising than all the cruel kings invented by the surrealists, so fond of tyrannies imagined but never suffered."[29] It was there perhaps that Carpentier first envisioned Ti Noël, the main character in *The Kingdom of This World*. Not a Toussaint, not a Dessalines, nor even a Christophe, this Ti Noël is an ordinary man, held as a slave alongside the legendary Mackandal – maroon, vodou priest, rebel whose spirit, according to legend, flew off freely just as French authorities were burning his body at the stake.

Carpentier's Ti Noël, like Mackandal, is also a rebel. He is a congregant at the ceremony of Bois Caïman and an insurgent from the first day of the revolution. Captured and ready to be hanged, he is spared by his master, who takes him to Santiago de Cuba, where he says the Spanish churches have a vodou warmth. After Haitian independence, Ti Noël returns to Haiti. There, in Christophe's northern kingdom, he is put to work on a palace under construction, carrying brick after heavy brick, laboring to avoid a thrashing. In 1820, he becomes a ringleader in the rebellion against Christophe that triggered the king's suicide. Later, from the ruins of his old master's plantation, Ti Noël watches as mulatto men arrive, commanding hundreds of black prisoners as they clear and plow the earth. "Mackandal had not foreseen this matter of forced labor,"

[28] Alejo Carpentier, "De lo real maravilloso americano" (1967), at http://www.literatura.us/alejo/deloreal.html.
[29] Ibid.

writes Carpentier. "Nor had Boukman, the Jamaican. The ascendancy of
the mulattoes was something new that had not occured to José Antonio
Aponte, beheaded by the Marqués de Someruelos, whose record of rebellion Ti Noël had learned of during his slave days in Cuba." Exhausted,
Ti Noël then does as Mackandal had done: he changes forms, becoming
a bee, a stallion, a wasp, a goose, and finally an old man again. A few
pages later, at the very end of the novel, a marvelous wind carries everything away. "From that moment Ti Noël was never seen again, nor his
green coat with the salmon lace cuffs, except perhaps by that wet vul-
ture . . . who sat with outspread wings, drying himself in the sun, a cross
of feathers which finally folded itself up and flew off into the thick shade
of Bois Caïman."[30]

There is perhaps an unwitting affinity between Carpentier's Ti Noël
(believed by some to have been based on a real person) and the unwritten
characters that C.L.R. James imagined as the rightful protagonists of a
Black Jacobins he never wrote. In 1971, speaking at the Institute of the
Black World in Atlanta, James pondered aloud what his monumental
book might look like if he had the chance to write it again in the present.
He suggested that the book he would have wanted to write in 1971 was
present implicitly in his already existing book, buried in the footnotes and
evident in his choice of original quotes. He shared some of those with his
audience. He read aloud from a Georges Lefebvre quote in a footnote:
"as in all the decisive days of the revolution: what we most would like to
know is forever out of our reach; we would like to have the diary of the
most obscure of these popular leaders; we would then be able to grasp,
in the act so to speak, how one of these great revolutionary days began;
we do not have it." James quoted Pamphile de Lacroix: "It was not the
avowed chiefs who gave the signals for revolt but obscure creatures."
He quoted General Leclerc, who wrote shortly after Toussaint's arrest in
1802: "*It is not enough to have taken away Toussaint; there are 2,000
leaders to be taken away.*" And then James made his point: "You see, in
1971 . . . I am concerned with the two thousand leaders who were there.
That is the book I would write."[31] He would write, in other words, not
Toussaint's book, or only Toussaint's book, but a book about the many
people left largely unnamed.

---

[30] Carpentier, *Kingdom of this World*, 176–177, 186.

[31] James, *Black Jacobins*, 338n, and C.L.R. James, "How I Would Rewrite *The Black
Jacobins.*" *Small Axe*, 8 (September 2000): 106–108. Emphasis in original.

Writing that book would allow him to tell a different history of revolution. That interest was already there in 1963, when he published the revised edition of the book.[32] But in 1971, he elaborated, confessing that the things he had confined to the quotes or footnotes of the book – the brief discussions of conflicts between leaders and rank and file, the latter almost always ahead of the former – were in fact the heart of the matter. James recalled the popular rebellions against Toussaint's labor regime (Ti Noël might have recalled the one against Christophe's, which he helped lead); he invoked "the black slaves in W.E.B. Du Bois's *Black Reconstruction* [who] were the ones who saw what should happen." Indeed, it was in reading that book, he said, that he "began to understand that this was a genuine historic part of every revolution."[33] James referred here not to some discreet "counterrevolution" nor even to some internal "betrayal" of revolution, but to a critical conflict at its core, comprehensible only if our lens takes in the history of revolutionaries like Ti Noël, alongside that of men like Toussaint.

James's lecture – like Ti Noël's subjugation to a forced labor regime unforeseen by the people who made the Haitian Revolution – raises important questions about the afterlives of revolution in Haiti itself. The Haiti imagined in Cuba (or Jamaica, or Charleston, or New Orleans, or Bahia), this Caribbean or Black Atlantic, this Haiti of liberation figurative and literal – was this also Haiti's Haiti?

The power and conviction of Haitian leaders' commitment to antislavery is without question, but as Michel-Rolph Trouillot and others have commented, the liberty to which they were committed did not always coincide with the liberty imagined by the people of Haiti. The Constitiution offered freedom and protection to enslaved foreigners, but other policies made it difficult for free workers to leave their place of work, or to avoid the demands of forced labor on public works, or of what scholars have identified as the "militarized agriculture" of early postcolonial Haiti, or later of the state's increasingly aggressive extractions in what Trouillot characterized as the "republic for the merchants." Many Haitians responded by becoming part of a counterplantation society,

---

[32] See David Scott's analysis of the ways in which the differences between the 1938 and 1963 editions of the book reflect a profound transformation in the structure of the book from romance to tragedy. *Conscripts of Modernity: The Tragedy of Colonial Enlightenment* (Durham: Duke University Press, 2004).

[33] C.L.R. James, "How I Would Write the *Black Jacobins* Today," 104–105. He was referring specifically to Dubois's *Black Reconstruction*.

building vibrant rural networks of cultivation and marketing that carved out spaces outside the purview of the state. Of course, these dilemmas around labor and autonomy in Haiti – the first postslavery nation in the modern world – had much in common with the problems faced in every subsequent postemancipation society.[34]

The Haitian state developed law and policy – including an antislavery foreign policy – with intellectual weight and political consequence. But the power of Haiti beyond its own borders was also more than a matter of state. It depended on black and brown people, enslaved and free, who assumed its challenges and victories as their own. They spoke about Haiti, used it to think about their own freedom and standing, and sometimes appointed themselves deputies of a project they imagined as shared. Many died or were hanged as a result.

Yet that Haiti – the one envisioned by Francisco Fuertes in Guara in 1806 or José Antonio Aponte in Havana in 1812 or a Jamaican sailor named Jem in 1817 or countless others whose names we do not know – did not always map easily onto the Haiti developing inside its own borders, onto the Haiti where Ti Noël labored, fought, and finally disappeared from view. Revolution abroad is not always the same thing as revolution at home. The story of how new forms of domination emerge out of a process of revolution is, however, another one. Indeed, it is the central question of Haiti's history in the nineteenth century, and of Cuba's in the twentieth.

---

[34] Michel-Rolph Trouillot, *Haiti, State against Nation: Origins and Legacy of Duvalierism* (New York, 1990); Sidney Mintz, *Three Ancient Colonies* (Cambridge: Harvard University Press, 2012), chap. 2; and Dmitri Prieto Samsónov, *Transdominación en Haití (1791–1826)* (Havana: Pinos Nuevos, 2010).

Bibliography

Archives

Cuba

Archivo Nacional de Cuba, Havana (ANC)
  Administración General Terrestre (AGT)
  Asuntos Políticos (AP)
  Comisión Militar (CM)
  Correspondencia de Capitanes Generales (CCG)
  Escribanías, Guerra
  Gobierno General (GG)
  Intendencia
  Reales Ordenes y Cédulas (RO)
  Real Consulado y Junta de Fomento (RCJF)
Archivo Histórico Provincial de Santiago de Cuba (AHPSC)
  Escribanía del Cabildo
  Escribanía de Raúl Manuel Caminero Ferrer
  Gobierno
  Juzgado de Primera Instancia
Archivo Histórico Municipal de Santiago de Cuba (AHMSC)
  Actas Capitulares
Archivo Histórico Provincial, Camagüey (AHPC)
  Fondo Ayuntamiento, Actas Capitulares
Archivo Histórico de la Oficina del Historiador de la Ciudad de la Habana
  (AHOHCH)
  Actas Capitulares (AC)
Biblioteca Nacional José Martí (BNJM)
  Colección Manuscrita (CM) Arango
  CM Morales
  CM Arredondo

Spain

Archivo Histórico Nacional, Madrid (AHN)
    Consejos
    Estado
    Ultramar
Archivo General de Indias, Seville (AGI)
    Arribadas
    Estado
    Indiferente General (IG)
    Mapas y Planos, Santo Domingo (MPSD)
    Papeles de Cuba (Cuba)
    Santo Domingo (SD)
    Ultramar
Archivo General de Simancas, Simancas (AGS)
    Secretaría y Despacho de Guerra (SGU)
Archivo General Militar, Segovia (AGMS)
    Expedientes Personales (EP)
Archivo del Museo Naval, Madrid (AMN)
    Guillén
    Campaña de Brest
    Departamento de Cartagena
Archivo del Ministerio de Asuntos Exteriores, Madrid (AMAE)
    Politica Exterior, Santo Domingo
    Política Exterior, Haiti
Archivo General de la Marina Álvaro Bazán, Viso del Marqués (AGMAB)
    Expediciones de América (EA)
    Corso y Presas (CP)
    Buques
Sección Nobleza del Archivo Histórico Nacional, Toledo (SN-AHN)
    Condes de Almodóvar
    Marqueses de Someruelos
Servicio Histórico Militar, Madrid (SHMM)
    Colección General de Documentos (CDG)
    Historiales de Regimientos
    Ultramar (Santo Domingo)

Haiti

Bibliothèque Haïtienne des Pères du Saint Esprit
    Séances du Sénat, Republic of Haiti, 1807

France

Service Historique de la Défense, Armée de Terre, Vincennes (SHD-DAT)
    2YE (Dossiers de personnel des officiers supérieurs et subalternes)
    B7/12 and 13 (Armée de Saint-Domingue, Affaires administratives)

Archives Nationales de France, Paris (CARAN)
416 AP 1 (Fonds Hector Daure)
DXXV (Comité des colonies, Îles sous le Vent et Saint-Domingue) 39

England

The National Archives, Kew (TNA)
Admiralty (ADM)
Colonial Office, (CO)
137 (Jamaica)
295 (Trinidad)
Foreign Office (FO)
High Court of Admiralty (HCA)
War Office (WO)

United States

Harvard University, Houghton Library
Escoto Collection
Hispanic Society of America New York
Cuban and Haitian Collection
South Carolina Historical Society, Charleston
Barbot Family Papers
Saint Michael's Church Records
University of Florida Library, Manuscripts and Archives Division, Gainesville
Rochambeau Papers

Newspapers

Cuba

Diario de la Habana
Memorias de la Real Sociedad Patriótica
Papel Periódico de la Habana

France

Journal des débats

Saint-Domingue/Haiti

Gazette Politique et Commerciale d'Haïti

Spain

Diario de Sesiones de las Cortes (Cádiz)
Espíritu de los Mejores Diarios que se Publican en Europa (Madrid)
Gaceta de Madrid (GM)
Semanario Patriótico (Cádiz)

United States

Alexandria Advertiser
Aurora General Advertiser (Philadelphia)
The Balance and Columbian Repository (Hudson, NY)
Charleston Courrier
Commercial Advertiser (New York)
Connecticut Herald
Daily Advertiser (New York)
Evening Post (New York)
Mercantile Advertiser (New York)
Philadelphia Evening Post
Poulson's Daily Advertiser (Philadelphia)
United States Gazette (Philadelphia)

Databases

Voyages: The Trans-Atlantic Slave Trade Database (Voyages) (http://www
.slavevoyages.org/)

Books, Articles, Dissertations

Adelman, Jeremy. *Sovereignty and Revolution in the Iberian Atlantic*. Princeton,
N.J.: Princeton University Press, 2006.
Aimes, Hubert. *A History of Slavery in Cuba, 1511 to 1868*. New York: G.P.
Putnam's Sons, 1907.
Álvarez Estévez, Rolando. *Huellas francesas en el Occidente de Cuba: siglos
XVI–XIX*. Havana: Ediciones Boloña, 2001.
Anstey, Roger. *The Atlantic Slave Trade and British Abolition, 1760–1810*.
Atlantic Highlands, N.J.: Humanities Press, 1975.
Aptheker, Herbert. *American Negro Slave Revolts*. New York: International Publishers Co., 1993 [1943].
Arango y Parreño, Francisco. *Obras*. Havana: Imagen Contemporánea, 2005.
Ardouin, Beaubrun. *Etudes sur l'histoire d'Haïti, suivies de la vie du général J.-M.
Borgella*. 11 volumes. Port-au-Prince: Dr. François Dalencour, 1958 [1853].
Artola, Miguel. "Los afrancesados y América." *Revista de Indias*, 15 (1949):
541–567.
Auguste, Claude Bonaparte, and Marcel Bonaparte Auguste. *L'Expédition
Leclerc, 1801–1803*. Port-au-Prince: Impr. H. Deschamps, 1985.
Azanza, Miguel José de and Gonzalo O'Farrill. *Memoria de D. Miguel José de
Azanza y D. Gonzalo O'Farrill, sobre los hechos que justifican su conducta
política. Desde marzo de 1808 hasta abril de 1814*. Paris: Impr. De P.-N.
Rougeron, 1815.
Baralt, Guillermo. *Esclavos rebeldes: conspiraciones y sublevaciones de esclavos
en Puerto Rico (1795–1873)*. Rio Piedras: Ediciones Huracán, 1982.
Barcia, María del Carmen. *Los ilustres apellidos: negros en la Habana colonial*.
Havana: Editorial de Ciencias Sociales, 2009.

————. "Influencias multiples: Cuba y la revolución haitiana." *Revista de la Universidad de la Habana*, 237, 1990.

————. "Los Batallones de Pardos y Morenos en Cuba (1600–1868). *Anales de Desclasificación*, 1, 2 (2006): 2–3.

————. "Otra vuelta de tuerca a la conspiración de Román de la Luz y los avatares de Joaquín Infante." Published online at http://www.academiahistoria.cu/index.php/Bitacora/Discursos-de-entrada-de-los-Academicos/Otra-vuelta-de-tuerca-a-la-conspiracion-de-Roman-de-la-Luz-y-a-los-avatares-de-Joaquin-Infante.

Barcia Paz, Manuel. *Con el látigo de la ira: Legislación, represión y control en las plantaciones cubanas, 1790–1870*. Havana: Editorial de Ciencias Sociales, 2000.

————. *Seeds of Insurrection: Domination and Resistance on Western Cuban Plantations, 1808–1848*. Baton Rouge: Louisiana State University Press, 2008.

————. *The Great African Slave Revolt of 1825*. Baton Rouge: Louisiana State University Press, 2012.

Barrett, Leonard. *The Rastafarians: Sounds of Cultural Dissonance*. Boston: Beacon Press, 1977.

Barthélemy, Gérard, and Christian Girault, eds. *La République haïtienne: Etat des lieux et perspectives*. Paris: Karthala, 1993.

Belaubre, Christophe, Jordana Dym, and John Savage. *Napoleon's Atlantic: The Impact of Napoleonic Empire in the Atlantic World*. Leiden: Brill, 2010.

Belcher, Wendy Laura. *Abyssinia's Samuel Johnson: Ethiopian Thought in the Making of an English Author*. Oxford: Oxford University Press, 2012.

Bell, Madison Smartt. *Master of the Crossroads*. New York: Pantheon, 2000.

————. *The Stone the Builder Refused*. New York: Pantheon, 2004.

Belmonte Postigo, Jose Luis. "El impacto de liberalización de la trata negrera en Santiago de Cuba." *Tiempos de América* (Castellón), 14 (2007), 35–47.

————. "Brazos para el azúcar, esclavos para vender. Estrategias de comercialización en la trata negrera en Santiago de Cuba, 1789–1794." *Revista de Indias*, 70, 249 (2010): 445–468.

————. *Ser esclavo en Santiago de Cuba: Espacios de poder y negociación en un contexto de expansión y crisis, 1780–1803*. Aranjuez: Doce Calles, 2011.

Benítez, Helena. *Wifredo and Helena: My Life with Wifredo Lam*. Lausanne: Acatos, 1999.

Bénot, Yves and Marcel Dorigny. *Le démence coloniale sous Napoléon*. Paris: La Découverte, 1988.

Benton, Lauren. *A Search for Sovereignty: Law and Geography in European Empires, 1400–1900*. New York: Cambridge University Press, 2010.

Berenguer Cala, Jorge. *La emigración francesa en la jurisdicción de Cuba*. Santiago de Cuba: Editorial Oriente, 1979.

Bergad, Laird, Fe Iglesias García, and María del Carmen Barcia, *The Cuban Slave Market, 1790–1880*. Cambridge: Cambridge University Press, 1995.

Blackburn, Robin. *The Overthrow of Colonial Slavery: 1776–1848*. New York: Verso, 2000 [1988].

————. *American Crucible: Slavery, Emancipation and Human Rights*. New York: Verso, 2011.

_____. "Haiti, Slavery, and the Age of Democratic Revolution." *William and Mary Quarterly*, 63, 4 (2006): 643–674.

Bogues, Anthony. "And What About the Human? Freedom, Human Emancipation, and the Radical Imagination." *Boundary* 2, 39, 3 (2012): 29–46.

Boisrond-Tonnerre, Louis Félix. *Mémoires pour servir à l'histoire d'Haïti*. Paris: France, Librarie, 1851.

Bolster, Jeffrey. *Black Jacks: African American Seamen in the Age of Sail*. Cambridge, Mass.: Harvard University Press, 1997.

Bonnet, Guy-Joseph. *Souvenirs historiques de Guy-Joseph Bonnet, général de division des armées de la République d'Haïti, ancien aide de camp de Rigaud. Documents relatifs à toutes les phases de la révolution de Saint-Domingue, recueillis et mis en ordre par Edmond Bonnet*. Paris: Auguste Durande, 1864.

Buck-Morss, Susan. *Hegel, Haiti, and Universal History*. Pittsburgh, Penn.: University of Pittsburgh Press, 2009.

Calcagno, Francisco. *Diccionario biográfico Cubano*. New York: N. Ponce de León, 1878.

Callejas, José María. *Historia de Santiago de Cuba*. Havana: La Universal, 1911.

Carpentier, Alejo. "De lo real maravilloso," 1967. Available online at http://www.literatura.us/alejo/deloreal.html.

_____. *El reino de este mundo*. Madrid: Alianza Editorial, 2004 [1949].

Carrera Montero, Fernando. *Las complejas relaciones de España con la Española: El Caribe hispano frente a Santo Domingo y Saint Domingue, 1789–1803*. Santo Domingo: Fundación García Arévalo, 2004.

Casimir, Jean. *Pa Bliye 1804 = Souviens-toi de 1804*. Port-au-Prince: Impr. Lakay, 2004.

Childs, Gregory. "Seditious Spaces: The 1798 Tailor's Conspiracy and the Public Politics of Freedom in Bahia, Brazil," manuscript in progress.

Childs, Matt D. "'A Black French General Arrived to Conquer the Island': Images of the Haitian Revolution in Cuba's 1812 Aponte Rebellion." In *The Impact of the Haitian Revolution in the Atlantic World*, edited by David Geggus, 135–156. Columbia: University of South Carolina Press, 2001.

_____. *The 1812 Aponte Rebellion in Cuba and the Struggle Against Atlantic Slavery*. Chapel Hill: University of North Carolina Press, 2006.

_____. "'The Revolution against the French': Race and Patriotism in the 1809 Riot in Havana." In, *Napoleon's Atlantic: The Impact of Napoleonic Empire in the Atlantic World, edited by* Christophe Belaubre, et al., 119–138. Leiden: Brill, 2010.

Chust Calero, Manuel. *América en las Cortes de Cádiz*. Madrid: Doce Calles, 2010.

Coatsworth, John. "American Trade with European Colonies in the Caribbean, 1790–1812." *William & Mary Quarterly*, 24 (1967).

Coradin, Jean. *Histoire diplomatique d'Haïti, 1804–1843*. Port-au-Prince: Édition des Antilles, 1988.

Cordero Michel, Emilio. "Dessalines en Saint-Domingue Espagnol." In *Saint-Domingue espagnol et la révolution nègre d'Haïti*, edited by Alain Yacou, 251–257. Paris: Éditions Karthala, 2007.

Córdova-Bello, Eleazar. *La independencia de Haití y su influencia en Hispanoamérica*. Caracas: Instituto Panamericano de Geografía e Historia, 1967.

Cornide, Teresa. *De la Habana, de siglos y de familias*. Havana: Editorial de Ciencias Sociales, 2003.

Cortes de Cádiz. *Colección de los decretos y órdenes de las Cortes Generales y Extraordinarias en 24 de septiembre 1810 hasta igual fecha en 1811*. Cádiz: Imprenta Real, 1811.

Craton, Michael. *Testing the Chains: Resistance to Slavery in the British West Indies*. Ithaca, N.Y.: Cornell University Press, 1982.

Cruz Ríos, Laura. *Flujos migratorios franceses a Santiago de Cuba (1800–1868)*. Santiago de Cuba: Editorial Oriente, 2006.

Cuba, Archivo Nacional. *Catálogo de los fondos del Real Consulado de Agricultura, Industria y Comercio y de la Junta de Fomento*. Havana: Siglo XX, 1943.

Davis, David B. *The Problem of Slavery in the Age of Revolution, 1770–1823*. Ithaca, N.Y.: Cornell University Press, 1999 [1975].

————. *Inhuman Bondage: The Rise and Fall of Slavery in the New World*. New York: Oxford University Press, 2006.

Debien, Gabriel. "Les colons de Saint-Domingue réfugiés à Cuba." *Revista de Indias*, 1 (1953): 559–605.

————. *Les colons de Saint-Domingue passés à la Jamaïque: 1792–1835*. Basse-Terre, Guadeloupe: Archives Départementales, 1975.

Deive, Carlos Esteban. *Las emigraciones dominicanas a Cuba (1795–1808)*. Santo Domingo: Fundación Cultural Dominicana, 1989.

Del Monte y Tejada, Antonio. *Historia de Santo Domingo*. 4 vols. Santo Domingo: Imprenta de García Hermanos, 1890–92.

Demostración de la lealtad española: colección de proclamas, bandos, órdenes, discursos, estados de exército . . . : publicadas por las juntas de gobierno, ó por algunos particulares en las actuales circunstancias. Madrid: Imprenta Repullés, 1808.

Deschamps Chapeaux, Pedro. *Los batallones de pardos y morenos libres*. Havana: Editorial Arte y Literatura, Instituto Cubano del Libro, 1976.

Dessalines, Jean-Jacques. *Lois et actes sous le règne de Jean-Jacques Dessalines*. Port-au-Prince: Éditions Presses Nationales d'Haïti, 2006.

Díaz, María Elena. *The Virgin, the King, and the Royal Slaves of El Cobre*. Stanford, Calif.: Stanford University Press, 2002.

Documentos de que hasta ahora se compone el expediente que principiaron las Cortes Extraordinarias sobre el tráfico y esclavitud de negros. Madrid: Imp. de Repullés, 1814.

Drescher, Seymour. "The Limits of Example." In *The Impact of the Haitian Revolution in the Atlantic World*, edited by David Geggus, 10–14. Columbia: University of South Carolina Press, 2001.

————. *Abolition: A History of Slavery and Antislavery*. New York: Cambridge University Press, 2009.

Dubois, Laurent. *Avengers of the New World: The Story of the Haitian Revolution*. Cambridge, Mass.: Harvard University Press, 2004a.

_____. *Colony of Citizens: Revolution and Slave Emancipation in the French Caribbean, 1787–1804.* Chapel Hill, N.C.: Omohundro Institute of Early American History and Culture, 2004b.

_____. "An Enslaved Enlightenment: Rethinking the Intellectual History of the French Atlantic." *Social History,* 31 (2006): 1–14.

_____. *Haiti: The Aftershocks of History.* New York: Henry Holt and Co, 2012.

Dubois, Laurent, and John Garrigus, eds. *Slave Revolution in the Caribbean.* New York: Bedford-St. Martin's Publishing, 2006.

DuBois, W.E.B. *The Suppression of the Atlantic Slave-Trade to the United States of America, 1638–1870.* New York: Social Science Press, 1954.

DVEAP. *Historia de la Isla de Santo Domingo continuada hasta los últimos acontecimientos durante la insurrección de los xefes negros, especialmente en el año 1800 (VIII de la República Francesa) y siguientes hasta el presente.* Madrid: Imprenta del Villalpando, 1806.

Eddy, Etienne. *La vraie dimension de la politique extérieure des premièrs gouvernements d'Haïti (1804–1843).* Sherbrooke, Québec: Éditions Naaman, 1982.

Edwards, Bryan. *A Historical Survey of the French Colony of St. Domingo.* London: John Stockdale, 1797.

Elisabeth, Leo. "Les relations." In *Haïti, première république noire,* edited by Marcel Dorigny, 177–206. Société Française d'Histoire d'Outre-Mer, 2003.

Eller, Anne. "'All would be equal in the effort': Santo Domingo's 'Italian Revolution,' Independence, and Haiti, 1809–1822." *Journal of Early American History,* 1:2 (2011a), 105–141.

_____. "'Let's show the world we are brothers': The Dominican Guerra de Restauración and the Nineteenth-Century Caribbean." PhD diss., New York University, 2011b.

Ellis, Joseph. *Founding Brothers: The Revolutionary Generation.* New York: Vintage, 2002.

Eltis, David. *The Rise of African Slavery in the Americas.* New York: Cambridge University Press, 2000.

Fabela, Isidro. *Los precursores de la diplomacia mexicana.* Mexico, D.F.: Secretaría de Relaciones Exteriores, 1926.

Farge, Arlette. *The Vanishing Children of Paris: Rumor and Politics Before the French Revolution.* Cambridge, Mass.: Harvard University Press, 1993.

_____. *The Allure of the Archives.* Translated by Thomas Scott-Railton. New Haven, Conn.: Yale University Press, 2013.

Fernández Duro, Cesáreo. *Armada Española desde la unión de los Reinos de Castilla y de Aragón.* Madrid: Museo Naval, 1972–73.

Fernandez Prieto, Leida. "Crónica anunciada de una Cuba azucarera." In *Francisco Arango y la invención de la Cuba azucarera,* edited by María Dolores González-Ripoll and Izaskun Álvarez Cuartero, 55–65. Salamanca: Publicaciones de la Universidad de Salamanca, 2009.

_____. "Joaquín Infante en el ideario político independentista americano: de lo local a lo continental." In *Discursos políticos de criollos ilustrados en las independencias americanas,* edited by Diana Soto Arango and Miguel Ángel Puig-Samper, Madrid: Doce Calles, 2014.

Ferrer, Ada. *Insurgent Cuba: Race, Nation, and Revolution, 1868–1898.* Chapel Hill: University of North Carolina Press, 1999.

———. "Noticias de Haití en Cuba." *Revista de Indias,* 63, 229 (2003a): 675–694.

———. "La société esclavagiste cubaine et la révolution haïtienne." *Annales,* 58, 2 (2003b): 333–356.

———. "Cuba en la sombra de Haití: Noticias, sociedad y esclavitud." In *El rumor de Haití en Cuba: Temor, raza y rebeldía, 1789–1844,* edited by María Dolores González-Ripoll, et al., 179–231. Madrid: CSIC, 2004.

———. "Cuban Slavery and Atlantic Antislavery." *Review, Journal of the Fernand Braudel Center,* 31 (2008a): 267–295.

———. "Talk About Haiti: The Archive and the Atlantic's Haitian Revolution." In *Tree of Liberty: Atlantic Legacies of the Haitian Revolution,* edited by Doris Lorraine Garraway, 21–40. Charlottesville: University of Virginia Press, 2008b.

———. "Speaking of Haiti: Slavery, Revolution, and Freedom in Cuban Slave Testimony." In *The World of the Haitian Revolution,* edited by David Geggus and Norman Fiering, 223–247. Bloomington: Indiana University Press, 2009.

———. "Haiti, Free Soil, and Antislavery in the Revolutionary Atlantic." *American Historical Review,* 117, 1 (February 2012): 40–66.

Ferrer Bosch, Diego and José Sánchez Guerra, *Rebeldía y apalencamiento en Guantánamo y Baracoa.* Guantánamo: Centro Provincial de Patrimonio Cultural, 2003.

Fick, Carolyn. *The Making of Haiti: The Saint-Domingue Revolution from Below.* Knoxville: University of Tennessee Press, 1990.

Filomeno, Francisco. *Manifiesto de la causa seguida a Manuel Rodríguez Alemán y Peña.* Havana: Imp. De Gobierno, 1810.

Finch, Aisha K. *Insurgency Interrupted: Cuban Slaves and the Resistance Movements of 1841–1844.* Chapel Hill: University of North Carolina Press, forthcoming.

Fischer, Sibylle. *Modernity Disavowed: Haiti and the Cultures of Slavery in the Age of Revolution.* Durham, N.C.: Duke University Press, 2004.

———. "Bolívar in Haiti." In *Haiti and the Americas: Histories, Cultures, Imaginations,* edited by Raphael Dalleo, et al., 25–53. Oxford: University Press of Mississippi, 2013.

Fouchard, Jean. "Quand Haïti exportait la liberté aux Antilles." *Société haïtienne d'histoire et de géographie,* 43, 143 (June 1984): 41–47.

Fouchet, Max-Pol. *Wifredo Lam.* Barcelona: Ediciones Polígrafa, 1976.

Franco, Antonio-Filiu and Clara Álvarez Alonso. *La cuestión cubana en las Cortes de Cádiz.* Mexico: Archivo General de la Nación, 2012.

Franco, José Luciano. *Documentos para la historia de Haití en el Archivo Nacional.* Havana: Archivo Nacional de Cuba, 1954.

———. *La conspiración de Aponte.* Havana: Consejo Nacional de Cultura, 1963.

———. *Revoluciones y conflictos internacionales en el Caribe, 1789–1854.* Havana: Instituto de Historia, Academia de Ciencias, 1965.

———. *Palenques de negros cimarrones.* Havana: Colección Historia, 1973.

———. *Ensayos históricos.* Havana: Editorial de Ciencias Sociales, 1974.

_____. *Las minas de Santiago del Prado y la rebelión de los cobreros.* Havana: Editorial de Ciencias Sociales, 1975.

_____. *Las conspiraciones de 1810 y 1812.* Havana: Editorial de Ciencias Sociales, 1977.

_____. *Comercio clandestino de esclavos.* Havana: Editorial de Ciencias Sociales, 1980.

_____. *Apuntes para la historia de la legislación y administración colonial en Cuba, 1511–1800.* Havana: Editorial de Ciencias Sociales, 1985.

Fraser, Lionel. *History of Trinidad.* 2 vols. London: Cass, 1971 [1891].

Frey, Sylvia. *Water from the Rock: Black Resistance in a Revolutionary Age.* Princeton, N.J.: Princeton University Press, 1992.

Fuente, Alejandro de la. "Slave Law and Claims-Making in Cuba: The Tannenbaum Debate Revisited." *Law and History Review,* 22, 2 (2004): 339–370.

_____. "Slaves and the Creation of Legal Rights in Cuba: *Coartación* and *Papel.*" *The Hispanic American Historical Review,* 87, 4 (2007): 659–692.

Funes Monzote, Reinaldo. *From Rainforest to Cane Field in Cuba: An Environmental History.* Chapel Hill: University of North Carolina Press, 2008.

Gaffield, Julia. "Complexities of Imagining Haiti: A Study of National Constitutions, 1801–1807." *Journal of Social History,* 41, 1 (Fall 2007): 81–103.

_____. "Haiti and Jamaica in the Remaking of the Early Nineteenth-Century Atlantic World." *William & Mary Quarterly,* 69, 3 (2012): 583–614.

_____. ed. *The Haitian Declaration of Independence.* Charlottesville: University of Virginia Press, forthcoming.

Gálvez, Gisela and José Novoa. *1812. Conspiración antiesclavista.* Holguín: Ediciones Holguín, 1993.

García Rodríguez, Gloria. *La esclavitud desde la esclavitud, la visión de los siervos.* Havana: Centro de Investigación Científica Ing. Jorge L. Tamayo, 1996.

_____. *Conspiraciones y revueltas: La actividad política de los negros (1790–1845).* Santiago de Cuba: Editorial Oriente, 2003.

_____. "Vertebrando la resistencia: La lucha de los negros contra el sistema esclavista, 1790–1845." In *El rumor de Haití en Cuba,* edited by Maria Dolores González Ripoll, et al., 233–320. Madrid: CSIC, 2004.

García Rodríguez, Mercedes. *Entre haciendas y plantaciones: orígenes de la manufactura azucarera en la Habana.* Havana: Editorial Ciencias Sociales, 2007.

Gaspar, David Barry and David Geggus, eds., *A Turbulent Time: The French Revolution and the Greater Caribbean.* Bloomington: Indiana University Press, 1997.

Geggus, David. *Slavery, War and Revolution: The British Occupation of Saint Domingue 1793–1798.* Oxford: Clarendon Press, 1982.

_____. "Slavery, War, and Revolution in the Greater Caribbean." In *A Turbulent Time: The French Revolution and the Greater Caribbean,* edited by D.B. Gaspar and D. Geggus, 1–50. Bloomington: Indiana University Press, 1997.

_____. "The French Slave Trade: An Overview." *William and Mary Quarterly,* Third Series, 58, 1 (January 2001a): 119–138.

_____, ed. *The Impact of the Haitian Revolution in the Atlantic World.* Columbia: University of South Carolina, 2001b.

———. *Haitian Revolutionary Studies.* Bloomington: Indiana University Press, 2002.

———. "The Caribbean in the Age of Revolution." In *The Age of Revolutions in Global Context, c. 1760–1840,* edited by David Armitage and Sanjay Subrahmanyam, 83–100. New York: Palgrave Macmillan, 2010.

———. "Haiti's Declaration of Independence." In *The Haitian Declaration of Independence,* edited by Julia Gaffield. Charlottesville: University of Virginia Press, forthcoming.

Geggus, David and Norman Fiering, eds. *The World of the Haitian Revolution.* Bloomington: Indiana University Press, 2009.

Gemon, Jean-Baptiste. "Précis des événements arrivés à la députation envoyée à Port-au-Prince." Available online at http://mornegue.free.fr/evenem.htm.

Genovese, Eugene. *From Rebellion to Revolution: Afro-American Slave Revolts in the Making of the Modern World.* Baton Rouge: Louisiana State University Press, 1979.

Ghachem, Malick. *The Old Regime and the Haitian Revolution.* New York: Cambridge University Press, 2012.

Girard, Phillip. "Napoleon Bonaparte and the Emancipation Issue in Saint-Domingue, 1799–1803." *French Historical Studies,* 32, 4 (2009): 587–618.

———. *The Slaves Who Defeated Napoleon.* Tuscaloosa: University of Alabama Press, 2011.

Godoy, Manuel. *Memorias.* 2 vols. Madrid: Atlas 1965 [1836].

Gómez, Alejandro. *Le spectre de la Révolution noire: L'impact de la révolution haïtienne dans le monde atlantique, 1790–1886.* Rennes: Presses universitaires de Rennes, 2013.

Gomez, Michael. *Exchanging our Country Marks.* Chapel Hill: University of North Carolina Press, 1998.

Gómez Robaud, Rafael. *Manifiesto documentado en respuesta a los hechos que se sientan en el papel del capitán de fragata José Luyando.* Cádiz: Imprenta de Don Diego García Campoy, 1813.

Goncalvès, Dominique. "Havana's Aristocrats in the Spanish War of Independence, 1808–1814." In *Napoleon's Atlantic: The Impact of Napoleonic Empire in the Atlantic World,* edited by Christophe Belaubre, et al., 81–95. Leiden: Brill, 2010.

González-Ripoll, Maria Dolores. *Cuba, la isla de los ensayos: cultura y sociedad, 1790–1815.* Madrid: Consejo Superior de Investigaciones Científicas, 1999.

———. "Dos viajes, una intención: Francisco Arango y Alejandro Oliván en Europa y las Antillas azucareras (1794–1829)." *Revista de Indias,* 62, 224 (2002): 85–102.

———. "Entre la adhesión y el exilio: trayectoria de dos cubanos en una España segmentada." In *Las Antillas en la era de las luces,* edited by José Antonio Piqueras, 343–363. Madrid: Siglo XXI, 2005.

González-Ripoll, María Dolores, Consuelo Naranjo, Ada Ferrer, et al. *El rumor de Haití en Cuba: Temor, raza y rebeldía, 1789–1844.* Madrid: CSIC, 2004.

Goveia, Elsa. *Slave Society in the British Leeward Islands at the End of the Eighteenth Century.* New Haven, Conn.: Yale University Press, 1965.

Griggs, Earl Leslie and Clifford H. Prator. *Henri Christophe and Thomas Clark-son: A Correspondence*. New York: Greenwood, 1968.

Guerra, François-Xavier. "'Voces del pueblo'. Redes de comunicación y orígenes de la opinión pública en el mundo hispano (1808–1814)." *Revista de Indias*, 62, 225 (2002): 357–384.

_____. *Modernidad e independencias: Ensayos sobre las revoluciones hispánicas* Madrid: Fundación Studium y Ediciones Encuentro, 2009.

Guerra, Ramiro. *Manual de historia de Cuba*. Havana: Editorial de Ciencias Sociales, 1973.

Hahn, Stephen. *A Nation Under our Feet: Black Political Struggles in the South from Slavery to the Great Migration*. Cambridge, Mass.: Harvard University Press, 2003.

Hall, Neville A.T. *Slave Society in the Danish West Indies: St. Thomas, St. John, and St. Croix*. Baltimore, Md.: Johns Hopkins University Press, 1992.

Hector, Michel and Laënnec Hurbon, eds., *Genèse de l'Etat haïtien, 1804–1859*. Paris: Maison des sciences de l'homme, 2009.

Hernández, Juan Antonio. "Hacia una historia de lo imposible: La revolución haitiana y el libro de pinturas de José Antonio Aponte." PhD diss., University of Pittsburgh, 2005.

Higman, B.W. *Slave Populations of the British Caribbean, 1807–1834*. Kingston, Jamaica: The University Press of the West Indies, 1995.

Hoffman, Léon-François "Un mythe national: la cérémonie du Bois-Caïman." In *La République haïtienne: Etat des lieux et perspectives*, edited by Gérard Barthélemy and Christian Girault, 434–448. Paris: Karthala, 1993.

Howe, Stephen. *Afrocentrism: Mythical Pasts and Imagined Homes*. London: Verso, 1998.

Humboldt, Alexander von. *Ensayo político sobre la isla de Cuba*. Paris: Jules Renouard, 1827.

Hurbon, Laënnec, ed. *L'insurrection des esclaves de Saint-Domingue (22–23 août 1791): actes de la table ronde internationale de Port-au-Prince, 8 au 10 décembre 1997*. Paris: Karthala, 2000.

Ibarra, Jorge. *Marx y los historiadores ante la hacienda y la plantación esclavistas*. Havana: Editorial de Ciencias Sociales, 2008.

Iglesia, Álvaro de la. *Tradiciones cubanas: Relatos y retratos históricos*. Havana: Ediciones Géminis, 1974 [1911].

Iglesias Utset, Marial. "Los Despaigne en Saint-Domingue y Cuba: Narrativa microhistórica de una experiencia atlántica." *Revista de Indias*, 71 (2011): 77–108.

Infante, Joaquín. "Proyecto de Constitución para la Isla de Cuba," 1811, http://biblio.juridicas.unam.mx/libros/2/808/10.pdf.

Jamaica Assembly. *A Report of a Committee of the Honourable House of Assembly of Jamaica presented to the House, December 10, 1817*. London: J. Darling, 1818.

James, C.L.R. *The Black Jacobins: Toussaint L'Ouverture and the San Domingo Revolution*. New York: Vintage Books, 1963 [1938].

_____. "How I Would Rewrite *The Black Jacobins*." *Small Axe*, 8 (September 2000): 99–112.

Janvier, Louis Joseph. *Les Constitutions d'Haïti (1801–1885).* Paris: C. Marpon et Flammarion, 1886.

Jean-Baptiste, St. Victor. *Le fondateur devant l'histoire.* Port-au-Prince: Presses Nationales d'Haïti, 2006 [1954].

Jenson, Deborah. *Beyond the Slave Narrative: Politics, Sex, and Manuscripts in the Haitian Revolution.* Liverpool: Liverpool University Press, 2011.

———. "Jean-Jacques Dessalines and the African Character of the Haitian Revolution," *William and Mary Quarterly,* 69, 3 (July 2012): 615–638.

Johnson, Sara. *The 'Fear of French Negroes': Transcolonial Collaboration in the Revolutionary Americas.* Berkeley: University of California Press, 2012.

Johnson, Sherry. "The Rise and Fall of Creole Participation in the Cuban Slave Trade, 1789–1796." *Cuban Studies,* 30 (1999): 52–75.

———. *The Social Transformation of Eighteenth-Century Cuba.* Gainesville: University Press of Florida, 2001.

———. "From Authority to Impotence: Arango's Adversaries and their Fall from Power during the Constitutional Period (1808–1823)." In *Francisco Arango y la invención de la Cuba azucarera,* edited by María Dolores González-Ripoll and Izaskun Álvarez Cuartero, 193–211. Salamanca: Aquilafuente, 2009.

Jordan, Winthrop. *Tumult and Silence at Second Creek: An Inquiry into a Civil War Conspiracy.* Baton Rouge: Louisiana State University Press, 1995.

Kiple, Kenneth. *Blacks in Colonial Cuba, 1774–1899.* Gainesville: University of Florida Press, 1976.

Klein, Herbert. "North American Competition and the Characteristics of the Slave Trade to Cuba" *William and Mary Quarterly,* 28, 1 (January 1971): 86–102.

———. "The Cuban Slave Trade in a Period of Transition, 1790–1843." In *The Middle Passage: Comparative Studies in the Atlantic Slave Trade,* 209–227. Princeton, N.J.: Princeton University Press, 1978.

Knight, Franklin. *The Caribbean: The Genesis of a Fragmented Nationalism.* New York: Oxford University Press, 1978.

———. "Origins of Wealth and the Sugar Revolution in Cuba, 1750–1850." *Hispanic American Historical Review,* 57, 2 (1977): 231–253.

———. *Slave Society in Cuba during the Nineteenth Century.* Madison: University of Wisconsin Press, 1970.

Kuethe, Allan. *Cuba, 1753–1815: Crown, Military, and Society.* Knoxville: University of Tennessee Press, 1986.

La Rosa Corzo, Gabino. *Los cimarrones de Cuba.* Havana: Editorial de Ciencias Sociales, 1988.

———. *Runaway Slave Settlements in Cuba: Resistance and Repression.* Chapel Hill: University of North Carolina Press, 2003.

Lamore, Jean, ed. *Les français dans l'Orient cubain.* Bordeaux: Maison des Pays Ibériques, 1993.

Lampros, Peter. "Merchant-Planter Cooperation and Conflict." PhD diss., Tulane University, 1980.

Landers, Jane. *Atlantic Creoles in the Age of Revolutions.* Cambridge: Harvard University Press, 2010.

Lartigue, Roberjot. *Rapport de la conduit qu'à tenue M. Roberjot Lartigue.* Paris: Impr. De Dubray, 1815.

Law, Robin. "La Cérémoie du Bois-Caïman et le 'pacte de sang' dahoméen." In *L'insurrection des esclaves de Saint-Domingue (22–23 août 1791): actes de la table ronde internationale de Port-au-Prince, 8 au 10 décembre 1997,* edited by Laënnec Hurbon, 131–147. Paris: Karthala, 2000.

Lipski, John. *A History of Afro-Hispanic Language.* Cambridge: Cambridge University Press, 2009.

Liverpool, Hollis. "Rituals of Power and Rebellion." PhD diss., University of Michigan, 1993.

Llaverías, Joaquín. "Unas décimas políticas." *Archivos del Folklore,* 1 (1924): 52–62.

Locke, John. *Two Treatises on Government.* New York: Cambridge University Press, 2010 [1821].

Logan, Rayford. *The Diplomatic Relations of the United States with Haiti, 1776–1891.* Chapel Hill: University of North Carolina Press, 1941.

López Mesa, Enrique. "Acerca de la introducción de esclavos en la Habana durante la ocupación británica (1762–1763)," manuscript in preparation.

Lubin, Maurice. "Les premièrs rapports de la nation haïtienne avec l'étranger," *Journal of Inter-American Studies,* 10, 2 (1968): 277–305.

Lucena Salmoral, Manuel. *Los códigos negros de la América Española.* España: Ediciones UNESCO, 1996.

Lynch, John. *The Spanish American Revolutions, 1808–1826.* New York: Norton, 1986.

———. *Simón Bolívar: A Life.* New Haven, Conn.: Yale University Press, 2006.

Maceo, Antonio. *Ideología Política: Cartas y otros documentos.* Vol. 1. Havana: SCEHI, 1950.

Madiou, Thomas. *Histoire d'Haïti.* Port-au-Prince: Edition Henri Deschamps, 1987–1991.

Madison, James. *The Writings of James Madison [1803–1807].* Vol. 7. Edited by Gaillard Hunt. New York: Knickerbocker Press, 1807.

Maffly-Kipp, Laurie. *Setting Down the Sacred Past: African American Race Histories.* Cambridge, Mass.: Harvard University Press, 2010.

Marrero, Leví. *Cuba: Economía y sociedad.* Vols. 9, 10. Madrid: Playor, 1983–84.

Martí, José. "Diario de Montecristi a Cabo Haitiano." In *Obras Completas,* 9: 184–212. Havana: Editorial de Ciencias Sociales, 1975.

Martín Zequeira, M.E. and E.L. Rodríguez Fernández, *Guía de arquitectura: La Habana colonial (1519–1898).* Havana and Seville: Junta de Andalucía, 1995.

Mercader Riba, Juan. *José Bonaparte: Rey de España.* Madrid: CSIC, 1983.

Mettas, Jean and Serge Daget. *Répertoire de expéditions négrières française au XVIIIe siècle.* 2 vols. Paris: Société française d'histoire d'outre-mer, 1978–84.

Mintz, Sidney. *Three Ancient Colonies.* Cambridge, Mass.: Harvard University Press, 2012.

Moïse, Claude. *Constitutions et luttes de pouvoir en Haïti, 1804–1987.* 2 vols. Montreal: Edition du CIDIHCA, 1990 [1988].

Monti, Laura. *Calendar of the Rochambeau Papers.* Gainesville: University of Florida Press, 1972.

Morales y Morales, Vidal. *Iniciadores y primeros mártires de la revolución cubana.* 3 vols. Havana: Cultural, 1931.

Moreau de Saint-Méry, Médéric-Louis-Elie. *Description topographique, physique, civile, politique et historique de la partie française de l'isle Saint-Domingue.* Paris: Société de l'histoire des colonies françaises, 1958.

Moreno Fraginals, Manuel. *El ingenio: Complejo económico social cubano del azúcar.* Havana: Editorial de Ciencias Sociales, 1978.

Morgan, Jennifer. "Accounting for the Women in Slavery: Numeracy and Race in the Early Modern Atlantic," manuscript in progress.

Moyn, Samuel. *The Last Utopia: Human Rights in History.* Cambridge, Mass.: Harvard University Press, 2010.

Mullin, Michael. *Africa in America.* Champaign: University of Illinois, 1992.

Muriel, Andrés. *Notice sur D. Gonzalo O'Farrill, lieutenant-général des armées de S.M. le Roi d'Espagne.* Paris: Bure Frères, 1835.

Murray, David. *Odious Commerce: Britain, Spain, and the Abolition of the Cuban Slave Trade.* New York: Cambridge University Press, 1980.

Naranjo Orovio, Consuelo. "La otra Cuba: colonización blanca y diversificación agrícola" *Contrastes,* 12 (2003).

———. "La amenaza haitiana, un miedo interesado." In *El Rumor de Haití en Cuba,* edited by María Dolores González Ripoll, et al., 83–178. Madrid: CSIC, 2004.

Nessler, Graham. "A Failed Emancipation?: The Struggle for Freedom in Hispaniola during the Haitian Revolution, 1789–1809." PhD diss., University of Michigan, 2011.

———. "'The Shame of the Nation:' The Force of Re-Enslavement and the Law of 'Slavery' under the Regime of Jean-Louis Ferrand in Santo Domingo, 1804–1809." *New West Indian Guide,* 86, 1–2 (2012): 5–28.

Nicholls, David. *From Dessalines to Duvalier: Race, Colour and National Independence in Haiti.* New Brunswick: Rutgers University Press, 1979.

Nuevo Reglamento y arancel que debe gobernar en la captura de esclavos cimarrones aprobado por S. M. en Real Orden expedida en San Lorenxo con fecha 20 de Diciembre de 1796. Havana: Impr. de la Capitanía General, 1796.

Orozco Melgar, María Elena. "Cuba et les îles sous le vent: La course comme facteur identitaire." In Christian Lerat, ed., *Le monde caraïbe: échanges transatlantiques et horizons post-coloniaux.* Bordeaux: Pessac, 2003, 97–116.

———. "La implantación francesa en Santiago de Cuba: Modalidades y consecuencias (1800–1810)." In *Les Français dans l'Orient cubain,* edited by Jean Lamore, 47–58. Bordeaux: Maison des Pays Ibériques, 1993.

Ortiz, Fernando. *Los negros esclavos.* Havana: Editorial de Ciencias Sociales, 1975.

Palmié, Stephan. *Wizards and Scientists: Explorations in Afro-Cuban Modernity.* Durham, N.C.: Duke University Press, 2002.

Pavez Ojeda, Jorge. "Expediente contra José Antonio Aponte, La Habana, 1812." *Anales de Desclasificación,* 1, 2 (2006): 717–768.

_____. "Lecturas de un códice afrocubano: Naturalismo, etiopismo y universalismo en el libro de José Antonio Aponte (La Habana, circa 1760–1812)." *Historia Crítica* (Bogotá), 45 (September–December 2011): 56–85.

Pérez, Louis. *Cuba: Between Reform and Revolution.* New York: Oxford University Press, 1988.

Pérez Concepción, Herbert Ramiro. "Haití en José Martí." *Ciencia en su PC*, 4 (2010): 61–72.

Pérez de la Riva, Francisco. *El café; historia de su cultivo y explotación en Cuba.* La Habana: Jesús Montero, 1944.

_____. "El negro y la tierra, el conuco y el palenque." *Revista Bimestre Cubana,* 58, 2–3 (1946).

Pérez de la Riva, Juan. "Cuadro sinóptico de la esclavitud en Cuba y de la cultura Occidental." In *Actas del Folklore*, Havana, 1, 5 (1961).

_____. "La implantación francesa en la cuenca superior del Cauto." In *El barracón y otros ensayos.* Havana: Editorial de Ciencias Sociales, 1975.

Perotin, Anne. "Le projet cubain des grands planteurs de la Havane, jalons pour une lecture de Francisco Arango y Parreño, 1769–1839." *Mélanges de la Casa de Velázquez*, Vol II (1974): 273–314.

Pezuela, Jacobo de la. *Historia de la Isla de Cuba.* Vol. 3. Madrid: C. Bailly-Baillière, 1878.

Pichardo, Esteban. *Diccionario provincial casi-razonado de voces cubanas*, 3rd ed. Havana: Imprenta la Antilla, 1862.

Pico, Fernando. *One Frenchman, Four Revolutions: General Ferrand and the Peoples of the Caribbean.* Princeton, N.J.: Markus Wienner, 2011.

Piqueras, Jose Antonio, "Los amigos de Arango en Madrid." In *Francisco Arango y la invención de la Cuba azucarera*, edited by María Dolores González-Ripoll and Izaskun Álvarez Cuartero, 151–166. Salamanca: Aquilafuente, 2009.

Ponte Domínguez, Francisco J. *Arango Parreño, estadista colonial cubano.* Havana: Imp. Molina y Cía, 1937.

_____. *La junta de la Habana en 1808.* Havana: Editorial Guerrero, 1947.

_____. *La huella francesa en la historia política de Cuba.* Havana: Academia de la Historia, 1948.

Popkin, Jeremy D. *You Are All Free: The Haitian Revolution and the Abolition of Slavery.* New York: Cambridge University Press, 2010.

Portuondo Zúñiga, Olga. *La virgen del Cobre: Símbolo de cubanía.* Madrid: Agualarga, 2002.

_____. *Entre esclavos y libres de Cuba colonial.* Santiago de Cuba: Editorial Oriente, 2003.

_____. *Cuba. Constitución y liberalismo (1808–1841).* Santiago: Editorial Oriente, 2008.

_____. "Santiago de Cuba, los colonos franceses, y el fomento cafetalero." In *Les Francais dans l'Orient cubain*, edited by Jean Lamore, 115–127. Bordeaux: Maison des Pays Ibériques, 1993.

Prévost, Julien. *Relation des glorieux événements qui ont porté leurs Majestés Royales sur la trône d'Hayti.* Cap-Henri: Chez P. Roux, 1811.

Prieto Samsónov, Dmitri. *Transdominación en Haití (1791–1826).* Havana: Pinos Nuevos, 2010.

Putnam, Lara. "To Study the Fragments/Whole: Microhistory and the Atlantic World." *Journal of Social History*, 39, 3 (2006): 615–630.

Rainsford, Marcus. *An Historical Account of the Black Empire of Hayti: Comprehending a View of the Principal Transactions in the Revolution of Saint Domingo; with its Ancient and Modern State*. London: J. Cundee, 1805.

Raynal, Abbé. *A Philosophical and Political History of the Settlements and Trade of the Europeans in the East and West Indies*. Glasgow: Mundell and Son, 1804.

Rediker, Marcus and Peter Linebaugh. *The Many-Headed Hydra: Sailors, Slave, Commoners and the Hidden History of the Revolutionary Atlantic*. Boston: Beacon Press, 2001.

Reis, João José. *Slave Rebellion in Brazil*. Baltimore, Md.: John Hopkins Press, 1985.

Renault, Agnès. *D'une île rebelle à une île fidèle*. Rouen: Université de Rouen, 2012.

Ribera, Nicolás Joseph de. *Descripción de la Isla de Cuba*. Havana: Editorial de Ciencias Sociales, 1975.

Rodigneaux, Michel. *La guerre de course en Guadeloupe*. Paris: L'Harmattan, 2006.

Rodríguez, Emilio Jorge. *Haiti and Trans-Caribbean Literary Identity*. Philipsburg, Saint-Martin: Jouse of Nehesi Publishers, 2011.

Rodríguez Campomanes, Pedro. *Reflexiones sobre comercio español a indias*. Edited by Vicente Llombart Rosa. Madrid: Instituto de Estudios Fiscales, 1988.

Rodríguez Demorizi, Emilio. *Invasiones haitianas de 1801, 1805, y 1822*. Ciudad Trujillo: Editorial del Caribe, 1955.

Rojas, Rafael. *Las repúblicas de aire: Utopía y desencanto en la revolución de hispanoamérica*. Mexico City: Taurus, 2009.

Saco, José Antonio. *Colección de papeles científicos, históricos, políticos y de otros ramos sobre la isla de Cuba*. Paris: Imprenta de D'Aubusson y Kugelmann, 1858.

———. *Historia de la esclavitud de la raza africana en el nuevo mundo y en especial en los países Américo-Hispanos*, 3 vols. Havana: Cultural, 1938.

Sagra, Ramon de la. *Historia económico-política y estadística de la isla de Cuba*. Havana: Arazoza y Soler, 1831.

Sánchez, Romy. "Enjeux politiques d'une circulation américaine des savoirs: la 'bibliothèque' abolitionniste de Jorge Davidson," forthcoming.

Santa Cruz y Mallén, Francisco Xavier de. *Historia de familias cubanas*. La Habana: Editorial Hércules, 1943.

Santamaría García, Antonio and Consuelo Naranjo Oviedo, eds., *Mas allá del azúcar*. Madrid: Doce Calles, 2009.

Sartorius, David. *Ever Faithful: Race, Loyalty, and the Ends of Empire in Spanish Cuba*. Durham, N.C.: Duke University Press, 2014.

Saunders, Prince. *Haytian Papers: A Collection of the Very Interesting Proclamations and Other Official Documents, Together with Some Account of the Rise, Progress, and Present State of the Kingdom of Hayti*. Boston: Caleb Bingham, 1818.

Schmidt-Nowara, Christopher, and Josep Fradera, eds. *Slavery and Antislavery in Spain's Atlantic Empire*. London: Berghahn Books, 2013.

Schneider, Elena. *The Occupation of Havana: Slavery, War, and Empire in the Eighteenth Century.* Chapel Hill: University of North Carolina Press/ Omohundro Institute, forthcoming.

Scott, David. *Conscripts of Modernity: The Tragedy of Colonial Enlightenment.* Durham, N.C.: Duke University Press, 2004.

Scott, Julius S. "The Common Wind: Currents of Afro-American Communication in the Era of the Haitian Revolution." PhD diss., Duke University, 1986.

———. "Afro-American Sailors and the International Communication Network: The Case of Newport Bowers." In *Jack Tar in History: Essays in the History of Maritime Life and Labour,* edited by Colin Howell and Richard Twomey, 37–52. Fredericton, N.B.: Acadiensis Press, 1991.

Scott, Rebecca. "Paper Thin: Freedom and Re-enslavement in the Diaspora of the Haitian Revolution." *Law and History Review,* 29 (November 2011): 1061–1087.

———. "Under Color of Law: Siladin v. France and the Dynamics of Enslavement in Historical Perspective." In *The Legal Understanding of Slavery: From the Historical to the Contemporary,* edited by Jean Allain, 152–164. Oxford: Oxford University Press, 2012.

Scott, Rebecca and Jean Hébrard. *Freedom Papers: An Atlantic Odyssey in the Age of Emancipation.* Cambridge, Mass.: Harvard University Press, 2012.

Sheller, Mimi. *Democracy after Slavery: Black Publics and Peasant Politics in Haiti and Jamaica.* Gainesville: University of Florida Press, 2000.

Sidbury, James. *Becoming African in America: Race and Nation in the Early Black Atlantic.* Oxford: Oxford University Press, 2009.

Sklodowska, Elzbieta. *Espectros y espejismos: Haití en el imaginario cubano.* Frankfurt/Madrid: Iberoamericana Vervuert, 2009.

Smallwood, Stephanie. *Saltwater Slavery: A Middle Passage from Africa to American Diaspora.* Cambridge, Mass.: Harvard University Press, 2007.

Smith, Matthew. "Port-au-Prince, I Love You," in *Haiti Rising: Haitian History, Culture, and the Earthquake of 2010,* edited by Martin Munro, 186–194. Liverpool: Liverpool University Press, 2010.

Soriano, Maria Cristina. "Rumors of Revolution: The Influence of Caribbean Turmoil in Venezuelan Political Culture (1790–1810)." PhD diss., New York University, 2011.

Stagg, J.C.A. "The Political Essays of William Shaler." In *William and Mary Quarterly,* 59, 2 (2002). Web Supplement, https://oieahc.wm.edu/wmq/Apro2/stagg.pdf.

Steedman, Carolyn Kay. *Landscape for a Good Woman.* New Brunswick, N.J.: Rutgers University Press, 1987.

Stein, Robert Louis. *The French Slave Trade in the Eighteenth Century: An Old Regime Business.* Madison: University of Wisconsin Press, 1979.

Stein, Stanley and Barbara H. Stein. *Silver, Trade, and War: Spain and America in the Making of Early Modern Europe.* Baltimore, Md.: Johns Hopkins University Press, 2000.

———. *Apogee of Empire: Spain and New Spain in the Age of Charles III, 1759–1789.* Baltimore, Md.: John Hopkins University Press, 2003.

———. *Edge of Crisis: War and Trade in the Spanish Atlantic, 1789–1808.* Baltimore, Md.: John Hopkins University Press, 2009.

Suárez Suárez, Reinaldo. "Repercusiones de la Constitución de Cádiz: Guridi y Alcocer y la esclavitud en Cuba." *Anuario Mexicano de Historia del Derecho,* 22 (2010): 339–365.

Tardieu, Patrick. "The Debate Surrounding the Printing of the Haitian Declaration of Independence." In *The Haitian Declaration of Independence,* edited by Julia Gaffield. Charlottesville: University of Virginia Press, forthcoming.

Thibaud, Clément. "'Coupé têtes, brûlé cazes': Peurs et désirs d'Haïti dans l'Amérique de Bolívar." *Annales,* 58, 2 (2003): 305–332.

Thomas, Hugh. *Cuba: The Pursuit of Freedom.* New York: Harper & Row, 1971.

Thomson, Sinclair. "Sovereignty Disavowed: The Tupac Amaru Revolution in the Atlantic World," manuscript in preparation.

Thornton, John. "'I am the Subject of the King of the Congo': African Political Ideology and the Haitian Revolution." *Journal of World History,* 4, 2 (Fall 1993): 181–214.

Tomich, Dale. "The Wealth of Empire: Francisco Arango y Parreño, Political Economy and Slavery in Cuba." *Comparative Studies in Society and History* 45 (2003): 4–28.

———. *Through the Prism of Slavery: Labor, Capital, and World Economy.* Lanham: Rowman & Littlefield, 2004.

Tonnere, Boisrond. *Memoires pour servir a l'histoire d'Haïti.* Port-au-Prince: Éditions Fardin, 1981 [1852].

Tornero Tinajero, Pablo. *Crecimiento económico y transformaciones sociales: esclavos, hacendados y comerciantes en la Cuba colonial, 1760–1840.* Madrid: Ministerio de Trabajo y Seguridad Social, 1996.

Torres Lasquetti,. *Colección de datos históricos-geográficos y estadísticos de Puerto del Príncipe y su jurisdicción.* La Habana: Imprenta El Retiro, 1888.

Trouillot, Henock. *Le gouvernement du Roi Henri Christophe.* Port-au-Prince: Imprimerie Centrale, 1972.

Trouillot, Michel-Rolph. *Haiti, State Against Nation: Origins and Legacy of Duvalierism.* New York: Monthly Review Press, 1990.

———. *Silencing the Past: Power and the Production of History.* Boston: Beacon Press, 1995.

"Un palacio entre sombras y luces." *Opus Habana,* III, 2, 1999.

Valdés, Antonio José. *Historia de la Isla de Cuba y en especial de la Habana.* Havana: Comisión Nacional Cubana de la UNESCO, 1964 [1813].

Van Norman, William. *Shade-Grown Slavery: The Lives of Slaves on Coffee Plantations in Cuba.* Nashville, Tenn.: Vanderbilt University Press, 2013.

Vastey, Baron de Pompee-Valentin. *An essay on the causes of the revolution and civil wars of Hayti, being a sequel to the political remarks upon certain French publications and journals concerning Hayti.* New York: Negro Universities Press, 1969.

Vázquez Cienfuegos, Sigfrido. "Cuba ante la crisis de 1808: El proyecto juntista de La Habana." In *IX Congreso Internacional de Historia de América,* edited by Fernando Serrano Mangas, et al., 1: 263–269. Mérida: Editora Regional de Extremadura, 2002.

_____. "*Omnia Vanitas*: Festejos en honor de Godoy en la Habana en 1807." *Ibero-Americana Pragensia*, 25 Supplement (2009a): 115–138.

_____. "Reacción de la población de color de la Habana ante los sucesos de 1808." In *El municipio indiano: relaciones interétnicas*, edited by Manuela Cristina García Bernal, et al., 351–368. Sevilla: Universidad de Sevilla, 2009b.

_____. "Anónimos en la Habana durante el verano de 1808: Un ejemplo de pensamiento conservador." *Araucaria. Revista Iberoamericana de Filosofía, Política y Humanidades*, 13, 26 (2011): 226–245.

_____. "El Almirantazgo Español de 1807: La última reforma de Manuel Godoy." *Hispania*, 72 (2012): 475–500.

Verna. Paul. *Pétion y Bolívar: una etapa decisiva en la emancipación de Hispanoamérica, 1790–1830*. Caracas: Ediciones de la Presidencia de la República, 1980 [1969].

Victoria Ojeda, Jorge. *Tendencias monárquicas en la revolución haitiana: el negro Juan Francisco Petecou bajo las banderas francesa y española*. México, D.F.: Siglo XXI, 2005.

White, Ashli. *Encountering Revolution: Haiti and the Making of the Early Republic*. Baltimore, Md.: John Hopkins University Press, 2010.

Williams, Eric E. *Capitalism and Slavery*. Chapel Hill: University of North Carolina Press, 1994 [1944].

Williams, Greg H. *The French Assault on American Shipping, 1793–1813: A History and Comprehensive Record of Merchant Marine Losses*. Jefferson, N.C.: McFarland & Co., 2009.

Yacou, Alain. *Saint-Domingue espagnol et la révolution nègre d'Haïti (1790–1822): commémoration du bicentenaire de la naissance de l'état d'Haïti (1804–2004)*. Pointe-à-Pitre: CERC, 2007.

_____. *La longue guerre des Nègres marrons à Cuba: 1796–1851*. Paris: Karthala, 2009.

_____. *Essor des plantations et subversion antiesclavagiste à Cuba, 1791–1845*. Pointe-à-Pitre: CERC, Université desl Antilles et de la Guyane, 2010.

Zeuske, Michael "Las Capitanías Generales de Cuba y Puerto Rico en el gran Caribe, 1808–1812." In *Los colores de las independencias iberoamericanas: Liberalismo, etnia y raza*, edited by Manuel Chust and Ivana Fresquet, 21–48. Madrid: CSIC, 2009.

_____. "Alexander von Humboldt in Cuba, 1800/01 and 1804: Traces of an Enigma." *Studies in Travel Writing*, 15, 4 (December 2011), 347–358.

Index

29028499R00219

Made in the USA
Middletown, DE
04 February 2016